Critical Anthropology Now

Unexpected Contexts, Shifting Constituencies, Changing Agendas

Publication of the Advanced Seminar Series is made possible by generous support from The Brown Foundation, Inc., of Houston, Texas.

School of American Research Advanced Seminar Series

Douglas W. Schwartz
General Editor

Critical Anthropology Now

Contributors

Donald Brenneis
University of California, Santa Cruz

T. David Brent
University of Chicago Press

James D. Faubion
Rice University

Michael M. J. Fischer
Massachusetts Institute of Technology

Kim Fortun
Rensselaer Polytechnic

Peter Dobkin Hall
Yale University

George E. Marcus
Rice University

Sherry B. Ortner
Columbia University

Paul Rabinow
University of California, Berkeley

Judith Stacey
University of California, Davis

Critical Anthropology Now

Unexpected Contexts, Shifting Constituencies, Changing Agendas

Edited by George E. Marcus

School of American Research Press
Santa Fe, New Mexico

School of American Research Press
Post Office Box 2188
Santa Fe, New Mexico, 87504-2188

Director of Publications: Joan K. O'Donnell
Editors: J. K. O'Donnell & Jo Ann Baldinger
Designer: Context, Inc.
Indexer: Douglas J. Easton
Typographer: Context, Inc.

Library of Congress Cataloging-in-Publication Data:
Critical anthropology now : unexpected contexts, shifting constituencies, changing agendas / edited by George E. Marcus.
p. cm. – (School of American Research advanced seminar series)
Includes bibliographical references and index.
ISBN 0-933452-50-0. – ISBN 0-933452-51-9 (pbk.)
1. Anthropology–Research. 2. Anthropology–Field work.
3. Anthropology–Methodology. I. Marcus, George E. II. Series
GN33.C74 1999
301'.07'2—dc21 99-41001
CIP

Manufactured in the United States of America. Library of Congress Catalog Card Number 99-41001. International Standard Book Numbers 0-933452-50-0 (cloth) and 0-933452-51-9 (paper). First paperback edition 1999.

Cover photograph: James D. Faubion at New Mount Carmel, on the outskirts of Waco, Texas, July 1995, by William R. Dull. Copyright © William R. Dull. Cover design by Context, Inc.

Contents

Critical Anthropology Now

1

Critical Anthropology Now

An Introduction

George E. Marcus

> The critique of the human sciences has had since the mid-1980s a peculiar fate, a fate that is burdened in one species of its knowledge by questions which as prescribed by its very nature it cannot ignore, but which as transcending its limitations it also cannot answer. Among these questions is the degree to which the language of critique itself has entered into those very discourses it was intended to transform.
>
> —*T. David Brent*[1]

The distinctiveness of the papers in this volume lies in the strangeness of the positions in which a number of the writers found themselves in the field. This is not the traditional, exotic strangeness of anthropological fieldwork, of being immersed in other worlds of difference that anthropology itself has prepared one for. It is rather the loss of this condition that provides the strangeness here, the strangeness of being immersed in writings, inquiries, and commitments that precede one, surround one, and to which one must define a relationship precisely in order to pursue one's ethnographic endeavors.

Some examples: James Faubion's effort to study the Branch Davidian/Waco conflagration was difficult to differentiate from the media coverage saturating the event; his treatment both portrays and problematizes this difficulty. Sherry Ortner investigates the contemporary lives of her Newark, New Jersey, high school class, connecting it to the popular "career" of "Generation X" and leading to a novel reconsideration of the always problematic notion of social class in the United States. Judy Stacey writes of the ways in which she was pulled into confrontation with conservative political agendas through the use their proponents made of her ethnographic work on Silicon Valley families (Stacey 1990). In extending her ethnography of activists at Bhopal to the corporate boardrooms of Union Carbide, Kim Fortun thoroughly blurs our conventional sense of the constituencies for anthropological knowledge. Paul Rabinow, in a searching account of his collaboration with a businessman/scientist at the center of his ethnography of the invention of the biotechnology PCR (Rabinow 1996), depicts a complex relationship in which the anthropologist's identification with the scientists he is studying is both irresistible and highly ambiguous. Donald Brenneis makes ethnography of his participation on a peer review panel of the National Science Foundation, probing the ways in which a major research bureaucracy is assimilating among other disciplines the same sorts of changes affecting the contemporary practice of anthropology. And Michael Fischer, from his academic base at MIT, examines how the complex technological changes evoked by the vision of cyberspace are transforming the stable contexts of society and culture on which research practices like ethnography have always depended.

When research interests are repatriated and refocused within US society, it is thus the strangeness of what is relatively familiar, but currently in dramatic transformation, that interrupts past efforts to simply reproduce anthropological methods developed in traditional societies (the "urban-neighborhood, clinic, or laboratory as analog of the tribe" syndrome). It is precisely the unexpected contexts, shifting constituencies, and changing agendas that anthropologists find themselves encountering and that alter classic conditions of fieldwork which emerged as the preoccupation of the School of American Research seminar and the papers presented here. This volume, then, captures something of the changes in the practice of anthropology that were first presaged in the critiques of anthropological writing and authority of the 1980s (Clifford and Marcus 1986; Clifford 1988), but that are now evident directly in the changing conditions of the research process itself.

Most anthropologists today are aware of and discuss among themselves these changes in the character and context of fieldwork. But only very recently have published discussions of these changing parameters begun to appear (see, for example, the edited volumes by Gupta and Ferguson [1997a, 1997b] and Marcus [1995]). The School of American Research seminar, originating in a particular concern about the legacies of the 1980s' critiques, was conceptualized as an effort to come to terms with these changes. It did so by examining how the participants' research projects became unexpectedly recontextualized, developed ambiguous relationships to other, sometimes competing forms of representation in the same field of activity, and shifted to agendas more complicated than the usual anthropological project of straightforward ethnographic description and interpretation. Together, the participants became interested in these experiences and writings not only as challenges to the traditional boundaries of the identity of fieldwork, but also as registers of what the situated gaze of the ethnographer in practice might be becoming.

At its most basic, this collection presents an array of current styles of critical anthropological research being done in and on US society at a time of widespread awareness of transformative change. As such, it contributes to the long and increasingly vibrant tradition of anthropological scholarship on the United States. We have decided not to synthesize these papers thematically in terms of this tradition, however, although many readers will want to read them primarily in this context. Instead, the papers are introduced according to what became the seminar's focus: the current predicaments in US academia that emanate from a quite remarkable infusion of provocative new ideas and styles of critical thought during the 1980s. The papers vary considerably in how they cleave to or depart from this intellectual trend, but all present research projects that are in various ways circumstantially and transitionally remaking basic understandings of ethnographic practice. In this sense, the papers just happen to focus on subjects within the (extended) geographic space of the United States; the changes in the research practices that we do emphasize are relevant to most other settings and regions in which anthropologists now work.[2] The purpose of the volume is to capture something of these ongoing changes through particular case studies of their occurrence.

THE ORIGINATING IDEA

The idea for this seminar arose in intermittent conversations between Paul Rabinow and myself since the early 1990s about the fate of the vibrant intellectual trend that had pervaded American academia in the 1980s. During that decade deep challenges emerged in this country to the founding assumptions of most of the disciplines that constitute the human sciences. The politics of knowledge of this era has been one of its defining features. Under the labels postmodernism and then cultural studies, a bracing critical self-examination was initiated by many practicing scholars in the social sciences and humanities. This examination of their own habits of thought and work involved reconsiderations of the nature of representation, description, subjectivity, and objectivity, reconsiderations even of the notions of "society" and "culture" themselves, as well as of how they have materialized objects of study and data about those objects to constitute the "real" to which their work had been addressed.

Therapeutic and personally transformative for some, excessively skeptical for others, this examination was conducted in the name of "theory" and "critique." The theory was largely diffused through literary studies, as that field tried to remake itself into a more interdisciplinary "cultural studies."[3] Currently we seem to be at a critical moment of intense interest in the ways we might deploy this intellectual capital in projects of long-term research as well as in interventions in contemporary public debates about politics, policies, and national problems. We are considering how to communicate and use in inquiry what was essentially a reformation of thought among scholars. Especially in self-described empiricist disciplines such as anthropology, there is interest in how the ideas and concepts of the past decade can be used to reformulate traditional protocols of research.

At the same time, we perceive a pervasive nervousness about the legacy of this self-critical ferment, a lack of confidence in the relevance of all the theory, a sense that maybe the so-called crisis of representation has been only an intellectual crisis, offering little possibility of effective theoretical or analytic engagement outside academia. This pessimism is easy to spot in conferences, publications, and corridor talk. In a volume of articles demonstrating the power of critiques of rhetoric and discourse in reanimating the work of geographers, for example, a characteristic hesitation about the involution of postmodernist debates appears toward the end of the volume's introduction:

> We would argue...that it is highly debatable whether the crisis of representation extends beyond a tiny coterie of hyper-educated intellectuals. Again, this is not to deny that a crisis exists; rather it is to situate it within its sociological context (the academy). If this is the case, and we believe it to be so, then the claims for a postmodern era are overdrawn in that they erroneously generalize from an intellectual elite to the population at large. (Barnes and Duncan 1992:251)

It is undoubtedly the case that the discussions among academics that developed the intellectual capital of the past decade ideologically and theoretically were indeed hermetic, but the precise legacy of this capital is now being determined in the kinds of research projects that it has inspired. Keeping in mind the effects of the 1980s' crisis of representation specifically on anthropology, Rabinow and I conceived of two urgent tasks that this seminar might take up. One was to address the changing research process itself: emergent styles of work within the paradigm of ethnographic research that reflect a combination of the influence of 1980s' critiques, the conception of new spaces and topics for work, and the quite pragmatic responses to obstacles that anthropologists have encountered as they try to practice traditional ethnography while addressing these new spaces and topics. The most appropriate legacy of the theoretical and conceptual critical discussions of the 1980s appears to be the changing nature of research practice itself, and this is what we sought to understand. Most of the papers in this volume report innovative projects of ethnographic research, case studies in the way that new and more complicated research locations are giving rise to shifts in the character of both fieldwork and fieldworker. We simply wanted to demonstrate that the impact of the so-called postmodernist critiques of anthropology lies not in further discussions of postmodernism, but in the enactments of new kinds of research projects in anthropology, differently problematized and innovatively conducted.

The seminar's second task was to address squarely—by a kind of experiment in the ethnography of knowledge—the creeping lack of confidence regarding the integrity, worth, and relevance of the critical ideas that had been introduced to American academics over the past decade and more. We wanted to test (and, frankly, undermine if warranted) the sense that critical reflexivity has been an insular activity, abstract and self-important. Our idea was not to try to bridge the gap between academic social scientists sympathetic to the 1980s' critiques and the ordinary people in everyday life who are the typical subjects of study of ethnographers, social historians, and sociologists. Rather, we sought to affirm that social scientists, including anthropologists, participate in a regime of power/knowledge (a term derived from Michel Foucault [1980] that we use to designate practices that exercise power through the creation and management of knowledge) and that the key alignment of self-critical trends in academia would be similar to trends in other power/knowledges, particularly those more directly concerned with the performance of instrumental functions in society: the professions, corporations, publishing, the military, finance, politics and policy, science and technology. Because any self-critical trend is unlikely to take the same form of discourse, consciousness, practice, or context of activity across such diverse sites of power/knowledge, the task of identifying self-critical trends in other arenas is eminently suitable for ethnography, a practice deeply familiar with subjects' views in the contexts within which it situates itself and oriented to translating across them in a comparative way.

By recruiting both scholars who had conducted ethnographies in institutions and practitioners within institutions, we hoped to provide a discussion about how widespread and relevant the crisis of representation has been. We expected from this experiment to find a strong affinity between some of the postmodernist concerns of academia and the more instrumental concerns of those lawyers, corporate officials, and scientists variously engaged with a profoundly transforming world. In so doing, we hope to dispel or qualify the loss of confidence among scholars at this crucial moment, just as possibilities for exploring these ideas in established research traditions occur and their future legitimacy is in the balance.

At the same time, we would assert an affinity between bureaucrats, officials, professionals, and left-liberal scholars that may be disturbing to the latter, but which progressive scholars would have to take self-consciously into account in pursuing future projects. Our experiment was thus meant to be an exploration in ethnographic terms of Bourdieu's provocative designation (1984) of academics and intellectuals as the "dominated segment of the dominant."

The relativization of academics along such a dimension of overlapping power/knowledges, often ignored or superficially acknowledged in our own self-identifications, would be an important by-product of addressing the fear that we are only projecting our own problems or habits of thought upon the world. It would be very interesting to know that the same "cracks" in concepts—a similar crisis of representation—has appeared in domains of power/knowledge far from the self-identifications or sympathies of left-liberal scholars.

Although we did not achieve the exact mix of scholars and practitioners that we had planned for the seminar, we did assemble a group of people with very diverse connections to the academy—an organizing scheme that turned out to have an equally illuminating result. As will be seen, virtually all of the participants have indeed gotten at the critically reflexive dimensions embedded within the institutional contexts and the very public issues and events that they probe—the contemporary anxieties, "cracks," and acknowledged indeterminacies in otherwise confident expert and common-sense discourses— the excavation of which was one of the seminar's tasks.

The association of this SAR advanced seminar with the one held in 1984 that led to the publication of *Writing Culture: The Poetics and Politics of Ethnography* (Clifford and Marcus 1986) is both irresistible and inevitable. The present seminar took place approximately ten years later in the same venue, included some of the same participants (Fischer, Marcus, and Rabinow), and certainly concerned issues that are directly connected to the legacy of that earlier effort. Indeed, *Writing Culture* came to stand distinctively for anthropologists as well as others outside the discipline both as a marker of anthropology's assimilation to, and as a sign of the general direction of, the 1980s' critical trend in social thought and the human sciences. Without harboring any nostalgia for that moment or hopes of equaling its impact, we recognize that the present volume does have direct links to that earlier one, and these must be addressed.

In our seminar discussions, we tried to define an alternative legacy for *Writing Culture,* one that had generally been under-acknowledged in the anthropological responses to it. *Writing Culture* originally generated three dimensions of response: one concerning its attention to poetics, one concerning its attention to epistemology, and one concerning its attention to politics. Certainly, the response to its emphasis on poetics was overplayed—the idea that this project was only a critique of ethnographic writing in narrowly literary terms. There was a certain therapeutic and positive effect in making anthropologists self-conscious about their rhetoric, but the effects of this critique seemed to be limited to ethnographic writing only. It did not extend to the empirical method that grounds such writing—the fieldwork process itself.[4]

The response to *Writing Culture*'s concern with epistemology—especially the practice of critical reflexive understanding—was often, albeit from a fundamentally sympathetic stance, to criticize the authors for being insufficiently reflexive themselves, or at least insufficiently representative (for the very strong and constructive feminist critique in this regard, see Behar and Gordon's *Women Writing Culture* [1995]). The implications of the *Writing Culture* critique for the political context and significance of contemporary anthropological research was perhaps the most overlooked of the three dimensions of response, and is now especially addressed in the ongoing reshaping of classic assumptions about the conduct of fieldwork.

The papers of this volume are distinctive for how each manages all three legacies of the *Writing Culture* project; all of the authors intermingle concerns about their own textuality and rhetoric, about their situated modes of knowing, and about the politics and political implication of research practice itself. In fact, among the seminar participants there was significant diversity in situated modes of knowing as well as political orientations. What we agreed upon was an intense interest in the positioning modalities involved in our various projects and the more general significance of these for the state of research in critical anthropology now. Amid the range and diversity of the poetics, politics, and epistemological preferences displayed in the papers, all represent attempts to constitute objects of study in new ways and to explore the complex relations of anthropological scholars to them.

REFLEXIVE MODERNIZATION: HOW POSTMODERN ARE WE?

Reflexive modernization is a social theoretical construct raised in response to the long-standing intellectual trend of the late 1970s through the present of speaking in terms of postmodernism and positing a present era of postmodernity. Although it incorporates the critical power of postmodernist discourse to disrupt the existing establishment of narratives and frameworks of social thought, reflexive modernization seeks to ground and systematize these critical initiatives in more sociological and empirical terms. Reflexive modernization thus does not so much oppose the idea of postmodernity as specify it for social thought. The construct is prominently developed in the recent writings of Ulrich Beck (1992) and Anthony Giddens (1990, 1991), and it is critically reviewed by Scott Lash (1993) under the guiding influence of Zygmunt Bauman (1991).[5]

Reflexive modernization is especially appropriate to introduce here because it conceptually frames what is at stake in one of the originating tasks of the seminar—that of exploring and assaying within their own contexts and terms of reference the levels of critical reflexivity exhibited in the operations of formal organizations and institutions of policy, government, science, and industry devoted to the pragmatic, rational control of social problems. In clarifying and amending theories of the postmodern, the construct of reflexive modernization proposes that the modernity characteristic of industrial society is succeeded by a modernity that involves living with irreducible contingency, living in a more complex and less controllable world. Reflexivity as a self-monitoring process on the level of both institutions and individual persons becomes not only a pervasive activity of society, but also a key focus of social thought itself, as presented in Beck's influential formulation of "risk society" (1992).

In one version of reflexive modernization (which Lash sees as characterizing both Beck and Giddens), however, self-monitoring retains close associations with classic ideas of social engineering and feedback; while contingency is considered to be profound, it is manageable, if not controllable, by increased learning. This version still has intellectual ties with the so-called Enlightenment project, and it sees reflexivity as a limited notion tied to the interests of problem-solving without sufficiently radical hermeneutic openness. In the other version of reflexive modernization, the failure of simple self-monitoring is acknowledged, contingency as a social condition is so profound as to be natural, and reflexivity is a far more critical enterprise with increased possibilities for the self-transformation of persons and systems in modernity.

In either version, though, the construct of reflexive modernization specifies and provides a theoretical context for the task of cultural critique that was suggested in this seminar. It is indisputable that reflexivity as a self-monitoring process is pervasive in contemporary rationalist organizations and institutions. Rather, the question worth addressing—both for the continued relevance of critical intellectual movements that have arisen in the academy over the past two decades and for the possibility of a future conversation of critical substance between the human sciences and the policy sciences—is how post-modern (how critically reflexive, how open, how shaken up in rationalist cognition) are the conditions of reflexivity within the operations of various institutions and formal organizations of contemporary late-twentieth-century life?

This is an eminently and urgent empirical question, one whose study requires the sensibility of ethnographers since reflexivity of the sort we are interested in assaying is unlikely to announce itself doctrinally or, say, in the planning departments and operations of organizations. Rather, it must be read as cracks, fissures, and shifts in cases and processes of dealing with phenomena, clients, and situations that don't fit operative categories and that resist easy fixes. The indications of reflexive modernization of the critical hermeneutic sort are likely to be registered not seismically, but in terms of tremors.

My own paper in this volume is an extended methodological exercise in relation to this task. It focuses on a recent historical example of such a tremor—the state of humanities thinking and strategic nuclear policy in the 1980s, in the years preceding the dramatic end of the Cold

War. I suggest the sort of genealogies that might establish affinities between these two "worlds apart" power/knowledge spaces, affinities that would allow mutually relevant discussions to take place among scholars and experts who might have thought they had little in common. The implications of this work go beyond relieving the anxiety of recent critical theorists that their concerns might have been insular and hermetic, merely projected upon the world. Once we have established convincing links through ethnographically sensitive translation, critical anthropology's agenda may become an attempt to exploit or explore those links in further dialogues across very strange, and estranged, boundaries of academic/expert intellectual discourse. What is at stake here, then, is the engagement of critical anthropology in a conversation with policy studies, but in a framework that critical anthropology has a substantial role in shaping.

Other papers in this volume reflect projects that more directly assay the level of critically reflexive modernization that appears in particular power/knowledge arenas. Here I think of David Brent's reflection on the state of academic publishing at a major American university press; of Kim Fortun's probing of the internal transformations in Union Carbide following the Bhopal disaster; of Peter Hall's consideration of major in-process changes in law, consultancy, and the work of "knowledge workers" generally in relation to a nonprofit sector that has rapidly and massively transformed its structural role in US political economy with the increasing importance of contracting regimes; of Judy Stacey's confrontation with the centrist shift of academic views of the family in league with the emergence of right-wing political movements; of James Faubion's and Sherry Ortner's studies of how contemporary media cover unusual events and new social formations, each of which registers efforts to come to terms with challenges that test the limits of what it has meant to do "reporting"; of Michael Fischer's consideration of the multiple expert and casual practices of communication that being involved with and in cyberspace calls into question; and of Paul Rabinow's meditation upon his collaboration with the scientist/businessman Tom White. Each of these pieces can be read as a measure of the crises of representation in various complexly intersecting domains: the manner and circumstances in which such crises are

Brenneis?

articulated; the degrees of explicit reevaluations of operative frameworks; the renamings of past practices and categories in response to such crises, at the level of official policy or of informal discussions of craft and corridor talk; and the degrees of detectable institutional resistance to change.

In this vein, Rabinow puzzles over what his work meant to scientists who welcomed him into their work environments and found what he was doing to be "useful." (But in what ways? And in what senses did Rabinow himself find what he did "useful"?). Fortun demonstrates that although the Bhopal disaster had profound consequences for Union Carbide and resulted in many shifts and transformations in the definition of what it was doing as a corporation, there was relatively little enunciation of these changes within the organization. Ortner reveals the sociological inadequacies of media representations of social trends like Generation X, but acknowledges that such media are nonetheless struggling with how to communicate massive cultural change to a popular audience. As Faubion shows, the media coverage of Waco—an odd collection of contradictory representations—became intimately a part of the events themselves, a kind of inclusion that the media was unable to deal with reflexively. Both Hall and Stacey demonstrate how cultural changes may reconfigure political domains—Stacey more directly through political alignments, Hall more ironically through emergence in legal cases in which new forms of organization become recognized and the very nature of private property, privacy, and neighborhood are subtly transformed. Brenneis presents a unique view of the crisis of representation within a key gatekeeping agency of the US government that through its funding decisions shapes intellectual trends and their terms of discourse.

Finally, working within another key gatekeeper of academic production, Brent assays the university press's assumption that everything changes but stays the same. His contribution is perhaps the most ironic: the press is intimately linked to the academic production of ideas, monitoring and exploiting them simultaneously for the often contradictory worlds of scholarship and business. Of the institutional and corporate sites considered in this volume the university press is perhaps the one most aware of critical reflexive trends, but it appears to be the least affected by this reflexivity. Brent's tone, not as academic but as businessman, is itself a datum of change, expressing a sense not so different after all from the unease in academia caused by the crisis of representation.

So the question is not the presence or absence elsewhere of critical reflexivity of the sort that has been fetishized in the academy during the 1980s, but rather its precise locale and articulation. Indeed, the future of critical ethnography itself depends on our ability to understand its affinities with critical sensibilities in other power/knowledge domains. Far from taking the distanced perspective on the "other" that has traditionally been ethnography's stance, ethnographers involved in such new locations are differently positioned altogether. Today, the fact of intellectual or cultural affinity between observer and observed is indeed "useful" knowledge, guiding us in new terrains and pointing up the need to modify standard fieldwork assumptions and settings.

EMERGENT CHANGES IN THE CHARACTER OF FIELDWORK

How did the seminar participants gain such keen inside perspectives on the shifting discourses of institutions, media, and corporations? Who were their informants, and what relationships did they have with them? The relationships reported on in this book have a qualitatively different tone and basis from the relationships with informants portrayed in "classic" fieldwork. The relative equality between or even superordination of informants in relation to ethnographers, for example, would alone make most of these cases exceptional. How did these writers participate in their research settings? What were the various constituencies for their projects? Here, I do not mean the possible audiences for the written product of the research, but those groups with an interest in the fieldwork itself. These kinds of questions led to discussions in the seminar of the changing agendas of research that often occurred unexpectedly in midcourse or at a later phase of fieldwork. We began to speak of the "citizen" anthropologist as a shorthand for our striving for a more defined sense of what these shifts in context, constituency, and agenda might mean for the practice of ethnography generally.

These considerations evoke the other preoccupation that emerged during the seminar, one that goes to the heart of the practices of research in contemporary anthropology and how they are changing as new domains and topics of work open up. What is distinctive about the projects represented in this volume is a new sense of the locations and spaces in which they operate. Anthropology has specialized largely in the study of everyday lifeworlds located outside the formal institutions of modernity: in communities, neighborhoods—sites of residence—have been the sites of fieldwork, with the surrounding "system"—state, economy, institutional order—constructed as context in an aggregate way. And when ethnography has defined its subjects within institutional arenas, as it has tended to do more frequently in recent years—in factories, schools, offices, hospitals, and corporations as circumscribed subcultures—it has tended to treat these sites as if they were like traditional places of study, as everyday lifeworlds.

What is distinctive, then, about the projects in this volume, as representatives of a whole generation of new work, is that they collapse the earlier distinction between "system" and "lifeworld" by constituting cultural formations as objects of study, formations defined by issues, problems, and dispersed features that require the fieldworkers to be mobile and multisited in their actual research trajectories. They operate in multisited spaces in which institutional and everyday life worlds are, if not collapsed, at least included in the same picture or frame of research and thus subject to the same intensive ethnographic treatment (see Gupta and Ferguson 1997a and 1997b; Marcus 1995).

Perhaps the most radical move required of this refiguration of the space of both fieldwork and the resulting ethnography is overcoming distinctions between elites and institutional orders ("others" whom anthropologists traditionally do not study), subalterns ("others" whom we do study), and anthropologists themselves, in the position of ethnographer as "other" to either elites or subalterns. As the compass of these ethnographic projects moves unpredictably across this segmented terrain, where the multiple sites of fieldwork and their connections must be reimagined, the concepts of elites, anthropologists, and subalterns get rearranged. Power structures and conspiratorial groups as the defining features of elites aside, the qualities that we have attributed to elites are not "other" or distant to us as scholars at all. Rather, reference to elites masks the play of institutional orders, which incorporates "us" as merely a different institutional interest, and a thoroughly elite one at that.

Operating within these new spaces of fieldwork has implications for the traditional sympathetic involvement of ethnographers with their subjects: these involvements are now multiple, conflicting, and more ambiguous. The nature and quality of fieldwork can be very different in different sites, requiring from a research persona (the ethnographer) a kind of resolution quite different from that which has normally characterized the anthropological fieldworker—a persona that was a major component of the much critiqued traditional conventions of authority in ethnographic writing (I know because "I was there"—I saw, I sympathized, etc.—see Clifford and Marcus 1986). The construction of a persona or identity both in fieldwork and in writing creates what I have called elsewhere a kind of circumstantial activism (Marcus 1995) in these new projects.

These new spaces of work entail new involvements, which make fieldwork so different and strange. And new involvements lead to circumstantial activism. This is not the traditional sort of activist commitment common in academic work; neither is it the traditional self-defined activist role claimed by the left-liberal scholar. It is not the activism claimed in relation to or affiliation with a particular social movement outside academia or the domain of research, nor is it the academic claim to an imagined vanguard role for a particular style of writing or scholarship with reference to a posited ongoing politics in a society or culture at a specific historical moment. Rather, it is activism quite specific and circumstantial to the conditions of doing multisited research itself. It arises from the various interventions that one makes in each of the fieldwork sites and the resulting issue of resolving the sometimes contradictory relationships among those interventions. After all, the anthropologist is not the presumed outsider that she or he was in traditional research. In order to work at all, she or he must make certain kinds of alliances or separations to define the very position of ethnographer. In certain sites, one seems to be working with, and in others, working against, changing sets of subjects.

Having to shift personal positions in relation to one's subjects and other active discourses in fields that overlap with one's own generates a sense of doing more than just traditional ethnography, and it provides a sense of being an activist in even the most "apolitical" fieldworker. This sense emerged frequently in our seminar discussions, as we tried to label and calibrate the integral activist side of these projects. Public issues were being addressed, but not necessarily in a public forum; rather, they were being addressed in the intimate, personal scenes of fieldwork. In whatever way the voice of the ethnographer might later be projected in the ethnography itself, seminar participants wanted to see what they were doing as the practice of a responsible form of activism, as at least the practice of citizenship. The "citizen anthropologist" was the term used in several of our discussions for this new kind of involvement in these projects. Nothing grandiose was being claimed for ethnography in the resonance of the term; rather, we were reaching for some articulation of the very politicized identity that was being shaped in the networks of multisited research.

The citizen ethnographer operates in a much expanded field where ethnographic positions are always implicated with others that are both like and unlike it. This kind of circumstantial activism is indeed the surrogate of the old sense of "being there" in some focused place or site with its own attendant politics and ethics. But it is made more complex by the fact that it must be performed multiply, necessitating some ethical, critical sense of the resulting fragmentation of ethnographic subjectivity. What emerges is a different sense of the politics of ethnography, a field in which the ethnographer will appear to be more engaged than in the past.

The papers in this volume reflect projects that are very much in transition in relation to these new trends; they are particularly interesting as case studies or barometers of this shift in research practices. Most of the projects evolved into their current positions, each in a different way, from work that began with more traditional assumptions. In other words, the trend was discovered along the way rather than being a matter of design.

Working in these new locations resulted in a certain seat-of-the-pants, ad hoc effort in our seminar discussions to name the new kinds of relations encountered by ethnographers in these unfamiliar spheres: terms like "new technologies of form-giving," "writing machines" (elaborated below), "human services contracting regimes," "new formations of extramural cum public structures," "para-public institutions," "knowledge workers." These terms have to do with the special congery of projects brought together at this seminar, but they reflect a striving to deal pragmatically with spheres in which standard framing concepts are no guide.

These papers show that the crisis of representation is not willed (or invented) by the scholar. Rather, it emerges most interestingly and substantively as a function of the conditions of work that seeks to treat cultural formations as something far more complex than those encompassed in the everyday lifeworlds of a limited set of subjects concentrated in an easily defined place. This had been the framing limitation of traditional ethnography.

In Paul Rabinow's paper, the conventional science studies site of a lab or workplace is expanded to the much more diverse terrain of a biotechnology company and process. His study takes into account the other genres of writing on this topic, of which he is keenly aware; the fascinating intersection of science with business that disrupts any stable, focused location of the mise-en-scène of fieldwork; and his own fascination with the similarities and differences between aspects of his personal sense of self and those of his subjects.

In James Faubion's study of the Branch Davidian conflagration at Waco, Texas, any hope of locating the aftermath of the events at Waco as a clearly delineated fieldwork site from which a conventional ethnographic account might be derived is dashed by the extraordinary media saturation of that place. The repetitive and thorough descriptions of events in redundant journalistic commentary make the locale itself a convincing case of postmodernist hyperreality. "Being there" amid such saturation, Faubion creates an account of the extraordinary cultural production of the events themselves through diverse representations.

As a result of her clearly delimited and focused ethnographic study of new family formations among the workers of Silicon Valley (Stacey 1990), Judith Stacey began to develop and locate her work in a broader and more dispersed sphere of contemporary American politics, which she is now treating both as an activist and a scholar. In a sense, her ethnography connected successfully with a context of reception that was there all along, and she was both pushed and pulled into an arena for academics of "new formations of extramural cum public structures." Here, the playing out of politics in terms of cultural issues like " family values" requires alignments and manipulations of academics as knowledge workers with diverse other functions and uses. As they find themselves in these sometimes uncomfortable positions, North American academics, in this case ethnographers, are discovering new dimensions to their work that affect every aspect of the research and writing process.

Peter Hall, a former academic historian, is now a full-time knowledge worker who consults and produces scholarship on the nonprofit sector where many of the new functions, uses, and pressures on traditional scholarship are being generated. His paper conveys the complexities of focusing an ethnographic concentration on this terrain, as well as his considerable agility in so doing. The bureaucratic-sounding subject of "human services contracting regimes" seems far from the issues of middle-class lives in places of residence and work—the neighborhood—wherein one expects ethnography to be developed. Hall make the stakes of such an organizational regime cogent for the lives of particular groups of people, following a path not merely of fine-grained description of a case study, but of considerable working through of issues concerning the legal and bureaucratic representation of that case. The ethnography at the heart of his piece thus has an unusual and complex structure of research and fieldwork contexts.

Kim Fortun's partially successful effort to develop the internal conditions of the Union Carbide corporation after Bhopal as a site for ethnographic investigation opened a much broader context of inquiry—determined by luck, by her own shrewd strategy, by what documents were available to her, and by whose doors were and were not literally closed to her. Her paper in this volume is integrally tied to other sites, especially in India, in which she has been situated as both fieldworker and activist. Her original project to focus ethnography upon the activist movements around Bhopal after the disaster mapped a much more complex object of investigation and compelled her to extend her fieldwork to law offices, corporate settings, and activist organizations in the United States and elsewhere. Hers is a prime example of a globally mapped project that begins with a local focus on a subject matter that compellingly pushes the fieldworker to probe elsewhere, to follow out other lines of inquiry.

Michael Fischer performs here a playful and profound internalization of the present and emerging conventions of Internet communication. In so doing, he evokes the crisis of representation that exists not only productively in the world of cyberspace but fearfully in the world of texts, a relatively static discursive medium. Writing here from within the long-standing textual confines of ethnography, Fischer reports on the ongoing immersion of ethnography's "writing machine" in the circuitry of a vast new "machine"—one that preserves the functions and spirit of ethnography while radically changing its forms and practice.

The ethnography in Don Brenneis's paper emerges from a professional task in which many scholars become involved, one that operates at a key interface between academia and the state's support for it. A kind of informal or chimerical ethnographic orientation toward events and situations in other contexts of their personal lives is a pose that anthropologists often adopt. In this volume, however, Brenneis—along with Ortner, Hall, Brent, and, to some degree, Fischer and Stacey—has extended this proclivity and made a somewhat more formal ethnography of aspects of his autobiography and work situation to create an unusual setting that productively suggests the shifting constituencies for and changing agendas of fieldwork. While Brenneis's piece remains an expert analysis of the ethnography of communication, its purpose may not be to pioneer an emerging field of specialization in anthropology (the anthropology of bureaucracies?) or to contribute to the anthropology of education, but rather to affect the bureaucratic process in question—a process in which Brenneis is as much, if not more, sometime member than sometime anthropologist.

Finally, in precisely the same way, Sherry Ortner defined for herself an unusual object of study—her Newark high school class—that was bound to explode the usual mise-en-scène of place-focused ethnographic research, giving her work dimensions as broad as US society itself. The shape of Ortner's research was defined by the demographic profile of her class cohort. Through tracking down its members and doing sets of ethnographic interviews, she has produced a study that has the grounded intensity of ethnography among interrelated subjects (in this case, not an existing community but a collective past experience), but with broad social and cultural scope. She thus provides one attractive and feasible model for the reconfiguration of ethnographic method.

WRITING CULTURE, WRITING MACHINES

One of the most interesting metaphors that emerged in our seminar discussions as a means of collectively characterizing our concerns was the notion of the "writing machine." By this we sought to express the sense that we were doing fieldwork in institutional and everyday contexts in which the production of representations, images, writing, and inscriptions in various modes was not only pervasive, but directly challenged the ethnographic task itself, at base a social practice of recording and representation. The omnipresence of such media—the writing machine—forced a fundamental rethinking of that task in the ways that this volume manifests from case to case.

This evocation of writing machines harks back to my earlier discussion of this seminar's relation to the 1980s' *Writing Culture* project, and the significance of the present volume as a commentary on the legacies of that project. Most of us who participated in the *Writing Culture* seminar saw ourselves primarily as researchers in the fieldwork paradigm, and we always viewed it as having deep implications for the ethnographic process that produced the writing. The act of "writing culture" is not merely writing but is the active process that moves the researcher from fieldwork to text. As is apparent from the research situations described in the chapters of this volume, any contemporary fieldwork project is deeply implicated in organizations of cultural production that are indeed writing processes. It is in this sense that the original critique of ethnography in its focus on writing had broader implications. It had much more to do with the ethnographic process than just the way monographs were written. This is what the references to writing machines pointed to.

One message, then, of the *Writing Culture* critique was not simply to explore more intensively the conventional authorial function of the fieldworker in relation to his or her subjects but to break the bounds of that frame altogether in the effort of constituting different and more complex spaces in which fieldwork/ethnography might occur. What's more, in defining these expanded spaces for specifically ethnographic research (which others in anthropology have been more accustomed to treating in classic languages of historical political economy), the notion of writing, far from being limited to the writing of monographs, becomes pivotal for thinking through how ethnography might construct and enter these more complex spaces.

The concept of the writing machine derives from Freud's attempt to model dreams and other psychic processes (Freud 1974[1925]). It has been filtered through French poststructuralism in various guises (primarily in the work of Deleuze and Guattari [1986], who created key distinctions around the notion of the machinic, but also in de Certeau's [1984] notion of scriptural economies and, to some extent, in Derrida [1978]). We take it up to refer to intersubjective and material modes of the production of both representations and the limits of representation. We were interested in this concept because most of our projects shared certain conditions that had to do with modifying or repositioning the writing functions of ethnography as we found our roles as fieldworkers and as writers to be inseparably linked.

There is virtually no space or scene of contemporary fieldwork that has not already been thoroughly mediated by other projects of representation. There is no longer any question of ethnographers entering these spaces as if these other layers and competing sectors of representation—often written or discursive in a quite literal sense—did not exist. The freshness of ethnographic perspective thus depends not on the recreation of an unmediated site of discovery of an "other": good literary journalists are likely to have been there already. Rather, any direct sense of others as subjects—a distinctive contribution of anthropology—must be preceded by disentangling dense webs of already existing representations, some of which are likely to have been produced by the subjects themselves. Ethnography thus becomes one kind of writing machine among others, and ultimately the literal events, actions, and behaviors that are the descriptive foci of study of ethnography must be negotiated as already having been heavily represented, inscribed, and written about.

Ethnographers employ a rather primitive and even naive organization or economy of writing in their work (symbolized iconically, perhaps, by the tattered, bug-stained field notebook of traditional ethnography—see, for example, the image of Stephen Tyler on the cover of *Writing Culture*) and may find intimidating these other structures of power and organization, understood as writing machines, with their much more complex productions of representation (legal opinions, corporate reports, news copy, or journalistic pieces, backed up by their elaborate divisions of labor for research, fact-checking, and editorial control). In the new fieldwork sites we encounter an image of the lone anthropologist with her notebook, tape recorder, and word processor, working amidst the massive corporate structures of law, media, science, and contemporary political movements. In virtually every paper in this volume, law and media as producers of powerful and sometimes authoritative representations intrude into the contexts of research, transforming the traditional isolated and circumscribed writing functions of ethnographers and giving them the kind of engaged political character that I have termed circumstantial activism.

Consider, for example, James Faubion reflecting the media glare of Waco; Judith Stacey resisting the "left-liberal" role created for her by the writing machine of the family values movement; Kim Fortun seeking her own truths amid the welter of memos, reports, and public relations initiatives within Union Carbide; Michael Fischer as pen-holding ethnographer nearly overwhelmed by the powerful new technology of writing in cyberspace; Paul Rabinow parsing the differences between his own intense commitment to analytic scholarly work and his scientific collaborators'/subjects' relative nonchalance, and at the same time between himself and the highly knowledgeable journalists treating the same topic; and Sherry Ortner critically objectifying and simultaneously engaging with the competing sociological writing within journalism concerning Generation X.

Each of these papers can be read as an experiment in overcoming the naive model of anthropological writing; all the authors have found themselves involved in other kinds of writing machines—not as a function of intellectual work separate from fieldwork but as an integral, inseparable part of it. This overlapping of highly structured projects of representation, of writing machines, in which the ethnographic process becomes engulfed is finally what it means to include institutional and everyday life worlds as parallel, complexly connected objects of study in the same frame of ethnographic inquiry. The writing machine is not just an interesting way to think about this more complex object of ethnography, it is a defining feature of fieldwork reflexive enough that it will not sustain the primitive writing machine of traditional anthropology in splendid isolation.

Ethnographic writing is thus what ultimately ties anthropologists reflexively to their contexts of study—those uncertain environments of response, reaction, reception, and competition in which they increasingly find themselves. "Writing culture" thus becomes a much broader exercise that not only signifies the production of texts in a certain controlled genre but also stands as a metaphor for the distinctive research process of fieldwork itself in these new locations.

ANTHROPOLOGY'S UNEASE: IS THERE REALLY A CRISIS OF REPRESENTATION?

The difference in perception among anthropologists about the future course of our discipline no longer revolves around hyperbolic claims to the rapidity and massiveness of transformation in late twentieth-century societies, as it still might have in the 1970s and 1980s. By the 1990s we seem to have reached consensus about the substantial changes that surround and have altered the nature of anthropology's objects of study. Where there remains considerable disagreement, as well as difference in scholarly sensibilities, is in how much change is required in methods, concepts, and theories in order to accommodate the study of these changes. Can current emergent transformations be understood in the frame of historical narratives? Is the concept of class, for example, even suitably modified, still useful as a tool for the study of society?

One set of preferences is for what we might call progressive conservation; another is for the development and exploration of radically different frames of work. Indeed, this was a major dividing line in our seminar discussions. Most of the participants were oriented toward new departures, but others were skeptical of the need to radically change methods and concepts of work in anthropology. Did the new proposals carry the same substance and strength of framework as did older perspectives that might be reformed, or did they contain more rhetoric than substance? One participant posed the underlying question: "Was there any room left for the problem of the 'durable' within the new?" Indeed, the durable seems to have been neglected in recent years with the influence of poststructuralism and the enthusiasm for a new sociological or cultural imaginary stimulated by the velocity and quality of recent globalizing social changes.

Indeed, there is a good deal of talking past each other on this issue, and what is being expressed, at least in terms of the worries over whether the crisis of representation is just rhetoric rather than substance, is a good deal of anxiety about the changing nature of anthropological work as well as some desire to resist it. The weight of the seminar and the projects it represented was to develop new grounds of work—to reconfigure the idea of the fieldwork process and the given range of analytic concepts, but there is no doubt that continuing stimulating work can be done by either set of preferences.

Acting on the perceived need for a revision of concepts and modes of work is more radical than simply supporting the call to replace one set of theories and methods with something better. We are not pursuing novelty for its own sake, some new aesthetic of theory. Ours is more a question of how the whole research enterprise might be repositioned in terms of changing constituencies and accountabilities; what this means can be quite variable in terms of the use of traditional concepts and methods. By this very repositioning, traditional concepts and methods are called into question, and this may be what the skeptics of a crisis of representation want to resist. They seek a more limited, circumscribed anthropology that leads to a specific sort of payoff.

Is the crisis of representation just rhetoric, or is it substantive? Most of the papers in this seminar demonstrated that the crisis of representation affects substance: it changes the basic nature of ethnographic research itself. No longer does it involve only the distanced scholarly specialist arguing with other scholars about the best theories and methods to use. Of course, scholarly communities remain one of the constituencies of ethnographic work, and pragmatically they are one of the most important since they are tied to academic institutions and define careers and rewards. But there are very clearly other constituencies for ethnographic work that break the frame of the isolated scholarly enterprise: again, circumstantial activism and the citizen anthropologist become an integral part of ethnography. Work slips in and out of parapublic settings; it is answerable to one's subjects in more substantial ways than in the past; it becomes thoroughly immersed in other kinds of writing machines in the space of its operations. Knowledge can be produced in this way also, but what sort of knowledge and for whom? Being open to this radical transformation of the research process is what is at stake in acting on a crisis of representation.

Resisting the sense of this crisis means preserving a distanced practice of scholarship for academics and whomever else it informs, and the considerable benefits it produces—it is creatively conservative, the result of a choice to remain only scholastic (see Bourdieu 1990). Resisting the crisis means preserving the tradition of the discipline, just as it is changing to meet new challenges. It means seeing certain things and missing others.

The second preference is more risky: to seek to develop new narratives of work that no longer occupy the same position or are circumscribed in the same way as the older disciplinary narratives. This change is based on the profound effect on research of recognizing certain affinities and identifications between the reflexive predicaments of the ethnographer and those she or he studies. It breaks the frame that holds analysis apart and in nervous reaction arouses questions and doubts (quite justified and self-fulfilling in this limited frame) about whether there is a crisis of representation.

In this way, the two tasks of this seminar project are intimately linked. Postmodernism is relevant not because it provides truer or more powerful explanatory models with which anthropologists can treat social facts among their subjects but rather because, in a sense, postmodernism is also differentially practiced "out there" on a widespread basis. This indeed is the crisis of representation—the breaking of the frame of conventional scholarly work altogether rather than the demise and replacement of specific concepts and methods characteristic of this academic frame—and it can be seen in the way that work such as the projects in this volume is evolving amid unexpected contexts, shifting constituencies, and changing agendas.

Notes

1. This is David Brent's paraphrase of the first sentence of Immanuel Kant's *Critique of Pure Reason.* This playful effort by Brent to thematize the seminar at one point in our discussions was met by the participants' unanimous and amused sense that he had succinctly captured what we had been trying to address. I therefore use it here as an appropriate epigraph to the Introduction.

2. In *Anthropology as Cultural Critique* (Marcus and Fischer 1986), we argued that in the typical ethnographic project there is always an "us" in the "there," the "us" referring in the case of US anthropologists to the implicit references in their research elsewhere to conditions in our own society. The project of critique we discussed was based upon amplifying this often underplayed relationship in ethnography. Now we would make the same argument in nonbinary terms. There are many frames, sites, and subject positions, the exploration of which becomes both the object and means of ethnographic research; there is no simple "us" orienting the reflexive dimension of critical work in anthropology. But multiplying the critical frame of reference does more than change the rhetoric of ethnographic representation. It destabilizes the conditions of fieldwork, the subject position of the fieldworker, and the ways that these have been typically imagined as well. This volume is about case studies of some of the destabilizations now underway.

3. To capture something of the spirit of this intellectual era, see the three related large volumes of readings by Grossberg and Nelson (1988), Grossberg, Nelson, and Treichler (1992), and Goankar and Nelson (1996), which both take the measure of and helped establish the trend.

4. Indeed, the volume *Recapturing Anthropology* (Fox 1992), based on a 1989 SAR advanced seminar, was intended politely to take in the *Writing Culture* critique and firmly move beyond it, by renewing faith in the revived vigor of traditional fieldwork and cultural historical approaches.

5. A composite discussion of the reflexive modernization construct is available in a useful volume (Beck, Giddens, and Lash 1994) that presents papers and responses by each of the three principal theorists.

2

Virtual Social Science and the Politics of Family Values

Judith Stacey

From the wild Irish slums of the nineteenth-century Eastern seaboard to the riot-torn suburbs of Los Angeles, there is one unmistakable lesson in American history: a community that allows a large number of young men to grow up in broken families, dominated by women, never acquiring any stable relationship to male authority, never acquiring any set of rational expectations about the future—that community asks for and gets chaos. Crime, violence, unrest, unrestrained lashing out at the whole social structure—that is not only to be expected; it is very near to inevitable.

—Daniel Patrick Moynihan, 1965

The way a male becomes a man is by supporting his children....What [the Democrats] cannot accept is that government proposals have failed. It is the family that can rebuild America....The dissolution of the family, and in particular, the absence of fathers in the lives of millions of America's children is the single most critical threat [to our future].

—Dan Quayle, September 8, 1994

That is a disaster. It is wrong. And someone has to say again, "It is simply not right. You shouldn't have a baby before you're ready, and you shouldn't have a baby when you're not married."

—President Bill Clinton, September 9, 1994

> I am flattered by Judith Stacey's view that my colleagues and I at the Institute for American Values are "central players" in a successful effort to "forge a national consensus on family values and to shape the family politics of the 'new' Democratic Party." As I understand it, we stand accused of persuading many people, including many in the media and in the Clinton Administration, to pay more attention to the problem of fatherlessness and the importance of the two-parent home. I believe that we are guilty as charged.
>
> —*David Blankenhorn, July 1994*

The discourse of family crisis in the United States has a history as long as that of the republic, but as the twentieth century draws to a close, its outpourings proliferate in terms more urgent, fractious, and ubiquitous than members of our fore-families could conceivably have imagined. David Blankenhorn, president of the Institute for American Values and director of the National Fatherhood Initiative, quoted above, figures prominently in the most recent, and least anticipated, development in this discursive history—a cultural campaign for "family values" waged primarily by social scientists operating outside the academy. The campaign claims the legitimacy of social science in a crusade to restore eroded privileges and prestige to fathers and the heterosexual, married-couple, nuclear families it wishes them to head (Stacey 1994a, 1994b). From the Institute for American Values, its offshoot, the Council on Families in America, and the American Family Panel of research scholars, which the Institute is cosponsoring with Rutgers University, to the Communitarian Network and the Progressive Policy Institute, social scientists lead a concerted effort to promote centrist family ideology and policies. Among the most visible of these academic, family-values activists are William Galston (formerly Deputy Assistant to President Clinton), Amitai Etzioni, the 1994–95 president of the American Sociological Association, David Popenoe and Jean Bethke Elshtain, co-chairs of the Council on Families, and Senator Daniel Patrick Moynihan, the forefather of late-twentieth-century family crisis discourse.

On December 26, 1992, this discourse "hailed" me, by name, from the op-ed pages of the *New York Times*.[1] Cast in the role of a dissident respondent, I began to map its institutional, rhetorical, and political frameworks (Stacey 1994a, 1994b). Extending that cartographical project, I offer here a reflexive, sociology-of-knowledge treatment of political and intellectual developments inside and outside the academy that drive and configure this eleventh-hour, twentieth-century campaign. After identifying historical forces that motivate some of the principal figures who produce and disseminate this family crisis talk, I assess the campaign's implications for emergent realignments of knowledge and power.

No geographer of family values discourse can survey the domain from a disinterested epistemological or political location. Fair disclosure principles prompt me to acknowledge my position as an increasingly active participant in contemporary representational struggles over family politics, particularly those operating at the boundaries of social science, the media, and political discourse. Indeed, hostile attention attracted by *Brave New Families* (Stacey 1990), my feminist ethnography about postmodern family life, drew me away from an ethnographic project on cultural studies and into the fray of public intellectual combat over family research and politics.[2] From this engaged and inevitably partial stance, I survey the shifting borderlines and fissures of fin de siècle family values terrain.

My overlay will suggest that a widely recognized, but largely untheorized, postmodern family condition has created genuine representational, material, and moral crises in the practice, knowledge, and politics of family life in the United States. Everyone in the nation experiences this postmodern family condition, which, in turn, impinges on virtually all significant domains and axes of power.[3] There is no longer a popular or scholarly consensus on how to define the boundaries of what constitutes a legitimate family. But neither does consensus exist to grant legitimacy, or even tolerance, to the implicitly pluralistic definition of family by which the nation's inhabitants, in fact, presently live. This gaping gorge between practice and consciousness signals the collapse of a once-shared family culture rooted in religious and naturalist narratives.

The popular representational crisis of family authority reverberates in the academy, where the ruling paradigms of nineteen-fifties sociology—structural-functionalism, modernization theory, and empiricism—have lost prestige and power, but where most sociologists remain aloof from challenges posed by debates about postmodern theory and cultural studies disturbing the peace in adjacent disciplinary corridors. Feminism, however, has had a profoundly unsettling impact on the field, one which almost no sociologist has been able to ignore. Some, like David Popenoe, have nearly abandoned academic sociology to feminists and liberal demographers, while creating independent institutions through which to deploy their academic status (and more than compensate for some of its decline) in circuits of power and knowledge with far greater reach and weight than engage most feminist, postmodernist, or cultural studies scholars. The gap in the degree of prestige that functionalist sociology enjoys in popular, as compared with professional, domains is also considerable, and growing.

Moreover, fin de siècle politicians of disparate ideological hues in the US also have come to perceive significant rewards in family values discourse, as the two excerpts above from back-to-back, and nearly interchangeable, 1994 election-season speeches by Dan Quayle and Bill Clinton indicate. A peculiar conjuncture of material, political, and academic dislocations has opened the door for collaboration between mainstream social scientists and electoral politicians. Revisionist family values scholars are supplying substantial ideology, rhetoric, and legitimacy to post–Cold War "New" Democrats and "moderate" Republicans alike.

Playing hooky from besieged and tarnished ivory towers, numerous social scientists, now including myself, are waging public cultural combat for weighty political stakes over the sources of and remedies to the fall of the modern family system. As the US approaches the third Christian millennium, its populace inhabits a world of contested family life whose everyday practices and conditions of social and material decline are increasingly at odds with a mythic discourse of virtual family values that envelops us.[4]

A VIRTUAL BEDTIME FABLE FOR THE AMERICAN CENTURY

Once upon a fabulized time, half a century ago, there was a lucky land where families with names like Truman and Eisenhower presided over a world of Nelsons, Cleavers, and Rileys. Men and women married, made love, and (in that proper order), produced gurgling, Gerber babies. It was a land where, as God and Nature had ordained, men were men and women were ladies. Fathers worked outside the home for pay to support their wives and children, and mothers worked inside the home without pay to support their husbands and to cultivate healthy, industrious, above-average children. Streets and neighborhoods were safe and tidy. This land was the strongest, wealthiest, freest, and fairest in the world. Its virtuous leaders, heroic soldiers, and dazzling technology defended all the freedom-loving peoples on the planet from an evil empire that had no respect for freedom or families. A source of envy, inspiration, and protection to people everywhere, the leaders and citizens of this blessed land had good reason to feel confident and proud.

And then, as so often happens in fairytales, evil came to this magical land. Sometime during the mid-nineteen-sixties, a toxic serpent wriggled its way close to the pretty picket fences guarding those Edenic gardens. One prescient Jeremiah, named Daniel Patrick Moynihan (1965), detected the canny snake and tried to alert his placid countrymen to the dangers of family decline. Making a pilgrimage from Harvard University to the White House, he chanted about the ominous signs and consequences of "a tangle of pathology" festering in cities that suburban commuters and their ladies-in-waiting had abandoned for the crabgrass frontier. Promiscuity, unwed motherhood, and fatherless families, he warned, would undermine domestic tranquillity and wreak social havoc. Keening to the tune of only black keys, however, this Pied Piper's song fell flat, inciting displeasure and rebuke.

It seemed that, overnight, those spoiled Gerber babies had turned into rebellious, disrespectful youth who spurned authority, tradition, and conformity and scorned the national wealth, power, and imperial status in which their elders exulted. Rejecting their parents' gray flannel suits and Miss American ideals, as well as their monogamous, nuclear families, they generated a counter culture and a sexual revolution, and they built unruly social movements demanding student rights, free speech, racial justice, peace, and liberation for women and for homosexuals. Long-haired, unisex-clad youth smoked dope and marched in demonstrations, shouting slogans like "Question Authority," "Girls Say Yes to Boys Who Say No," "Smash Monogamy," "Black Is Beautiful," "Power to the People," "Make Love, Not War," "Sisterhood Is Powerful," and "Liberation Now!" Far from heeding Moynihan's warning, many young women drew inspiration from the "black matriarchs" he had condemned, condemning Moynihan instead for blaming the victims.

Disrupting families and college campuses, the young people confused and divided their parents and teachers, even seducing some foolish elders into emulating their sexual and social experiments. But the thankless arrogance of these privileged youth, their unkempt appearance, provocative antics, and amorality also enraged many, inciting a right-wing, wishful "moral majority" to form its own backlash social movement to restore family and moral order.

And so it happened that harmony, prosperity, security, and confidence disappeared from this once most-fortunate land. After decimating black communities, the serpent of family decline slithered under the picket fences, where it spewed its venom on white, middle-class families as well. Men no longer knew what it meant to be men, and women had neither time nor inclination to be ladies. Ozzie had trouble finding secure work. He was accused of neglecting, abusing, or oppressing his wife and children. Harriet no longer stayed home with the children. She too worked outside the home for pay, albeit less pay. Ozzie and Harriet sued for divorce. Harriet decided she could choose to have children with or without a marriage certificate, with or without an Ozzie, or perhaps even with a Rozzie. After all, as front page stories in her morning newspaper informed her, almost daily, "Traditional Family Nearly the Exception, Census Finds" (Shogren 1994).

As the last decade of the century dawned, only half the children in the land were living with two married parents who had jointly conceived or adopted them. Twice as many children were living in single-parent as in male-breadwinner, female-homemaker families. Little wonder few citizens could agree over what would count as a proper family. Little wonder that court chroniclers charted the devolution of the modern family system in books with anxious titles like *The War Over the Family* (Berger and Berger 1983), *Embattled Paradise* (Skolnick 1991), *Disturbing the Nest* (Popenoe 1988), *Brave New Families* (Stacey 1990), *The Way We Never Were* (Coontz 1992), *Fatherless America* (Blankenhorn 1995), and *Families on the Faultline* (Rubin 1994). The clairvoyant Daniel Patrick Moynihan found himself vindicated at last, as political candidates from both the ruling parties joined his hymns of praise to Ozzie and Harriet and rebuked the selfish family practices of that rebellious stepchild of the Nelsons, Murphy Brown.

The era of the modern family system had come to an end, and few felt sanguine about the postmodern family condition that had succeeded it. Unaccustomed to a state of normative instability and definitional crisis, the populace split its behavior from its beliefs. Many who contributed actively to such postmodern family statistics as divorce, remarriage, blended families, single parenthood, joint custody, abortion, domestic partnership, two-career households, and the like still yearned nostalgically for the "Father Knows Best" world they had lost. "Today," in the United States, as historian John Gillis (1994) so aptly puts it, "the anticipation and memory of family means more to people than its immediate reality. It is through the families we live by that we achieve the transcendence that compensates for the tensions and frustrations of the families we live with." Not only have the fabled modern families we live by become more compelling than the messy, improvisational, patchwork bonds of postmodern family life, but as my bedtime story hints, because they function as fixed elements in our distinctive national imaginary, these symbolic families are also far more stable than any actual families in which future generations ever dwelled.

Similar evidence of the decline of the modern family system appears throughout the "advanced" industrialized world, and for similar reasons, but thus far, in no other society has the decline incited responses so volatile, ideological, divisive, or so politically mobilized and influential as in the US.[5] Only here, where the welfare state was always underdeveloped and is now devolving, where religious fervor and populist movements flourish and organized labor languishes, has the beloved bedtime fable begun to evoke so many nightmares. Now the popular representational crisis of family order incites acrimonious conflicts in every imaginable arena—from television sitcoms to Congress, from the Boy Scouts of America to the United States Marines, from local school boards to multinational corporations, from art museums to health insurance underwriters, from Peoria to Cairo, and from political conventions to social science conferences.

SOCIAL SCIENCE MARCHING ON

> Contrary to expectations many of you may have of historians, I'm not here to tell you that we have seen it all before. The current obsession with family values seems to me, if not entirely new, then peculiar to the late twentieth century, and I will argue that what we are experiencing is yet another dimension of what David Harvey has called the "postmodern condition," and an example of what Anthony Giddens has identified as the late-twentieth-century capacity for intimacy at a distance.
>
> —*John Gillis, "What's Behind the Debate on Family Values?"*

> What lies behind the family values debate is that the family is in Big Deal trouble. No child would understand John Gillis's talk. A child wants to know, Will my mommy and daddy still be there?...I'm working to help make putting children at the very highest level of personal and public priority. And it's been gratifying seeing this liberal intelligentsia gradually shift. Most recently, Donna Shalala even said, Yes, when she was asked if Dan Quayle was right. I urge you to join in this new national bandwagon for the family.
>
> —*David Popenoe, "What's Behind the Debate on Family Values?"*

> The essential integrity of at least a large proportion of American family social scientists is evidenced by the fact that as the evidence accumulated on the effects of family changes, the originally sanguine views of the changes began to change to concern.
>
> —*Norval Glenn, "The Re-Evaluation of Family Change by American Social Scientists"*

Just as no new family system has yet succeeded in attaining the kind of hegemonic status that the modern, male-breadwinner, nuclear family order enjoyed at mid-century, likewise the ruling paradigms of 1950s' sociology have been dethroned but not supplanted. Probably no discipline felt the disruptive impact of the social movements of the 1960s and early 1970s more strongly than sociology. Seeking to understand and critique their own society and to explore alternatives, militant students with left-wing commitments, including draft resistors in search of student deferments, entered sociology in droves. Infatuated with romantic versions of Marxism, Leninism, Trotskyism, Maoism, and Frankfurt School theory, radical young sociologists rejected positivism, Parsonsian structural-functionalism, and modernization theory as apologias for US racism and imperialistic ventures and for the conformity and "false promises" of the Cold War era.

A feminist onslaught on the discipline pursued the left-wing attacks on structural-functional sociology and modernization theory. During the late 1960s and early 1970s, the grass roots women's movement spurred a wave of feminists to enter academic careers, where the left-liberal cast and the diffuse intellectual boundaries of sociology in its stage of crisis (Gouldner 1970) attracted many, like myself, to the discipline. Feminists organized professional caucuses, conferences, journals, and subspecialty sections in the American Sociological Association (ASA), rapidly transforming the demographics, intellectual preoccupations, and the leadership of both the professional organization and the discipline. The explicitly feminist Sex and Gender section, formed in the early 1970s, rapidly outdistanced the older, far more mainstream section on family sociology in membership, intellectual dynamism, and appeal. By 1992, it had become the largest subfield section in the ASA.[6]

Marxist and feminist interventions challenged value-free, empiricist pretensions throughout the discipline, but few subfields were quite so dislocated as family sociology. During the mid-1970s, sociology of the family experienced what Canadian sociologist David Cheal (1991:8) terms "a Big Bang in which feminism played a conspicuous part." I share Cheal's view that the "explosion blew the field apart, and the separate pieces have been flying off in different directions ever since."

Parsonsian sociology had posited the universality of the nuclear family and theorized that the gender structure of its Ozzie and Harriet, male-breadwinner–female-homemaker genus evinced an ideally evolved "functional fit" with modern industrial society and political democracy (Parsons and Bales 1955). In 1963, William J. Goode's *World Revolution and Family Patterns* predicted that modernization would accomplish the global diffusion of the superior Western variety of family life and, thereby, of the democratic society it was thought to nurture.

Feminist scholars, however, rapidly subjected 1950s' families and family sociology alike to trenchant critique. Influenced by demographic evidence of rapid family transformations in the US, by countercultural communal experiments, and by the anti-housewife ethos of the early women's liberation movement, feminist scholars exposed ethnocentric and androcentric foundations of functionalist and modernization theories of family life. Betty Friedan's scathing attack on "the functionalist freeze" in *The Feminine Mystique* (1963) had directly launched such a project, and it was but a short leap from there to Jessie Bernard's academic work on His and Her marriages (1972), or from incendiary movement classics like Pat Mainardi's "The Politics of Housework" (1970) and Ann Koedt's "The Myth of the Vaginal Orgasm" (1970) to scholarly treatments like Ann Oakley's *The Sociology of Housework* (1974) and Gayle Rubin's "The Traffic in Women" (1975).

Meanwhile, outside the embattled groves of academe, a right-wing profamily movement rapidly polarized popular discourse on family change into feminist vs. antifeminist, left vs. right, and fundamentalist vs. "secular humanist" camps. This forced the largely liberal ranks of mainstream family scholars, many of them predisposed to sympathize with Moynihan's earlier, ill-timed critique of black family decay, to confront uncomfortable ideological choices.[7] Initially most accommodated their work to liberal feminist values, but the conditions under which they did so implanted an embryo of resentment that would come full term in the backlash against "political correctness" of the 1990s. While remaining firmly wedded to an empiricist, value-free paradigm that failed to engage the theoretical challenges of feminist and materialist critiques of family sociology, during the 1960s and 1970s most scholars in the subfield supported liberal feminist critiques of the modern nuclear family. Embracing a relativistic tolerance of family experimentation as well as elements of the sexual revolution, many in the functionalist lineage produced research findings on subjects like divorce, maternal employment, day care, single parenthood, and sexual experimentation that gave comfort to the rising numbers of people involved in such practices.

Norval Glenn (1994:2), a prominent, senior, family sociologist in the US and a member of the Council on Families in America, surveys this disciplinary history as participant-observer:

> Social scientists in the United States generally took a sanguine view of the family changes that started or accelerated in the mid-1960s. Although the label of "family decline" was often attached by social scientists to the family changes that occurred early in the century, the prevailing view in the 1960s and 1970s was that the family was only adapting to new circumstances, not declining.

For example, sociologists promoted a pollyanna-ish assessment of rising divorce rates, interpreting the trend both "as a sign that marriage had become more, not less, important" to adults, because they were no longer willing to settle for unhappy unions, and as beneficial in the long run for children released from the hostile environment of an unhappily married parental home (Glenn 1994:3). Glenn confesses that he and his colleagues felt "strongly inclined to express positive views of recent family changes" then, because, the changes coincided with a feminist movement which "viewed family change and the trend toward gender equality as parts of the same bundle. Being human," sociologists sought "the approval of those whose opinions matter to them, and those persons are largely liberals" who embrace "the ideal of male-female equality" (Glenn 1994:4–5). Andrew Cherlin (1988:138), a prominent demographer and family sociologist who does not support the family-values campaign, confirms Glenn's assessment of feminist influence on family sociologists: "It is above all the wish to avoid sounding like an antifeminist, I think, that causes liberals to downplay the costs of the recent trends."

Since the late 1970s, however, the ideological force field within which scholars investigate the consequences of family change has veered decidedly rightward. Glenn demonstrates, with less reflexivity than above, that his own views have kept pace. Speaking in conjunction with the United Nations International Year of the Family in 1994 to prominent governmental, religious, and academic bodies in Australia, Glenn (1994) applauded social scientists for a voluminous "second thoughts" literature recanting earlier, uncritical stances on family change, especially concerning the social effects of divorce, fatherlessness, and single motherhood. Psychologist Judith Wallerstein's widely popularized work (Wallerstein and Blakeslee 1989), which finds that divorce inflicts substantial, lasting, and harmful effects on children, has been particularly influential, as has demographer Sara McLanahan's (1994; McLanahan and Bumpass 1988) revised assessment that single-parent families harm children. Adding his voice to "most of the more prominent family social science researchers," who, Glenn claims, now evaluate such changes "in distinctly negative terms," Glenn (1994:10) recounts his personal conversion to what he considers to be the now "virtually unanimous" social scientific view that "the best family situation for children and adolescents is one in which there is a successful, intact marriage of the biological (or adoptive) parents," and that single-parent and stepfamilies are "far less than ideal."

Whereas Glenn perceptively identifies the ideological context informing earlier, uncritical social scientific appraisals of family change, he shifts to an "objectivist," scientific narrative to account for current pessimistic verdicts. His tribute to "the essential integrity" of family social scientists (included in an epigraph above) claims that the weight of cumulative data compelled this intellectual conversion. I believe, in contrast, that just as was true during the 1960s and 1970s, reconfigurations of power and knowledge provide more illuminating explanatory pathways than does the autonomous march of (social) science. The metamorphosis occurred as a New World Order of global capitalism and economic crisis brought the glory days of sociology as a discipline to a halt, while the modernist liberal theories that had sustained its humanitarian progressivist ethos began to falter in postmodernist, neoliberal, and postfeminist currents.

If feminism unleashed a "Big Bang" in family sociology, postmodernism and cultural studies have yet to provoke much more than a whimper. Even though most family scholars are enmeshed in an ideological crisis of representation over the meaning of "family" under postmodern conditions of patchwork intimacy, very few participate "in discussions about so-called postmodern conditions of society and thought" (Marcus 1993). Like most US sociologists, they remain remote from these discourses, still wedded to a realist epistemology, to empiricism and to an unproblematic view of the transparency of discourse, texts, and representation. Feminist sociologists, European theorists like Foucault, Giddens, and Bourdieu, and infrequent visits from colleagues in other disciplines, like historian John Gillis who spoke at a session on the family values debate at the 1994 meetings of the American Sociological Association, provide mainstream sociologists with their principal, still marginal, and often defensive exposure to such questions.[8]

Fending off the intellectual challenge of Gillis's (1994) reading of postmodern family developments and discourse on the ASA panel, for example, Popenoe (1994) resorted to an anti-intellectual, populist rhetorical mode pervasive in family values discourse.[9] Amidst lingering echoes of appreciative applause for Gillis's paper, Popenoe (1994) mounted the podium of the Hotel Bonaventure's cavernous auditorium and declared, "I guess I'm the right wing here, but that's not true outside of sociology." Popenoe positioned himself against the elite world of academia and with "most Americans [who] agree with what I just said, except for the liberal intelligentsia I've been battling."

A singular lack of reflexivity about the changed historical conditions for knowledge production governing the "new locations" in which we operate renders many family social scientists, particularly senior white males like Popenoe and Glenn, responsive to the rewards of the revisionist campaign. Since the 1970s, the discipline of sociology has become increasingly feminized, but the massive feminist Sex and Gender section remains a female ghetto—alien, unfamiliar territory to most mainstream family scholars.[10] Academic feminism has been institutionalized and, thereby, has become both intellectually respectable, and, as any student familiar with Weber's (1946) analysis of the routinization of charisma might have predicted, partly de-fanged. It is unsurprising that displaced male scholars might now feel freer to expel feminist perspectives they once had been force-fed and never fully digested.

Moreover, the crisis in Marxism and loss of faith in materialist explanations for social change provoked by the collapse of Communism had particularly strong effects in sociology. Today, regardless of theoretical or ideological affinities, only comatose sociologists can escape "anxieties about the social field in which they operate" (Marcus 1993). However, debates in family sociology remain empirical and ideological, rather than philosophical, and few doubt that these signal more than an academic predicament. The nation's generalized right-wing political shift, the diffusion of postfeminist culture (Rosenfelt and Stacey 1987), and the organized movement against "political correctness" in higher education have offered family scholars compelling inducements to hopscotch over challenges to academic family theory posed by the postmodern family condition to land directly in the public political fray.

The centrist campaign for family values offers displaced, formerly liberal scholars an opportunity to reclaim positions of intellectual authority without appearing to be antifeminist. Adopting the power-evasive, postfeminist rhetoric of "a new familism," the campaign distances itself from reactionaries intent on restoring Ozzie and Harriet to the frayed upholstery of their suburban throne. New familism, in Glenn's (1994:12) formulation, represents a return to the belief that stable marriages, two-parent families, and putting children's needs before those of adults are desirable and important. It differs from the older familism in its espousal of male-female equality and the rejection of economic dependence as a basis for marital stability.

Migrating ideologically from Moynihan (1965) to Friedan (1963) and then only somewhat farther back than Friedan (1981) herself has since traveled, revisionists applaud phantom signs "at the mass level" of a "return toward more traditional family values (excluding the ideal of male dominance)" (Glenn 1994:12).[11]

A few social scientists whose scholarly work never achieved major academic acclaim have found the centrist campaign a route to public influence, media celebrity, and even renewed academic attention. For example, speaking at a Peder Sather Symposium, "Gender Equality,

Children, and the Family: Evolving Scandinavian and American Social Policy," at the University of California, Berkeley, on April 6, 1994, Popenoe acknowledged that his book *Disturbing the Nest* (1988), which criticizes the impact of social democratic policies on family change in Sweden, had earned him little respect in Scandinavia: "My book did not start a dialog in Sweden. I wasn't even invited back." As if to confirm Popenoe's self-report, prominent Scandinavian scholars and officials in attendance gave his critical analysis of Scandinavian family policy a chilly, dismissive response. Karin Stoltenberg, the director-general of the Norwegian Ministry of Children and Family Affairs, for example, termed "insane" Popenoe's belief that welfare state policies were the source of rising divorce rates (see also Sandqvist and Andersson 1992). Likewise, an anti-intellectual polemic that Popenoe delivered "from the heart" at the August 1994 American Sociological Association meetings confronted nearly a solid wall of disapproval from co-panelists and the audience. Session organizer Frank Furstenberg, among the most prominent demographers and family sociologists in the US, publicly chastised Popenoe's "unhelpful us/them approach" to sociologists and the family values debate. In response, Popenoe portrayed most sociologists as out of touch with popular concerns and invited listeners sympathetic with his views to accompany him to the nearby conference of the Communitarian Network.

Since Popenoe became a major organizer of the centrist family values campaign, he has been "invited back" again and again to deliver his lament for family decline in venues that range from the "Jim Lehrer News Hour" to the US Department of Transportation, from the *New York Times* to the *Chronicle of Higher Education,* in addition to academic conferences and meetings such as at UC Berkeley and the American Sociological Association. Blankenhorn, who claims the mantle of social science despite his lack of such academic credentials or status, has achieved even greater celebrity with the National Fatherhood Tour he launched in conjunction with the release of his book *Fatherless America* (1995). From Oprah to CNN's "Talkback," from the cover pages of *Time* magazine to syndicated feature stories in hundreds of local newspapers, Blankenhorn has blazed an extramural trail to academic podiums.[12] Likewise, the family values campaign has offered William Galston, Amitai Etzioni, and their colleagues access to extensive public and professional recognition. Etzioni's public campaign as founder and director of the Communitarian movement, for example, coincided with his successful bid to become president of the ASA, and Galston took leave from his professorship at the University of Maryland to serve as deputy assistant to the president.

The rhetoric of the few women scholars, like Jean Bethke Elshtain and Sylvia Hewlett, who are visibly active in the revisionist campaign suggests more personalized resentments against academic feminists. Hewlett (1986) blames the antimaternalist ethos of second wave feminism for compounding the tribulations she suffered with her pregnancies when she was an assistant professor of economics at Barnard College in the 1970s. Elshtain complains, more plausibly, that she is "hooted out of the room" by feminists whenever she talks "about not ceding the issue of family values to the right" (quoted in Winkler 1993:A7). It is true that few academic feminists sympathize with Elshtain's support for heterosexual marital privilege or her disapproval of single motherhood, particularly as Elshtain herself once divorced while her children were young (see Heller 1995).[13] Feminists have personal and political stakes in these judgments as profound as Elshtain's, and thus, few respond to her public challenges with scholarly dispassion.[14]

It seems ironic, and in my view unlucky, that the crisis of representation which decentered mainstream family social scientists within the academy, a crisis induced by radical family change and feminism rather than by postmodernist philosophy, propelled quite a few of them into center stage in the public sphere. There, aloof from even the modest constraints of peer review, they deploy social scientific authority to influence political responses to postmodern family representational struggles by disseminating selective readings of the very functionalist research on family change that feminist sociologists imagined we had discredited. Family sociology, after all, never had been the site of too many power lunches within the academic arena, not even for feminists, let alone for postmodern or cultural studies theorists. In an era of academic retrenchment when universities like the University of Rochester, Washington University, Yale University, and San Diego State University have abolished or slashed their sociology departments, dining halls outside the ivy pastures beckon with more gratifying fare. Modernist family social scientists (and pretenders, like Blankenhorn) can often enhance their academic status in the public domain, where they enjoy much more intellectual esteem and influence than do any postpositivist or feminist theoreticians.

Unfazed by late-century epistemological quagmires, they have developed an extramural social science apparatus with which to wage their cultural crusade for centrist family values. Through interlocking networks of think tanks, organizations, periodicals, and policy institutes, these social scientists have been constructing a "virtual" scholarly and popular consensus in the media supporting the very narrative about universal family values that succumbed to feminist and other forms of deconstructive scrutiny in academia. Saturating the media-beltway world they now inhabit with this virtual new familism, they misleadingly maintain that social science has confirmed Moynihan's warning about the socially destructive effects of single motherhood, "illegitimacy," and fatherless families. However, scholars do not now, and likely will not ever, achieve consensus on the relative significance that family structure, material circumstances, the quality of parental relationships, and psychological factors play in shaping children's lives. While it is true that most sociologists in the US do express some uneasiness over mounting rates of single parenthood, the predominant scholarly view is that single-parent families are more often the consequence than the cause of poverty, unemployment, emotional distress, and other negative correlates (e.g., Cherlin 1988; Furstenberg and Cherlin 1991; and even McLanahan 1994). Ironically, right-wing historian Allan Carlson (1990:194) offers a critique of "the use and abuse of social science" that he believes Gunnar and Alva Myrdal employed to promote social democratic family policies in Sweden that Carlson dislikes, which could apply at least as well to the contemporary family values campaign he supports in the US:

> In short, it is difficult to see social science in this episode as little more than a new tool for rhetorical control and political advantage. Weak and inconsistent data, confusion over cause and effect, and avoidance of experimentation proved to be no obstacles to the construction and implementation of policy.

The family values campaign admixes its flawed functionalist framework with an untheorized notion of culture. It presumes that the truth about the relative merits and effects of diverse family structures—be they intact married-couple families, stepfamilies, single-parent families, extended families, adoptive families, not to mention gay families—is singular, knowable, and extricable from its social, economic, and political context. Although some revisionists, like Glenn, concede that at times (always past times), ideological and cultural convictions interfere with the capacity of social scientists to perceive this truth and temporarily distort social scientific knowledge, still truth and virtue triumph in the end. Most social scientists are sufficiently scientific to listen when "the data" speak to them in robust and uniform tones.

Secondly, the singular truth is also a timeless one—a happy marriage in the 1990s is the same as one in the 1950s, and divorce has the identical negative effects. "Culture" intervenes simply to affect the frequency of these structures by rendering each more or less attractive or despised and by sustaining or subverting individual submission to a regime of duty, propriety, and self-sacrifice. Culture functions as an untheorized, grab-bag category—a black hole ready to absorb all messy, unexplained causes and consequences. Here it trumps material circumstances, collective struggles, and institutional constraints as the source of the decline of stable and "happy" marriages and families that rising rates of divorce, unwed motherhood, and "deadbeat dads" index. Culture becomes an exogenous, unproblematic, remarkably flexible category from which an aggregate of individuals, like savvy shoppers, can select timeless garments—like marital commitment, fidelity, responsibility—and discard their unfashionable accessories—like male dominance.

Revisionist social scientists certainly do harbor anxieties about the social fields in which they operate. Somewhat regretfully, perhaps, most have accepted the demise of the 1950s-style, male-breadwinner family and the likely permanence of a level of postmodern family instability, diversity, and change.[15] Recognizing that working mothers, at least, are "here to stay," they promote a new (post)familism that evades power and justice conflicts embedded in family transformation.[16] However, revisionists have not conceded the decline of positivism, if they have even noticed its infirmity. Instead, following the successful example set by right-wing intellectuals (Messer-Davidow 1993), Parsonsian family social scientists have regrouped outside the academy to provide a middle course between ideologies of the religious right on one side and feminism and gay liberation on the other. They proffer eager politicians a social science narrative to fill the vacuum created by weakened naturalist and divine justifications for the contested, modern gender and family regime.

SITCOM SOCIOLOGY FOR A DISAFFECTED ELECTORATE

Post–Cold War politicians from both moribund parties have compelling cause to grasp at this outstretched academic hand. With a shrinking, increasingly cynical electorate, one described in a study by the Times Mirror Center for the People and the Press (Berke 1994b) as "angry, self-absorbed and politically unanchored," the volatile balance of electoral power rests in the hands of those illusive "neglected, middle-class" voters, who are disproportionately white (Yoachum 1994).[17] The Democratic Party, weakened by the erosion of its traditional liberal and working-class base, has particularly urgent need to court this constituency. The family values campaign offers "New Democrats" a way to exploit the ideological stranglehold that religious, right-wing, profamily crusaders have secured on the Republican Party in efforts to lure Reagan Democratic defectors back to the fold. As one political journalist (Brownstein 1994) quipped, "Democrats Find the Right's Stuff: Family Values."

During the 1994 election season, Republicans, for their part, worked to shed the unpopular, intolerant, profamily image emblazoned on the national unconscious by their televised 1992 national convention. Dan Quayle, William Bennett, and even some leaders of the right-wing Christian Coalition retreated from the militant profamily rhetoric they had imposed on the 1992 party platform, such as hardline opposition to abortion and gay rights. Asked for his views on abortion and homosexuality just before he addressed the Christian Coalition in September 1994, Quayle told reporters, "That's their choice" (Berke 1994a:A8). Bennett's speech to the Christian conference advised participants to constrain their homophobic passions: "I understand the aversion to homosexuality. But if you look in terms of damage to the children of America, you cannot compare the homosexual movement, the gay rights movement, what that has done in damage to what divorce has done to this society" (Berke 1994a:A8). Quayle defended this political regression toward the mean in explicitly instrumental terms: "The political situation has changed in this country. There's not the political support to make it illegal, so we should focus on reducing the number of abortions, and we want to change attitudes" (Berke 1994a:A8).

Mirror-image speeches delivered during the 1994 election season by Quayle and Clinton previewed campaign rhetoric that was to dominate the last presidential election of the millennium, when the electorate was treated once again to primetime combat for the family values crown. Richard Sennett (1994:490) suggests that "the popular language of 'family values' and of 'values' per se is a barely disguised language of sexual prohibitions," which imagines "the breakdown of family values and community standards to be synonymous with sexual explicitness." Voters overwhelmingly view Republicans rather than Democrats as defenders of this symbolic domain.[18] Perhaps, in consequence, Clinton ceded so much ideological and political ground to the family values crusade—from instantly pledging to sign the Republican-sponsored, anti-gay "Defense of Marriage Act" to signing a reactionary welfare bill whose preamble begins with the congressional "finding" that "Marriage is the foundation of a successful society"—that by the time he had been reelected, there were few issues beyond the legal right to abortion separating the family politics of his administration from those of the Republicans.

The rhetoric of family values provides an infinitely malleable semiotic resource that is understandably irresistible to politicians from both major parties in the age of corporate-sponsored, mass media politics. A floating signifier, the language of family values functions more like those potent, "innocent" images analyzed by Foucault than like verbal communications subject to rational debate. Little wonder, therefore, that Murphy Brown (but not Candice Bergen) enjoyed star billing in the 1992 presidential campaign when Quayle castigated the sitcom heroine for glamorizing unwed motherhood. In a moment of supreme irony, anchorwoman Murphy took to the sitcom airwaves to chastise the former vice president for being out of touch with the problems of "real" families. Millions of voters watched this well-hyped episode, and ensuing responses to Murphy's sermon provided by Quayle and the small group of "real" single mothers he had selected to join him, on camera, in viewing this electoral spectacle (see Fiske 1994). Most political commentators at the time echoed the sitcom heroine's scorn for the vice president's inability to distinguish virtual from actual families. Because the Quayle-Brown spectacle underscored the message of the Republicans' 1992 nominating convention that the Grand Old Party was "out of touch" with ordinary families, it assisted Clinton's slim margin of victory.

Breathtakingly soon, however, Dan Quayle began to enjoy the last laugh-in, as even President Clinton joined the "Dan Quayle Was Right" brigades (Stacey 1994b, 1996). Quayle's campaign against single mothers scored such a dramatic comeback victory over Clinton, the reputed comeback king, because the former vice president's campaign scriptwriters were quick to grasp the virtual character of contemporary family values. They recognized that Murphy Brown could function symbolically as a wayward stepdaughter of Ozzie and Harriet Nelson, the mythic couple who lodge, much larger than life, in collective nostalgia for the world of 1950s' families.

The decade of the 1950s was the originary moment of the fable of virtual family values. Those halcyon days of the modern nuclear family were also the years when television became a mass medium, indeed an obligatory new member of "the family." From its hallowed living room perch, the magic box broadcast the first generation of domestic sitcoms, emblazoning idealized portraits of middle-class family dynamics into the national unconscious. From "Ozzie and Harriet" to "Murphy Brown," from "Amos and Andy" to "The Cosby Show," from "The Life of Riley" to "Roseanne," the world of TV sitcoms saturates popular imagery of family life. Ozzie and Harriet and their kin serve as the Edenic families of our century's bedtime fable, because the apogee of the modern family system coincided with television's own originary Golden Age.

Family sitcom programming was created in the post–World War II period to construct a mass viewing audience for the nascent television industry and its corporate sponsors. The programs did not simply reflect, or even merely romanticize, the existing structure and values of the family audience they sought to entertain. As cultural historians have demonstrated (Spigel 1992, 1995; Taylor 1989), the introduction of television played an active role in constructing, and later in deconstructing, the boundaries of the isolated nuclear family it depicted in such sentimental tones. Because the 1950s was also the first Cold War decade, the years when the US emerged as the dominant global superpower, images of an invincible family and nation mingle inextricably in the national imaginary of the "good old days" (see May 1988). Clinton, Quayle, Newt Gingrich, and the primary constituencies of the electorate they address, as well as many of their academic counselors, all were reared in the first generation of families who learned to spend their evening hours huddled together watching family TV in their newly conceived "family rooms," designed as small shrines for the magic box.

This semiotic history of family sitcom TV, which evolved while the modern family it celebrated devolved, renders the idiom of family values a potent, inescapably visual and emotional register. Addressing psychic rather than cognitive frequencies, family values discourse offers politicians and populace a brilliant defense mechanism with which to displace anxieties over race, gender, sex, and class antagonisms that were unleashed as the modern family regime collapsed (see Stacey 1994b). No wonder that as the century ends, "it's all in the family."

During the 1994 and 1996 political seasons, the most popular sitcom social science plots furnished simple, emotionally resonant motivations and resolutions for those spectacles of normative fin de siècle violence, crime, and social decay that the networks broadcast nightly, in Technicolor, for the pleasure and edification of home viewers. Serial killers, crack babies, gang rapists, carjackers, dope dealers, drive-by shooters, school dropouts, welfare queens, arsonists, wife beaters, child abusers, sex offenders, kidnappers, runaways, pregnant teens, gang warriors, homeless vagrants, terrorists—all social pathologies begin in a broken home. Her parents divorced, or they never married. His mother was hooked on welfare and drugs, or she dumped him in day-care. No one taught them family values. We need to stop coddling these criminals and con artists. From the punitive, anticrime fervor of "three strikes and you're out" to "two tykes and you're out" welfare caps, family values ideology plays to the privatistic, antigovernment sentiments and the moralistic and vindictive appetites of our dismal, late-millennial political culture.

An unholy alliance of academic and political networks produces and sponsors this sitcom sociology. Fending off competing networks on the channels to their right and their left, mainstream family scholars and politicians work to keep the public tuned to the center-right channels of the dial. Unwilling or unable to analyze the social sources of postmodern family and civic disorder, or to address the manifold injustices these upheavals expose and intensify, they resort to reruns of old family favorites. Religious and naturalist treatments of virtuous family order continue to play to substantial numbers of viewers in their specialized market niches. However, aging scholars, allied with "new" Democrats and "moderate" Republicans alike, have hitched their hopes for robust Nielson and ballot box ratings to narratives featuring a prodigal society returning to conjugal family virtue after suffering the painful consequences of self-indulgent rebellions. The production company has assembled a postmodern pastiche of social science, fable, advanced technology, and (dis)simulation to script and enact the serial melodrama. The plot line, imagery, and production values owe more to television archives, and to power and knowledge shifts in the academy, economy, and polity, than they do to ethnographic, demographic, or analytical acumen. We seem unable to conclude the season of sitcom sociology—designed to distract a disaffected public from the daunting familial and social realities that the United States confronts as an ignoble century expires.

Notes

1. A widely circulated op-ed piece by David Popenoe (1992), "The Controversial Truth: The Two-Parent Family Is Better," identified me as an ideological exception to an emergent consensus among social scientists that two-parent families are superior.

2. I had been collaborating with Judith Newton in a study of male cultural critics (see Newton and Stacey 1992–93, 1995, and 1997) when the op-ed mentioned above appeared, followed quickly by other articles by family values advocates (see Popenoe 1993a, 1993b; Wilson 1993) that identified *Brave New Families* as an example of misguided liberalism.

3. The postmodern family condition has generated new controversies and challenges that bear on all five of the domains George Marcus (1993) identified in his proposal for the School of American Research seminar that generated this volume. For example, political struggles over gender, sexuality, and family policy affect local school boards, workplaces, international population conferences, immigration policies, and funding for public broadcasting and the National Endowment for the Arts.

4. John Gillis (1996) is one of the first to employ the concept "virtual family values."

5. However, recently politicians in Britain and elsewhere in Europe have initiated efforts to stir public concern over single motherhood, divorce, and family instability (see Tuula Gordon 1994; Millar 1994). For example, "The Crumbling of Family Life," the headline story by Paul Crosbie run by London's *Daily Express* on June 23, 1994, seems a direct replica of US rhetoric.

6. In 1994 the Sex and Gender section of the ASA had 1,271 members, over two hundred more than the next largest section, Medical Sociology, with 1,033 members (ASA Governance Sections).

7. After all, Moynihan's analysis of black family decline (1965) had built quite directly on the sociological work of E. Franklin Frazier (1939), and even *Tally's Corner*, Elliot Liebow's (1967) decidedly liberal and sympathetic ethnography of urban black families, supported the thesis of black family pathology.

8. For example, at an evening plenary session attended by more than one thousand sociologists at the American Sociological Association meetings in Los Angeles in August 1994, Patricia Hill Collins delivered a polemical assault on postmodern theory and was rewarded with rapturous applause.

9. For a discussion of this populist rhetorical device, see Stacey (1994b). For additional examples, see Wilson (1993) and Elshtain (quoted in Heller 1995).

10. While the proportion of doctoral degrees awarded to women in all fields in the US rose only from 30 percent in 1980 to 36 percent in 1990 (National Research Council 1991), in sociology, women's share of Ph.D. degrees rose much more substantially, from 33 percent in 1977 to 51 percent in 1989

(National Science Foundation 1991). These data on completed degrees understate feminization trends evident among currently enrolled graduate students in sociology departments.

11. Friedan's *The Second Stage* (1981) celebrated the reappearance of familism among feminists. For an early critical discussion of the emergence of this perspective within feminism, see Stacey (1983, 1986).

12. For example, Blankenhorn co-convened an academic conference on family change at Stanford University and then co-edited the resulting conference volume (Blankenhorn, Elshtain, and Bayme 1990). Blankenhorn also spoke at a Santa Clara University conference, "Ethics, Public Policy and the Future of the Family," on April 18, 1995.

13. Etzioni's complex marital history, for that matter, includes two divorces and children with different wives.

14. However, Elshtain herself rarely forfeits an opportunity to raise the animus ante. In a letter to the editor which *The Nation* published in abridged form, Elshtain (1994) responded to my critical discussion of the centrist campaign (Stacey 1994a) in quite personalized, and purple, prose: "I was pleased to see that Judith Stacey is on the job. Not having been attacked by Ms. Stacey in print for a few years, I wondered if she was still up to the ideological stalking so characteristic of her efforts a few years back. Then, if memory serves, Stacey expended a good bit of energy before finally landing on the label, 'New Conservative Feminist' for a few of us and now, to my surprise, I get to be something brand new and exciting, a 'New Family Values Crusader.' Stacey seems to believe nothing can be discussed unless you first line people up in team jerseys. This labeling fetishism, alas, has long been characteristic of segments of the sectarian left and this same infantilizing urgency has infected a good bit of academic feminism."

15. Glenn (1994:11–12), for example, depicts himself as "among the relatively small number of American family social scientists who believe that some of the changes can be halted if not reversed. Reconstitution of the American family of the 1950s—a goal of some conservatives—is indeed unrealistic and, in my view, undesirable."

16. *Here To Stay* (Bane 1976) is the title of an early, misleadingly optimistic assessment of nuclear family stability in the US that is a frequent foil for the family values campaign.

17. In California, whites constituted only 57 percent of the adult population in the state, but they cast 83 percent of the votes in the 1994 election.

18. Indeed, survey data indicate an alarming anomaly. On the one hand, since the 1980s "the electorate as a whole moved in a clearly liberal direction on three issues besides gay rights: abortion, the role of women, and, to a lesser extent, on the role of government in guaranteeing jobs and living standards" (Strand and Sherrill 1993:9). Nonetheless, in a November 1994 poll sponsored by the Democratic Leadership Council, more voters identified the Republicans than the Democrats as the party that "would do a better job strengthening families" (Greenberg Research 1994).

3

Generation X

Anthropology in a Media-Saturated World

Sherry B. Ortner

> The cultural ubiquity of the professional middle class may seem to make it an easy subject for a writer. There is no need to travel to offbeat settings or conduct extensive interviews to find out what is on its mind. One does not need to consult specialists—sociologists or anthropologists—to discover how people in this class order the details of their daily lives. Their lifestyles, habits, tastes, and attitudes are everywhere, and inescapably before us...Who can presume to step "outside" of it? Its ideas and assumptions are everywhere, and not least in our own minds.
>
> —*Barbara Ehrenreich,* Fear of Falling

My problem for the present paper concerns the relationship between "public culture" on the one hand, and ethnographic inquiry on the other, in the contemporary United States. By "public culture" I mean all the bodies of images, claims, and representations created to speak to and about the actual people who live in the US: all of the products of art and entertainment (film, television, books, etc.), as well as all of the texts of information and analysis (all forms of journalism and academic production). "Public culture" includes all the products of what is commonly called the "media" but much more as well.

Public culture in this sense stands in a very complex relationship to "ethnography." First, public culture is both subject and object vis-à-vis the ethnographer. It claims, and the ethnographer must grant, that it stands as a competing subject, a competing author(ity): much of journalism, as well as many academic fields, are jostling with ethnography to tell "the truth" about American culture. As we shall see when we turn to the public representations concerning Generation X, journalists and academics are constantly trying to subsume one another, to claim the position of subject and to turn one another into objects, data. Journalists quote both native informants and academic experts to weave a story about the here and now; academics do the same with journalists, as I will do in this paper. Ethnographers' "data" are part of the journalists' stories; journalists' reporting is part of the public culture and thus part of the ethnographic data.

In trying to think through this relationship, one needs to avoid several temptations. The first is the unmodified "cultural studies" or "media studies" temptation—the fantasy that one can understand the workings of public cultural representations solely by interpreting/deconstructing the representations. The second is the reciprocal of the first—the ethnographic fantasy that doing fieldwork in and of itself provides the kinds of "data" necessary to correct for the cultural studies illusion. As already noted, ethnography and public culture—at least in the United States—are deeply intertwined and therefore cannot be set against one another in any clear-cut way.

It will be useful here to reintroduce the distinction between anthropology and ethnography. "Ethnography," or at any rate a variety of "qualitative research" practices operating under that sign, is now going on in many disciplines and in many interdisciplinary arenas (including some arenas of cultural studies and media studies). But anthropology has always been more than ethnography. For one thing, anthropologists themselves do extensive work on "public culture"; that was in part what the Geertzian revolution of the sixties (and since) was all about (Ortner 1984). For another, both interpretive cultural work and on-the-ground ethnographic work (and more) have always been carried out in relation to larger theoretical frames that both shape such work and are revised by it.

In recent years there has been a tendency to parcel out these components—cultural studies scholars are seen as the specialists on public culture, literary critics and philosophers have claimed the zone of "theory," and anthropologists are increasingly identified simply with "ethnography." There are complex academic and intellectual politics in play here, and this is not the place to try to address them. Perhaps the most contested of the terms is "theory." What counts as theory? Which disciplines are producing theory, and which are merely consuming? My own sense of what counts as theory is very broad, as I will discuss in more detail below. In any event, I resist the idea that anthropology's contribution to the current intellectual division of labor is simply ethnographic; in this chapter I seek to reappropriate a larger anthropology in which ethnography, theory, and public culture are held in productive tension.

For the past few years I have been looking at class and culture in the United States in the second half of the twentieth century.[1] The ethnographic population for the study is my own high school graduating class (the class of 1958 of Weequahic High School in Newark, New Jersey) and their grown children.[2] The children of the Class of '58 were born in the sixties and early seventies, and thus qualify at least demographically as authentic members of what has come to be called Generation X. Generation X has been the subject of extensive media coverage, as well as films, novels, television series, and so on. At first I did not think of the children of the Class of '58 as Generation Xers, even though technically they were. My twentysomething "natives" were, for the most part, hard-working and success-oriented, while Xers—I had already picked up the stereotypes—were "slackers" and "whiners." But then I realized that my category failure raised some interesting questions about doing anthropology in contemporary media-saturated societies, and this realization opened the subject of this paper.

GENERATION X: THE PUBLIC CULTURE

I will begin by drawing a picture of Generation X as an ideal type. It should be noted at the outset that virtually every statement in the following description has been contested at one point or another, by one writer or group or another. Moreover, the characterization of Generation X has shifted over time, as different groups temporarily gained control over the image. Although it would be interesting to try to interpret the shifting imagery in relation to shifts of various kinds in the real world, unfortunately this will be impossible within the scope of the present chapter. Here I simply provide a somewhat simplified overview of Generation X imagery as it has appeared since the mid-1980s.

The idea of the emergence of a distinctive generation in the mid-1980s began in the hands of demographers and marketing interests, and the initial journalism was mostly in demographic and economic journals like *American Demographics* and *Fortune.* In a second stage the image was picked up by popular magazine journalism (including *Newsweek, Business Week, The New Republic,* and *The Atlantic Monthly*), which addressed a more general public across the political spectrum. By now it is probably fair to say that the Xers themselves control the representation (e.g., Holtz 1995; Nelson and Cowan 1994; Rushkoff 1994), although it has already been shaped by all the hands it has passed through.

One can see the play of various positionalities, interests, political claims, and marketing intentions at work in the competing representations. One can see as well that Generation X is quite literally brought into being in the play of these representations. Finally one may come to feel—as the images never stabilize—that there is a kind of Baudrillardian process at work, a free play of signifiers with no referent, really, at all. In a way the discussions that follow are an attempt to move away from that vertiginous position and to articulate an alternative standpoint.

We begin, then, precisely with the question of the referent: Who or what, out there, is being designated "Generation X" and loaded up with (varying) meanings and attributes? The early referent was narrowly defined by demographics as the generation born between 1965 and 1976 (*American Demographics* 1987). Nineteen sixty-five was the first year the birth rate started dropping after the baby boom (which began right after World War II, in 1946); 1977 was the first year the birth rate began to rise again (*American Demographics* 1992). The earliest label for this group was drawn from the boom/bust opposition in economics: They were the Baby Busters who followed the Baby Boomers.

The narrow demographic parameters for the cohort have now been replaced, however, with much wider ones. It is now generally accepted—for reasons that are not entirely clear—that the generation in question begins with those born in about 1961 and ends with those born in about 1981 (Howe and Strauss 1993:12–13). The difference makes a difference. When the cohort was defined demographically (i.e., 1965–76), its most prominent feature was the fact that it was much smaller than the preceding Boomer generation. Its small size seemed to mean that things would be easier for the Busters in almost every way: There would be less competition for jobs and for promotions (Williams 1985:122), colleges would be competing for Busters' enrollments (Edmondson 1987b), and when they hit the home-buying market there would be a glut of starter homes at depressed prices as the larger Boomer population traded upward in housing (*American Demographics* 1992:27). "Demographers and economists forecast golden opportunities for this [graduating] class and for those that follow..."[3] (Williams 1985:122).

When the parameters were redrawn to include everyone born between 1961 and 1981, however, the picture of the generation changed. And here we come to the supposed characteristics of the cohort. The most prominent characteristics are economic: There are not enough jobs, there are certainly not enough well-paying jobs, there are particularly not enough quality jobs available for the level of education and qualification many members of the cohort have achieved. People are basically overeducated (or anyway overcertified)[4] and underemployed.

Part of the problem with the economy derives, it is claimed, from a variety of government spending patterns and programs in preceding generations. Preceding administrations, presumably in tune with wider sentiments, have run up the national debt to grotesque proportions and have shifted the wealth of the middle class to (choose your target) the poor, the rich, the old, or some combination of these (e.g., Holtz 1995; Howe and Strauss 1993).

More tangibly, and for a variety of reasons including but not limited to those just noted, the wages of the American male had been dropping for some time. A *Business Week* article in 1991 reported that "the median income of families headed by someone under 30 is now 13% lower than such families earned in 1973" (*Business Week* 1991:80). The article concludes that some socially undifferentiated group called "America's young people" are going to "mature in a less affluent world. And that spells trouble for all Americans, young and old alike" (p. 85).

A careful reading of the *Business Week* article shows that these predictions will not apply to everyone equally. It turns out that families of this age-group headed by college graduates actually show a 16 percent gain in income, and not a 13 percent loss, but this is dismissed because it is only the effect of "working wives." The real impact is on families headed by people with only high school degrees (16 percent decline) and families headed by dropouts (33 percent). There are large racial differentials as well.

The significance of these differences will be clear later in this paper. The point for now, however, is that according to these accounts, "the middle class" has been very hard hit by falling male wages, which forces both spouses to work just to stay even. Even then, a couple has great difficulty keeping up economically. In particular, they are going to have great difficulty buying that hallmark of middle-class status, a house, and they will certainly not be buying one of the quality in which they were brought up. The consequence of all this is the doomsaying prediction that has by now become one of the hallmarks of Generation X: "[T]he baby busters may never match their parents' living standards. And that...would make them the first US generation ever not to do so" (*Business Week* 1991:80; see also Newman 1993).

It is not at all clear what, if any, of this is objectively true. Take the issue of whether or not Generation X will be able to afford a house. In both 1992 and 1993 *American Demographics* insisted that there was no problem. Not only was there said to be "a glut of starter houses" (*American Demographics* 1992:27), mortgage rates were falling to "their lowest levels in 20 years" (*American Demographics* 1993:35) and indeed have remained very low since then. But objective reality is not precisely what is at issue.

In addition to generating a bleak future for the Busters, the bad economy generates boring, low-paying, non–career-track jobs in the here and now. This was a major aspect of Douglas Coupland's novel, *Generation X: Tales for an Accelerated Culture*, which was published in 1991 and which provided the name that would henceforth label the cohort: Generation X. Coupland described his characters as working in "McJobs," a phrase that has by now gained a permanent place in the vocabulary. McJobs—"low-pay, low-prestige, low-dignity, no-future job[s] in the service sector" (Coupland 1991:5)—would be tedious and poorly paid by many people's standards, but they are particularly galling for Xers who had put in the time, effort, and money to gain an education that was supposed to yield something more rewarding in every sense.

In addition to encountering difficult economic conditions, Generation X is described as encountering extremely problematic social conditions, including a soaring divorce rate, high rates of working mothers and latchkey children, ecological disaster, the AIDS epidemic, and so forth. This is particularly the theme of *13th Gen: Abort, Retry, Ignore, Fail,* by Neil Howe and Bill Strauss, which came out in 1993 (see also *Business Week* 1992; Holtz 1995; Howe and Strauss 1992). Howe and Strauss are concerned to shift the blame for all these problems from the preceding Boomer generation, where it is usually targeted and which includes themselves (their E-mail moniker is "2boomers"). Instead they spend a lot of time blaming the senior generations: "[W]hen Thirteeners [their term for Xers] were ready to enter the adult labor force, the politicians pushed every policy lever conceivable...to tilt the economic playing field away from the young and toward the old" (Howe and Strauss 1993:78). They also specifically blame the parents of Xers, whom they see as having been self-indulgent, anti-child parents, who sacrificed their children's psychological well-being for the fulfillment of their own selfish needs and desires.

Most other writers focus the blame not primarily on the parental generation but on the adjacent Boomer generation. The Boomers themselves are also very contradictorily portrayed, but this cannot be explored here. Suffice it to say that the category includes both the counterculture/antiwar generation and the greedy Reagan/Bush generation, both hippies and yuppies (see, e.g., Russell 1993). To someone who lived through both, and who thought first of all that the yuppies were a historically distinct cohort, and second of all that yuppie values were entirely antithetical to those of the counterculture/antiwar generation, the combination is rather startling.[5] Nonetheless what unites them, in these arguments, is the notion of self-indulgence. And in at least some portrayals, the hippies and political activists of the sixties are even worse than the yuppies, because they claim greater moral purity. It was this collective self-indulgence in turn that generated the economic, social, sexual, and psychological problems—everything from the deficit to the divorce rate to AIDS—that GenXers have inherited. Howe and Strauss (1993:12) call Generation X "the clean-up crew."[6]

Descriptions of Generation X then move from characterizations of the pathologies of the world to characterizations of the pathologies of GenX consciousness. Living in a ruined world, GenXers manifest (it is claimed) a range of problematic attitudes. One set of attitudes clusters around anger and frustration over their plight; this shades into complaining and—as seen by others—"whining" (e.g., *Business Week* 1992; D. Martin 1993; Newman 1993) Another cluster of attitudes takes the form of ironic distancing from their situation, renouncing ambitions and ideals, becoming "slackers," and taking refuge in cyberspace and in a television-generated world of soap operas, quiz shows, and MTV. This is the stance portrayed in some of the most visible sites of GenX expressive culture, including Coupland's *Generation X* novel, Rushkoff's *Generation X Reader*, and Richard Linklater's film *Slacker.* A final cluster is organized around the idea that GenXers are truly damaged by the world in which they find themselves: They feel themselves to be worthless losers (one anthem of the generation is a song by Beck, of which the refrain is, "I'm a loser, baby, so why don't you kill me"; the band in *Slacker* is called the Ultimate Losers), and are deeply depressed. The suicide of rock star Kurt Cobain (of the group Nirvana), and the empathetic responses to it, epitomized this cluster of images (Freedland 1994; O'Connell 1994).

As noted earlier, every one of these images is contested. Among the journalists themselves there is a fair amount of dissension as to whether Generation X has this or that characteristic. For example, in June 1994, *Newsweek* came out with a cover story called "GenerALIZation X," which argued that although the world was indeed in bad shape, Generation X did not have all the bad attitudes that had been projected upon it (Giles 1994; see also *American Demographics* 1993). On the contrary, *Newsweek* cited a recent poll to show that there is virtually no difference in attitudes between Xers and Boomers:

> Our extensive research shows "*there are no significant national or personal mood differences separating young and old.*" Twenty-five percent of the twentysomethings polled said that they were unhappy with their lot in life; 26 percent of the baby boomers agreed. Sixty-three percent of the twentysomethings said that they were "dissatisfied with the way things were going in the US"; 71 percent of boomers said the very same thing. (Giles 1994:65; italics in original)

Others have questioned the generational framing as well. In a piece on Kurt Cobain following his suicide, Alex Ross called "the nation's ongoing symposium on generational identity...a fruitless project blending the principles of sociology and astrology" (Ross 1994:102; see also Ratan 1993). The most searching critique of the generational framing was offered by Alexander Star, whose remarks are worth quoting at some length:

> This kind of generational packaging continues even as the actual bases of generational cohesion erode. Changing family roles and occupational hierarchies, the universal accessibility of the mass media to all age groups, early exposure to work and sex, gadgets and crime, have made age a less, not more, reliable indicator of taste, values, and behavior. The idea of generational culture is itself largely a byproduct of the considerable leisure and prosperity that young people enjoyed in the '50s and '60s, together with the existence of overarching causes like Vietnam. Today, a generic youth culture has been assembled from above precisely because it doesn't exist down below...As young people acquire adult responsibilities (and adult vices) at an earlier age, their distinctness as a group diminishes. They do not stamp a unique sensibility on society so much as mirror its disarray. (Star 1993:25)

Yet these arguments perhaps go too far in the direction of denying that a Generation X consciousness exists. There is enough in both the public culture and in my ethnographic data to suggest that it is really out there in some part(s) of social space, and the question is one of locating it correctly rather than denying its existence. They also go too far in claiming that this consciousness is imposed from the top; popular thought and public culture exist in a fairly tight loop, each reworking the other in an ongoing process. I agree, however, that the idea of a single generational consciousness is highly implausible, especially in an era as conscious as this one about social difference.

It is perhaps time to declare my argument, which is that the idea of "Generation X" is an attempt to deal with profound changes in the American middle class in the late twentieth century. Before getting to the class argument, however, a few words must be said about race.

THE WHITENESS OF GENERATION X

Relatively early on in the Baby Buster literature, back in 1991, we were told that the economic downturns that were so problematic for the future of Generation X in fact hit minorities much harder than they hit whites. The 1991 *Business Week* article quoted earlier made it clear that the long decline in male wages may have put a squeeze on the white middle class but had been "devastating"—their term—to many minorities (*Business Week* 1991:80, 85).

Yet this point is quite literally never raised again within the framework of the Generation X public culture. Race is virtually absent from further discussions of the supposed characteristics of Generation X, except for some relatively flimsy references to "diversity." The first came in 1992, when *Business Week* pointed out that the Baby Buster generation was "more ethnically diverse, and they're more comfortable with diversity than any previous generation" (*Business Week* 1992:75). *Newsweek* made the same point in 1994:

> Generation X most certainly is not [white]. The stereotypical Xer, as he's[7] trotted out in movies and in the media, is white and privileged and living in a suburb near you. But twentysomethings are actually the most racially diverse of

> any generation to date: they're [only] 70% white...Xers may also be the least racist. "We are the first generation to be born into an integrated society," writes Eric Liu, a foreign-policy speechwriter for President Clinton. (Giles 1994:65–66)

The point of these comments in both cases is quite unclear, as they never get integrated into some larger discourse about Generation X. They have a somewhat congratulatory tone, as if being demographically more diverse were some sort of (white) achievement or as if it guaranteed a growth of tolerance, which may or may not be the case—no evidence is presented. In any event, despite these indications of greater diversity, the actual Generation X public culture—the journalism, the novels, the films—is almost entirely white. And despite the vast influence and popularity of African-American performers in popular music, most of the musicians and groups taken as epitomizing Generation X—Nirvana, Beck, Hole, and Offspring[8]—are white.

For a long time it appears that nobody spoke to African Americans and other minorities about their relationship to this category. Finally, the 1994 *Newsweek* article, which was concerned to sort the GenX representations into "myths" and "realities," pointed out that the category had virtually no relevance for minorities:

> The phrase "Generation X" doesn't mean much to twentysomethings of color...Allen Hughes, co-director of the inner-city coming-of-age story *Menace II Society* [said], "I mean, the media isn't aiming that at us. Our film had the same demographics as [the GenX classic] *Reality Bites,* but they didn't call it a Generation X film, they called it a damn gangsta film. Call it racist, or whatever, but we don't count when it comes to Generation X." (Giles 1994:66)

Or, as rapper Dr. Dre put it, "I haven't heard anyone in my 'hood talking about [Generation X]...The only X I know is Malcolm X" (Giles 1994:64).

My point is not so much that the Generation X representation "excludes" blacks, as if Generation X were some club to which African

Americans or other minorities would like admission. Rather it is that the racialization of the representation, white-not-black/brown/other, hides more significant class divisions at work. In my own ethnographic data, young African Americans in their twenties who were stuck in prime GenX locations (I will get to what those are in a moment) sounded virtually indistinguishable from young white twentysomethings in the same situation; it is the locations that are obscured by the racialization of the categories. Which brings us finally to class.

THE TRANSFORMATIONS OF THE MIDDLE CLASS

Whatever else Generation X has been about—social problems, ecological disasters, AIDS—it has always been, first and foremost, about identity through work: jobs, money, and careers. The issues have been economic from the very beginning—declining male wages and family incomes, working harder for less money, shrinking job markets, expensive degrees that lead nowhere, McJobs. And although one or another of these economic issues affects everyone in this society, it seems fairly clear that both the source and the target of the Generation X imagery is the middle class. That is, although poor people, mostly minorities, have actually been hit even harder than the middle class, the whiteness of the GenX imagery just discussed indicates that these are not the people the public culture is worrying about. The centrality of the home-ownership issue suggests the same thing.

Yet "the middle class" is not some empirical object that can be found lying around in the world, and this brings us back to the question of theory. By "theory" I mean a range of types of thought-frames—narratives, maps, categories, perspectives, positionalities—that operate as the conditions for allowing us to see and talk about social and cultural phenomena at all. Most theorizing in the late twentieth century is quite eclectic, drawing on a variety of master theoretical narratives but rarely signing up for any one of them in full. Yet these master narratives, claiming to describe/explain/represent how the social/cultural world is put together and why things are the way they are and not otherwise, remain the (sometimes hidden) condition for the ongoing bricolage of contemporary theory-work. With respect to the questions for the present paper, then, I draw on theorizing about "late capitalism" and its entail-ments, about class reproduction as seen primarily from feminist perspectives, and most generally about the ways in which public cultural representations operate in and through social practices and social anxieties. I begin with class transformations under late capitalism.

Recent theorizing of the postmodern condition, and the global/transnational turn, have somewhat overshadowed another major arena of theoretical activity, the attempt to retheorize late capitalism as a social structure, or in other words to retheorize "class." A major part of this attempt derives from constructing a new narrative of capitalist transformation, one that builds on Marxist theory but takes account of the further historical/institutional/cultural changes that have taken place in the century and a half since Marx wrote.[9] The new narrative, in turn, constructs a new map of what Bourdieu (1984) has called "social space," a field of both locations and trajectories, possibilities of movement, defined by economic and cultural capital. Here, then, a quick version of the story.

As a result of various forces unleashed by capitalism itself, as well as certain historical specifics of American capitalism (e.g., the high proportion of illiterate immigrant labor), the notion of "management" and the emergence of a managerial class became a central aspect of the capitalist process starting relatively early in the twentieth century. As this class grew and became more powerful over the course of the twentieth century, theories of capitalist process had increasingly to take into account the dynamics of the middle class. Much of recent class theory, then, has sought to understand what has happened to the middle class over the course of the century and how changes in the middle class in turn have affected the structure of capitalism as a whole. A major dimension of what is called "late capitalism," including changes in capital/labor relations and changes in the social characteristics of both the capitalist and working classes, is seen in many ways as a product of the expansion and transformation of the middle class.[10]

Much of this expansion and transformation was generated at a certain point in time by boosting up a large sector of the working class. Following the Second World War, the GI Bill allowed thousands of US veterans to go to college virtually free and to get virtually free mortgages. The general level of prosperity in this period was extraordinarily high.[11] This set of factors had many effects, which have all been well documented elsewhere. Here it is important to note that the homeownership program, along with changes in the occupational structure of the economy (the gradual reduction of "blue-collar" jobs and the continual growth of "white-collar" ones), created or vastly enlarged a zone in the class structure that the folk call the lower middle class. The lower middle class is really, one might argue, the working class in middle-class clothing (i.e., housing, as well as other aspects of middle-class material culture); alternatively, it is the middle class with a working-class income.[12] Either way, it is a fundamentally insecure and interstitial place, and it is highly vulnerable to economic shifts.

Within the era of postwar prosperity, basically through the 1960s, people occupying this zone felt securely part of the middle class. They made good money. They were able to buy houses and consumer goods, and also save for the future. They began to send their kids to college, and they bought heavily into "the American dream." They saw themselves mirrored in the new mass genre, television sitcoms, as the very type of what it means to be American (Lipsitz 1990). The culture of "the fifties," with its conservative politics and its repressive gender and sexual relations, was arguably their culture, hegemonized in part by the growth of television.

The popular image of "the middle class" as a large and relatively seamless whole, constituting the core of American society, was created in this era and seemed infinitely sustainable. Starting in the seventies, however, and accelerated by Reagan/Bush policies in the eighties, the middle class started pulling apart at the middle. The economy suffered a series of setbacks, and the overall level of prosperity began to slip. But Reagan/Bush policies favored and protected the top of the structure. The top and the bottom of the middle class began pulling away from one another. Since that period, the upper middle class has done better and better, while the lower middle class has been slipping down into more and more difficult straits. The old adage has absolutely applied: In this era, "the rich got richer and the poor got poorer" (Duncan, Smeeding, and Rodgers 1992:38).

It is to this widening abyss in the middle class, I would argue, that the Generation X imagery is addressed. The most consistent aspect of the representations involves pointing at and constructing the characteristics of the social and economic abyss. Since the abyss is in many ways real, it takes no sleight of hand for the representations to be convincing. What is elided about the idea of "generation," however, is that people's relationships to the middle-class abyss are very different. Depending on which edge one is standing on, the configurations of anger, fear, anxiety, and resentment will vary. Yet all of Generation X can agree that it is "there." As the next move in this discussion, then, we need to look at the structures of feeling generated around this abyss. We begin with the view from the lower edge.

GENERATION X AS THE CHILDREN OF THE LOWER MIDDLE CLASS

Katherine Newman's *Declining Fortunes* was one of the pioneering works in establishing the argument that the generation that followed the Baby Boom was getting a raw deal.[13] Newman never uses the phrase "Generation X," but her portrait of "Pleasanton, NJ" maps almost perfectly onto one dimension of the GenX literature. The book opens with (and contains throughout) quotes from informants that embody the anger and frustration over "declining fortunes" that is the hallmark of Generation X. For example: "In Cathy's life, financial limitations create what she calls a 'low burning thing,' a subtext of constraint, a feeling that she is not free. This above all is the meaning of the intergenerational slide: the freedom to consume is cut short, the ability to plan for the long run is limited, and the bitter sense of rules turned inside out makes people feel, to use Cathy's words, like 'it was all a big lie'" (Newman 1993:20).

Or again, from "Lauren": "I'm living a lifestyle that's way lower than it was when I was growing up and it's depressing...Even if you are a hard worker and you never skipped a beat, you followed all the rules, did everything they told you you were supposed to do, it's still horrendous. *They lied to me*" (Newman 1993:3; italics in original). Newman's "Pleasanton" is described as embodying the full spread of the middle class, but various scattered indicators (occupational, ethnic) show that the bulk of the town, or perhaps the bulk of Newman's informants, were from the lower middle class. One indicator here is that there is a large Catholic sector to the population, and that "Jews were a decided minority" (Newman 1993:10); within the ethnic/religious spread of New Jersey, however, one knows that the Jews are strongly represented in the upper middle class, while the Catholics are the locus classicus of the lower middle class.

With respect to occupation, the town is represented as "middle class," with occupations ranging from "white-collar professionals [to] skilled blue-collar craftsmen" (Newman 1993:x). Nonetheless, most of the informants quoted by Newman as specifically feeling the effects of "the withering of the American dream" (Newman's subtitle) seem to be upper working/lower middle class. Lauren's father was "a quiet man of working class origins and modest means" (Newman 1993:2); Simon Rittenberg was a salesman for security devices (Newman 1993:12); "Martin's father was a blue-collar man through and through" (Newman 1993:14).

Moreover, informants themselves were quite aware that the "middle-class" facade of the town contained an incipient split: "[My son] could always go to Michael's and play big shot over there. He made these friends. But I noticed that when he got in college...his friends seemed to be those who were more [like us]. Some did go to college, but one had a landscaping business, or an upholstery business. Some joined their fathers' trades" (Newman 1993:78). Another informant alluded to a variant of the contradiction that is always lurking within the lower middle class, what I referred to earlier as the working class in middle-class clothing: She described her family as "a Sears Roebuck family living in a Bloomingdale's community" (Newman 1993:77).

It is worth noting that Newman's community is not only "lower middle class" but also white. I noted earlier the degree to which "Generation X" does not seem to embody a black referent (Coker 1994; James 1994; as well as individuals quoted in Giles 1994). The whiteness of "Pleasanton" explains particularly the sense of betrayal one hears in Newman's informants. African Americans are certainly just as angry as whites in this situation, if not more so, but they never felt they had really been promised more, that they had been "lied to" in the first place.

It makes sense that people who feel that they are slipping economically, despite their best efforts, would be frustrated and angry.[14] It is more of a puzzle to hear GenX-type noises from the other side of the abyss, to which we now turn.

GENERATION X AS THE CHILDREN OF THE UPPER MIDDLE CLASS

As part of the larger project noted earlier, I had been interviewing Generation Xers in the early 1990s, that is, during the period in which the GenX representation was taking shape and gaining visibility in the media. I was actually referred to the book, *Generation X,* by one of my interviewees, who recommended it to me as capturing important aspects of his own experience.

I interviewed about fifty young people in their twenties, all of whom were children of my own high school classmates. They were scattered around the country, but most of the interviews were done in New York City, the New Jersey suburbs, Ann Arbor, Michigan, and Los Angeles, California. Most of their parents, and most of these kids, were Jewish, although that will not play much of a role in the present discussion.[15] More important, for present purposes, are class factors: Their parents, the Class of '58 of Weequahic High School in Newark, New Jersey, had been lower- to middle-middle class in the fifties; many of them had done very well financially and were well up into the upper middle class by now. This meant in turn that many of their kids, the Xers I interviewed for the study, had grown up with a good bit of economic and cultural capital. Not all of them were either Jewish or had grown up in privileged circumstances, and the range of young people I interviewed had at least some diversity in terms of ethnicity, race, and class. I concentrate here, however, on the children of what is now the upper middle class.

What I found striking—astonishing, even—about these young people was that despite all their capital—money, fine schools, self-assurance—they were just as upset about their economic situations as Newman's informants. Rather than being angry at the system, however, they expressed their distress as tremendous fear and insecurity about holding on to what they have. Take, for example, David, the son of a wealthy businessman. He was twenty-four years old at the time of the interview (1993), living in New York, and trying to launch a career as an artist.[16] David went to an elite college, was still being supported by his parents, and knew that he was very privileged. Every possible safety net was in place: his education, his parents' money, and a sense of plausible alternatives (law school, graduate school) in case his present career hopes did not work out. But David was still worried about the future:

> Look, I am willing to put in hard work, that has never been a problem...There is this one guy, Edward, who is twenty-nine I think, graduated years before me and he is [also trying to succeed as an artist]. He has these small shows, sometimes he gets a good crowd, sometimes not...and I look at him and I'm thinking, "Oh my God, I do not want to be twenty-nine, I do not want to be thirty, I don't want to be thirty-one and still having no money at all and being no further along than I was when I was twenty-four"...To me that still sets in a panic attack of "Oh my God," and I try to think, that is not just my parents doing this to me, that's me. Part of it is this expectation of growing up [with everything] the way I did. You know, I don't really want to be thinking, "God we really need to get away. Oh that's right, we have no money, we can't go [skiing] for three days." It's not fun.

David viewed his anxieties as specific to his GenX positioning; it was he who recommended the novel *Generation X* (Coupland 1991) to me.

And then there was Karen, age twenty-seven, the daughter of a very successful doctor. She also went to an elite college but at the time of the interview did not quite know what she wanted to do with her life. She moved back with her parents for a while after college while trying out various jobs in the New York–New Jersey area. But she came to feel that she needed to go someplace completely new and get a fresh start. Her parents agreed and were footing most of the bills for her to live in California while she figured out what she wanted to do. Karen had much the same configuration of anxieties about privilege, work, and success that we heard from David. In particular she felt guilty about her parents' unending flow of financial support, while at the same time she saw no real career possibilities for herself. She began by talking about a roommate who was also supported by his parents:

> [About] my roommate in New York—how did he not work for a whole year? How much money did his parents send him over that year? I mean how much does it take for a person to live, rent was nine to twelve thousand a year, cash. So we have a lot of guilt... [She thus insists on paying part of the rent herself]... and my dad says, "Are you sure, can you pay your rent?" and I say yes because I am working three jobs. And I could take the money [he offers] and party out here and go on hikes and paint, do my thing, but I always know that I owe it to myself to keep making the effort to make my own living.

Yet Karen too seemed to have little confidence that she would succeed. Although she was evidently an extremely talented writer, she was not pursuing a writing career. As I wrote in my summary of the interview, "The biggest part of her story was basically an unhappy history of boring and unfulfilling jobs. She [said that she] and her friends talk about Generation X all the time; they feel it really describes them."

As a final example, take Charles, twenty-six, the son of a wealthy businessman. Charles went to an elite undergraduate college as well, and then went on to take an MBA before joining his father's well-established and highly profitable business. At the time of the interview (1994) he had only been in the business for a year but had been doing very well, both in terms of making internal managerial improvements and in terms of bringing in new accounts. Moreover, not only were his own parents wealthy; his fiancée's parents were very wealthy too. Nonetheless, he described himself as "terrified, absolutely terrified" of the possibility of financial ruin. Here is one of many long riffs on the subject:

> Now my dad gave me his old Jaguar, I mean this is like a fifty-thousand-dollar car that I'm driving around... I told my dad, I said, "Dad, look, this car is way beyond me, if you want this thing back I would not feel bad."... I don't care what the fuck I am driving, you just have got to pro-

> duce something. Am I status conscious? Yeah. Do I feel great driving that car? Yeah. Does it make me feel good, do I love having good things, and I am wearing a Rolex watch? Shit, that's great, I have had it since I was fifteen years old, I mean, come on, this is the best life. But have I earned it? Have I deserved this? I am very aware of the fact that I deserve none of the shit that I have, I am very grateful. I am very aware of the fact that [my father] could fall over and die and then I am on my own and nobody is going to step in there and pick up. That's it, it's over.

I must confess at this point that for a long time I failed utterly to hear these texts as examples of Generation X anxiety. As I presented earlier versions of this paper as talks at various universities and colleges, I argued that these privileged and materially secure kids could not possibly be the "real" Generation Xers; that they have bought into representations that came from elsewhere and that did not really describe them; that what we were hearing in these texts was just recycled Protestant-ethic anxiety, soon to be well sublimated in hard work and more material success; that if they were GenX at all it was only because any complaining from people with this much capital has to be heard as "whining."[17]

Yet every time I gave a talk arguing that the real embodiment of Generation X was the children of the lower middle class, and that the children of the upper middle class had been in effect terrorized by the media, there were howls of pain from the numerous GenXers (that is, graduate students) in my audiences. Finally I reminded myself of the cardinal rule of ethnography: The informant is always right. Even if, "objectively," these kids had nothing to worry about, there was something experientially real to them about the doom-saying forecasts of the GenX literature, and this needed to be captured by the argument.

FURTHER CLASS THEORIZING: REPRODUCTION AND REPRESENTATIONS

At this point we must pull into this interpretive arena another active body of theorizing: the question of class reproduction via family and gender relations. This has become much more central to class theory than it used to be, a fact that may be seen as an effect of twenty-five years of feminist social and cultural thought. This includes, among other things, renewed attention to "youth culture" (Brake 1985; Gaines 1990; Hall and Jefferson 1975; Ortner 1992; Willis 1977). It also includes the recognition of the deep centrality of family politics, including gender and, most pertinent to the present paper, generational politics, for understanding class reproduction. Although questions of family dynamics and politics in class reproduction are not missing from other recent works of class theorizing, like Bourdieu's *Distinction* (1984), they have been much more deeply explored in such feminist-inspired works as Barbara Ehrenreich's *Fear of Falling* (1990), Judith Stacey's *Brave New Families* (1990), and Elizabeth Traube's *Dreaming Identities* (1992).

Let us start this time with the upper middle class. The characteristics of the upper middle class have by now been well described, because it is in some sense the growth of this class—what the Ehrenreichs call the "professional-managerial class" or the "PMC"—that is generally thought to have driven many of the transformations of late capitalism (Bourdieu 1984; Ehrenreich and Ehrenreich 1979; Ehrenreich 1990; Mandel 1978; Pfeil 1990; Walker 1979). Although the entire middle class is in some sense built on "managerial" functions (and hence is "white collar"), a large sector of the upper middle class specifically occupies those positions that depend on high levels of specialized education; they are the professionals of society—doctors, lawyers, judges, planners—as well as the managers of business and finance.

As Ehrenreich and others have emphasized, the middle class in general and the upper middle class in particular cannot pass on its status to its children. This is distinctive of middle-class positionality: The lower classes find it all too easy to pass on their "status," while the upper classes have elaborate institutional means of preserving money and status for the group (e.g., Marcus 1992). Middle-class parents can only pass on to their children the means—economic, educational, and psychological—with which to (try to) reproduce their status. But ultimately the children must do it themselves.

The process is never secure. There are always some kids in danger of, as it is frequently put, getting off the track. Not every child can do well in school, not every child internalizes the work ethic or the commitment to "success." Although the upper middle class is downclassing slightly less than it did before 1980, the figure is still around 25 percent (Duncan, Smeeding, and Rodgers 1992), a figure well within the range documented for much of the twentieth century (see Lipset and Bendix 1957; Ortner 1991). Downclassing at the lower end of the middle class is surprisingly less likely overall (around 10 percent), though slightly more likely than it was before 1980 (Duncan, Smeeding, and Rodgers 1992). In any event it is clear that all middle-class parents have good reasons to worry about the trajectories of their particular children. But these anxieties are differently dealt with in the upper middle and the lower middle classes.

Among the upper middle class, what comes through strongly in my ethnographic data is that parents will provide almost unlimited and unending support for their children, well into adulthood. It is important to remember that the postwar period, in which the parents of current twentysomethings came of age, was a time of great prosperity, seemingly for all. Howe and Strauss call the parents of Generation X "the wealthiest generation in the history of America, maybe the world" (1993:39). This, of course, included the Class of '58 of Weequahic High School, my original ethnographic population and the parents of the upper-middle-class Xers discussed in this paper. These parents did very well indeed.

In turn they told me stories of almost unlimited support for their kids.[18] The support took many forms, but certainly material benefits were front and center: a materially comfortable life style while growing up, a college education, a professional education beyond that, a generous four- or five-figure wedding present, the down payment on a house, and perhaps a trust fund for the grandchildren's educations.[19]

In general, parents spoke of these things as part of loving their children and wanting them to be happy, and there is no question in my mind that that was how they experienced what they were feeling and doing.[20] But at another level a kind of adaptationist logic lies behind this: Several fathers said to me that they spoiled their kids by design, that they wanted them to become attached to the good things of life, so that they would want to work hard to get them. At the same time I also heard, from parents as well as grown children, about an amazing array of what I came to think of as "rescuing mechanisms" (Ortner 1992) on behalf of children who seemed to be in trouble—counseling, therapy, rehab programs, tutoring, booster courses, abortions for pregnant daughters, expensive legal services for sons in trouble with the law, and on and on.

The sum of these points is that upper-middle-class parents, in trying simply to do the best for their children out of the deepest sentiments of love and caring, were also enacting a refusal to let their kids slide downclass if they could possibly afford it. Virtually all the kids in my project, like the Xers of the public culture, had at least BAs and in some cases advanced (usually law) degrees. But those who were having trouble finding the jobs they wanted or hoped for, or having trouble starting on some career track that they sought, or finding it difficult to get a position consistent with their level of education and self-image, were being supported by their parents. In a few cases they were living at home, part of that large wave of "boomerang children" that is another piece of the GenX picture. But for the most part these twentysomethings were living on their own (at least physically), with a large part of the rent and other expenses covered by parents while they, the kids, sought the ideal (and not merely acceptable) job, or pursued the auditions and casting calls for careers in the arts and/or show business, or simply marked time until they decided what they wanted to do. The parental financial cushion, and their willingness to use it, meant that these young people had the luxury of a very extended period of uncertainty and openness about their own futures, and were not forced to lock themselves into McJobs. This is indeed cultural capital, backed up by the other, more old-fashioned, kind.

But all of this, which I found hard for a long time to view as anything but extreme privilege which should be protecting and defending these kids from anxiety, was also precisely the key to their anxieties. As the split opened up in the middle class, these kids felt like they were looking into the abyss, protected only by the safety net provided by their parents.[21] On the one hand they felt very grateful, which comes through in their texts. On the other hand they felt like they were in fact hanging over an abyss; hence the terror. As yet another GenX informant said, "I adore working at [a certain upscale publishing house], but there's not a day when I don't think my happiness won't be pulled out from under me like a rug. And I have a trust fund!"

Let us return now to the lower middle class. We have seen that the upper middle class enacts a pattern of supporting its kids relatively lavishly, well into adulthood. The general idea, in a sense, is to front-load their potential for success, to go all out early in their careers and give them the strongest possible start. When we turn to the lower middle class, we see precisely the absence of this pattern of class reproduction. Here we must turn again to Katherine Newman's valuable ethnography of a lower-middle-class community. Newman discusses at length the fact that her informants grew up in nice houses with plenty of material comforts. They expected to do as well as, or better than, their parents. And now they realize (or fear) that they will not, which is why they are angry at the system.

Newman then raises the question of why the parents do not help out their kids. She argues that they cannot, that they are basically house-poor, and they need whatever resources they have to support their own retirements. At the same time she indicates that such massive aid to the next generation is in effect not part of the class culture, that there is a commitment to a much more classic kind of economic individualism: "There are those—even in Pleasanton—who might ask why the postwar parents do not help out. Having benefited so much from the boom years, do they not have the resources to rescue their kids? *Even if Pleasanton parents were inclined toward rescue missions,* inclined to ignore the cultural prescription that calls for every generation to stand on its own two feet, they lack the wherewithal to prop up their adult children" (Newman 1993:21; italics added).

I am not suggesting here that lower-middle-class parents do not adequately support their growing children. Nor am I suggesting that there is no variation; there is indeed a great deal of racial and ethnic variation that I have to gloss over here in the interests of space. But I am suggesting that the patterns are different. There is, as just indicated, a greater emphasis on the idea that kids should stand on their own two feet, and the earlier the better. Within that emphasis (and of course in a context of scarcer economic resources), help is more likely to take the form of sharing goods and pooling services, rather than transferring large amounts of cash.[22] There is also more emphasis on backing children up in case of failure than on proactively endowing them with a lot of start-up capital and cultural boosting.

There are at least two ways in which these patterns would have worked well enough to produce "success" in times of prosperity and relative social stability, but would be problematic under current social and economic conditions. The first is simply that in better times the public sector picked up a bigger part of the tab, in the form of a better economic environment in general and in the form of specific middle-class perks like student loans, for example.

But the second way in which lower-middle-class family economic practices have been rendered problematic relates to the specific patterns of the launching of adult children just discussed. The lower-middle-class pattern is heavily dependent on the maintenance of relatively stable family relations, on the availability of family members for backup child care, housing, and job connections. Yet the period in which the upper and lower middle class pulled apart economically was also the period of the tremendous growth of the two-earner family, the galloping divorce rate, the declining fortunes of divorced mothers, and so on and so forth. That is, what was attenuated in this period was not only a larger structure of economic resources and opportunities, but the specific form of the safety net upon which the lower middle class depended. This, then, is certainly a recipe for frustration and rage.

In the worst cases we see some social pathologies that are not normally recognized as part of the Generation X phenomenon, but that I would suggest might fruitfully be looked at in that light. For example, Joan Didion (1993) wrote a riveting piece on the "Spur Posse," a gang of youth in white, "middle-class" Lakewood, California, who engaged in systematic gang rape and other forms of terrorism in their own community. Didion situates the phenomenon within the massive unemployment generated by the collapse of the aerospace industry, including a large amount of white-collar unemployment. For another example, Donna Gaines (1990) powerfully explored the dead-end conditions for lower-middle class youth in Bergenfield, New Jersey, in order to understand what led four teenagers collectively to commit suicide there in 1987. We are not far here from the widespread fascination, among self-professed GenXers, with Kurt Cobain's suicide.

Lower-middle-class rage and depression, and upper-middle-class terror and whining, are thus two sides of looking into the same abyss, an abyss portrayed in the public culture and theorized in accounts of class transformation and class reproduction. From the lower side this abyss seems increasingly impossible to cross; from the upper side it seems all too easy.

At this point a shift in analytic strategy is called for. Thus far I have portrayed the problematic as having three virtually independent pieces—the public cultural representations; the ethnographic accounts of informants' lives and talk; and a theoretical frame (or parts of one) that lets us see how class works and how it has been changing. This strategy has allowed us to see a number of useful things: that the public culture hides social difference even as it reveals (a certain picture of) social reality; that the amorphousness of the representational process (GenXers are angry, depressed, whining, and slacking, all at once) hides the ways in which different parts of the mix of images actually apply to different and indeed antagonistic social locations; that a theorized framework allows us to begin to sort out what goes where.

Yet this strategy itself obscures other questions. In particular, I have so far failed to ask in any systematic way about the production of these representations. In addition, apart from an early passing reference to "interpellating" (Althusser 1971) or constituting Generation X, largely as a marketing target, I have not asked what kinds of productive work these representations might be doing in the social process. Here then we need to recall that the middle class in general, and the upper middle class in particular, are not only the referents and objects of GenX imagery, but also its makers. Who, after all, writes the screenplays, the novels, the advertising copy, the journalistic reports, the demographic surveys? If at one level the public culture stands over and against what is going on on the ground, at another level it is one of the things that is made on the ground. This brings us to the final section of the essay.

THE PROBLEM OF THE SLACKER

In addition to the angry young lower-middle-class people with college degrees working in McJobs, and the privileged but highly anxious children of the upper middle class who come across as "whiners," there is one other classic GenX figure that needs to be addressed: the "slacker." The image of the slacker derives from Richard Linklater's 1990 film by that name (published later as a book, Linklater 1992), in which a series of seemingly bright, young, downwardly mobile twentysomethings carom off one another ironically, absurdly, funnily, for an hour and a half. All are either unemployed or working in jobs that are beneath their abilities/educations/inherited class positions. As Linklater said in an interview, "It's not that everyone in *Slacker* is unemployed, it's just that their little slave job isn't what's motivating them in the world" (Petrek and Hines 1993). This is classic GenX stuff, another version of McJobs. But as Linklater himself says, most people think a slacker is simply "someone who's lazy, hangin' out, doing nothing" (Petrek and Hines 1993).

Every Xer I have talked to, across the class spectrum, has hated the "slacker" label for their generation. All felt that they worked hard, and that their problems about their futures were not of their own making. Many, however, knew a slacker or two—recall Karen's roommate who lived in their expensive New York apartment and didn't work for a whole year.

Let me suggest that the referent of the slacker image is the falling upper-middle-class child, but the power of the image is not simply in its referent. Recall here the figures for downward mobility in the upper middle class: One out of four kids will not make it, and in really bad times, one out of three. If, as we have seen, the kids are terrified about failure, their parents are equally (or more) frightened for their kids. One indicator of the depth of their fears is the degree to which it was difficult to get parents to acknowledge, no less discuss, children with serious problems. Along with criminality, this was certainly the most sensitive area of my fieldwork. Kids with serious problems were not the ones who sent back their questionnaires. And parent-talk about kids was almost entirely and unrelievedly upbeat: All the kids were reported to be doing unbelievably well at whatever it was they were doing. One is reminded of Garrison Keillor's Lake Wobegone, where all the children are above average. I do not think there was a single interview in which a parent actually volunteered a story about a child in trouble.

Yet one way or another I was able to collect at least fragments of the stories these middle-class parents did not tell, about the kids who got into drugs, who did poorly in school, who became pregnant at a young age, who got in trouble with the law, who did not finish college and wound up as hairdressers or secretaries or mechanics. (These are, of course, perfectly respectable occupations, but from the point of view of the upper middle class, they represent failures of "achievement.") These kids are sources of great pain to their parents because the parents love them and do not want to see them damaged. They are also sources of conflict, as parents try to change their lives over and against the children's resistance. And they are sources of embarrassment verging on humiliation, as they stand in for and embody the parents' own anxieties about personal success in the world.

The degree to which upper-middle-class parents are sensitive about problems with and about their children, and the kinds of intense feelings generated around a problematic child, gives some sense of the anxieties behind the production and reception of a representation like the slacker. Slackers are images of (the possibility of) these kids, downwardly mobile and not even caring. More than markers of a social type, slackers are models of parental anxieties, pictures of upper-middle-class parents' worst fears for their kids. Moreover, for these parents, slackers are contradictions waiting to happen: When (if ever) does the parental support run out? When does one cut these kids loose financially? After all, the support was meant to be in the service of launching upward mobility, giving the kids the time to wait for the big break. If this period goes on too long, it becomes apparent to the parents that they have in fact financed downward mobility instead.

From the point of view of anxious young GenXers, on the other hand, either locked into McJobs or hanging in the safety net, the slacker is a more complex figure—a figure of repulsion and resentment, but also of envy. Slackers' lives may be empty, but at least they have stopped feeling the pain. Or have they? Although the characters in the film *Slacker* appear to have adopted this stance, the characters in Generation X spend the entire novel in a desperate quest to fend off a sense of meaninglessness. As one of the characters says, "We know that this is why the three of us left our lives behind and came to the desert—to tell stories and to make our own lives worthwhile in the process" (Coupland 1991:8).

SOME CONCLUSIONS

Anthropology increasingly operates in the midst of the contemporary world. Whereas once upon a time it was the hallmark of anthropologists to leave the world, to go far away, to seek the untouched and the pre-modern, it is now much more common for anthropologists to work in their home societies, or in sites of the "modern" wherever it happens to be. Even when they did not go far away, even when they worked in their home societies and/or on "modern" phenomena, the anthropological trick in the past was often to treat the community under study as if it were distant and exotic.

One implication of the shift to the here and now (or to recognizing the hereness and nowness of everything) is the fact that anthropology becomes only one voice, one entry, within an enormously complex and multivocal universe of "public culture." In this context, what—if anything—is its distinctive contribution? One obvious answer derives from the richness of ethnographic data, a product of doing long-term, in-depth, whole-self (or much-self) fieldwork. Ethnographic understanding is built up through density, "thickness" of observation, over an extended period of time. Perhaps the most extreme opposite of this kind of understanding is to be seen in some forms of television journalism, with its reliance on quick visual cuts and chopped sound bites. For all the attacks on elevated claims of "ethnographic authority" (some of which I agree with; see Clifford and Marcus 1986), I would still make the argument that classic long, deep ethnographic fieldwork produces some kinds of truth that a quicker and thus shallower journalism cannot produce.[23]

Yet in the end, ethnography is not enough. Ethnography is not the whole of anthropology, and it is important for the field to resist being confined to that box. Ethnography always takes place in explicit or implicit interaction with theory, that is to say, with competing bigger pictures of how things are "really" put together (regardless of what the natives say) and why.

It is theory that allows us to map the world in such a way that we can understand the relationship between various (journalistic and/or ethnographic) claims, rather than engaging in a competitive struggle for authority. At least this is how I have proceeded in this paper. I have argued that a range of recent theoretical thinking allows us to locate the diverse representations about twentysomethings—including (diverse) representations of "Generation X" and my own ethnographic data—within a larger picture, a picture of changing class relations in the United States under "late capitalism." "Theory" in this case includes rethought narratives of capitalist development in the late twentieth century, feminist arguments concerning the centrality of intimate relations to the reproduction of all relations of inequality, including class, and theories of representation from Geertz and Althusser to the present.

Theories of representation, in turn, compel us to think not only about the relationship between a signifier and its referent, but about representations as produced and consumed within a field of inequality and power, and shaped as much by those relations of production and consumption as by the nature of the supposed referent. Thus I have suggested, if only briefly, that the idea of Generation X in part tells us as much about the anxieties of upper-middle-class parents as it does about some set of young people out there in the world. Indeed we may think of the public culture on Generation X in part as the product of a cultural scouting expedition on behalf of these people, a trip to what to them is the edge of social space, and a set of postcards from that edge.

Notes

A slightly revised version of this paper appears in *Current Anthropology: The Journal of the Society for Cultural Anthropology* 13(3) (August 1998). Funding for the larger project of which this is a part has come from the University of Michigan, the Wenner-Gren Foundation for Anthropological Research, the University of California, Berkeley, and the John D. and Catherine T. MacArthur Foundation. I am extremely grateful to all these agencies. For excellent library searches, thanks to Lynn Fisher, and amazing Internet searches, thanks to Tim Taylor. For insightful comments on earlier drafts of this paper, I wish to thank James Faubion, Marc Flacks, Judith Rothbard, Roger Rouse, Judith Stacey, Tim Taylor, and the members of the SAR seminar. And finally, a special vote of thanks to Rick Perlstein, Xer native, generous commenter, and vociferous critic—if I still haven't got it right, it is not his fault.

1. The fieldwork with the Class of '58 has been discussed briefly in Ortner 1994 and 1997. The results of that work will be treated extensively in other publi-

cations. I present only the tiniest fraction of my ethnographic data here. I have just completed the interviewing and am only just beginning to sort the material for a full ethnography.

2. The ethnography of New Jersey is building up nicely. Gaines's (1990) youth study was in Bergenfield, not far from Newman's "Pleasanton" and not far from the epicenter (though not the only site) of my study. Moffatt's *Coming of Age in New Jersey* (1989) should also be mentioned. David Halle's (1984) study of chemical workers was done in Elizabeth; *The Class of '66* was based in a town on the south Jersey shore (Lyons 1994; Lyons is a graduate of Weequahic High School, Class of '60); the research for *Ritual Healing in Suburban America* was conducted in Essex County (McGuire 1988). Varenne, Goldman, and McDermott (n.d.) worked in New Jersey and have a similar footnote to this one listing yet other New Jersey–based ethnographic work.

3. In terms of college graduating classes, the first one by this reckoning was the class of 1985.

4. See Bourdieu 1984 on the inflation and devaluation of higher educational certification.

5. Some famous hippies and/or antiwar political activists later became yuppies, of course. But this was a secondary convergence.

6. Writers vary on the degree to which they acknowledge the countercultural and antiwar generation as having made any positive changes. Most recognize to some degree that that generation produced some important kinds of social and cultural progress: social advances for women, gays, and minorities; the ecology movement; the legitimation of rock music and many other forms of contemporary popular culture. But depending on the writer's political stripe (which is quite variable), these are either not really gains or they are gains which are irrelevant to today's world and Xers are tired of hearing about them (see Rushkoff 1994 for the more appreciative end, Howe and Strauss 1993 for the more negative end).

7. Despite the male pronoun, Generation X does not seem to be particularly gendered.

8. Thanks to in-house music consultants Gwen Kelly and Tim Taylor. The genre is sometimes called "whiny white-boy rock."

9. The discussion begins with Mandel 1978. See also Harvey 1989, Lash and Urry 1987, Rouse 1995.

10. The other major force in the emergence of "late capitalism" is globalization, which gives the economy its increasingly decentered and transnational character. This aspect of the question cannot be pursued in this paper.

11. As several observers have pointed out (e.g., Sacks 1994), today's "middle class" is not aware of, or does not wish to recognize, the degree to which it was created by what would now be seen as "government handouts." The minority scholarships, fellowships, and other forms of affirmative action created in the seventies and eighties are clearly analogues of those earlier programs, and they have had analogous positive effects. They are currently (and foolishly, in my opinion) being dismantled.

12. Working-class studies frequently—and correctly in my view—differentiate between the homeowning and nonhomeowning working class (e.g., Chinoy 1955; Halle 1984). See also Ortner 1991 on this split within the working class.

13. Although it is clear from context that Newman is talking about the group that came to be called "Baby Busters" or Generation X, she locates them as the latecomers or tail end within the Baby Boomers, which she sees as a split generation. This produces some confusion for readers (e.g., Callinan 1993), as her classification is out of synch with what have now become the established categories. This does not affect the present argument.

14. For an excellent portrayal of lower-middle-class rage in this era, from a different angle, see Rieder 1985.

15. See Ortner 1998 for a preliminary discussion of some aspects of the Jewish factor in relation to class in the US.

16. Quite a few of the twentysomethings in this project were trying to "make it" in one or another of the arts, and I hope to write a separate paper on the subject.

17. Thanks to tremendously responsive and thoughtful audiences at Princeton, University of California, Berkeley (Sociology), and University of California, Santa Cruz. In the same way, thanks to my Practice Theory seminar at UC Berkeley in the spring of 1996.

18. I benefited from a goodly level of this sort of privilege myself, and take this opportunity to thank my parents again for everything they have done for me.

19. It may be suspected—given the Jewish bias in my ethnographic data, as well as various folk beliefs about these matters—that the extremes of (financial) support for grown children is a particularly "Jewish" pattern, and not characteristic of the upper middle class as a whole. While I do think there are some subcultural differences between ethnicities, including Jews, in America, I would resist an argument posed in terms of Jewish exceptionalism. Again, see Ortner 1998.

20. On love and American kinship, see Schneider 1980.

21. The idea of the safety net is central to the Generation X novel. Coupland uses it to signify several different points—that being a GenXer can be a pose, when one really has parents and resources one can fall back on, but also that middle-class people carry around the idea of safety nets that may not in reality be available any more (Coupland 1991:113 and passim; Carden 1995).

22. I am grateful to Judith Stacey for stressing this point in her comments to me.

23. There are of course some great ethnographic journalists. Frances FitzGerald is at the top of my personal list, which also includes Jane Kramer. *The New Yorker* in general has long supported this kind of work.

4

Figuring David Koresh

James D. Faubion

The events that transpired at the Branch Davidian compound near Waco, Texas, between February and April of 1993 have continued to haunt us. Even before the bombing of the Federal Building in Oklahoma City, they were the stuff of an ever-increasing array of popular legends: tragic, grotesque, exotic, conspiratorial, always titillating, never quite convincing or complete. They allow nearly as great a variety of anthropological diagnoses. They pass easily enough as yet another epiphany of that expectant religiosity with which the Abrahamic tradition has so long been infused, the recrudescence of ancient passions and ancient visions still lurking in the untended cracks and crevices of a bland and supposedly secular present. Or they pass, just as easily, as yet another epiphany of that irresolute clash of values and authorities in which Max Weber discerned a quintessentially modern "war of the gods." They can even sustain the familiar formulae of postmodernist farce. Their inevitable bevy of docudramatists accordingly had little need of imagination. The real was already virtually ideal: a rock guitarist turned messiah who was as skilled with a rifle as he was with biblical quotation; psychological commandos who hoped that an amplified medley of Buddhist chants and the screams of dying rabbits would crack the intransigent sectarian spirits with whom they found themselves in a protracted standoff; and Janet Reno, the nation's first woman attorney general, a self-proclaimed "old maid" who would encamp her troops on the southern prairie under the banner of "family values."

What happened near Waco was, in short, an ambiguous affair, but also an affair that has remained outstanding for its narrative and diagnostic as well as its practical excess. It was at once a train of mute events and the spate of portraits and tales it inspired, at once history and story, at once act and representation, each of its double planes every bit as causally effective as the other. In what follows, I survey some of the accidents and some of the more systematic processes by which millenarianism once again became "news" and a small gathering of adherents brief, if dark, celebrities. I preface a structural account of both the ambiguities and the excesses of the Waco affair with a reconstructive review of three of its most abiding hallmarks.

The first if also the least accessible of these hallmarks is epistemic. From the outset of the standoff and still today, it inscribes a vector of what, following Baudrillard, might be called "simulation."[1] Indeed, the standoff remains the stuff of so many legends because it has refused with such stubborn consistency to yield up its realities, its genuine facts. Who, after all, could be trusted to ascertain them? Throughout a conflict in which all the usual, all the official agencies of investigation were themselves often cast as partisan, were perhaps often compelled to be partisan, sheer information had little if any consistent conduit. Denotata were obscure from the outset. "Theory" very soon had the pride of place that it has yet to relinquish.

The second hallmark, which I spell out at some length, is technological. The standoff was not merely news. For more than three months, it was the constant topic of an unprecedentedly elaborate and unprecedentedly efficient "writing machine" and "imaging machine" that has continued ever since to generate far more than mere reports from the scene.

The final hallmark is—not metaphorically—demonological. In the past half century, the United States has concentrated its attention on a diverse array of "public enemies" and "threats to the fabric of society," from communists to homosexuals, from the ethnic (and other) radicals of the sixties and seventies to the urban gangs of the eighties and the present. Both the media and the behavioral scientists who served as consultants during the unfolding of the standoff, however, made of David Koresh a quite singular but also quite exemplary figure around whom the anxieties and the psychosocial symptomatologies dominant at the time, dominant at present, and likely still to be dominant at the beginning of the next millennium, could coherently coalesce. A public that has become increasingly ambivalent about many of the values it has long held may be inclined today to look back on the standoff as an epitome of the government's readiness and willingness to serve itself at the expense of liberty, even as it continues to regard Koresh as reprehensible precisely for his abuse of liberty, for all his arrogant pretensions to absolute sovereignty.[2] A public whose increasing sensitivity to the rhetoric of corruption has gone hand in hand with the increasing embrace of a distinctly deterministic and distinctly "pandemic" comprehension of the sources and the perpetuation of corruption might even today regard Koresh as monstrous precisely for his alleged "abuse" at once of the laws regulating the sale and possession of weapons and of the children around him. Whatever might accurately be said of the man, the figure of a supremely hubristic and supremely abusive Koresh in any case constitutes an archetype of the demonic, an archetype of the deviant, that has lost none of its disturbing resonance. It is a figure of a structural transition still unfolding. It still echoes the ever more patent exhaustion of the institutions of welfarist governmentality. It also echoes a potentially adaptive redirection of the discourses and practices of welfarist policing. Or so much, by way of concluding, I argue.

THE MACHINICS AND THE POETICS OF DEVIANCE

The tabloids were content to treat both the standoff and its leading dramatis personae as sensations. The tropology that governed their exegeses and exposés was, as always, hyperbolic. Television would, throughout the standoff, frequently compromise itself in its quest, if not for sensation then at least for the "scoop." But the tropology it adopted was, in the long run, also the tropology of its slightly more respectable counterparts, those printed dailies and weeklies and monthlies of recognizably high standards and of national and international circulation through which—if through anything—something like a public doxa continues to be reflected and to be formed and reformed.[3] In lieu of voluminous quotation, I present a cross-sectional sampler of what they produced. The sampler is not itself to be found in the media. It is a *fictio.* It reveals the modest diversity of points of view typical of contemporary doxa, but its scope is grounded in my own, "native" judgment of the limits of "respectable," "reasonable," "mainstream" public doxa itself. Though marked with the signatures of its multiple authors, its stuff is the stuff of redundancy, of words and images shared among the various media, repeated and repeated again, most of them resting just on the edge of anonymity. It is not the only pastiche that might have been constructed. But it is, I think, an illustrative example of prevailing rhetorical trends. Even so, the Common Reader can hardly confront it in toto as anything other than pastiche. For all its disparities, for all its seams, the sampler at least reveals a strong penchant for metonymy. Kenneth Burke recognized metonymy, and especially the metonymic reduction of complex wholes to one of their exemplary parts, as the great trope of modern science. The sampler confirms Burke's insight, but shows that metonymy can have its moral utility, and moral force, as well.

LOCALES

Waco, ***heart of Texas,*** is ***the buckle of America's Bible Belt.*** It ***enjoys one of the highest concentrations of religions anywhere in America, more than 100 at the last count*** (Ben MacIntyre [BM], *London Times* [*LT*] 3/6/93:14b).[4] It is ***the eternal city of the Baptists*** (Larry McMurty [LM], *New Republic* [*NR*] 6/7/93:16). But Waco also has ***14 museums, a new zoo and other attractions*** (Sam Howe Verhovek [SHV], *New York Times* [*NYT*] 3/6/93:A8). The director of its Convention and Visitors Bureau declares it ***"bigger"*** than ***what will surely go down as one of the strangest episodes in the country's law-enforcement history*** (SHV, *NYT* 4/4/93:IV:7). Even so, ***most Texans have never seen anyone who isn't Texan; and many, politely but firmly, do not want to*** (BM, *LT* 4/7/93:13a). ***What you are is what you wear*** in Waco, ***although what you are is also accurately reflected by what you drive and what you shoot*** (BM, *LT* 4/7/93:13a). ***The "High Noon" philosophy survives intact... if a man reaches for his gun, you can shoot him dead*** (BM, *LT* 3/15/93:9a). ***Waco must be one of the few places in the world where you can still buy adult-sized, Osh Kosh B'Gosh dungarees, of the sort usually worn by infants*** (BM, *LT* 4/7/93:13a)—or so presumes the journalist whom the *London Times* conveyed to cover the standoff firsthand.

The fateful compound stood about seven or eight miles from Waco's city center. By February of 1993, it was ***a compact fort*** (Richard Lacayo [RL], *Time* [*T*] 3/15/93:37), ***dominated by a tower with lookout***

windows facing in all directions (SHV, *NYT* 3/1/93:B9). ***Cult members*** had once ***discussed renaming the place Ranch Apocalypse.*** Among its buildings were ***an underground bunker and an armory—adjacent to the chapel*** (RL, *T* 3/15/93:37). The property included ***a well with undrinkable water*** and ***a storage tank for fuel*** (SHV, *NYT* 3/5/93:A16). By the second week in April, the fort had begun to look ***like a prison.*** It had been surrounded ***with razor-sharp barbed coils*** (SHV, *NYT* 4/13/93:A1). A week later, it would become a ***tar-paper, yellow-pine and plasterboard crematorium*** (Nancy Gibbs [NG], *T* 5/3/93:32). ***Flimsy construction and... 30 mph winds*** (Michael deCourcy Hinds [MCH], *NYT* 4/28/93:A16) would abet the flames that destroyed it.[5]

GENEALOGIES

Only in Texas? The casual portraiture of a region where ***commerce still yields to faith, at least until after church*** (LM, *NR* 6/7/93:16), through which the sometimes native sons and daughters of the press sought to locate the Branch Davidians in space, falls short of either environmental or cultural determinism, however often it might indulge in the tonalities of sociological reductionism. A portraiture at once more sober and less settled would locate the community in time. The more distinguished national magazines would invite such religious scholars as Paul Boyer and Bill Pitts to offer their reflections on the millennial tradition to which the community was attached. A professor of the history of religion at Waco's Baylor University, Pitts would also offer his expertise to the legion of observers assigned to watch a particular moment in the history of religion unfold. Scholarly voices would point to spiritual sources and constitutional principles that tied good citizens of the United States more closely to the separatism in their midst than they might at first have cared to admit. At least a few among them would question from the outset whether the strategists of the FBI had an adequate comprehension of the doctrinalism and devotionalism they were confronting. They seem, however, to have won at most an ephemeral hearing, either in the wider media or among the strategists of the FBI themselves.[6]

The apical ancestor of the community is Victor Houteff, ***a Bulgarian immigrant who joined the Seventh-day Adventist Church in 1918*** but was excommunicated some 11 years later ***for disrupting an Adventist Sabbath School with his dissident views*** (*NYT* 3/1/93:B9). Houteff, ***a Maytag washing machine salesman*** (Peter Steinfels [PS], *NYT* 3/6/93:A9), ***claimed that he had been sent to "cleanse" the Adventist denomination*** (*Christian Century* [*CC*] 3/17/93:286).[7] In 1935, he led a small group of acolytes from his home in Los Angeles to a settlement known as Old Mount Carmel, which lay just outside Waco. In 1942, he decided that his group would be known as the ***Davidian Seventh-day Adventists... because he believed the restoration of David's kingdom in Palestine was imminent*** (*NYT* 3/1/93: B9). In 1955, Houteff died. Since then, ***the cult's history has been marked by turmoil and violence*** (*CC* 3/17/93: 286). Houteff's wife, Florence, ***assumed power and predicted that the new kingdom would come on April 22, 1959*** (*NYT* 3/1/93:B9). ***She also predicted that a divinely inspired slaughter of "wicked" Seventh-day Adventists would occur*** (*CC* 3/17/93:286). Her message attracted a substantial following. In 1957, the Davidians disposed of their original acreage and moved a few miles farther from Waco, to the "New Mount Carmel" or "Mount Carmel" at which the 1993 standoff would take place.

But after April 1959, the group splintered (*NYT* 3/1/93:B9). Davidians who claim strict loyalty to the Houteffs might still be found ***peacefully proselytizing in upstate New York, California, South Carolina, and elsewhere*** (PS, *NYT* 3/6/93:A9). Most of those who had gathered at the Old Mount Carmel Center, however, shifted their loyalty to ***a rival prophet, Ben Roden, who called his group the Branch Davidians*** (*NYT* 3/1/93:B9) and ***styled himself the literal successor to King David*** (RL, *T* 3/15/93:36). ***When Roden died in 1978, his wife, Lois, took over leadership*** (*NYT* 3/1/93:B9), a role that she shortly began to share with her son, George. A certain Vernon Howell ***joined them in 1984, after he was expelled from a conventional Seventh-day Adventist congregation*** (RL, *T* 3/15/93:37). Howell ***began a sexual relationship with... Lois, then in her late 60's*** (Adam Nossiter [AN], *NYT* 3/10/93:A14). ***Before long he was locked in a power struggle with George.***

At one juncture, Howell was ***driven from the sect at gunpoint*** (RL, *T* 3/15/93:37), ***with virtually all of Mr. Roden's followers*** (AN, *NYT* 3/10/93:A14). ***He briefly established his own desolate congregation, living with them in tents and packing crates in nearby Palestine, Texas*** (RL, *T*

3/15/93:37). But ***Mr. Roden seethed*** at Howell's ***influence over the several dozen members of the sect who had followed him. And in 1987, he challenged*** his adversary *to* ***a ghoulish contest: whoever could bring back the dead deserved to be the true leader*** (AN, *NYT* 3/10/93:A14). ***Roden*** accordingly ***disinterred the*** coffin and ***corpse of a female church member with the intention*** of reviving her (RL, *T* 3/15/93:37). He failed. Instead of ***taking up the challenge,*** Howell went to the police and denounced Roden for committing ***corpse abuse*** (AN, *NYT* 3/10/93:A14). Told to obtain proof, he summoned seven companions and executed an armed raid on New Mount Carmel. In the exchange that ensued, Roden was wounded in the hand and chest.

Howell was accused of attempted murder, but the jury he faced could not agree on a conviction. His trial ***is still remembered in the domed, turn-of-the-century McLennan County Courthouse for its circus atmosphere....*** Howell's ***lawyer wanted to introduce the coffin, complete with the skeleton, as evidence. Before the coffin was taken to the courthouse,*** Howell ***tied a pink bow around the skeleton's neck, to dress it up*** (AN, *NYT* 3/10/93:A14). Roden recovered from his wounds, but was not long at Mount Carmel. In 1989 he was declared mentally unfit to face charges after having murdered a man in Odessa, Texas, and was promptly delivered to the high-security ward of an institution for the insane. He continues to be detained in a similar institution to this day.

With Roden out of the way, Howell became undisputed leader of the Branch Davidians in Waco, completing their transition from congregation to cult. He and a few select followers began recruiting new members on trips around the U.S., Britain and Australia. In 1990, he legally changed his first name to David (after King David) and his last ***to Koresh, Hebrew for Cyrus, the Persian king who allowed the Jews to return to Israel after their captivity in Babylon*** (RL, *T* 3/15/93:37). David Koresh, whose ***business card*** said ***"Messiah,"*** who once asserted that ***if the Bible*** were ***true,*** then he was ***Christ*** (SHV, *NYT* 3/6/93:A8), who later insisted that he was only a prophet, was leader of the Mount Carmel Branch Davidians until he died on April 19, 1993, shortly after the breakout of the fire that would bring the standoff, and some seventy-five to eighty other lives, to an abrupt end.[8]

Those who might seek comfort in the idiosyncrasies, either of Koresh or his community, would be disappointed. ***Koresh was...a crea-***

ture of his time and place, an archetypal anti-establishment figure of the American present and past (Paul Boyer [PB], *NR* 5/17/93:30). ***To many Americans,*** his ***talk of "breaking open the seals" was as unfathomable as a foreign language*** (PS, *NYT* 4/25/93:I32). But in fact, ***the general contours of*** his ***beliefs were neither unique nor particularly unusual. His rambling hour-long sermon broadcast early in the siege (as part of the deal he struck with negotiators) was in important respects indistinguishable in tone and content from the presentations of other apocalyptic preachers who now crowd the airwaves. From Michigan comes the durable Jack Van Impe, known as "The Walking Bible"; from Tulsa, Oral Roberts. Charles Taylor's "Today in Bible Prophecy" radio show... airs on more than twenty stations nationwide and globally via the Spacenet, SATCOM and Galaxy communications satellites... Pat Robertson's Christian Broadcasting Network (CBN), which fully believes in the apocalyptic Scriptures, serves some 3,000 cable t.v. systems*** (PB, *NR* 4/25/93:30–31). The Seventh-Day Adventist Church from which Koresh was expelled has itself long been ***a bastion of prophecy teaching.*** So, too, The Assemblies of God Church, ***which grew by 121 percent from 1965 to 1989*** and has a current membership of some ***2.2 million*** (PB, *NR* 5/17/93:31). Consider also ***Hal Lindsey, whose premillennial popularization*** **The Late Great Planet Earth** ***(1970) ranks as*** <u>***the***</u> ***nonfiction bestseller of the 1970s; the book has sold upwards of 20 million copies in various editions and translations*** (PB, *NR* 5/17/93:32).

Indeed, ***from Puritan days, American Christianity has been suffused with...millennialist belief, which*** stems ***especially*** from ***the Book of Revelation, the last book of the New Testament,*** and ***has counterparts in Judaism and Islam*** (PS, *NYT* 3/3/93:B10). Asked for his opinion after he conducted his Easter service, ***Rev. Angelo Bertini*** of Waco's ***St. Mary's Catholic Church*** avowed that the Book of Revelation ***"has nothing to do with the Apocalypse"*** (*NYT* 4/12/93:B11). ***For 1,900 years,*** however, ***Revelation... has exercised an almost hypnotic power over some Christians, particularly the dispossessed, the persecuted and those desperately trying to make sense of personal or social turmoil*** (PS, *NYT* 4/25/93:I32). ***From the earliest centuries, church leaders recognized the explosive character of this intoxicating brew of puzzling and ferocious images.*** After the destruction of Mount Carmel, ***several scholars, including Ronald F. Thiemann, Dean of the Harvard Divinity School, and James Richardson, a sociologist of religion at the***

University of Nevada at Reno, questioned...whether the authorities...really recognized how deeply (PS, *NYT* 4/25/93:I32) Koresh and his entourage—***who were not living within reason,*** but rather ***within belief*** (LM, *NR* 6/7/93:19)—might have ***believed that the last book of their Bible provided a script for the last hours of their lives*** (PS, *NYT* 4/25/93:I32).

Koresh was solidly a player in ***American history*** not, however, merely because of his engagement with the Book of Revelation, but also because of ***his creation of a cult...If the People's Temple and the Branch Davidians are products of America's uniquely* laissez-faire *religious culture, so, too, were John Woolman, Harriet Beecher Stowe, Jane Adams, Henry J. Cadbury, A. J. Muste, Dorothy Day and Martin Luther King Jr.*** (PB, *NR* 5/17/93:33). Not all "cults"—a term ***often...used pejoratively and imprecisely***—live in expectation of ***violent conflict.*** Only a few of ***maybe more than a thousand*** carrying on ***almost invisibly around the United States today*** are ardently separatist, and most of those opt for ***pacific retreat.*** What ***exactly sends them one way or another remains puzzling...David C. Rapoport, a professor of political science at the University of California at Los Angeles who has studied links between religion and terrorism,*** observes that in a few cases, ***isolation intensifies the belief of the group and its leader that they are exempt from society's norms and laws...Michael Barkun, a political scientist at Syracuse University who has studied white supremacist and anti-Semitic Christian groups,*** observes that separatist ***sects*** are ***inherently unstable... Defections...often breed internal repression. Inquiries and accusations...breed paranoia.*** But Rapoport notes ***that clashes between sects and the Government* have *become more common in recent decades. "These groups don't get violent until the 1960's when everyone else gets violent...Several scholars argue that greater knowledge about these sects could help prevent violent confrontations*** (PS, *NYT* 3/3/93:B10).

THE FLOCK

In June of 1993, Michael Barkun emphasized to the readers of *The Christian Century* that ***as bizarre and misguided as...*** the ***beliefs*** of the Branch Davidians ***might have seemed, it*** is ***necessary to grasp the role these beliefs played in their lives*** (Michael Barkun [MB], *CC* 6/2–9/93:596). In the middle of March 1993, a writer for *U.S. News and World Report* would urge even greater empathy. ***Most Americans, of course, are not in extremist***

cults. But they belong to other groups—companies, families, churches—with their own rules and value systems. And in small, undramatic ways, as psychiatrist Arthur Deikman argues in "The Wrong Way Home," we all cross the line into "cult" behavior, conforming our views to those of others (Erica E. Goode [EEG], *U.S. News and World Report* [*USNWR*] 3/15/93:5).[9] In early May, *The New Yorker* could suggest in retrospect that there are distinctively American features of the ***Koresh phenomenon,*** and that Americans perhaps especially ***tend to channel*** their ***most radical impulses through religious enthusiasms rather than through politics, philosophy, or art.*** It also suggested that the Branch Davidians were part of ***the worldwide fundamentalist upsurge.*** Yet they ***were not Al-Jihad. They did not train themselves for an assault on society; they trained themselves to resist an assault by society*** (*New Yorker* [*NY*] 5/3/93:6). In July, an essayist for the libertarian journal *Reason* would publish his suspicion that those who perished in ***the Waco tragedy*** are likely never to garner their eulogies, much less encomia, only because ***there aren't enough Branch Davidians left to preserve a proper memory*** of them (Jacob Sullman [JS], *Reason* [*R*] 7/93:5).

In fact, the residents of Mount Carmel came not only from the United States but from such distant countries as Israel and Australia. Perhaps because several Britons were also among them, *The London Times* would monitor the standoff with unusual vigilance. If the view from afar can be condescending, it can also be accommodating in its own right. Approaching Easter of 1993, *The Times* relegated half a page to Ian Robertson's reflections on the ***"Voices of Sweet Unreason."*** Robertson wasted few words: ***Britons pride themselves on their rationality, but are they really that rational? Take superstition, for instance: how many of us would balk at taking room 13 in a spooky hotel? Or avoid walking under a ladder? Or prefer not to "tempt fate" by mentioning something we fear or desire?*** (Ian Robertson [IR], *LT* 4/6/93:17a). What, moreover, of Anglican theology itself? What of ***believing in such things as virgin births, bread turning into human flesh ...?*** Indeed, even the ***average British rationalist-materialist-humanist citizen*** is startlingly partial to ***such exotica as aromatherapy, acupuncture, reflexology, astrology and aura-massage.*** The predilections of even the average British citizen reveal ***that rationality is simply not enough for the human mind*** (IR, *LT* 4/6/93:17a), at least not always.

Even so, rationality is a very stubborn taskmaster, and ***does not easily***

tolerate odd behaviour and experience, and likes to tidy it up by labelling it as "sick", and calling in the doctors (IR, *LT* 4/6/93:17a). Indeed, slightly more than a month before Robertson's Eastertime reflections were published, another writer for the *London Times* does just that. ***Why do cults flourish in America particularly? Because of a prevalent sense of exclusion, according to Dr. David Eddy, a clinical psychologist whose patients include teenagers growing up in the Washington suburbs*** (Ian Brodie [IB], *LT* 3/2/93:17). And in the immediate aftermath of the destruction of Mount Carmel, similar estimations appeared: ***The joyless family that arose around David Koresh sought... authority, certainty, community*** (*LT* 4/21/93:15). Those who died in the fire, ***denied method elsewhere in their lives,*** must have ***found method in*** their prophet's ***madness.*** Not all were Americans, ***but to seek solace in lunacy makes sense only when nothing else does,*** and ***this is what Americans fear most: that their most treasured institutions are bankrupt, that their freedom has turned to riot, and that the moral revolution of the 1960s has finally torn out society's deepest roots*** (*LT* 4/21/93:15). In the next issue of the *Times,* readers learn that ***the bizarre behaviour of the followers of David Koresh at Waco*** merits a quite specific diagnosis. In ***their fascinating book*** **Uncommon Psychiatric Syndromes,*...Dr. David Enoch and Sir William Trethowan...make a case for relating*** such behavior ***to a condition known as*** **folie à plusieurs,** ***where a leader, however deluded, finds support from people who are usually comparatively simple, idealistic and disaffected. These followers seek self-esteem and a sense of being needed and belonging*** (*LT* 4/22/93:17a).

Should it thus come as any surprise that the government agents at Waco were so concerned that ***the Texas cult was contemplating mass suicide*** (*NYT* 3/6/93:A8), in spite of the denials of its spokesmen? Who were the Branch Davidians, after all, but ***people who had lost jobs, lovers or simply a sense of belonging to the world in which they lived*** (SHV, *NYT* 3/3/93:A1)? Who were they, after all, but people ***distressed and lonely,*** likely to be bound to one another by ***an addictive excitement*** and ***a shared paranoia of outsiders*** (Daniel Goleman [DGO], *NYT* 4/21/93:A21)? This ***misguided paramilitary community*** (and cf. Wolfgang Münchau [WM], *LT* 5/5/93:12a) included the ***empty and afraid*** (James M. Wall [JMW], *CC* 5/5/93:476), ***the disenfranchised*** and ***the weak-willed,*** some of whom had ***compared the experience*** of listening to Koresh's teachings to

being on drugs (Jan Jarboe [JJ], *Texas Monthly* [*TM*] 6/93:152). ***"It was difficult to leave because you were so brainwashed," said Robyn Bunds, 23*** (SHV, *NYT* 3/2/93:A16).

Consider Steve Schneider, who emerged early in the standoff as Koresh's chief deputy: ***a disappointment, if not to himself, then to some of the people who wanted to use him*** (David Van Biema [DVB], *T* 5/3/93:39). Consider Kathy Andrade. Like Schneider and many of the other Branch Davidians, she had past connections with the Seventh-Day Adventist Church. But ***she was, as her generation would put it, in a search mode,*** and when she ***began investigating her religious options, she even interviewed a...rabbi*** (DVB, *T* 5/3/93:41). Consider Sherry Jewell. ***"Her childhood was pretty happy,"*** or so her mother thought. But her ex-husband recognized that ***she wasn't emotionally secure... "She had a desperate need to be led"*** (Richard Zoglin [RZ], *T* 5/3/93:42). Consider Louis Anthony Alaniz, who succeeded in breaching the barrier that the government had set up around the perimeter of the Mount Carmel compound in order to join the community inside. An FBI agent announced that Alaniz ***"was described as a religious fanatic by his own mother"*** (SHV, *NYT* 3/26/93:A14). Koresh soon decided that Alaniz was too troublesome, and sent him back out to the wider world. Schneider, Andrade, and Jewell died with Koresh. Alaniz alone is still alive.

For the dead, as for more and more of the living, the rhetoric of psychological symptomatology is a particularly persuasive rhetoric of excuse. But it also comes at a cost: it tends to undermine the maturity and the moral integrity of the very persons and very acts for whose pardon it argues. For all its currency and for all its modernity, it accordingly tends to confirm a moral suspicion of religious separatists that is quite constant and quite ancient. In his *Annals of Imperial Rome,* Tacitus writes disapprovingly of Nero's fabrication of "scapegoats" in order to dispel rumors that the burning of Rome was an official act of arson. Among Nero's worst-abused victims were a sect which Tacitus describes as "notoriously depraved." He explains that "their originator, Christ, had been executed in Tiberius's reign by the governor of Judaea, Pontius Pilatus"—thus the only reference to the crucifixion in all of pagan Latin literature. The crucifixion was "a temporary setback," but not long after "the deadly superstition had broken out afresh, not only in Judaea...but also in Rome."

Tacitus underscores his remarks with the sage observation that "all degraded and shameful practices collect in the capital" (Tacitus 1971:365). He adds that "despite their guilt as Christians, and the ruthless punishment it deserved," those who were tortured and put to death "were pitied. For it was felt that they were being sacrificed to one man's brutality rather than to the national interest" (Tacitus 1971:366).

Libertarians might point out that ***any demanding religion can be made to seem sinister. Hassidic Jews, for example, obey and revere their leader, limit outside contact, run their own schools, and even dictate what their kids may eat*** (JS, *R* 7/93:5). Relativists might propose that ***the parents in Koresh's cult were unusual in only one respect: they did not accept the norms of postmodern child rearing, which prizes rights, autonomy and personality development of children*** (Kenneth Woodward [KW], *Newsweek* [*NW*] 5/3/93:30). But the contemporary bearers of the Tacitan sensibility were the greater force. One of the latter cites a professional opinion that the twenty-one Branch Davidian children who were released before the fire would probably fare well, so long as they received ***even a "modicum" of such things as loving, setting of rules and teaching.*** Without them the children would be ***in jeopardy. But of course, the jeopardy was there from the time their parents sought the false comfort of a cult*** (David Gelman [DG], *NW* 5/17/93:54). After the fire, rumors abounded that the children who had remained inside had been given lethal injections. Another rumor was more persistent: ***Some Koreshians may have committed the most unforgivable sin...Top-ranking FBI officials...believe virtually all of the children at Ranch Apocalypse, 17 of them under age ten, almost certainly were killed before the first flames from the Davidian compound were spotted. FBI observers stationed on the compound grounds reported that less that two minutes before the first flames were sighted, they heard a 20-to-30-second burst of automatic-weapons fire...One top official says the theory is that the shooting was directed at the children because they were easy to round up*** (Harrison Rainie [HR], *USNWR* 5/3/93:26). Of the twenty-three bodies later officially identified as being those of minors, three had in fact died of gunshot wounds, and one of a stab wound. Coroners were able to establish that fifteen had died either of suffocation, of smoke inhalation or carbon monoxide poisoning, or of burns. The precise cause of the death of the remaining four was unclear (cf. Scruggs et al.

1993:320–28). But whether or not the Koreshians could uniformly be condemned for what they had inflicted upon their children, ***72 percent*** of the Americans who responded to an ABC news poll ***said they believed that the Federal Bureau of Investigation had done the right thing*** when it finally moved against the compound; ***78 percent thought that the standoff would have ended in violence sooner or later anyway*** (Stephen Labaton [SL], *NYT* 4/23/93:A20).

CHARISMATICS AND CON ARTISTS, MESSIAHS AND MADMEN

An even greater number of Americans, ***95 percent,*** showed their Tacitan side in holding David Koresh largely responsible ***for the catastrophic end to the siege*** (SL, *NYT* 4/23/93:A20). The members of his flock had their troubles, their weaknesses. But Koresh ***preyed on*** them (NG, *T* 5/3/93:43). ***The authorities in Waco*** may have ***failed to grasp the nature of charismatic leadership*** (MB, *CC* 6/2–9/93:598). They may consequently have underestimated and misconstrued Koresh, that ***charismatic guitar player and beer drinker who*** claimed ***to be Christ*** (*LT* 3/1/93:13e). But they ***understandably treated*** him ***as a thug and a terrorist*** (JMW, *CC* 5/5/93:476). He was a ***notorious liar and con man*** (JJ, *TM* 6/93:152). ***After two days of negotiation that followed the*** initial ***shootout, Koresh promised to surrender himself peacefully if he could deliver a statement on radio. But after his rambling 58-minute address was broadcast on Christian stations around the country, he reneged, saying he was still awaiting "further instructions from God"*** (RL, *T* 3/15/93:39). He ***never doubted that he was a law unto himself*** (John Berry [JB], *Esquire* [*E*] 7/93:54). Koresh ***held over*** his congregants ***the power of the Apocalypse; he was the Lamb of Revelation, who alone could open the seven seals and foresee the end of the world*** (NG, *T* 5/3/93:39). But he was also a ***dyslexic*** who ***spent elementary school in the special-education room and dropped out of Garland High School*** in Dallas ***in the ninth grade*** (JB, *E* 7/93:54).

To be sure, Koresh had always been ***an avid reader of the Bible who prayed for hours and memorized long passages of Scripture*** (RL, *T* 15/93:36). He claimed to have ***had a mystical conversion in a Tyler***, Texas, ***graveyard*** (JB, *E* 7/93:54). Many of those who knew him would remark on his remarkable gifts as a preacher. ***"No one,"*** said ***Oliver Gyarfas, a***

twenty-one-year-old Australian who came to Mount Carmel after his father had already established himself there, ***"ever put such beautiful phrases together out of Scripture"*** (JB, *E* 7/93:55). ***"He had this amazing ability to recite verse," said Robyn Bunds...who joined the sect in California*** but left after bearing one of Koresh's ***many children. "He just has a good way of interpreting the Scriptures"*** (SHV, *NYT* 3/3/93:A1). If with many qualifications, at least one or two theologians, including the University of North Carolina's James Tabor (1994), could concur.

But such theologians were a decided minority. Most who heard Koresh speak took him to be spouting ***biblical gibberish*** (HR, *USNWR* 3/3/93:28), some of it quite salacious. ***For example, the "oil of gladness" mentioned in the Forty-fifth Psalm as the substance of choice when anointing the king was a reference to vaginal secretions—at least according to Koresh. When it came to sex, no suggestion seemed too outrageous, no line of reasoning too vulgar. "There's only one hard-on in this whole universe that really loves you and wants to say good things about you," he reportedly assured his female followers, comparing their relationship to him with that of Mary's to God*** (JJ, *TM* 6/93:151). Nothing out of the ordinary, perhaps, for the figure of a man who told an interviewer from the Waco *Tribune-Herald*: ***"If the Bible is true, then I'm Christ. But so what? Look at 2,000 years ago. What's so great about being Christ? A man nailed to a cross. A man of sorrow acquainted with grief. You know, being Christ ain't nothing. Know what I mean?"*** (*LT* 3/1/93:13e).

Not merely salacious, the figure of Koresh was rapacious as well. When young he was ***prone to excessive masturbation*** (JB, *E* 7/93:54). At Mount Carmel he ***indulged liberally in sex with the women in the cult, including young teenage girls—all of whom he said he could claim as wives and none of whom were permitted to have sexual relations with their husbands or anyone else*** (HR, *USNWR* 5/3/93:20). ***And for anyone who thought it odd that a holy man lived out a teenage boy's sexual fantasy, Koresh had managed a theological rationale. He was...Christ in sinful form, who because he indulged the flesh could judge mankind with insights that the first, more virtuous Messiah had lacked*** (RL, *T* 5/3/93:34).[10] He demanded self-denial from the men of the community that he never dreamed of demanding from himself. ***Once in the cult, Davidians surrendered all the material means of personal independence, like money and belongings, while***

Koresh seemed to have unlimited funds... The grounds around the compound were littered with old automobiles that the faithful cannibalized for parts to keep their clunkers running while Koresh drove a black Camaro muscle car... Even as he bedded their wives and daughters...in his comfortable private bedroom on the compound's ***second floor, the men were confined to their dormitory downstairs. Behind the mind games and the psychological sadism,*** moreover, ***lay the threat of physical force. In addition to...paddlings, administered in a utility area called the spanking room*** or whipping room, ***offenders could be forced down into a pit of raw sewage, then not allowed to bathe*** (RL, *T* 5/3/93:35).

Nor was this ***madman*** (*LT* 4/21/93:15) Koresh slow to take offense. ***Once he caught one of his followers, whom he had sent into Waco on an errand, sneaking a hamburger at McDonald's. He flew into a blind rage*** (SHV, *NYT* 3/5/93:A16). ***In a tactic common to cult leaders, Koresh made food a tool for ensuring obedience*** (RL, *T* 5/3/93:35). ***To ensure his control,*** he ***undermined family attachments. The children were told to consider him their only father—their parents were called "dogs"*** (Sophronia Scott Gregory [SSG], *T* 5/17/93:54). The ***mad messiah of Waco*** (SSG, *T* 5/17/93:54) ***preached that the world was full of "bad guys," hurtful unbelievers out to kill the Davidians*** (SSG, *T* 5/17/93:54).

The psychologists and psychiatrists who reviewed Koresh's ***strange and brutish behavior*** (JJ, *TM* 6/93:151) inclined to similar, if more precise, assessments. The *London Times* was not alone in comparing Koresh to such ***charismatic but maniacal*** figures as Charles Manson. The FBI solicited a wide array of criminological evaluations. There was near consensus that Koresh was a ***psychopath*** (RL, *T* 5/3/93:34). Dr. Murray Miron, a psychology professor at Syracuse University, may have erred with many of his colleagues in drawing up ***a profile of*** Koresh ***that all but precluded suicide... "We thought this was an individual who was extraordinarily vain and very fearful of physical injury"*** (SHV, *NYT* 4/22/93:B13). Miron in any event speculated that ***Mr. Koresh had become so delusional that his final order*** to set the compound buildings afire ***may not have been inconsistent with a desire to protect himself. He said the cult leader*** had ***alluded, in at least one exchange with negotiators, to the Old Testament figures of Shadrach, Meshach and Abednego who, according to the Book of Daniel, were thrown into a fiery furnace only to "come forth of the midst of the fire"***

unscathed. Even as the flames surrounded him . . . Mr. Koresh may have believed that the same thing would happen to him (SHV, *NYT* 4/22/93:B13). He seems not in fact to have taken his own life. He may, however, have commanded that it be taken for him. He died of a gunshot wound to the head that forensic analysts doubted could have been self-inflicted. Even President Clinton would deem Koresh ***dangerous, irrational, and probably insane.*** But could it be denied that Koresh was also the one to be held largely accountable for having placed so many ***children in harm's way*** (NG, *T* 5/3/93:43)?

DEVIANT COUPLES

After six weeks, the government personnel at Waco had become frustrated with Koresh's apparent inconsistencies. They had grown tired of his uninvited teachings, which they had neither will nor means even to begin to engage. They were increasingly alarmed at what they saw as his hardened resolve to last them out. After Mount Carmel burned, their tactics and decisions would be subjected to lengthy scrutiny. The report that was finally delivered by the US Department of Justice would absolve them of any attempt either to conjure or to find a convenient motive for the aggressive maneuvers that, once approved by newly seated Attorney General Janet Reno, were eventually undertaken (cf. Scruggs et al. 1993:216 and 264–74).

The report argues that the rationale for the maneuvers was sound, compelling, and complex. It makes a special point of stressing that "while one of the FBI representatives made one misstatement indicating that Koresh was continuing to beat children during the standoff, that misstatement did not materially influence the Attorney General's decision" to approve the injection of tear gas into the compound's interiors. It makes a point of stressing that even more generally, "the issue of child abuse represented only one of the many factors that influenced the Attorney General" (Scruggs et al. 1993:216). It declares definitively that "no single factor was determinative," and that the attorney general was in fact "more influenced by other significant issues, such as the difficulty in maintaining perimeter security at the compound, the unanimous conclusion of the negotiators and experts that Koresh was not coming out, the Davidians' plentiful food and water supply, the deteriorating sanitary conditions inside the compound, the safety precautions included in the tear gas plan, and the unanimous agreement of her top advisors in the Justice Department and the FBI that the tear gas plan represented the only viable option left for the government" (Scruggs et al. 1993:216–17). Even so, the report discusses allegations of abuse at notable length, and marshals a substantial corpus of testimonials in support of them (Scruggs et al. 1993:217–26).

The authors of the Justice Department report are aware that their exposition of the role that suspected child abuse played in urging Attorney General Reno and the FBI toward interventionism is in almost complete contradiction to expositions widely promulgated in the press. Whether or not theirs is the more exact exposition, it is effective in minimizing the dimensions of the conflict that erupted between Reno and FBI Director William Sessions over whether or not abuse was ongoing at Mount Carmel during the standoff. Reno soon accepted Sessions's pronouncement that the FBI had evidence only of a history of abuse and had little more than circumstantial or hearsay evidence even of that. The report's insistence on plural reasons, plural authorities, and plural actors minimizes other conflicts as well: between the Bureau of Alcohol, Tobacco, and Firearms (BATF), whose agents were ultimately excluded from the scene, and the FBI, which asserted its primacy early on; between the FBI, which sought above all to resolve the standoff, and local law enforcement, which hoped to prosecute the guilty once they were in custody; and between regional and local executives of the US Attorney's Office (cf. Scruggs et al. 1993:250–58). The leitmotif of the report is one of coordination and compromise.

Throughout the standoff at Mount Carmel, the fourth estate has less interest in compromise than in apologue. Not only its interests but its discursive position are distinctive. The "public sphere" may in the strict sense be dead, but the press survives, indeed fluoresces, in its place. It is in part an industry, designed like so many of its latter-day counterparts to produce not simply goods and services but also beliefs and desires. Predictably, the media would be brought generally to task for having risked divulging evidence that ought to have remained secret. Just as predictably, they would be brought to task for having induced and having fed Koresh's craving for publicity as much as the public's craving for Koresh, and so—less observer than player—for having prolonged a standoff that might have come to a close far sooner and perhaps more peaceably than it did.[11]

The media had heard similar accusations, just or unjust, on many earlier occasions, not the least of them the occasion of the Gulf War. Indeed, they had very likely already acquired all the skills that the standoff would require of them during that war. Their coverage of both the standoff and the war was, however, exemplary of the relatively recent enhancement of their apparatuses for the production of salable and consumable texts and images. In spite of all the strictures to which they were subjected, their coverage of both was remarkable for its virtually symphonic simultaneity. The Mount Carmel compound was accordingly remarkable for being at once a "scene" and a simulacrum. A replica of it, constructed on the Oklahoma prairie, would be the site of the production of an NBC docudrama that would be the first ***about a horrific disaster filmed while the disaster was still unfolding*** (Harry F. Walters [HFW], *NW* 5/24/93:58). Some two weeks before the April 19 fire, David Koresh's lawyers would seek bids for the rights to their client's biography. Many worried psychological diagnosticians were hopeful. Koresh's apparent interest in striking a deal, which his lawyers said that they expected to have ***"a floor of two and a half million dollars"*** (Esther B. Fein [EBF], *NYT* 4/7/93:C19), seemed anything but suicidal.

At Mount Carmel and elsewhere, the media prove also to be something of a moralistic demimonde, proudly open and above board but even at their loftiest by no means obliged to maintain the standards of judgment expected, if rarely realized, in the academy or the courts. In the "traditional" villages in which so many anthropologists used to pass so much of their time, the staff of the contemporary media have their most typical functional analogues in those solid, respectable, but frank matrons and patrons who make a special business of assessing the character of prospective brides and grooms, young wives and old bachelors, mistresses and masters of house. Their medium is almost entirely oral. Their verdicts are rarely constrained by the principle that all are innocent until proven guilty. If sometimes disparaged as "gossips" and "rumormongers," they contribute actively to the definition and maintenance of a moral order. If only informally, they can by most accounts serve as perfectly effective moral police. Their methods are predominantly those of the tête-à-tête. Of necessity, their counterparts in the contemporary media, whose most direct precursors might be found among such "muckrakers" as Lincoln Steffens, have other, increasingly oralist but also increasingly efficient, means of communication. The actual moral impact of the media remains obscure, but can hardly be dismissed. The moral *fictio* of what unfolded at Mount Carmel, which the media surely helped to compose, is clear enough.

The hero, or rather, the anti-hero of both the Justice Department report and the media's *fictio* is of course David Koresh, but the media's pivotal characterological master trope is not pluralist. It is once again metonymic, and if it figures Koresh to be sick, it makes him the sufferer not of mental but of social and sensual illness. Koresh's "charlatanry," his overweening "egoism" and "delusions of grandeur," his "despotism" and his "salaciousness" are all so many derivatives of a far more fundamental disposition. In the media's prevailing final analysis, Koresh is essentially an abuser of children. During the standoff, he had not only put children in harm's way. He had considered those children who remained within the compound ***hostages*** (HR, *USNWR* 5/3/93:28). Long before the standoff, ***allegations surfaced that Koresh physically abused the children with frequent harsh beatings for infractions as minor as crying after a nap*** (RL, *T* 3/15/93:38). Released from the compound in early March, one ***young Branch Davidian girl was*** reportedly ***fascinated with the hot running water, flush toilets,*** and ***heated food*** that she found in the home of her new guardians. Discovering the home's basement, she asked, ***"Do you have a whipping room down there?"*** (SSG, *T* 5/17/93:54).

Under the observation of Baylor College of Medicine psychiatrist Dr. Bruce Perry, the rest of the surviving children would reveal even more. ***The children learned songs filled with violent apocalyptic imagery. War and martial-arts films proliferated in the cult's video library*** (SSG, *T* 5/17/93:54). ***To train for the final battle, they were instructed to fight each other, and if they did not fight hard enough, they were paddled*** (Sara Rimer [SR], *NYT* 5/4/93:B11). ***One of*** their ***most disturbing qualities...was the... apparent weakness of*** their ***attachment to adults*** (SSG, *T* 5/17/93:54). Yet ***even after their release, and as they described their treatment by Mr. Koresh, all the children...talked about their love for him*** (SR, *NYT* 5/4/93:B11).

They had ***learned,*** Perry surmised, ***to substitute the word love for fear*** (SSG, *T* 5/17/93:54).[12] ***Denied traditional family bonds and subjected to Koresh's warped teachings, the children became compliant playthings*** (SSG, *T* 5/17/93:54). ***A whole variety of techniques were used including shame, coercion,... intimidation, humiliation, guilt, overt aggression and power*** (SR, *NYT* 5/4/93:B11). Koresh's ***son Cyrus, when he was three years old, once refused a command and, according to a former cult member, was starved for two days and forced to sleep on a garage floor where Koresh told him large rats prowled*** (SSG, *T* 5/17/93:54). *The New York Times* thus raised no questions when Attorney General Reno suggested ***that there was a particular urgency in the decision to move*** upon Mount Carmel on April 19. ***"We had information that babies were being beaten," she said. "I specifically asked, 'You really mean babies?' 'Yes, that he's slapping babies around.' These are the concerns that we had"*** (SHV, *NYT* 4/20/93:A20). Then White House communications director George Stephanopoulos would state categorically that the government had ***mountains of evidence that there was child abuse going on*** at Mount Carmel ***over a long period of time*** (BM, *LT* 4/22/93:11a).[13]

In 1992, Texas Child Protective Services had in fact investigated the compound, but ***were met with a brick wall of denial from cult members and children alike*** (Melinda Beck [MBE] et al., *NW* 5/17/93:51). In 1991, however, Koresh had made frequent visits to La Verne, California, ***where in a gated house he established what police called a "women's dormitory" for 18 "wives." When neighbors reported that one of them was 12 years old, police launched a child-molestation investigation*** that was never closed (RL, *T* 3/15/93:38). ***"It was an intrinsic part of*** Koresh's ***teachings that he would have sex with young girls,"*** said ***David Bunds, a former member*** of the community. Bunds said ***that when Koresh took up with one girl, he "was having trouble penetrating her, because she was so young and little. He told her to start using tampons...to make herself larger"*** (Ginny Carroll [GC] et al., *NW* 5/17/93:50). ***Girls as young as 11 were given a plastic Star of David, signifying that they had "the light" and were ready to have sex with the cult leader*** (SR, *NYT* 5/4/93:A1).

At times, Koresh did try to control his own sexual impulses toward children—and the impulses of other men in the cult...Koresh once ***decreed that no Branch Davidian man could change a girl baby's diaper, because they might***

become aroused (GC et al., *NW* 5/17/93:50). Controlling his tongue was reportedly another matter. ***Younger children, boys and girls, were exposed to sexually explicit materials in*** his ***"sermons." Perry, the psychiatrist, has an audio-tape of one Bible-study session where he says children were present. In it, Perry says, Koresh "talks about stripping off the clothes of a young girl and 'whacking' it to her right there"*** (GC et al., *NW* 5/17/93:50).

For several months after the fire at Mount Carmel, Koresh and the Branch Davidian children would appear and reappear in the press—less singly, however, than as a worrisome, an increasingly inextricable, couple. Koresh, predator and victimizer, might just have been trying to win sympathy when ***he would complain to FBI negotiators about his awful treatment at the hands of his stepfather, Ray Haldeman, and tearfully regret the loss of life in the February 28 shootout***...He ***made it clear that he was deathly afraid of going to prison for fear of being raped by inmates—a fate that often befalls child abusers*** (HR, *USNWR* 5/3/93:28). But was the abuser quite so afraid only because his reputation might precede him? Had the abuser perhaps also been among the abused? So it seemed: ***he was an aloof kid, preyed upon and sodomized by older boys*** (JB, *E* 7/93:54). The surviving Branch Davidian children were, for their part, as likely as any other ***victimized children...*** to ***show signs of Post-traumatic Stress Disorder...a syndrome marked by nightmares and psychic numbing, among other problems*** (DG, *NW* 5/17/93:52).

Experts would articulate further complexities. ***Clinical psychologist Margaret Thaler Singer, of the University of California, Berkeley,*** had ***treated hundreds of ex-cultists. She*** thought ***it a kind of "intellectual mistake" to equate sexual abuse in outside society with sexual abuse in cults... "Children may resent it, they may hate it, but they see it happen to other children and they don't feel they're the only one—which is such an important aspect of the way it's experienced on the outside. And, Singer adds, she has interviewed scores of abused former cultists who grew up to be well functioning adults*** (DG, *NW* 5/17/93:54). Still, the likelihood that Koresh and the children were bound together in a single nexus, the likelihood that perversion would continue to generate perversion in spite of all efforts to check it, was frequently underscored. ***"So often...a person seeks a way of turning the passive-victim experience into the active mode of being a perpetrator,"*** said ***child psychiatrist Dr. Spencer Eth...As many as 70 percent of child***

abusers and wife beaters... turn out to have been abused children themselves (DG, *NW* 5/17/93:52).

It did not, then, really matter whether Attorney General Reno had acted on faulty information. It did not really matter what precisely led her to approve the final breaching of Mount Carmel's buildings. With a uniformity that could not possibly have been intentional, the press at once disseminated and dignified the portrait of an executive for whom the specter of ***precious, innocent children*** (NG, *T* 5/3/93:36) being battered and corrupted was too much to tolerate, too much to bear. What the press proffered, the vast majority of the public seems readily and unambivalently to have embraced. For several months after the fire at Mount Carmel, Reno was far and away the most popular official in Washington. Or so the media's opinion polls had it.

AFTER WELFARE?

Sociologists remind us that just about anything might, in principle, pass as deviance. They also remind us that deviance has its functions. It lends concreteness to our normative order; it offers us bad examples against which and in light of which we might make better ones of ourselves. At least a few sociologists are further prepared to suggest that deviance has its natural limits in (and only in) the limits of the collective resources that can be devoted to their policing (see, e.g., Erikson 1966). But if correct as far as it goes, such structure-functionalism risks endowing both the figure of David Koresh and his sociocultural milieu with far more determinate outlines than they actually have. The figure of Koresh is a figure of "monstrous" transgressions. He is further a figure of "monstrous" amalgams, of contradictory attributes and contradictory urges. He seems to have been the object of so widespread an outpouring of fascination and repulsion, of such widespread ambivalence, less because his essence was transparent than because it remained persistently vague and elusive. We might think we know that David Koresh was a child abuser. But we have not—at least, not quite yet—come to terms with what child abuse itself "really" is.

As Ian Hacking points out in a recent conceptual history, the very notion of what we now tend to refer to as "child abuse" is of very recent origin.[14] Hacking dates its emergence no earlier than 1961, the year in which Dr. C. H. Kempe and his associates introduced clinical evidence of a "battered baby syndrome" to the American Medical Association (Hacking 1995:61). He argues that it differs from its most familiar, Victorian predecessor, "cruelty to children," in at least four respects. First, child abuse is distinctive of no particular socioeconomic class. Numerous counterexamples notwithstanding, cruelty to children would always be an index of poverty. Child abuse is the potential failing even of the wealthy, the potential nightmare even of the most genteel. Nor is it merely one potential failing among others. As Hacking puts it, "cruelty to children was bad; child abuse is an ultimate evil" (Hacking 1995:58). At its thematic core, it is also a sexual evil. Incest, pederasty, and cruelty to children would generally be conceived as quite different, if by no means mutually exclusive, iniquities. Incest and pederasty now constitute child abuse by both legal and popular definition. Cruelty to children would, moreover, generally remain merely bad, merely objectionable, merely punishable. Child abuse is all of that. But it is also a symptom, a sickness that might yield to therapy, a pathology that might be subject to cure (Hacking 1995:56–58). So construed, child abuse will have come into full-fledged notional being by the middle 1970s. It acquires its characteristically "autopoietic" etiology, its self-reproducing causality, during the same period.[15] Even a decade earlier, however, it had already become the focus of an ever-increasing share at once of media scrutiny, behavioral research, and governmental legislation.[16] It continues to be the focus of vigorous scrutiny, vigorous research, and vigorous legislation today.

If "much less interesting than sex, class, or evil," the medicalization of child abuse is, as Hacking rightly insists, of great epistemic consequence (Hacking 1995:59). With its medicalization, child abuse wears the trappings of a natural kind, and the child abuser a (natural) kind of person, "about whom scientific knowledge is [presumed] possible" (Hacking 1995:59). Precisely with its medicalization, child abuse can acquire its etiology. With its medicalization it can be the hypothetical effect of specifiable causes, and the cause of such specifiable effects as itself. With its medicalization, it promises an ever more precise division into subtypes, each with its own dispositional and etiological profile. But Hacking notes that such hypotheses and promises have far less often been subject to test than they have been treated as already fulfilled. "Knowledge" about child abuse is "peculiarly a priori" (Hacking 1995:60). Consider the almost inexhaustible array of shadowy gray eminences and gray emanations whose actions, whether in Satanist covens or daycare centers, whether purported or real, have more and more systematically been presumed to lie behind every terrifying memory or daydream, every pedophilic or incestuous fantasy or desire, behind sexual precocity and sexual promiscuity, behind depression and low self-esteem. The conceptual and the rhetorical dynamics of "child abuse" are driven by the assumption "that there is knowledge to be had." But "that," Hacking suggests, "may be a mistake," and not merely because the etiological a priori of child abuse itself is so often without or even at odds with "empirical" evidence:

> There may be no true general answers to the question "Why do parents X-abuse their children?" where X is a defined type of child abuse...The concept of child abuse may itself be so made and molded by attempts at knowledge and intervention, and social reaction to these studies, that there is no stable object, child abuse, to have knowledge about. (Hacking 1995:60–61)

The suggestion is phrased with telling delicacy.[17] Its crux is nevertheless plainly Foucaultian: Not irreal, but not a natural kind, either, child abuse is less an object of knowledge than it is an object, and an operative, of power/knowledge.[18]

Hacking's subsequent consideration of the "truth-effects" of child abuse owes much to Barbara J. Nelson's *Making an Issue of Child Abuse* (1984). Hacking reiterates the most decisive implication of Nelson's research: From the mid-seventies forward, "child abuse" is the trump card of liberal politicians and policymakers who are less and less willing and less and less able to trust the rhetorical power that once resided in "poverty" (Hacking 1995:64). Precisely because it "knows no class," child abuse escapes becoming the partisan issue into which poverty has recently devolved. It remains all the more politically potent as a consequence. Hacking recognizes, however, that child abuse is more than merely the latest liberal cause célèbre. He accordingly recalls several contemporary commentaries that note the regularity with which child abuse effectively obscures the current burgeoning of poverty and the regularity with which the child abuser stands as an individual "scapegoat" for systematic inequities and collective wrongs (Hacking 1995:65). He recalls a crucial correlation: Child abuse emerges as a central collective concern and a central collective preoccupation precisely as the organizational and institutional infrastructure of welfarist redistribution begins to be dismantled.[19] Or to carry the correlation farther than Hacking would perhaps approve: Child abuse constitutes the personalization of systemic injustice; it favors the pursuit of personalistic over collective solutions, of therapies over collective reform. Where and when child abuse begins, welfarism comes, more or less abruptly, to an end.

Or does it? If Hacking himself does not explicitly declare the ascendance of child abuse to be the death of welfare, he at least regards its ascendance as indicative of a period of "radical moral change" (Hacking 1995:67). For all the relative novelty of such latter-day deviants as David Koresh, however, and for all the relative novelty of child abuse, constants remain, moral constants among them. For all the relative novelty of its latter-day extensions, no precept seems in fact to have had greater constancy over the last half-century than the precept that has governed the growth and the agenda of welfarism itself. Indeed, there may today be no more compelling precept than welfarism's own: health. Nor does there seem to be a precept more widely diffused, or more widely embraced, at once as a collective and an individual good. As both collective and individual good, health is contingently but nevertheless regularly at odds with liberty. Its contemporary idealization is an unambiguous indication of a corresponding debasement of liberty, of the good of being able to do whatever one pleases (however unhealthy it might be). Health further possesses a normative potency at which the ardent libertarian would surely take alarm. Health is not any longer merely an ideal, a value, a thing to be cherished. Whether collective or individual, whether psychical or physical, it is also increasingly obligatory, its absence less and less excusable and more and more the license not simply of the dissolution of any solid division of what is public from what is private but also of "interventions" as drastic even as those with which the standoff at Mount Carmel came to an end.

Welfarist moralism is still very much with us, then, even if liberty is presently of shifting fortunes. The welfarist apparatus of policing is still very much with us as well. The complex of administrative and interventive institutions that has since the middle fifties been addressed to the welfare of children may presently be disintegrating rapidly.[20] The psychojuridical nexus from which "social work" has long drawn both its intellectual and its practical authority, however, seems at least as intact now as it was throughout the standoff at Mount Carmel. The experts whose opinions about David Koresh and his followers circulated in newspapers, on radio, and on television were very often the very experts whose opinions were specifically sought by the FBI and the attorney general's advisors. Most of them—and certainly most of those who had the greatest strategic influence—were "behavioral scientists" of one specialization or another: psychiatrists, psychologists, psycholinguists, criminologists, "threat assessors," and "profilers." The Justice Department report specifically mentions a dozen such scientists in its roster of principal consultants and principal contributors.[21] It mentions few theologians, most of whom felt that they should have been consulted more regularly and that their interpretations and recommendations should have been taken more seriously (cf. Tabor 1994; Arnold 1994). Predictably enough, it makes no mention of either sociologists or anthropologists.[22]

In the face of ever more severe budgetary cuts, not even the enduring integrity of the psychojuridical nexus of the authority of social work is likely to save the careers of our current staff of social workers. The standoff at Mount Carmel, however, has been only the most spectacular of many other indications that welfarist policing has already acquired a far vaster and better-equipped front line of surveillance and enforcement. Neither social workers nor the legions of more intimate witnesses such as friends and neighbors, teachers and physicians, have been entirely superseded. The media have nevertheless joined them, with all their means of production and all their systemic curiosities in train. As a consequence, child abuse and its fellow evils have not simply received a wider airing. They have captured, and sometimes perhaps stimulated, a wider imagination.[23] On a proliferating array of talk shows and televised news magazines, they have become the textual and imagistic matrix both of anonymous rumor and of the more personal articulation of private suffering with public confessions and public accusations. In their various contemporary forums, the media invite each one of us to participate in the quotidian routine of a welfarist assessment, at once of others and of ourselves. If there are indeed many signs of the institutional death of welfarism, there are thus as many signs of a collective revival, and a revival the scope of which is already virtually ecumenical.

Another expansion appears to go in tandem with the expansion of collective involvement in welfarist policing and welfarist self-policing. As Hacking notes, the notion of child abuse becomes strikingly more inclusive with its subsumption of incest and pederasty (Hacking 1995:62). Nor does its inclusiveness stop there. Like the scope of welfarist policing, the scope of child abuse itself currently approaches the ecumenical. Not only have many time-honored practices of "corporal punishment" come, especially in the past ten years, to be deemed abusive. So, too, have a still multiplying array of acts and gestures, from intentional slights to thoughtless omissions, the scars from which may remain entirely "invisible." The abused must often be induced to remember the damage done to them.[24] But the medicalization of child abuse in any case allows for a diagnostics quite independent of actual "illness," actual suffering. Even should they fail to remember, even should they profess not actually to have felt wounded by what their diagnosticians determine their injuries to be, the abused are still "carriers." They still have a "disease."[25]

"Radical" or not, the proliferation of the sufficient conditions and the tokens of child abuse undoubtedly signals a change, not simply in the institutions of welfarism but also in what might until recently have been described as their characteristic practical logic. Hacking has remarked on the abstraction of child abuse from class. One should further remark its abstraction from any other differential category, whether ethnic or demographic. If the object of consistent feminist attention, child abuse is not a "women's" issue. Because its victims remain victims throughout their lives, it is not even a "children's" issue.

Institutionalized welfarism has always had its target populations, and hence, always relatively limited ambitions. Our new, ecumenical welfarism has no such restrictive target. It has much grander ambitions. In principle and, it seems, in practice, its targets are individuals, each and every one of them.

To be even more precise, its targets are the relations between individuals. If the proliferation of the modalities and tokens of child abuse does not in this respect signal a rupture, it signals a substantial refinement of institutionalized welfarism's cruder and more casual cartography of human relations. Nor is it the only signal of such refinement. The conceptual history of child abuse has very close parallels in the conceptual history of many of its partial synonyms, a few of which have garnered an equal share of public attention and politico-epistemic scrutiny. Like child abuse, "harassment" has rapidly lost any specific populational index that it might once have had, and has become the byword of a new statutory movement. Like child abuse, "violence" has been the inspiration for several new genres of ecumenical policing, in the establishment and facilitation of which the media have played not an exclusive but still an especially pivotal role. For at least a decade, it has also been the object of both epidemiological and endocrinological modeling.[26] Like child abuse, harassment and violence both encompass an ever more baroque universe of potential and actual "incidents" in the midst of which innocence has perhaps been irretrievably lost. Hacking observes that "no man in his right mind today would help a strange child in a park trying to reach the water fountain" (Hacking 1995:66). It goes without saying that no man in his right mind would do anything more than dream—perhaps would dare no longer even to dream—of behaving like such a figure as David Koresh.

But David Koresh should not, I think, thus be seen as the quintessential Other, the prince of the darkness of a moral or politico-epistemic regime that is already securely in place. He might better be seen as having stood precisely at the cusp of moral and politico-epistemic possibilities still unrealized. The final conflagration at Mount Carmel was itself less regimental than the manifestation of the failure of routine and patience alike. It punctuated an irresolute antagonism between one would-be sovereign and another. In its aftermath, Koresh and his followers would rapidly assume the stature of martyrs for the largest contingent of antigovernmental separatists to have been active since the twenties. Some number of those separatists would allegedly choose to commemorate the second anniversary of the conflagration with the execution of the Oklahoma City bombing. Some number of them, would-be sovereigns in their own right whether nor not inclined to terror, will surely still be with us long after the new millennium is launched. All of them will surely continue at length to evoke very much the same valuational ambivalence that Koresh himself evoked.

A less dramatic, but presently more widespread and perhaps even more enduring politics of sovereignty is concerned, however, with dominion not over geographical or administrative territories but rather over the territories of the body itself. In its most extreme expressions, it is a politics for which the sovereign body is an inviolable body, and for which every unwanted instance of contact, every uninvited mark, every trace of either psychical or physical incursion, is at once a stigma and a provocation. In its less extreme expressions, it appears to have intimate affinities with the welfarist policing of human relations, all the more intimate as such policing grows even more ecumenical and more baroque. But if the political and epistemic marriage of the inviolable body with its disciplined habits is the new custom of our workplaces, the conflagration at Mount Carmel is indication enough that it is burdened with tension and sometimes with quite terrible paradox. The standoff and the conflagration at Mount Carmel are both indications of just how costly such a marriage can be, at least when it falls short of perfection. The same must be said of ecumenical welfarism itself. Not even the prodigious eye and the prodigious seductiveness of the media would appear to be sufficient to sustain in the long run quite so gargantuan and so sedulous a police force. The question of its moral or ethical value quite aside, such a force is structurally and functionally in dire need of severe jurisdictional strictures if it is to survive at all. With the passing of target populations and with the private sphere at least as much under erasure as its public counterpart, it is by no means clear whence such strictures might derive.

So, then: We, too, are left, at the end of this and the dawn of the next millennium, wondering what is to become of us.

Notes

I would like to thank Peter Dobkin Hall for leading a discussion of an earlier draft of this essay during the SAR seminar. I would also like to thank George Marcus, Paul Rabinow, and all the other participants in the SAR seminar for their comments and advice. Finally, thanks to Gail Kelly.

1. That is, imitation in the absence of any original. For a sustained treatment of the concept, see Baudrillard 1983.

2. A second round of congressional hearings on the standoff was held during the summer of 1995. Its revelations were minimal, but its tenor was far less friendly to the government's agencies and decision makers than the first, and only in part because the Republican leadership was apparently hoping to use them as another opportunity to embarrass President Clinton. At least until the Oklahoma City bombing, suspicion that the government had overstepped itself at Waco (as elsewhere) had steadily been growing in the press and, it would seem, in the public at large. For a journalistic expression of such suspicion, see Reavis 1995.

3. Compare Jacques Derrida's remarks on the press as reflection and as formulator of opinion and doxa (1992:88–89).

4. In the interest of conserving space, I adopt an abbreviated style of citing the authors, newspapers, and journals from which I have constructed my sampler. Sources are cited in full only in their first occurrence. Thereafter, they are represented by initials. All quotations from journalistic sources appear in boldface type and (with the exception of a few book titles and foreign phrases) in italics.

5. Tourists who visit the site of the standoff would (at this writing) still find charred rubble and fragments of cement gathered into four or five high, neat piles. They would see an abandoned motorcycle, and an inoperative bus that formerly served as the station of a pair of security guards, under government contract, posted in shifts extending around the clock. Until early 1995, the rubble, a few pieces of heavy equipment, the motorcycle, the bus, and the guards were all enclosed within a cyclone fence. For all but the guards, entrance was forbidden. The Texas Water Commission had determined that the area formerly occupied by the community's central buildings was contaminated with lead. After a cleanup the fence came down. The families and friends of those who died in the fire subsequently supplied the landscape with a planting of crepe myrtles. The funding of the memorial, which includes small granite headstones bearing the name of each of the Branch Davidians who died during the standoff, was provided by a local militia organization. Here and there, a souvenir of battle

remains recognizable: a bathtub, riddled with bullet holes; the rusted frame and shattered windows of yet another bus. On a knoll near the road that gives access to Mount Carmel, Amo Paul Bishop Roden tends an office and maintains the papers and posters and artifacts of a museum she has built herself. A handwritten sign announces that she likes to talk and is happy to answer questions. Other signs offer readings of passages from the biblical books of Isaiah and Ezekiel, hermeneutical analyses of prophetic dreams, speculations on what really brought about the destruction to which she daily bears witness, and denunciations of the courts, the president, and other officials. The wife of the man from whom David Koresh seized control of the Branch Davidian community, Roden maintains her trust that a "Present Truth" will continue to be disclosed and continue to offer guidance to her widely scattered fellow congregants, all of whom had left the compound long before the standoff began.

6. For one scholar's rather embittered, first-hand account of scorned expertise, see Tabor 1994.

7. Journalists revealed some confusion over Houteff's occupation. In a book-length reprise that appeared only a few months after the standoff came to an end, for example, one journalist reported that the founder of the Davidians worked as a "lay preacher and assistant superintendent at the...Sabbath School" after taking up residence in Los Angeles (Leppard 1993:55). In fact he sold washing machines beforehand. For the most accurate account of the history of the Branch Davidians to date, see Tabor and Gallagher 1995:23–51.

8. Simulation operates with particular obstinacy at this juncture. Four agents of the BATF died, and sixteen were wounded, during the initial raid of the Branch Davidian compound. The government's Report to the Attorney General issued in October of 1993 states that five members of the Branch Davidian community were presumably killed (or mortally wounded) at the same time. It states further that seventy-five members of the community "died during the April 19 fire" (Scruggs et al. 1993:7). Thus the official toll. But in part because the Branch Davidians themselves have disputed the government's reckoning, the total number of dead reported in the media continues even today to remain unfixed. It might be added that Amo Paul Bishop Roden herself suggests the number of dead to be "about ninety" (Roden, personal communication 1994).

9. Many other writers would object to referring not simply to the Branch Davidians but to any other religious community as a "cult," even were the term always enclosed within quotation marks.

10. The "sinful messiah" in fact has a biblical locus—in Psalm 40. See Tabor 1994:16.

11. Cf. Kamen 1993. Though Kamen's essay appears in the *American Journalism Review,* arguably a specialists' periodical, the wider media were by no means disinclined to self-reflection. Indeed, the media's inclusion as one among many of the dramatis personae of the standoff was itself an ongoing part of the story. It, too, was news.

12. The rather dramatic Bruce Perry quoted in this article stands in marked contrast to the Bruce Perry who appears in Peter J. Boyer's contribution to the May 15, 1995, issue of *The New Yorker.* In Boyer's article, Perry "found socialization problems" among the twenty-one children of the community who were released from the compound before the final fire; but "he concluded in his report that 'the children released from Ranch Apocalypse do not appear to have been victims of sexual abuse' or of physical abuse severe enough to warrant state intervention" (Boyer 1995:42). Is it Perry or merely doxa that we see shifting here?

13. In the same article mentioned in the preceding note, Peter Boyer has also reviewed the inconsistencies between press reports of Reno's overriding concerns about child abuse and the later, official Report to the Attorney General. Boyer is not alone in suggesting that certain FBI agents may have intentionally misinformed Reno in order to compel her to approve their intervention. See Boyer 1995:42.

14. The point should perhaps originally be credited to Stephen Pfohl. See Pfohl 1977.

15. As Hacking notes, such an etiology has nevertheless been under scientific dispute for nearly a decade. For a concise review, and critique, of the autopoietic hypothesis, see, e.g., Kaufman and Zigler 1989.

16. Barbara Nelson has documented what amounts to a veritable politico-epistemic explosion with some care. On the almost two-thousandfold increase in medical and scholarly publications concerning child abuse after 1951, see Nelson 1984:65–66; on the multiplication of both state and federal statues concerning the victims and their abusers, see Nelson 1984:81–121. On the media's attention to child abuse, see again Nelson 1984:52–75. For a survey of similar currents in Great Britain, see Jenkins 1992.

17. Like virtually all public critics of the concept and construction of "child abuse," Hacking is very concerned that his audience not presume him to be denying that children are, in fact, frequently and horribly abused. Without such dis-

claimers, the critic might perhaps seem—or at least, might fear himself to seem—to be protesting too much.

18. In what may be a further exercise of all due caution, Hacking makes no explicit mention of Foucault's work at this juncture. But the debt is real in any case. See especially Foucault 1979 and 1980.

19. Hacking 1995:65. The first sustained freeze of the funding of programs directed to child welfare began in the United States in 1972 and lasted for at least four years. Cf. Newberger and Daniel 1979:19.

20. From the middle fifties forward, child abuse has been the official concern of the federal Children's Bureau (Nelson 1984:32) and under the specific jurisdiction of various state departments of child protection or "children's protective services." There is considerable evidence that many states had ceased to be able to sustain the good working order of such departments even a decade ago. Caseloads had come to overwhelm a diminishing pool of both technical and human resources. For a selective but telling review of the crisis, see Wexler 1990:240–42.

21. Only one, psychiatrist C. Di Giovanni, declined to declare Koresh either psychotic or neurotic. See Scruggs et al. 1993:168–69.

22. See Scruggs et al. 1993:159–85. The secular media would seek out theologians and sociologists sporadically; they would seek out anthropologists even more rarely.

23. The capacity of the media and of many other of our modern writing and imaging machines to give form and content to vague fantasy is of course the topic of increasing politico-epistemic concern in its own right. Causality here is a very vexed issue.

24. The exceptionally controversial and exceptionally divisive debates over the reality of "repressed memory" and "multiple personalities" is in fact Hacking's primary interest in the text on which I am relying here. If altogether relevant, those debates are nevertheless far too complex for me even to be able to begin to summarize them here.

25. For the source of this distinction between (experienced) illness and (physiological) disease, see Eisenberg 1977.

26. For the endocrinological data, see, e.g., Svare 1983. Such data are the frequent focus of the burgeoning field of "evolutionary psychology," in which several contemporary anthropologists are intimately involved. An epidemiological model of violence has had a hearing in this decade among at least some of the ranking officials of the Alcohol, Drug Abuse, and Mental Health Administration, due not least to the influence of the former head of the administration, Frederick Goodwin.

5

New Lexicon, Old Language

Negotiating the "Global" at the National Science Foundation

Donald Brenneis

> Bureaucratization of the imaginative..."Bureaucratization" is an unwieldy word, perhaps even an onomatopoeia, since it sounds as bungling as the situation it would characterize. "Imaginative" suggests pliancy, liquidity, the vernal. And with it we couple the incongruously bulky and almost unpronounceable.
>
> —*Kenneth Burke*

In his characterization of bureaucracies as "bungling...bulky and almost unpronounceable," Kenneth Burke (1964:76) captures a widespread opinion. In few other contexts, to his view, are innovation, creativity, and fluid adaptation to a changing world less likely to flourish. Indeed, Burke drew upon the seemingly contradictory juxtaposition of bureaucracy and imagination as a prime topic for the analytical method he termed "perspective by incongruity" (Burke 1964:76). Pace Burke, in this article I suggest that federal bureaucracies provide arenas within which imagination is crucial: New knowledge is produced, new problems are recognized, new languages sought for their definition, and new options pursued, foreclosed, or not even considered for their comprehension and, occasionally, remedy. At the same time, and with the irony to which Burke's comment points, such agencies are also sites in which imagination must be disciplined—translated, routinized, compared, and evaluated—to succeed, that is, to lead to new understanding. Although frequently characterized by considerable institutional and conceptual inertia, such bureaucracies have also been exceptionally significant in shaping our sense of crisis and change. This essay presents a primarily ethnographic exploration of one such bureaucratic locus in which questions of power, knowledge, and novelty are implicated.

The National Science Foundation (NSF) provides a particularly telling case study in this regard. Charged with funding and thereby guiding innovative basic research in the natural, behavioral, and social sciences (despite recent legislative attempts to shift its focus to more immediately relevant and applied work), NSF is consistently faced with pursuing new knowledge—and new kinds of knowledge—through established disciplinary and organizational frameworks. NSF constitutes a critical if often unrecognized nexus for the institutionally inflected negotiation of new understandings.

This essay focuses on the development of a new NSF funding initiative in the social sciences. The initiative, "Global Perspectives on Sociolegal Studies," is an offshoot of the standing program on Law and Social Science, a multidisciplinary program within the social and behavioral sciences at NSF. At the core of the Global Initiative was the recognition that many of the issues central to sociolegal studies could no longer be comprehended within the framework of one state's legal and social control systems, a framework which had defined the broadest appropriate ambit of most previously funded research. Such diverse "problems" as international labor migration, cross-border environmental crises, multinational corporations, and human rights were seen as demanding that formerly assumed boundaries, both political and intellectual, be rethought.

The genesis of the Global review panel in some ways represents the recognition of new and problematic phenomena, legal and social control issues no longer considered comprehensible in terms of "the state." Characterizing these issues as "global" defined both a new class of research issue and a newly legitimated topic for research funding. It also gave this new category a label, as well as introducing to NSF funding discussions a host of related terms such as "transnational," "regional," and "internationalization." At the same time, the broader range of evaluative practices through which funding decisions were made under this new rubric, the ways in which the imaginative was disciplined, remained much the same as they had long been for other NSF panels. New concepts—or at least new labels for them—were introduced, but the institutional communicative patterns within which they came to figure remained relatively unchanged.

My purpose here is to examine the tension between the novel, in this instance the topicalization of the global as a current and pressing issue, and the routine, that is, those ways of comparatively evaluating research applications with an eye to the concerns of both "science" and fairness. After locating my approach vis-à-vis some of the intellectual perspectives informing this volume as a whole, I will turn to a brief historical account of the genesis of the Global Initiative and a discussion of the "Belmont Report," a planning conference paper which became its foundational text (National Science Foundation 1990b). Central to the Belmont Report is the recognition of a dramatically transformed world and of the necessity for new, imaginative, and unorthodox ways of defining research problems and of pursuing them. The ethnographic core of the paper focuses on an analysis of funding panel meetings as reading events. In this part of the discussion, I will draw primarily on my own experience as a knowledge worker, a member of the Global panel during its first three years. What ways of reading and of talking about reading shaped our recommendations, and how did we bring our sense of the explicitly innovative goals of the initiative together with our negotiated rankings of particular proposals? Finally, I will return to the Burkean tension between routine practices and novel ideas.

READING THE READINGS

As Marcus noted in his original proposal for this seminar, the topic "power/knowledge shifts" represents in several ways a reappraisal of the issues at the heart of *Writing Culture* (Clifford and Marcus 1986) and subsequent related approaches to the intersections of text, power, and cultural criticism. I want to draw on one part of the complex set of arguments in that volume, specifically the introduction and essay by James Clifford (1986a, 1986b), as a starting point here. At the core of Clifford's analysis is an examination of the production of particular forms of scholarship and the knowledges they implicate. The relationships between formal and representational conventions, on the one hand, and what we take to be fact, on the other, are clearly and suggestively explored. In his illuminating focus on the complex interactions of author, generic form, and contingent knowledge—and more markedly in some of the less-nuanced studies that these essays inspired in others—however, three consequential and complementary issues remain unaddressed.

First, the focus of analysis remains primarily the completed, published text. Articles, monographs, and published research reports provide the raw material and are where the interpretive action lies. Embedded here is, to my view, something of a fiction that the published product is indeed a finished one. Linked to this focus on finished texts is a central concern for the interplay of generic assumptions and authorial strategies. The writer is at the heart of such work, and it is primarily through a community of writers that the joint production of such generic conventions is effected. Surprisingly little attention is paid to the role of editorial and review processes, interventions, and negotiation, for example, although such considerations might well strengthen the underlying critical argument.

As the apparently finished text is the focus, informed "reading" in the classical literary critical sense often serves as a principal methodology. What is left as unproblematic is the reception of these texts; their effects and implications are usually assumed rather than pursued. Clifford briefly hints at the importance of a (perhaps) imagined audience, noting that among the ways in which ethnographic writing is "determined" is its institutional character; in his words, "one writes within, and against, specific traditions, disciplines, *audiences* (my emphasis)" (Clifford 1986a:6). He does not, however, pursue the issue of reception further, other than to cite Asad's comment that "Allegories are secured...by teaching people to read in certain ways" (Clifford 1986b:119). What ways of reading there are and how readers are taught to use them—and by whom—are crucial and unasked questions. The neglected audience is, I should note, a recurring problem in a wide range of rhetorical analyses. Detailed, insightful, and compelling accounts of what writers—and speakers—are up to are fortunately becoming more common (as in the contemporary renaissance of rhetorical approaches to scholarly writing by such scholars as Bazerman

1988; McCloskey 1985; Nelson, Megill, and McCloskey 1987), but equally effective accounts of how, why, and to what extent such texts "succeed" with audiences, whether of readers or listeners, are infrequent. (For examples of several different audience-focused approaches see Boyarin 1993; Brenneis 1987; Duranti and Brenneis 1986; Radway 1984; Schieffelin 1985.)

At the heart of my broader research project lurk some particular forms of scholarly writing and reading, ones in which the three concerns noted above cannot be elided. These forms of writing are the social science research funding proposal (and some cognate forms in the humanities) and related fellowship support applications (Brenneis 1988, 1994; see also Swales 1990). Before "writing culture," many of us must also "write money"; that is, compete and obtain support for ourselves and our research projects. Our grant proposals can be seen neither as finished products nor as texts with inconsequential and unproblematic readers. An analysis that focuses solely on the writing practices and textual features characteristic of such writing, while potentially revelatory, clearly cannot tell the whole story. Any account of the "writing machine" behind grant proposals must be complemented by an investigation of the "reading machine" that is brought to bear on them.

How we as authors craft such proposals and how we as reviewers read, interpret, and evaluate them are crucial and connected processes in shaping our scholarly discourses—in the defining and policing of disciplinary boundaries, in the support of some kinds of research at the expense of others, and, more subtly, in the ongoing negotiation of the complex links between language and epistemology: links between what we can know, how we can come to know it, and how it can be represented and conveyed. Grant writing, reading, and rewriting have also come to occupy increasingly larger portions of our scholarly work time. And for many, the funded proposal has replaced the refereed acceptance of a manuscript as the definitive mark of serious scholarly accomplishment. As a colleague once commented to me, "Anyone can publish an article somewhere or another these days, but getting funded by NSF or NIH [National Institutes of Health] means it's good science." In writing money we also write status.

At the same time a quotidian practical concern for academics and an analytically invisible cluster of social practices, the funding nexus is one through which many of us as scholars are engaged in producing knowledge, not only as funded researchers but also as active readers and reviewers of the proposed work of others. Such agencies as NSF are clearly bureaucratic institutions, but they are remarkably porous ones, as they depend absolutely on the intermittent but consequential participation of scholars from outside the foundation. In this instance, to paraphrase Pogo, we have met the bureaucrats, and they are us.

THE GLOBAL INITIATIVE

In this section I briefly trace the development of the "Global Perspectives on Sociolegal Studies" initiative within NSF. I am primarily concerned with the foundational text for the initiative, a document that is both rhetorically positioned and substantively significant in shaping subsequent definitions and discussions on the panel.

The initiative emerged within a particular institutional context in which a catalytic role was played by Felice Levine, then program officer for the Law and Social Science panel, an interdisciplinary program within what was then the Social and Economic Sciences (SES) Division of NSF. The broader NSF context is significant, as this was the second such interdisciplinary initiative within SES. The first initiative, "Human Dimensions of Global Environmental Change," involved program officers from economics, geography and regional science, law and social science, political science, sociology, and other programs. In setting up the "Human Dimensions" initiative, SES was following the lead of programs in biological and ecological science at NSF and drawing directly on the perception of widespread environmental risk as a new problem and topic. Levine has noted to me that the "Global Perspectives" initiative would not have worked without "Human Dimensions" as a prototype, in large part because the earlier initiative essentially foregrounded human agency and response within an already well-established scientific discourse about the environment, one in which themes of interdependence, inflected at times by metaphors drawn from chaos theory, were salient. "Human Dimensions" both established a rhetoric of interdependence (along the lines of more purely biological theories) and legitimated the enterprise as "science," a critical consideration within NSF.

Heartened by the success of the "Human Dimensions" initiative, as measured by both its funding level and the number of applications received, Levine organized a conference, held in Belmont, Maryland, in mid-1990. The purpose of the meeting was twofold: "(1) to examine how a global perspective extends or alters traditional ways of conceptualizing and studying law and law-related processes and behaviors; and (2) to provide guidance on the implications of a transnational perspective for research strategies and support" (National Science Foundation 1990a:1). In short, Levine asked the twenty participants, drawn from a wide range of disciplines and intentionally including a number of scholars who had not worked extensively in sociolegal studies, to consider "both the global dimensions of sociolegal phenomena and sociolegal dimensions of global phenomena" (National Science Foundation 1990a:1).

At the core of their discussions was an assumption of increased interaction and interdependence in the world—among people and across institutions, organizations, and economies. Participants saw the character of global life as undergoing a major substantive transformation: "Even with issues that seem to be local, processes of international diffusion and interaction have become so common that it is no longer useful to think of events as independent. Not only are legal agreements, treaties, and innovations diffusing...but so too is culture being transmitted across national boundaries by the movement of people or the rapid transmission of ideas" (National Science Foundation 1990b:3). Such a change required recognition as a consequential new phenomenon; it also demanded an appropriate epistemological transformation on the part of researchers. As the Belmont Report argued, "Events around the globe demonstrate the importance of thinking transnationally if our understanding of sociolegal phenomena is not to become limited and parochial" (National Science Foundation 1990b:3).

While the "Human Dimensions" panel fit relatively well within a global environmental paradigm, "Global Perspectives" suited the underlying ecological model less comfortably. Interdependence was a recurrent theme, but much of the impetus behind discussions in

Belmont had to do with the somewhat different recognition that earlier units of analysis were insufficient for dealing with current issues. The states—or statelike entities—which had historically been central to sociolegal inquiry had become problematic, acting more frequently not as the arenas for and forces of social control but as parties in broader conflicts. Multinational organizations, international institutions, and new forms of transnational governance and social control all were taken to challenge the nation-state as the appropriate primary unit for description and analysis. The interdependence metaphor, however necessary initially for in-house funding arguments, became a bit strained when applied to questions of conflict.

Situational factors such as the transformation of Eastern Europe and the former Soviet Union and "uncertainty in the Middle East" were also offered as further significant incentives for the timeliness of such funding. These discussions were located within a context in which a dramatically changing world was a recurring theme.

In preparing for the Belmont Conference, Levine identified five themes and asked each of the participants to prepare a memorandum concerning a particular theme. These topics, chosen to represent domains where "globalization" seemed especially marked and of particular sociolegal consequence, complemented the broader theoretical perspective of the Report. Although these themes were explicitly not intended to constitute an exhaustive inventory, for subsequent readers they became particularly important signposts, staking out much of the territory of the "global." The core of the Report proper provides a fairly detailed account of group discussions of these five themes, which included (National Science Foundation 1990b:9) the following:

1. Commercial and economic transactions
2. Immigration and population shifts
3. Social and ethnic conflict
4. Regulation of the environment
5. Transnational governance

The Report also provided a discussion of theoretical opportunities suggested by the recognition of the "global interdependence of sociolegal phenomena," among them the "reinvigoration of extant concepts, expansion and generalization of theories and models, the development of new theories and models, and the reassessment of some of our basic assumptions" (National Science Foundation 1990b:15). Again, the summary of conference discussions called strongly for new methods to suit a transformed world situation: "A revolution in research must follow the revolution in world events and the increasing globalization" (National Science Foundation 1990b:16).

Central to these discussions was the development of a new vocabulary within which apparently new problems could be conceptualized, explored, and interpreted. Much of this vocabulary was borrowed from other scholarly and institutional contexts, but new and frequently contested, or at least implicitly contradictory, meanings also emerged, both in the Belmont Report and in its subsequent interpretations over the ensuing three years of funding discussions.

Due in part to the success of the Belmont Conference and Report and in part to Levine's remarkable intellectual vision, political acuity, and organizational energy, a new funding initiative[1] was approved under the aegis of the Law and Social Science program. The initiative was announced in the winter of 1990 with a submission deadline of March 15, 1991; it has been continued on an annual basis every subsequent year. The language of the announcement drew heavily on the Belmont Report. In specifying the range of appropriate topics for funding, the announcement noted that

> Proposals are welcome that advance fundamental knowledge about legal interactions, processes, relations, and diffusions that extend beyond any single nation as well as about how local and national legal institutions, systems, and cultures affect or are affected by transnational or international phenomena. Thus, proposals may locate the research within a single nation or between or across legal systems as long as they illuminate or are informed by global perspectives. (NSF 1990)

The Belmont Report and the initiative announcement jointly framed a broad understanding of globalization as a process and provided a range of exempla for how it was transforming the sociolegal realm. How this wide-ranging and innovative perspective was to be put into practice, however, fell to the peer review panel appointed to fund research sponsored by the initiative.

REVIEWING PEER REVIEW

NSF review procedures are built around the notion of peer review, an institution associated not only with research funding but also with the refereeing of manuscripts for journal and scholarly press publication, ethical self-regulation within disciplines, and a range of other professional activities. Some types of grant review rely almost solely on ad hoc mail reviewers. Program officers request commentary and recommendations on specific proposals from up to ten scholars, but the reviewers never meet to discuss the proposals, and few individual reviewers will have read more than at most a handful of them. The most usual practice within SES is for a standing panel with a number of members serving multiyear terms to meet twice a year. Ad hoc mail reviews are solicited from specialists on the subject of each proposal, and at least two of the panel members read, write evaluations of, and take responsibility for shaping the panel's discussion of each proposal. The entire panel participates in comparative discussion and, most critically, the relative ranking of the full array. Finally, in some instances, as on the Global panel, there are no mail reviewers. Each proposal is read and reviewed in writing by three or four panelists, who also start off discussion. The entire group, again, usually joins in, and all collaboratively construct priority rankings for all the proposals.

In this essay I am concerned primarily with the practices of the Global panel, but several general points from the peer review literature are worth noting. First, while peer review is central to much civilian federal research funding, both the military and private foundations often rely on quite different methods of decision making, usually involving a "strong manager" who may be advised by outside scientists but is not limited by their opinions. The two most thorough historical studies of how research funding has affected the development of particular scientific fields, in both instances focusing on the guided rise of molecular biology (Kay 1993; Kohler 1991), have concentrated on prewar private foundations in which particular individual administrators acquired—

and then used—enormous discretionary power. Both are exceptionally compelling and perceptive studies, but the stories they tell are in many ways classic hero tales with brilliant and determined if at times problematic protagonists. Perhaps not surprisingly, no comparable account exists for NSF, apart from discussions of debates at the time of its founding. Influenced by the overtly powerful personalities who figure centrally in his own narrative, Kohler has suggested that, in peer review–dominated institutions such as NSF, program officers may end up as little more than "secretaries for the panelists" (Kohler 1991:404). As my brief description of review practices above hints, and as my consideration of panel meetings stresses, program officers are far from mere recorders of scholarly discussion; their power, however, is subtly exercised and, without careful observation, can be easily overlooked.

Peer review at federal agencies has been the subject of considerable critical study. Some literature concentrates on particularly flagrant ethical abuses (for example, Bell 1992), but most scholarship is concerned with more everyday structural and procedural problems within the system (Brooks 1978; Chubin and Hackett 1990; Chubin and Jasanoff 1985; Cole and Cole 1981; Cole, Cole, and Simon 1981; Cole, Rubin, and Cole 1978; Gillespie, Chubin, and Kurzon 1985; Harnad 1985; Porter and Rossini 1985; Rip 1985; Roy 1985; Salter 1985). Several themes recur in these critiques, including a concern that there is no way of predicting from a proposal the quality of the scientific knowledge to be gained (a focus in the work of the Coles and their colleagues) and the sense that review by scholarly peers, rather than elected representatives, is antidemocratic.

Two other themes are particularly helpful for thinking about the Global panel. First, Rustum Roy, an especially outspoken critic, has argued that "the system is intrinsically inimical to innovation; this situation occurs because few leading scientists are willing to expose their best ideas to their competitors, and because it often takes between 9 and 18 months to get funds, and because radically new ideas will always be viewed critically by the majority" (Roy 1985:74). While Roy does not provide much evidence to support these claims, it is clear that he sees intense competition driving the production of knowledge; exposure, delay, and resistance make the process unattractive to the best competitors. A somewhat more sober and empirically grounded appraisal (Porter and Rossini 1985) suggests that interdisciplinary proposals have had a significantly lower rate of support than those clearly identified with one discipline; they attribute this finding to the discomfort of reviewers in evaluating proposals beyond their immediate expertise.

A second recurrent concern is for the fairness of the peer review process. A recent General Accounting Office report, for example, focused on questions of bias in the "selection of peer reviewers, the scoring of proposals by reviewers, and the final funding decisions of agencies" (GAO 1994:2), examining the work of NSF, NIH, and the National Endowment for the Humanities with an eye to disproportionate patterns of representation along racial, ethnic, gender, regional, or institutional lines. The results were generally positive, although relatively few younger scholars were used as reviewers. Apart from issues of general group bias, critics have often considered the question of whether it is possible for proposals to be evaluated solely on their own merits and compared equitably with each other, a concern often shared by panelists themselves.

Chubin and Hackett (1990:43–48) provide a thoughtful analysis of these critical themes, noting that the stated desiderata of rationality, fairness, validity, and reliability are often competing and incompatible goals and that frustration with peer review derives in part from a lack of clarity and agreement as to the purposes of funding.

All these studies deal with aggregate characterizations of peer review practices, whether more or less anecdotally (as in Roy 1985) or through more systematic consideration. One striking consequence of this approach is that, as the peer reviewers themselves and their behavior hold center stage, the program officers vanish from view, just as in the historical accounts discussed above. There has, furthermore, been little attention to what actually goes on in panel discussions. Although peer reviewers are treated in terms of aggregate features, they are also implicitly regarded as more or less independent actors. Chubin and Hackett (1990:48) have suggested that a serious study of the "group dynamics" of such meetings would be very helpful, but apparently no one has taken up the challenge of taking panel interaction seriously. In turning now to my own fieldwork, I will provide a somewhat fuller account, not of "group dynamics" per se, but of the discussions as "reading events," jointly structured and accomplished occasions within which shared understandings are disputed and negotiated.

TABLE TALK

NSF review panels take place within a bureaucracy of a particularly porous sort. At NSF a professional program officer or a scholar on a two-year visiting position, usually assisted and guided by an administrative associate, coordinates the review process and writes up the final recommendations. Most participants in the evaluation, however, are academics engaged elsewhere in their own teaching and research. If serving as ad hoc reviewers, faculty might read one or two proposals a year, providing a written evaluation for consideration by the standing panel. As a panel member, one reads and writes up considerably more proposals (often forty for NSF and more at NEH) and spends several days a year in Washington in face-to-face discussions of the entire range of applications. In short, NSF is staffed primarily, though not permanently, by what I have elsewhere (Brenneis 1994) called "nonce bureaucrats," a shifting cast of visiting academics. Although panel discussions and final decisions about funding take place in Washington, a comprehensive understanding of the entire process calls for truly multisited ethnography (Marcus 1995). Many of the participants are never together in the same place, but all are linked through their shared though scattered engagements as authors, readers, critics, gatekeepers, and researchers. The process coalesces, taking form and acquiring visible participants, in recurrent but relatively ephemeral events such as panel meetings.[2]

My own research is based on considerable time spent as one of these nonce bureaucrats, that is, as an active participant in such critical reading events. To return to Marcus's original vision for this seminar, I represent, at least in part, an insider in the institution that I'm discussing. While I am far from a full-time and fully initiated practitioner, one of the striking characteristics of such sporadic participation is its intensity and the surprisingly strong identification that it occasionally catalyzes. This sense of serious engagement in the review process (or perhaps the suspicion of one's own complicitous coperformance of institutional agendas) is critical in shaping both the tenor and the responsiveness of reading panel discussions.

I began serving on such review panels six or so years ago (and I've now logged three years on the Global Initiative at NSF, four years on the college and independent scholars panel for anthropology at NEH, and five years evaluating NSF graduate fellowship applications). I was invited to join the NSF panel primarily because I am one of a quite small number of legal anthropologists of my cohort who has worked extensively outside the United States. I had never applied for NSF funding, but had evaluated numerous proposals for the Law and Social Science panel as a mail reviewer. Most of my fellow panel members were chosen in part because they had received NSF funding in the past.

Given the global dimensions of our subject matter, panels included a variety of disciplines. In 1991, the first year, eleven panelists (including two deputized from the Law and Social Science panel) evaluated fifty-five proposals. The panelists' disciplines ranged from demography and economics to anthropology and legal history, with three political scientists constituting the single largest group. Subsequent panels were somewhat smaller but included a similarly diverse group. In 1991 three women and eight men served on the panel; a similar gender ratio continued in following years. The first year Felice Levine, a sociologist, long-term professional NSF staff member, and the catalyst for the Global Initiative, served as our program officer. Levine left to become Executive Director of the American Sociological Association and was succeeded by two Visiting Scholar/Administrators with extensive sociolegal research experience, Michael Musheno and Susan White.

Early on it became clear to me that panels such as ours constituted consequential audiences indeed, not only for the funding of specific research but in the broader shaping of what we take knowledge to be. It also became evident that the audiences we imagine when "writing culture" are quite different from those we must address in "writing money." Many of us in anthropology imagine our extradisciplinary audience to be involved in literary, historical, and cultural studies, a range of interpretive communities (cf. Rabinow 1986) demanding a particular range of styles and strategies. For the funding that makes our work possible, however, we often must turn to quite different kinds of interlocutors and draw on very different forms of discourse.[3] At times, in fact, our interlocutors may be the same individuals, but how they read and what they expect can change with their roles. The speed and relative ease with which such transformation often occurs speak both to the compelling qualities of the evaluation process itself and to deeper underlying notions of coherence, method, fairness, and the "studyable" that we as readers discover we share, at times to our considerable surprise.

One of the rhetorical consequences of my dual roles as active participant and critical observer is the pronominal limbo in which I've found myself while writing this essay. At times I write about what "we" do, at times of what "they" are up to. Such deictic shifts are not intended to assign culpability to the third person, however strong the temptation. They primarily reflect the extent to which I've had to rely on introspection as an empirical strategy.

I should also note here that I've been quite open with both full-time administrators and my panel colleagues about my dual roles as reader and researcher. My fellow nonce bureaucrats found my interest generally antic but harmless; many have been quite generous with their time and thoughts. Program officers have been exceptionally supportive and forthcoming, in large part because they are often looking for strategies for adjusting and improving the present system of review, ameliorative moves which I'm not sure my research can suggest.

This section focuses on those reading events in which I was both active participant and ethnographer, that is, the three two-day meetings of the "Global Perspectives" panel from 1991 to 1993. These sessions were consequential in part because of the individual funding decisions made during them. They also provided a recurring context in which we actively negotiated the meanings of the "global" and its implications for focus, method, and interpretation[4]—and quite directly shaped the forms and topics through which "global" knowledge was to be produced. We were actively engaged in taking and translating several foundational texts—the Belmont Report and the Call for Proposals—in terms of specific cases. Every year, for example, the question of how strictly we should interpret the Belmont document arose: Would comparative studies, ones in which the units remained the nation-state, be fundable under the global rubric, or could we only support proposals that truly embodied the new "transnationalism"? This was a recurrent source of amiable but spirited disagreement, concerning which each of the three different program officers with whom we worked also had different views. One program officer in fact confessed to some irritation with the panel because it seemed we had "sacralized" the Belmont Report. One reason some of us adopted such a "strict constructionist" perspective might well be not so much a substantive commitment to the idea as the response of readers driven to make decisions among too many good proposals. Relying on external criteria, in this instance goodness of fit with particular programmatic goals, was often exceptionally useful.

Beyond these formative documents, however, we were also engaged in interpreting individual proposals—couched, not surprisingly, in the jargons of a dozen different disciplines—and in trying to translate them into the terms of the Belmont Report. A critical conundrum for us was the dual mandate to take each proposal on its own terms and to compare it with all the others, at times an internally incompatible enterprise.

A further issue is the nature of funding panel discussions as communicative events.[5] I want here to address two critical dimensions: first, the role of the program officer, and, second, the general characteristics of panelist participation. In marked contrast to the weak or almost invisible figure other studies have suggested, the program officer is pivotal. She recruits panel members and determines who will read which proposals. In a multidisciplinary panel in which at most a very few members will be specialists in the proposer's discipline, such decisions are particularly consequential. The program officer also controls the agenda. Although there is a general trajectory from report and discussion to comparison and ranked recommendation, lots of variation is possible. Some program officers start with what they think are prima facie the strongest proposals and then move on to less promising ones. Other officers will move back and forth among proposals of variable perceived quality. Only the program officer has had the opportunity to read all panelists' comments on each proposal and therefore has some sense of initial rankings. Within the discussion of a proposal, the program officer may choose to have several more positive reviews read, followed by more negative ones, or she might choose to begin with the most positive and the most negative reviewers, calling upon other respondents only if necessary. This latter approach often led to the creation of particular antiphonal roles within the discussions more generally. I recurrently found myself, for example, paired with—and speaking amiably against—one particular colleague as we jointly staked out the theoretical and epistemological antipodes of a particular research idea. Such disclosure strategies clearly influenced the "group dynamics" of our discussions.

The program officer controlled a great deal of information to which panelists had no direct access. As noted above, only she knew beforehand what each respondent thought of every proposal and could play those cards as she saw fit. She also was familiar with the budgetary possibilities. Exact dollar figures were rarely discussed in the panel; we pursued financial questions only in the case of exceptionally expensive proposals, where we might recommend cuts. Generally, however, attempts on panelists' part to learn how many proposals might actually be fundable were discouraged; we were to compare and rank in terms of intrinsic merit and promise and to keep money out of the picture.

It is important to point out that panels in themselves do not make funding decisions; they rather make recommendations to the program officer as to priorities for funding. A composite list placing each proposal into one of a number of priority groupings, usually organized in terms of "Fundable," "Possible," "Deferred," and "Declined," is advisory rather than binding on the program officer. She is our principal interlocutor and audience. The program officer actually makes decisions as to final recommendations for funding, but she also has a further audience in mind, here comprising both more senior administrators and the implicit audience of congressional oversight committees.[6]

After the panel meeting, two documents concerning each proposal are prepared. One, "Form 7," is written by the program officer for future audiences within NSF and would be seen by panel members only in subsequent years if a previously rejected proposal has been resubmitted. These paragraph-long reports address various aspects of each proposal to provide reasons for particular recommendations: the number and quality of proposals reviewed that year, the importance of the issues, investigators' track records, the clarity of the proposal, how well it fit with the topical definition of the panel, the "ripeness" of the proposed work for funding, and the nature of the panel's recommendation. In these documents the program officer translates talk into text, abstracting a clear and concise message from often lengthy and complex conversations. The power to clarify and articulate here is considerable and highly consequential. At no time during my panel experiences did I think program officers were doing anything other than trying to represent our discussions; at the same time, completing Form 7 does inherently shape the outcome of our deliberations, especially in a funding context where only about a third of the proposals could be funded.

The other documents prepared after panel meetings consist of the "panel summaries," a series of individual accounts of the written and oral responses to each proposal which are to be sent to the respective Principal Investigators. Some program officers ask individual panel members to write these, while other program officers write the summaries themselves. To quote one program officer, each such summary should provide "a simple description of what was said," one that necessarily highlights particular points of praise and criticism in the written reviews and discussions as salient and leaves others unaddressed. Panel summaries are to focus solely on the merits and limitations of each individual proposal, rather than explicitly considering the broader comparative framework, which is often in fact quite consequential. These panel summaries are particularly critical documents for those applicants whose proposals have failed; the ideal summary should provide candid feedback and give positive indicators of the potential merit of the project.

A second crucial dimension of panel discussions as communicative practice has to do with the tenor of our talk with each other. In marked contrast to the image suggested by Roy (1985) and others—and to the picture some of us might have had in mind before the panels actually began—our conversations were marked not by explicit and antagonistic competition but by remarkable amity and cooperation. One way of thinking about this is to return to the polysemic notion of peer review. We were both reviewing the work of others as peers and, in our discussions, concerned with being peers. We became, in the context of the meeting, "nonce peers"[7] as well as nonce bureaucrats. Participation in such decision making made one, for the moment at least, an "equal." In peer review we jointly constituted an ephemeral peership among ourselves as reviewers as well as vis-à-vis those whom we were evaluating.

Such civility is clearly not singular to the Global panel. Shapin's recent (1994) detailed examination of the influence of gentlemanly codes of conduct among scientists in seventeenth-century England is exemplary in this respect; what was taken as "true" information depended in large part on who presented it and how they did so. Mutual trust was considered indispensable for creating scientific knowledge. It inhered in particular relationships—that is, among those who were equals as "gentlemen"—and became attenuated as scientists were forced to rely on the findings of individuals who were not their peers. In contemporary scholarly discourse, where "gentle" origins are no longer in explicit play, there may in fact be an even greater premium on enacting equality and the trust it both engenders and reflects.

The importance of sustaining amiable discussion at panel meetings was evident. In those instances where disagreement was present, panelists often relied on humor, and particularly on the strategy of exaggeratedly embracing those roles which might have been suggested for them by the program officer. Making such role parody work required more than one performer; I could have played the defender of highly qualitative if methodologically underspecified research successfully only if my opposite took on an archpositivist persona. In Bateson's terms (1972), argument was often reframed in terms of play; potential "bites" were prophylactically performed as "nips." Such reframings required coperformance, as well as an attuned audience that knew what was going on. Hedging and disclaimers were also common in introducing our written comments; for example, "Well, you know what I'm going to say," or "I don't really know much about this."

As striking as the general commitment to civility was the degree of interdisciplinary deference shown. In part this reflected the necessarily interdisciplinary definition of sociolegal studies as a general field and of the particular call for innovative methods issued for the Global Initiative. We also had no highly specialized external reviewers on whose opinions we could count for knowledgeable advice and were constantly consulting with each other, again, with frequent disclaimers of our own expertise. A further element muting potential overt competition was the fact that we were explicitly discouraged from talking directly about money, with the exception of some egregiously expensive proposals.

In short, our discussions were generally characterized by amiability and a willingness to listen to what others had to say.[8] Ironically, this willingness to listen often served to limit what one might say or how strongly one might be willing to say it. My sense is that it was much easier to raise doubts about proposals—through questions, brief and often indirect critiques, or humorous comments—than it was to make an impassioned argument for them. Panelists rarely went out on a limb on which they might find themselves alone; intellectual passion often conflicted with our commitment to civil conversation. While Roy and others see individual competitiveness as a core limitation on the efficacy of peer review, especially in regard to innovative work, I'd suggest the opposite: that the highly collaborative nature of panel work makes disagreement difficult.

One of the most striking features of panel sessions has to do with how the discussion of individual papers and our comparative discussion would come to an end. Quite frequently the panel officer would say something like, "I hear a consensus developing," or "The sense of the meeting seems to be…" Usually what she would literally be hearing would be silence rather than any overtly articulated panelist commentary. She was responding to the end of open disagreement and the apparent unwillingness of panelists to push the discussion any further. Silence is clearly polysemic here; often motivated by the topic having been exhausted, it could also be "heard" as a sign of panel agreement. Panelists could respond to the program officer by claiming they'd heard no such agreement, usually with tongue patently in cheek to mark the comment as play, but such cavils were very rare. Coming to closure through silence and the open-ended interpretive possibilities it engendered were critical features of our discussions—and left a great deal of play for the program officer.

I have elsewhere (Brenneis 1994) explored some of the processes of socialization and self-discipline that lie at the heart of becoming a bureaucratic reader and a participant in such panel discussions. I want here to note one further feature of our table talk, the development of a putatively common language for comparison and evaluation. Transparency of goals and means was considered important, and proposals that might be thought-provoking but "noisy" (to borrow a term from communications theory) were often considered incomparable and therefore difficult to fund in good conscience. A frequent comment at panels ran along these lines: "It's a terrific idea, but I don't really know how to compare it to the other proposals." Such engaging if troubling proposals were frequently tabled for later discussion but rarely were returned to with enthusiasm. At the same time, we were expecting applicants to be working in an uncommon, or at least highly innovative, language as they struggled to get an empirical handle on what were seen as pressing and novel problems. How we used a common language to discuss proposals which were, at their best, likely to be fairly uncommon, was a constant if usually unspoken tension in our discussions.

This notion that both the language of proposals themselves and that of the evaluative talk about them should be referentially transparent—that is, that they should carry meaning assumed to be independent of rhetorical or idiosyncratic baggage—has to do with views of both science and fairness. Informing the peer review system is what I see as the heuristic fiction of interrater reliability, of decisions not being the result of a majority view but the closest possible approximation of some external, objective standard. In peer review, we are not agreeing with each other but, through disciplined reading and discussion, coming into agreement with and about the phenomenon at hand.

Concerns about fairness also figured critically here. Procedural regularity, that is, treating each proposal equally, was seen as critical. Such an "equal protection" procedural model also presupposed the commensurability of proposals. We often assumed that the ability to make sense of a particular proposal vis-à-vis other proposals was indispensable for a fair determination of comparable merit. Innovation, truly novel approaches, and those that are not clearly argued—or, particularly, those for which methodological strategies are left underspecified—were unlikely to be read as comparable and therefore unlikely to be recommended for funding.

A final issue in this section has to do with the outcomes of our discussions over the three years of Global panels. Perhaps most surprising is how unsurprising the recommended projects were, a comment not on their scientific merit but on the novelty of their topics (a situation that is, by report, changing for the better as potential applicants get a stronger sense of the possibilities the initiative affords). While some proposals clearly focused on the new initiative, for example, a study of specific problems of policing across borders, or one studying through survey research the legitimacy of the Court of Justice in the European Community, many represented "older" issues: the effects of race in eyewitness testimony, internal ethnic conflict, and classical comparative studies. A secondary goal of the initiative had been to encourage joint research with non-US scholars, but very few such proposals were funded—a clear instance, I think, of the application of assumedly universalistic criteria for evaluation across quite disparate intellectual communities.

CONCLUSIONS: GLOBAL ISSUES AND GLOBALIZING DISCOURSE

I want here briefly to consider lexical innovation as only one part of the broader discursive activity associated with research funding discussions. Language is more than lexicon (Brenneis 1995). While the vocabulary may be new, in short, the ways in which that vocabulary is used are consistently under negotiation and, more signally, are embedded in usually much more conservative linguistic practices. How we talk about these issues and how institutional concerns and constraints shape and discipline the style as well as the terms of our discussion has proved much less susceptible to transformation. How we think about language, and particularly the quite specific ways in which we turn to assumptions of the importance of referential transparency in NSF discussions, has not changed markedly, although the subjects to which we turned our discussions are innovative. In part this is because the "global" as topic is considered within an already "globalizing" discourse, one in which fairness, science, and notions of universal and objective criteria figure critically.

In regard to one of Marcus's framing questions for this volume, that of the response of institutions to a possibly radically transformed world, the NSF provides a complex but basically limiting case. The new vocabulary is there, in large part due to the real intellectual vision of several critical actors, most notably Felice Levine, who is clearly the hero figure in this account. And, of even more consequence, so is the money. How these new terms and the conceptualizations they imply are deployed and how they actually affect outcomes (and especially, how their innovative implications are frequently muted by the weight of ongoing panel discursive practices) remain central and quite open questions. To return to Burke's incongruity, How and to what extent can the imaginative flourish? New words have been found, but they are often used as part of a much older story.

Notes

I would like to thank George Marcus for organizing the advanced seminar and for inviting me to participate; fellow members of the seminar for their lively and generous conversation; Douglas Schwartz, Duane Anderson, and the staff at the School of American Research for making a remarkable week all the more memorable; and Felice Levine, Bonnie Sheehan, Michael Musheno, Susan White, Patricia White, and my fellow panelists at NSF for their candor, insight, and collegiality. Earlier versions of this paper were also presented at the 1994 annual meetings of the American Anthropological Association, where Rayna Rapp was an exceptionally insightful discussant, and as a talk at Indiana University; many thanks to Bev Stoeltje, Dick Bauman, Stephanie Kane, and Carol Greenhouse for providing both the opportunity and the stimulating conversation. Joel Kuipers made a further presentation possible at George Washington University, and I would like to thank him, Stuart Plattner, Paul Chapin, and Sally Nerlove for their very astute and knowledgeable comments on that version. At Pitzer College Dan Segal, Lee Munroe, Ronald Macaulay, and James Bogen provided very helpful and timely readings, and Wynne Furth has been an insightful and stimulating interlocutor throughout.

1. Within NSF, the term "initiative" indicates a somewhat exploratory funding opportunity, often renewed on an annual or biennial basis. It is distinguished from standing programs (such as the Law and Social Sciences Program), which have ongoing organizational and funding status within NSF. Appointments to Program panels are usually made for a three-year term, while participation in

initiative funding is on an annual basis. Some initiatives represent a coalition of standing Programs and Program Officers; the Global Initiative is much more clearly linked to one Program.

2. In a germinal article, De Solla Price and Beaver (1966) characterize such dispersed scholarly "communities" as the "invisible college." While their perspective is, in my view, overly optimistic and was confined to a much smaller range of characters, i.e., "researchers," than more recent accounts, it remains a useful heuristic notion.

3. For stimulating considerations of the implications of funding audiences for the focus and definition of suitable research projects see Rafael (1994) and several of the essays in Gupta and Ferguson (1997a and 1997b).

4. Kearney (1995) provides a particularly thought-provoking account of just how diverse, contradictory, and indeterminate current uses of notions such as "global" are.

5. While there have been at least two interesting analyses of the language of written peer evaluations (He 1993; Johnson and Roen 1992), I know of no consideration of oral evaluatory discussions. Grimshaw (1989) and some of the articles in Drew and Heritage (1992) touch on some kinds of related practices.

6. The congressional audience was taken very seriously. One program officer noted to me that the most difficult part of the job was working with successful applicants to rewrite their titles and proposal abstracts to make them intelligible and compelling for a lay audience. While Senator Proxmire's "Golden Fleece Awards" have been discontinued, the fear that what to scholarly eyes was an excellent proposal might seem to others a senseless boondoggle remained.

7. I am indebted to Craig Calhoun for suggesting the phrase "nonce peers."

8. Stuart Plattner, NSF program officer for cultural anthropology, confirmed this interpretation for me by noting that he and his colleagues select potential participants with an eye to their capacity for working well together, and that panelists who are other than amiable in meetings are rarely asked to return.

6

Blurred Boundaries, Hybrids, and Changelings

The Fortunes of Nonprofit Organizations in the Late Twentieth Century

Peter Dobkin Hall

For twenty years I have been trying to describe and analyze the historical development of the "third," "independent," or "nonprofit" sector. My earlier attempts (Hall 1982, 1987) treated the phenomenon as a straightforward historical narrative: I began at the beginning and worked my way to the end, from Elizabeth I's Statute of Charitable Uses to the 1969 Tax Reform Act and beyond. Sometime in the late 1980s, I became increasingly uncomfortable with this approach. How could I write the history of something—the "nonprofit sector"—that only began to be defined as such a decade earlier and in the recognition of which my colleagues and I had played a central role?

So I turned my energies to writing about the "invention" of the nonprofit sector, describing the historical development of its various institutional strands—the arts, charity, education, health care, social welfare, and religion—and devoting increasing attention to why scholars, policymakers, and social activists had, beginning in the 1970s, needed to construct conceptual frameworks that would enable them to treat the whole range of eleemosynary activity as a coherent and definable "sector" of organizations and activities (Hall 1992a, 1992b). In the course of this work, I became aware that virtually the whole community of scholars studying philanthropy, voluntarism, and nonprofit organizations, myself included, had overlooked a very important fact. We had all assumed that Tocqueville was right when he wrote that

> Americans of all ages, all conditions, and all dispositions constantly form associations. They have not only commercial and manufacturing companies, in which

> all take part, but associations of a thousand other kinds, religious, moral, serious, futile, general or restricted, enormous or diminutive. The Americans make associations to give entertainments, to found seminaries, to build inns, to construct churches, to diffuse books, to send missionaries to the antipodes; in this manner they found hospitals, prisons, and schools. If it is proposed to inculcate some truth or to foster some feeling by the encouragement of a great example, they form a society. Wherever at the head of some new undertaking you see the government in France, or a man of rank in England, in the United States you will be sure to find an association. (Tocqueville 1945 II:114)

I already had good reason to suspect that Tocqueville's iconic assertion was wrong. My 1973 dissertation on Boston merchant families had shown that most of Boston's associations, proprietary and eleemosynary, had been established only a decade or two before the Frenchman's visit to America. My 1982 book, *The Organization of American Culture*, had focused on the debate over the status of associations and corporations as a central feature of early American politics. And, during the late 1980s, I had written detailed accounts of the emergence of "organizational cultures" in early-nineteenth-century Connecticut, Ohio, and Pennsylvania, all of which demonstrated that the establishment of private associations had been fiercely resisted and, in most places outside New England, had taken very different forms from the standard civil privatist model delineated by Tocqueville (Hall 1987b, 1988).

But the statistics on charitable tax-exempt organizations included in Burton Weisbrod's important 1989 book, *The Nonprofit Economy*, really made the point. The appendices to the volume, which contained the IRS figures for nonprofit organization establishments from the mid-1960s to the mid-1980s, showed that the charitable tax-exempt universe had grown from 300,000 organizations to nearly a million in a twenty-year period. Other information, such as the testimony of

Treasury Department officials to Congress, pushed these numbers backward. In 1940, the IRS commissioner testified, there had been only 12,500 registered tax-exempt organizations; in 1950, he estimated their number at about 50,000. Pushing Weisbrod's statistics forward added to the panorama of an explosion in the population of nonprofits. By the early 1990s, they were estimated to number over one and a quarter million. Setting aside quibbles about the meaning of government registration statistics (clearly, changes in the tax code during and after the Second World War gave many already extant organizations incentives to apply for tax-exempt status), it seemed clear that the "nonprofit sector"—the universe of charitable tax-exempt organizations—was not a venerable although largely unrecognized organizational domain but instead had largely come into being in our own time.

Weisbrod's statistics, when combined with the work of policy scientist Lester Salamon, produced another unsettling insight. Beginning with Tocqueville, conventional understandings of voluntary organizations had always portrayed them as alternatives to government. And it was generally believed that, as the welfare state grew, voluntary associations, and the distinctive civil society based on them, would whither away. Ronald Reagan took conventional wisdom at its word and, upon being elected, set about to enact massive cuts in federal social expenditures, expecting that voluntary action would not only "take up the slack" but would provide services more cheaply and responsively than could government.

Salamon, then at the Urban Institute, was commissioned by a group of nonprofit executives to project the impact of the proposed budget cuts (Salamon and Abramson 1982). He found that the impact would be devastating because direct and indirect subsidies from the federal government comprised the largest single component in nonprofit revenues, ranging from 55 percent for human services organizations to 42 percent for community development, 36 percent for health care, 22 percent for education and research, and 12 percent for arts and culture (Salamon 1987a:104). Salamon suggested that the characteristic relationship between government and nonprofits in the United States, rather than being antagonistic, as in a conventional model, had been complementary—had been, to use his term, a "partnership."

Salamon recognized that his findings were more than just new data; they posed a fundamental challenge to the way we had gone about understanding our institutions. "The partnership between government and the nonprofit sector has been overlooked," he wrote,

> not because of its novelty or because of a lack of research, but because of a weakness in theory. It is the role of theory, after all, to direct attention to facts that are most relevant to a particular process ... Lacking a valid theory, crucial facts can therefore be overlooked or misperceived. "Facts do not speak for themselves," Stephen Jay Gould had observed, "they are read in the light of theory."

"It is the argument here," Salamon continued,

> that "basic progress in the technology of thinking" is very much needed in the analysis of the voluntary sector and its relationships with government. Our failure to perceive the reality of extensive government-nonprofit ties is, I believe, in substantial part a product of the limitations of the conceptual lenses through which this reality is being perceived. Both the theory of the "welfare state" and the theory of the voluntary sector, moreover, have been at fault. Neither leaves much conceptual room for a flourishing government-nonprofit partnership. To the contrary, both suggest quite strongly that such cooperation could not, and should not, exist. Equipped with such theories, it is no wonder that observers have tended to overlook such cooperation or question it when it appears. (Salamon 1987b:32–33)

Writing in the mid-1980s, Salamon still assumed, as did virtually all scholars interested in the subject, that nonprofits had always been around in pretty much the same form they have today. But the publication of Weisbrod's statistics shed a different light on the matter. Rather than the kind of long-term, ongoing partnership which Salamon posited, organizational demography suggested a direct relationship between the emergence of the post–World War II welfare state and the explosion in the population of charitable tax-exempt entities. Taken together, Salamon's and Weisbrod's work suggested that, while nonprofit/voluntary associations may have existed at least since the early nineteenth century, in terms of their numbers and significance they had only assumed real importance as a form of collective action very recently—within the previous quarter century. This, in turn, shed some light on why, on the one hand, scholars had ignored nonprofits before the 1970s, and, on the other, why the concepts and terminology of a third, independent, or nonprofit sector only came into being at that time.[1] My initial analyses attributed the growing self-consciousness of the sector to the nonprofit industries' efforts to defend themselves from legislative attack by subsidizing scholarship that would show them to be a legitimate and historically sanctioned part of the American polity (Hall 1992a:243–56).

But this was only part of the story. More important was the fact that nonprofits themselves were the fastest growing and most rapidly evolving organizational domain in the US. While the scholars might have been responding to industry incentives and the industry was responding to congressional and regulatory pressure, Congress itself—and, as it turned out, public opinion—was responding to an awareness that a set of organizations that no one understood was growing rapidly in numbers and influence. In the 1950s, critics directed their attention to foundations because of their highly visible wealth. But it turned out that the growth rate of foundations was a proxy for a population explosion in the whole domain of charitable tax-exempt organizations. In the 1970s, scholars and policymakers began to invent new terms in an attempt to capture the phenomenon and anchor it in existing knowledge and theory. By the late 1980s, it became apparent, as Salamon so eloquently put it, that existing knowledge and theory could not encompass what was happening.

Around this time, management guru Peter Drucker published *The New Realities* (1989), a remarkable book that combined intuitive insights based on cutting-edge historiography about the rise and fall of the liberal corporate state between 1890 and the 1980s with a set of bold pronouncements about the emergence of a new class—"the knowledge class." "The new pluralist institutions of society," Drucker wrote, "are organizations of 'knowledge workers.'" Though employees of organizations, they are not tied to organizations in the traditional sense, nor is their status defined by their occupation. Moving from accounting work in business to accounting work in a hospital to teaching accounting in a university does not involve a fundamental change in social or economic position. "Knowledge workers have mobility," Drucker continued. "They are 'colleagues.' They have both social and economic status. They enjoy the bargaining power that results from social equality and from becoming economically essential" (Drucker 1989:94).

Changing criteria for the success of organizations, Drucker argued, further enhanced the importance of these individuals not merely as technical specialists but as intellectuals. "The more knowledge-based an institution becomes," Drucker noted, "the more it depends on the willingness of individuals to take responsibility for contribution to the whole, for understanding the objectives, the values, the performance of the whole, and for making themselves understood by the other professionals, the other knowledge people, in the organization" (1989:97). In other words, active intellectual commitment had become a crucial element in the effectiveness and efficiency of organizational functioning.

Drucker's analysis of the emerging "knowledge society" pointed to an especially important role for "the non-profit organizations of the so-called third sector" (1989:195). These organizations, Drucker believed, "are rapidly becoming creators of new bonds of community and a bridge across the widening gap between knowledge workers and the 'other half.'" Increasingly, he argued, "they create a sphere of effective citizenship," "spheres of personal achievement" in which the individual "exercises influence, discharges responsibility, and make decisions."

"In the political culture of mainstream society," Drucker suggested, "individuals, no matter how well-educated, how successful, how achieving, or how wealthy, can only vote and pay taxes. They can only react, can only be passive. In the counterculture of the third sector, they are active citizens. This may be the most important contribution of the third sector" (1989:205). Though unaware of either the changing organizational demographics of nonprofitdom or Salamon's theories of third-party government, Drucker boldly argued that fundamental changes were occurring at the deepest levels of American culture, and he placed the emergence of the "third" sector, rather than business, at the center of those changes. The new brave world he projected would be based on "values quite different from those of the 'business society.' They bespeak a society in which economic satisfactions are a means rather than a good in themselves, and in which business is therefore a tool rather than a way of life" (1989:178).

There is one final element to this panorama: the beginning of a transformation of academic understandings of what organizations are and how they work. This transformation is perhaps best summarized by Paul DiMaggio and Walter Powell's 1991 anthology, *The New Institutionalism in Organizational Analysis*, which brought together the editors' own work with that of contemporaries and senior scholars to challenge and replace "rational theories of technical contingency or strategic choice with alternative models that are more consistent with the organizational realities that researchers have observed" (DiMaggio and Powell 1991:3). These alternative models stressed the problems of cognitive limits, incomplete information, and unintended consequences, and shifted levels of analysis from individual firms to "organizational structures that [were] industry-wide, national or international in scope" (1991:9). Conventional distinctions between public, private, and nonprofit domains disappeared in the face of organizational field analyses, which focused on interactions between "those organizations that, in the aggregate, constitute a recognized area of institutional life: key suppliers, resource and product consumers, regulatory agencies, and other organizations that produce similar services or products" (1991:64–65). Most importantly, the "new institutionalism" focused on the importance of ideas and values. "Institutionalized arrangements," Powell and DiMaggio (1991:10–11) wrote,

> are reproduced because individuals often cannot even conceive of appropriate alternatives (or because they regard as unrealistic the alternatives they can imagine). Institutions do not just constrain options; they establish the very criteria by which people discover their preferences. In other words, some of the most important such costs are cognitive.

I was struck by the coincidence between Drucker's bold pronouncement of the end of corporate liberalism and the persuasive and wide-ranging attack by Powell, DiMaggio, and their colleagues on conventional rationalistic understandings of collective action. It was not insignificant in my view that both Powell and DiMaggio had spent much of their careers studying and writing about nonprofit organizations. And it seemed clear that the "new institutionalism" might be seen as a kind of manifesto for the emergence of the knowledge class and its favored organizational vehicle, the nonprofit organization.

In agreeing to participate in the School of American Research seminar, I originally intended to write a nifty little paper that would have provided a sort of Gramscian overview of the intertwined emergence of a new class of knowledge workers, an organizational domain (the "nonprofit sector") to which the new class was particularly attracted, and a new way of understanding organizations (neo-institutional organization theory) that served, among other things, to legitimate the new class and its favored vehicles of collective action. At that point, I still thought that the issues could be dealt with using standard historical narrative and conventional, albeit challenged, concepts. I wanted to get at the story-behind-the-story of nonprofits and how they were understood. But I still did not appreciate how deep the fin de siècle crisis of institutions and understanding went and how little it was leaving untouched. It took a completely pedestrian event—a crisis involving my neighborhood—to lead me to begin to grasp the extent to which events had outstripped conventional narratives and conventional concepts of even the most commonplace things like "family" and the boundaries between public and private spheres.

DISMANTLING THE LIBERAL STATE, THE RISE OF THE CONTRACTING REGIMES, AND THE CRISIS OF THE NONPROFIT SECTOR

The dismantling of the liberal state is conventionally dated from the election of Ronald Reagan, the first president in half a century to make reducing the size of government the centerpiece of his campaign. In fact, the process began earlier—perhaps as early as 1954, when the Supreme Court declared racial segregation unconstitutional.

The decision in *Brown v. Board of Education of Topeka* had a number of unusual features. First, it was a class action suit, broadly applicable to a wide group of persons, not an appeal to remedy injustices suffered by a specific individual; second, as the court conceded, because school desegregation would require remedies tailored to the circumstances of particular localities, consent decrees would have to be crafted by the lower courts with the help of special masters appointed to recommend specific terms for such decrees. In so constitutionalizing a disability—in this case, the civil disability attached to race—the federal courts took the first steps toward becoming the primary arenas for social policy making.

The success of the desegregation litigations of the 1950s encouraged liberal activists to mount class action suits on behalf of a broad range of groups whose constitutional rights were believed to be violated by state laws. Chief among these groups were the mentally disabled, who, under the laws of most states, were warehoused in vast, isolated institutions ("philanthropic monasteries," as they had been called by their turn-of-the-century proponents, designed to contain "the gelatinous mass that simply eats and lives" [Warner 1894:23–24, 336]) where, hidden from the public eye and abandoned by their families, they were subjected to abuse and neglect. Rather than seeking reform through Congress or the state legislatures, where they were bound to be frustrated, advocates for the mentally disabled successfully persuaded the federal courts to consider the situation of patients in state mental institutions and training schools for the retarded from a constitutional perspective, arguing that, as citizens, they enjoyed rights to habilitation and treatment (Chayes 1976, 1982; Gardiner 1977; Rothman and Rothman 1984:45–65).

The movement experienced its first successes in 1972, when an Alabama federal district court ruled that mentally retarded inmates in one of the state's institutions were constitutionally entitled to "the least restrictive conditions necessary to achieve the purposes of habilitation" and ordered the state to move them from "(1) more to less structured living; (2) larger to smaller facilities; (3) larger to smaller living units; (4) group to individual residence; (5) segregated from the community to integrated into the community; (6) dependent to independent living" (*Wyatt v. Stickney* 1972:387). The effort received high visibility in

January of 1972, when television newscaster Geraldo Rivera broadcast an exposé of conditions at New York's Willowbrook School for the Retarded, which featured vivid images of naked, often battered, children lying in pools of their own excrement. That broadcast sparked a furious outcry—and a class action suit on behalf of Willowbrook patients that, in terms of its ultimate impact, would do for the mentally disabled what *Brown v. Board of Education* had done for victims of segregation.

Although the judiciary—out of tradition and a keen awareness of the awesome challenges of trying to implement remedial orders—was reluctant to follow the procedures imposed in the school desegregation cases, by the 1970s jurists found that the spectacle of officially sanctioned neglect and suffering made it increasingly difficult to sustain the "rule of abstention" (Joint Hearings 1985). Beginning in the mid-1970s, a series of court challenges brought by coalitions of human services professionals and legal activists forced the state-by-state deinstitutionalization of disabled children and adults and required their placement in communities and, where possible, in family settings. Most importantly, the court orders required that treatment plans be tailored to the needs of individual clients according to the nature of their disabilities—a requirement that gave rise to a system of almost unimaginable complexity.

Deinstitutionalization transformed the nonprofit sector but, because it occurred on a state-by-state basis, it is difficult, even two decades later, to capture the scale and scope of the process. In New York, for example, the number of group homes grew from a few dozen in the mid-1970s to more than a thousand by the mid-1980s. Faced with deinstitutionalization, officials in Connecticut, a relatively small state, estimated that they would have to create more than nine thousand housing units—group homes, apartments, and single-family dwellings—to implement federal court orders (Hamilton 1984; Libov 1988; UPI 1981, 1988). By 1990, more than three hundred nonprofits, a substantial proportion of the state's tax-exempt entities, would be serving the mentally disabled.

The financial scale of the transformation was, and remains, incalculable. In 1994, the State of New York was spending $35,000 annually for each of the thirteen thousand clients lodged in group homes—a total of $104 million (Winerip 1994:3–4). But this figure captures only a small part of the cost, since it includes neither disability and other federal outlays to clients nor the capital costs of acquiring and renovating community-based facilities. In little Connecticut, the latter absorbed 85 percent of the state's entire economic development budget for the years 1988 to 1991—a sum amounting to more than $200 million in state loans and grants to individuals and nonprofit organizations (Connecticut 1992; Cockerham 1992a, 1992b; Megan 1992; Paznoikas 1992). The complexity of contracting regimes is suggested by Kirsten Gronbjerg's study of social services delivery in Cook County, Illinois, where a single midsized nonprofit agency serving urban youth with an annual budget of about $1.5 million received its revenues from six federal agencies (the Departments of Housing and Urban Development, Health and Human Services, Justice, Labor, and Education, and the National Endowment for the Arts), seven state agencies (the Illinois Departments of Public Health, Public Aid, Mental Health, Children and Family Services, and Commerce and Community Affairs, the State Board of Education, and the State Arts Council), five local government agencies, 73 corporations and foundations, and 299 individual donors, plus income from endowment and miscellaneous earned revenues (Gronbjerg 1993:3–6).

Placing this complexity in a broader framework does not make its contours any easier to discern. Because deinstitutionalization required that treatment plans be tailored to the needs of individuals, states did not simply contract with nonprofits to provide services in bulk to clients, but contracted on a client-by-client basis; for example, a blind, orphaned, HIV-positive, mentally retarded individual would be entitled to a different cluster of benefits than an elderly, emotionally disturbed client. According to Gronbjerg, Cook County alone issued more than 100,000 human services contracts to hundreds of nonprofit and proprietary providers—a situation whose very complexity made it impossible to monitor (Beacon Hill Institute 1992).

The capacity to monitor or even grasp the impact of the system of privatized (usually nonprofit) community-based treatment and care for the disabled was impaired not only by its decentralized character and its complexity, but by the fact that the academic and policy enterprise was ill-equipped to observe and analyze changes on the state and local level. The social and policy sciences had grown in close association with the rise of an emphatically national central government. (Such community- and state-level studies as the Lynds' work on "Middletown" in the 1920s and Lloyd Warner's "Yankee City" project in the 1930s and '40s were, in the decades following the Second World War, deemed marginal.) Preoccupied with emergent federal government agencies and interventions, the social and policy sciences were similarly unable to grasp either the growing centrality of nonprofit agencies in service provision or (as Salamon would point out in 1982) the extent to which the American welfare state depended on them even before deinstitutionalization.

If all but a handful of students of public policy were ignorant of the larger dimensions of nonprofit service provision and the significance of deinstitutionalization on the already burgeoning (but largely ignored) "nonprofit sector," they were even less aware of the processual dimensions of the constitutionalizing of disability and the privatization of service provision. Creating contracting regimes required legal innovations. Because one of the primary goals of the system was to "mainstream" the disabled, placing them in residential neighborhoods where zoning regulations often restricted multifamily and institutional uses, lawmakers came up with the idea of "permanent family residences." These entities were defined by statute as state-sponsored (though usually privately operated) service providers, which local authorities were required to treat as single families. To prevent localities from excluding group homes, separate statutes were passed exempting such facilities from conformity to municipal zoning, building, fire, safety, and other codes (see Appendix for the example of Connecticut).

Thus, in a stroke, legislatures created entities that were simultaneously state agencies, private corporations, and families. At the same time, the planning and zoning powers of communities, long established in law, were entirely superseded. Citizen efforts to protest these changes were effectively silenced through SLAPP suits (Strategic Lawsuits Against Public Participation) brought by service providers backed by the considerable resources of the state and federal governments. Any citizen or citizens' group that petitioned, spoke at public meetings, leafleted, wrote letters to the press, or expressed any opinion critical of efforts to establish group homes risked a federal housing discrimination suit (Gugliotta 1994; Sills 1993). By early 1994, more than three dozen of these suits were pending in federal courts throughout the United States (Mariano 1990, 1992).

A HOUSE? A HOME? A FAMILY? A NONPROFIT CORPORATION?

Despite my deep professional involvement in the study of nonprofits and my personal interest as a civic activist in land use issues, I was unaware of the transformation taking place around me until the winter of 1992, when a housing discrimination suit was brought against the neighborhood association on whose board I served. One hundred fifty Huntington Street is a large brick Tudor-style residence on the edge of New Haven's Ronan-Edgehill neighborhood, a twelve-block area of large, tree-shaded streets and yards, the kind of generic upper-class enclave built in almost every city at the turn of the century. The property was a private residence until twenty-five years ago, when it was acquired by Albertus Magnus College for use as a dormitory. At that time, the Board of Zoning Appeals granted a conditional-use variance which permitted this nonconforming use subject to continuing review.

Late in 1991, the college put 150 Huntington and the adjacent property on the market. At a meeting in January of 1992, college officials and their real estate broker assured residents that the properties would be sold for residential purposes. The first sign that something was amiss came when they were listed and advertised as commercial properties. Within a short time, rumors began to circulate among neighborhood residents that 150 Huntington Street had been placed under contract to a group home. No one really knew what kinds of clients the home had, though it was said that it served disabled children.

In April of 1992, a number of Huntington Street residents called a meeting to discuss the proposed sale of the property to There's No Place Like Home, Inc., and to explore their legal options in regard to it. About thirty people attended this gathering, which was held in a resident's living room. In the course of the meeting, residents aired their questions and concerns. Officers of the neighborhood association (including myself, as chair of its Zoning Enforcement Committee) were invited to outline our general policy on zoning compliance and describe our practice of having the residents most immediately affected in zoning disputes take the initiative in pursuing legal and administrative remedies.

Several weeks later, the prospective purchaser of 150 Huntington became known. Marjorie Eichler operated a "permanent family residence" for disabled children under the name of There's No Place Like Home, Inc. (a nonprofit corporation) in another part of the city (Bascom 1987; Weaver 1987). She reportedly had ten clients in residence—six adopted and four foster children. Early in May, four residents whose properties adjoined 150 Huntington Street retained legal counsel and petitioned the Connecticut Superior Court for an injunction that would require the proposed change of use to be reviewed by the Board of Zoning Appeals. The issue in the case concerned only the question of zoning review; at no time was the proposed use as a group home opposed, nor was any mention made of the race or disabilities of those who might live at 150 Huntington.

I did not attend this session, since I regarded the matter as a routine request for zoning review. I was astonished to learn afterwards that when the neighbors' lawyers entered the courtroom, they found sitting alongside the attorney for the group home three Connecticut assistant attorneys general (representing the state agencies affected by the proposed zoning review) and two federal officials, one from the Department of Housing and Urban Development (HUD) and one from the Department of Justice (DOJ). Representatives for the group home endeavored to have the proceeding removed to federal court, alleging that in requesting the zoning review neighborhood residents had violated the federal Fair Housing Act and had discriminated against their clients on the basis of race and disability. The federal court refused jurisdiction and sent the case back to the state court.

While the presence of such legal artillery on the other side surprised me, neither I nor anyone else connected with the neighborhood association, whose board included half a dozen eminent attorneys and legal scholars, guessed that we were entering uncharted territory and that the stakes were infinitely greater than anyone supposed. Late in

May, the association decided to enter the case directly as a co-litigant. This decision was based on our concern that the state's efforts to circumvent the review and public hearing requirements of the New Haven zoning ordinance constituted a fundamental threat to the integrity of the ordinance and its future enforcement.

For us, the issue was not the possible occupancy of 150 Huntington Street by disabled people. Human services agencies had long been located in the neighborhood: Highland Heights, a Catholic facility for the profoundly retarded, had been operating in one form or another (at one point as an orphanage with more than 200 residents) since the 1880s; Ben Haven, a residential facility for autistic adolescents, had occupied two buildings since the 1960s; other agencies included Green Briar, a sheltered workshop for the retarded, the Cedarhurst School, a high school operated by the Yale Psychiatric Institute, and a slew of day schools, nursery schools, kindergartens, and churches (Hall 1995). Because the neighborhood was overwhelmingly liberal in its political orientation and many of its residents were involved in health care and education, it had always welcomed these facilities, asking only that those in charge respect residents' concerns about traffic, parking, and other routine zoning matters. Accordingly, the neighborhood association's position on the Huntington Street group home was not to oppose it, but to request that it be subject to the same rules and procedures affecting all properties under the city's zoning ordinance.

The association and the Huntington Street residents withdrew their suit against There's No Place Like Home, Inc., in early June, upon learning that the funds with which the facility had hoped to make the purchase had not yet been approved by the state bonding commission. Unbeknownst to most residents and to the association, HUD investigators, acting on Eichler's complaint that neighborhood protests amounted to violations of the antidiscrimination provisions of the federal Fair Housing Act, had been combing the neighborhood, pressing individual residents to give depositions about statements their neighbors had made about the group home in private conversations and private meetings. This evidence became the basis for a formal charge of housing discrimination by the DOJ.

On June 15, the association and a number of individual neighborhood residents were notified by the Civil Rights Division of the DOJ that they were subjects of suit. The government alleged that the residents and the association had, by requesting zoning review of the proposed change of use, discriminated against the Eichlers (the operators of There's No Place Like Home, Inc.) "by seeking to bar them from their neighborhood, through litigation and by other acts, because of their status as a foster family for four children" (United States 1992a; *U.S. Newswire* 1992). The government further alleged discrimination against the Eichlers because of the children's race and disabilities. It sought damages "on behalf of the Eichler family and each of the foster children for economic loss including emotional distress, and punitive damages because of the intentional and willful nature of the defendants' actions."

The defendants named in the case were John Levanthal, a pediatrician and youth advocate (he had brought the class action suit which led to the reorganization of the state's Department of Children and Youth Services); his wife, Beverly Hodgson, a superior court judge and outspoken civil rights advocate; Duncan Robinson, curator of Yale's British Art Center, and his wife; Roberta Pooley, the city's outstanding civic gadfly and president of the neighborhood association; and the Ronan-Edgehill Neighborhood Association (C. Bass 1992a). The individual defendants were a representative cross-section of the neighborhood, whose residents were perhaps the most politically liberal and civicly active group in the city (C. Bass 1993b; *Hartford Courant* 1993; Span 1993a, 1993b; Waldman 1992) and included much of the senior faculty of the Yale Law School, the president of one of the country's most liberal foundations, Congresswoman Rosa DeLauro (a liberal Democrat) and her husband, Stanley Greenberg (Bill Clinton's pollster), and Zoe Baird (chief counsel for the Aetna Insurance company and eventual nominee for US Attorney General in the Clinton administration).

The government was seeking total damages of $68,00: $33,000 to cover the Eichler's legal fees, $10,000 for emotional harm, and a $25,000 civil penalty. In addition, the association would be required to sign a consent decree in which it would pledge to refrain from engaging in certain practices governed by the Fair Housing Act. In addition to these formal threats, a representative of the Justice Department's civil rights division suggested in a telephone conversation with the neighborhood association's attorney that resistance to the suit would lead the government to take legal action against its officers, directors, and individual members. The association's attorney was also threatened with being called as a witness, which would bar her from further participation in the case.

The association's board instructed its attorney to discuss possible scenarios for the resolution of the matter and learned that the DOJ would consider reducing its financial demands to $10,000 in exchange for the association's signing a consent decree (US 1992b). When the draft consent decree was received, it became clear that the government did not seriously intend to settle the case. Lawyers familiar with such documents declared that they had never seen anything like this one. It would have permitted the government to treat any future effort to enforce zoning against any member of a "protected group" as a discriminatory act; any statement or expression of opinion made by individual citizens with regard to zoning issues, whether in private conversation, at informal neighborhood gatherings, or at association meetings, could be used as the basis for a future federal suit; the neighborhood and its residents would be placed under federal monitoring for an unspecified period, enabling government agents to inquire into their private opinions and actions; the injunction against discriminatory speech and acts would apply to individuals affected by the decree even if they were no longer resident in the neighborhood; and the injunction would require all directors and officers of the association and a third of its membership to attend "educational seminars" on "the application of the Fair Housing Act to neighborhood opposition to residence of persons, because of disability and familial status."

The extraordinary legal pressure being brought to bear against the neighborhood association for what appeared to be a minor matter piqued my curiosity. The fact that it involved nonprofits was further intriguing. I began a database search on group homes, zoning, and related matters. It didn't take long to discover that the issues involved—deinstitutionalization, privatization, housing discrimination, and the growth of a huge and largely unrecognized nonprofit industry—were very significant indeed. I brought these matters to the attention of the neighborhood association board but, curiously, they had little impact on its deliberations. More concerned about the extraordinary restrictions the consent decree might impose on neighborhood residents who had neither knowledge of nor opinions about the case, the board reluctantly decided to oppose the government's allegations. (Still, a number of members evidently knew that something important was afoot. Three of the attorneys on the board quietly resigned after this vote was taken).

Although subjects of a single lawsuit, the individual defendants and the association were warned by their respective attorneys not to discuss the case. The association was further warned not to keep detailed minutes of meetings at which the case was discussed, since these would be liable to seizure by the government. The association was, accordingly, unable to inform its members about the legal entanglement in which it was becoming ever more deeply enmeshed. In September of 1992 the association and the individual defendants filed a motion for dismissal of the complaint on the ground that the association's actions were protected and privileged under the First Amendment.

EMBATTLED MOMS, TONY NEIGHBORHOODS

While the suit slowly wound its way through the courts, press reports were frequent and uniformly negative. The association and its members were characterized as a stereotypical NIMBY (Not In My Backyard)—as "prominent residents" of a "tony neighborhood" who sought to prevent an "embattled mom" from buying a home for her disabled children. A *Connecticut Law Tribune* story was typical. Under the subhead "21 Rms, Money Vu," it stressed the contrast between the neighborhood's "large, gracious older homes with immaculate clapboard exteriors and natural-woodwork interiors" which were "home to a congresswoman and the local chamber of commerce president," and adjoining Newhallville, "a neighborhood of working-class homeowners and poor renters plagued by drug gangs and ubiquitous street violence." "On one side" of the hill, the writer declaimed, "lie Newhallville's poverty and despair;" go a few blocks to the east, she continued, "and you're surrounded by tile-roofed stucco or brick mansions" (C. Bass 1992a). The article portrayed Eichler as a woman currently living in an impoverished neighborhood who only "wants the 21-room red-brick mansion for herself and her extended family: her grown son and daughter-in-law, her six adopted kids and four foster children, whom she's in the process of adopting."

Under the subhead "The Zoning Dispute That Wasn't," the article portrayed the neighborhood's zoning complaint as a sham, behind which lurked purely discriminatory motives:

> The complaint, presented as a zoning challenge, sought to prevent Eichler and her family from moving into 150 Huntington. The house falls in a single-family residential zone, and New Haven's zoning ordinance defines "family" as people "related by blood, marriage or adoption" or up to four people "who need not be so related."
>
> Leaning heavily on that "or," the Robinsons argued that the Eichler family doesn't fit the bill, since it includes members from both defined categories. In fact, the Robinsons' pleadings argued, Eichler and her children would be setting up "essentially a group residence," disrupting the neighborhood with noise and traffic.
>
> "Despite that the defendants may desire to live essentially in the same manner as a traditional family, the intended use is simply not permitted under New Haven zoning ordinances at 150 Huntington Street," the Robinsons maintained.

Much was made of the political liberalism of those defending the neighborhood:

> "Discrimination" is a familiar word to Arterton and Garrison, whose firm of Garrison & Arterton is well-known for its plaintiffs-side employment work: age discrimination, sex discrimination, race discrimination, disability cases. Their reputation has led some to wonder why they represented opponents of a foster family, why they

> argued in pleadings that the neighborhood's "private pools, aesthetically pleasant stone walls and other architectural details...will overnight become the source of continual anxiety, worry and potential liability for the acts of so many young children."
>
> "It's certainly a fascinating role reversal here," says Breetz, Eichler's lawyer. "Joe and Janet are well-regarded in [*The Connecticut Law Tribune*] and elsewhere as the white knights of the civil-rights movement. I think they're on the wrong side of this."
>
> Garrison and Arterton aren't the only members of New Haven's liberal legal establishment entangled in this matter. (C. Bass 1992a)

The press came down with particular viciousness on Superior Court judge Beverly Hodgson and John M. Leventhal, associate professor of pediatrics at the Yale School of Medicine and a director of the Ronan-Edgehill Neighborhood Association, who was one of the named defendants in the federal suit. Levanthal and Hodgson had earned reputations as advocates on women's, children's and civil-rights issues (C. Bass 1992a, 1992b, 1992c).[2] *New York Newsday* ran this item under the headline "Doc Who Cleared Woody Faces Suit":

> The head of the Yale–New Haven team who signed the report clearing Woody Allen of sex abuse is being sued by the federal government for having threatened and intimidated a family very much like Mia Farrow's.
>
> This is a story about a big doctor from Yale who went to war on a little nurse. The big doctor is John Leventhal, with Yale credentials as long as your arm, Pediatrics professor, Yale Medical School, medical director of the Yale–New Haven Child Sexual Abuse program, attending physician Yale–New Haven Hospital, head of the Yale–New Haven team.
>
> Marjorie Eichler is the little nurse, who served and was promoted in the military, did graduate work in public health, adopted children, then tried to move into the

same neighborhood as Leventhal. That's when Leventhal went to war. Eichler brought with her her family, which is amazingly like Mia Farrow's.

Like Farrow, Eichler has 11 children.

Like Farrow, she adopted most of them.

Like Farrow, she adopted several children who are handicapped.

Like Farrow, she adopted children from multiracial backgrounds. Eichler, like Farrow, is white. She's about the same age as Farrow. She lives in Connecticut, where Farrow has a house.

And she had special dealings with Dr. John Leventhal that didn't turn out so great.

This is what the U.S. Attorney General, in a complaint filed in federal court in Connecticut, says the big doctor did to the little nurse and to her children to try to keep the lot of them out of his neighborhood:

He "interfered with, threatened, intimidated, and coerced" the Eichlers. Along with his wife, Beverly Hodgson, a Superior Court judge, he "discriminated against the Eichler family because of handicap and familial status...by soliciting and orchestrating support for a lawsuit to bar the Eichlers from purchasing their home..." unless they got a zoning variance or permit "which other families are not required to obtain."

They did this "to interfere with the Eichlers' fair housing rights, because of the handicaps of the Eichler children and the foster status of some of the children..."

The feds filed this suit against Leventhal and some of his neighbors last fall, about the same time Leventhal started investigating the Allen/Farrow household. The suit was still in force on March 18, when the report came out...

Now none of this stuff—even if every word of it were true—casts doubt on the Leventhal team's central finding: That Woody Allen didn't molest his daughter.

But it sure raises some questions about other matters

> the report went into, like the parenting ability of Mia Farrow, her fitness to deal with matters in the household, whether or not she ought to be in therapy.
>
> And it raises the whole question of whether Farrow's household ought to be judged by a man who is accused of "discriminating" against just this kind of household. (Agus 1993)

The tone taken by the august *New York Times* varied only slightly from that of the tabloid *Newsday*. A story in its Metro section referred to "Yale touchy-feely liberals and people who fancy themselves as progressives" who live in "one of [New Haven's] last predominantly white professional enclaves" (Yarrow 1993). The article, suggesting that Eichler and her clients had been physically threatened, stated that "members of the church, which Eichler attends, are building a fence around her yard to protect her children."

The local press was no kinder. The *New Haven Register* printed DOJ and HUD press releases verbatim, making no effort to verify the government's claims. The weekly tabloid, the *New Haven Advocate*, took every available opportunity to lambaste the residents of the "ritzy white Ronan–Edgehill area" (P. Bass 1992). Coverage of the case in the state's legal press, written by the wife of the *Advocate*'s editor, echoed similarly hostile and scornful sentiments.

In January of 1993, the neighborhood received additional negative attention from the press when resident Zoe Baird was nominated by President Clinton to be Attorney General of the United States. A peculiar partnership of liberals, led by Ralph Nader, and conservatives, led by the *Washington Times*, was formed to make the Ronan-Edgehill case an issue in the confirmation hearings. Nader compiled a twenty-page packet of information on the neighborhood, which he circulated to the Senate Judiciary Committee and to selected members of the press. Within days, the national media were trumpeting stories under such headlines as "Baird May Be Grilled on Housing-Bias Lawsuit" (*Washington Times*), "Confirmation Could Pit Baird against Neighbors" (*Hartford Courant*), "Zoe 'N' the Hood" (*Connecticut Law Tribune*) ("Baird Facts" 1993; C. Bass 1993a; "Confirmation" 1993; Seper 1993; Span 1993a,

1993b). Although Baird was not directly involved in the case, had never attended a meeting of the neighborhood association, and, indeed, was unknown to most residents (she and her husband had lived in the neighborhood for only three years, and she worked in Hartford, not New Haven), the case—along with the controversy over her au pair arrangement with an undocumented alien—did its part in handing the new president the first major defeat of his administration.

DOING THE RIGHT THINGS FOR THE WRONG REASONS? DOING THE WRONG THINGS FOR THE RIGHT REASONS?

Following the Zoe Baird flare-up, the press lost interest and the judge set the matter aside. Early in the summer of 1994, however, the national press began to focus on the larger issue that framed the case: HUD's suppression of citizens' First Amendment rights in its enforcement of the Fair Housing Act.

Renewed press interest in the matter was not accidental. With an increasing number of suits being brought by the government on behalf of the group home industry, the subjects of these prosecutions began to become aware of one another, either by stumbling on stories in newspapers or through database searches. A number of groups, notably the communitarian American Alliance for Rights and Responsibilities, took up our cause, put us in touch with one another, and lobbied vigorously with Congress and the press. Other groups helped out, including Connecticut's Center for First Amendment Rights. And the right-wing press, scenting an opportunity to attack the Clinton administration—and, in particular, a chance to bash the outspokenly gay HUD fair-housing enforcement chief Roberta Achtenberg—entered the fray with gusto in the summer of 1994. As events unfolded, the instinctively liberal Ronan-Edgehill neighborhood found itself allied with some very unlikely partners!

The story moved from the op-ed offerings of the right-wing columnists and the editorial pages of the *Wall Street Journal* and the *Washington Times* to the mainstream features of the *New York Times* and the *Washington Post* late in the summer, when the federal district court in northern California ruled against the government in a suit it had brought against a group of Berkeley residents fighting the location of a group home in their neighborhood. The case was notable not only because it took place in ultraliberal Berkeley, but also because it was the only such case in which a major civil liberties group had vocally defended citizens' First Amendment rights (Achtenberg 1994a, 1994b; Cheshire 1994; "Free Speech" 1994; "Free Speech?" 1994; Gugliotta 1994; "Henry Cisneros" 1994; Hentoff 1994; Holding 1994; "Housing" 1994; HUD 1994; "HUD-Nail" 1994; "HUD Plays" 1994; "HUD Releases" 1994; "In Berkeley" 1994; Leo 1994a, 1994b, 1994c; Ludlow 1994; Price 1994; Raimondo 1994a, 1994b; Roberts 1994a, 1994b; "Statement" 1994; Wells 1994a, 1994b, 1994c, 1994d, 1994e; "Whoa" 1994).

Faced with a firestorm of criticism, HUD made a strategic retreat. Achtenberg admitted that HUD investigators had been overzealous and announced that the department was adopting new guidelines to prevent further rights violations and dropping ongoing suits that involved First Amendment rights ("HUD Drops" 1994; "Statement" 1994; Achtenberg 1994c). HUD's actions, as it turned out, were designed primarily to silence criticism. The new guidelines were difficult to obtain and proved to contain a major loophole: No individual or group who had litigated against a congregate living facility would enjoy constitutional protection. In their wisdom, HUD and DOJ legal staff had decided that the First Amendment right of citizens to petition their government for redress of grievances did not include the right to go to court. As a result, most of the cases that HUD had said it would drop were being pursued with renewed vigor. While the prosecutions continued and the right-wing press and communitarian groups ranted and raged, the *Times* and the *Post* wrote editorials congratulating HUD and promptly dropped all mention of the matter ("HUD Plays" 1994; "HUD Gets" 1994). "Sixty Minutes" likewise dropped the inquiry it had initiated.

In the meantime, the government's suit against Ronan-Edgehill dragged on. In October of 1994, a magistrate judge issued a decision against the neighborhood, but attorneys for the association and the individual defendants demanded that the federal district court hear oral arguments on the First Amendment grounds for dismissing the suit. The judge accepted written arguments. Months went by while he pondered his decision. In December of 1995, two days after Christmas, a fire, started by a spark from an unscreened fireplace, gutted 150 Huntington Street. Eichler and her family were taken in that night by two neighbors who were named defendants in the discrimination suit.

THE STORY BEHIND THE STORY?

As I researched the background of the suit, the inadequacy of existing language and concepts to describe and explain institutions and institutional processes became increasingly evident. Such familiar ideas as "family," "home," "voluntary/nonprofit organization," as well as conventional boundaries between public and private action, were taking on meanings that I couldn't quite grasp.

This epistemological confusion was nowhere more evident than in the concept of the "family" as I found it being defined in the context of new forms of human service provision. In the 1980s, Connecticut's legislature had enacted a statute providing for the establishment of new kinds of foster care facilities—"permanent family residences"—state-licensed entities whose purpose was "to provide permanent care to handicapped children in a home environment and family setting" (Connecticut 1990:17a-154). In ordering local zoning authorities to treat these facilities as families, the legislature unknowingly challenged both the conventional idea of the "traditional" nuclear family (parents and children) and the somewhat more liberal version (no more than two persons unrelated by blood or marriage) set forth in 1974 by the US Supreme Court in a landmark decision on the power of local zoning authorities to regulate density (*Village of Belle Terre et al. v. Boraas,* 416 US 1; 94 S. Ct. 1536 (1974). Justice William Douglas, writing for the majority, upheld municipalities' power to regulate density while balancing their desire to maintain enclaves of single-family residences with a definition of family which permitted persons unrelated by marriage—a provision he singled out as being protective of "alternative life styles."

Justice Thurgood Marshall wrote a powerful dissent which, in retrospect, clearly anticipated the subsequent erosion of conventional conceptions of the family. Marshall argued that the efforts of municipalities to define the nature of families and regulate where they might live placed unnecessary burdens on First Amendment rights of association and privacy. The ordinance upheld by the majority, Marshall charged, was discriminatory because

> it permits any number of persons related by blood or marriage, be it two or twenty, to live in a single household, but it limits to two the number of unrelated persons bound by profession, love, friendship, religious or political affiliation, or mere economics who can occupy a single home. Belle Terre imposes upon those who deviate from the community norm in their choice of living companions significantly greater restrictions than are applied to residential groups who are related by blood or marriage, and compose the established order within the community. The village has, in effect, acted to fence out those individuals whose choice of lifestyle differs from that of its current residents.

In limiting the occupancy density of only those homes occupied by unrelated persons, the Belle Terre ordinance reached beyond control of the use of land or the density of population and undertook to regulate the way people choose to associate with each other within the privacy of their own homes. The ordinance, Marshall noted, imposed no restriction on the number of persons who might live in a house as long as they were related by blood or marriage, no matter how distantly. But it specifically restricted the number of unrelated persons who might live in a home to no more than two. Within the majority's reasoning, an extended family of a dozen or more might live in a small bungalow, while three unrelated elderly and retired persons could not occupy the large manor house next door. "By limiting unrelated households to two persons while placing no limitation on households of related individuals," Marshall concluded,

> the village has embarked upon its commendable course in a constitutionally faulty vessel. I would find the challenged ordinance unconstitutional. But I would not ask the village to abandon its goal of providing quiet streets, little traffic, and a pleasant and reasonably priced environment in

which families might raise their children. Rather, I would commend the village to continue to pursue those purposes but by means of more carefully drawn and evenhanded legislation.

From Marshall's standpoint, "family," as an expression of the constitutionally protected right of association, could be anything people wanted it to be; hence the use of zoning powers to regulate family composition rather than mere density was a clear violation of the rights of association and privacy.

In Belle Terre, the court did not consider the knottier question raised by the Ronan-Edgehill case: whether the corporate rather than familial status of those occupying a residential property affected its treatment under municipal zoning ordinances. Eichler's family certainly fit Marshall's definition of a constitutionally protected "alternative lifestyle"; but did its corporate status as a licensed human services provider render it a commercial and, thus, a nonconforming entity requiring zoning review?

New Haven's land use ordinances accorded special treatment for eleemosynary uses. Places of worship, for example, were entirely exempt from the zoning ordinance; they could locate wherever they pleased and carry on virtually any activities they wished.[3] Similarly, child day-care centers could locate anywhere in the city. Within this framework, was Eichler's family/nonprofit corporation an eleemosynary or a commercial entity? A number of leading nonprofit scholars, notably economists Henry Hansmann (1987) and Burton Weisbrod (1989), had argued that there are important differences between "traditional" nonprofits—voluntary organizations supported by donations—and "commercial/entrepreneurial" nonprofits, which derived their revenues from earned income (sales of services, grants, and contracts); they did not believe that the latter should enjoy the tax-exempt and largely unregulated status of genuinely charitable enterprises.

Clearly, there was no simple answer to the question of how an entity like There's No Place Like Home, Inc. (TNPLH) should be treated. It had many of the characteristics of a traditional voluntary entity: Eichler, a public health professional, had acted on her convictions and established a facility to deal with a pressing need—the growing number of HIV-positive "children of AIDS" whose parents had either died of the disease or were unable to care for them. Like many of the community-based nonprofit service providers established in the wake of deinstitutionalization, TNPLH was an expression of its founder's deep personal commitment and willingness to pioneer new forms of treatment and care for the disabled and dependent. Given the outrageous discrimination to which AIDS sufferers and those seeking to care for them had been subjected, Eichler's willingness to sue her neighbors and the neighborhood association rather than negotiate with them was understandable.

At the same time, I discovered that TNPLH was a part of a complex contracting regime that had come to dominate the provision of human services in Connecticut, and most other states, over the past decade and a half. Eichler's "family," along with several hundred other community-based service providers, was tied to a giant nonprofit holding company, the Corporation for Independent Living (CIL), which used state funds to purchase, renovate, and lease properties to service providers. CIL's financial services arm managed the financial assets of the service providers' clients and had a profitable sideline of selling and leasing special equipment for the disabled to service providers.

The scale of CIL's operations was suggested by a 1992 report from Connecticut's Office of Legislative Research, which showed that over a three-year period, 85 percent of the state's entire economic development budget of more than $200 million had been allocated to private nonprofit corporations involved with developing community-based facilities for the disabled ("Helping Connecticut's Businesses" 1992). CIL received the lion's share of these funds—a total of some $134.7 million (Pazniokas 1994). Further research suggested that this was only a fraction of the funds taken in by CIL since its establishment in 1979. In 1987, a year not covered by the OLR report, CIL received $77 million in bonded funds (Reports of Negotiated Bond Sales 1987–1990). Furthermore, the OLR report did not monitor operating revenues received by CIL or its affiliates, nor did it include figures on development activities being undertaken by CIL in other states as the corporation began to follow the lead of other nonprofit human services providers into operations on a national scale (CIL 1991a).

For a nonprofit enterprise, CIL broke new ground in terms of structural complexity. It was a nonprofit real-estate holding company that leased its properties (numbering 275 in 1991) to perhaps as many as ninety-three affiliated provider agencies, each of them incorporated separately. The latter could not be regarded merely as client agencies, however, because eleven of CIL's officers and directors were executive directors of member agencies to which CIL, its subsidiaries, and related firms leased furnishings and supplies and provided financial and property management services. In this sense, the company had features of a consumer cooperative, though it was not formally incorporated as such. The CIL's board more resembled that of a trade association or for-profit business than a charitable organization, since it included no representatives of state government, client groups, or the general public but rather was dominated by social service professionals, most of them officers and directors of provider agencies with which the holding company did business.[4]

From newspaper stories and fugitive materials produced by unions and client advocates, I learned that the CIL also departed from the conventional donative nonprofit profile in its impressive political power. As reports of its financial activities suggested, building the privatized human services infrastructure was the largest public works project undertaken by the state since the construction of the interstate highway system—and, like the highway system, it inevitably became entwined with Connecticut's quasi-feudal system of political patronage. According to a report compiled by union activists unhappy with the company's "open shop" stance, it was standard practice for CIL insiders and political favorites to receive advance information about properties the corporation intended to purchase (Service Employees International Union 1992). These insiders could gain control of such properties, which they then sold to CIL for hefty mark-ups. The union charged that renovation contracts and legal services, which were seldom bid out, followed a similar pattern of political favoritism. Such charges seemed partially substantiated when it was revealed that Edward Marcus, chair of the state's Democratic Party, was not only a major operator of group homes but also had sold properties to the service providers he controlled and, acting as attorney for both seller and purchaser, had charged enormous amounts of money for handling property transactions between himself and the group homes (C. Bass 1994b, 1994c; Bixby 1994b, 1994c; Christofferson 1994).

CIL's political clout stemmed also from its capacity to mobilize powerful organized interest groups. With membership including service providers in nearly every municipality in the state and statewide advocacy groups such as associations of retarded citizens, Catholic charities, disabled veterans, and so on, CIL was able to fill hearing rooms with vocal partisans and mount letter-writing campaigns. Its power was such that no elected official in the state was willing to speak or act against it; in fact, Connecticut's politically ambitious attorney general, Richard Blumenthal, had been one of the CIL's most active partisans.

Above all, CIL's political clout came from its aggressive litigation activities on behalf of the disabled. Following the 1988 amendments to the Fair Housing Act, which broadened the definition of housing discrimination and put in place a process through which those who complained of discrimination had access to the full resources of the federal government, the group home industry appeared to have framed an agenda to eradicate efforts by municipalities, citizens groups, and individuals to oppose or even question the location of group homes ("State Sues Landowner" 1988; "Group Home to Get Land" 1988; Hamilton 1990; Mariano 1990, 1992). With assistance from the Connecticut Civil Liberties Union, CIL-affiliated groups introduced a new element into the struggle for the rights of the disabled by adapting a technique pioneered by for-profit developers of housing and commercial properties—the "SLAPP suit" (Strategic Lawsuit against Public Participation) (Sills 1993).

The group home industry's first foray into litigation following the passage of the 1988 amendments involved a suit with striking similarities to the Ronan-Edgehill case. In 1988, the nonprofit Stewart B. McKinney Foundation proposed to locate a facility for homeless AIDS sufferers in a residential neighborhood of suburban Fairfield, Connecticut (*Stewart B. McKinney Foundation v. Town Plan and Zoning*

Commission of Fairfield 1992). Neighbors brought pressure on town officials to review the zoning status of the proposal, which they viewed as a change of use from residential to institutional. At private meetings and public hearings, citizens expressed their opinions freely and often indiscreetly. Facing a rising tide of opposition to their plans, backers of the facility initiated a housing discrimination complaint that was ultimately decided by the federal district court. The judge, relying on the 1988 fair housing amendments as well as two decades of civil rights decisions, pointed out that it was not necessary for plaintiffs to prove that the town was "motivated by some purposeful, malicious desire" to discriminate against the disabled or that its officials "were motivated solely, primarily, or even predominantly" by concerns about the disabilities of the facilities' future tenants; they merely needed to demonstrate that the disabilities were a "motivating factor." In effect, the court ruled that public hearings at which citizens expressed opinions that could be construed as discriminatory tainted the proceedings and rendered the municipality liable for practicing housing discrimination. Such liability proved to be so costly that public hearings in Connecticut on the location of group homes effectively ceased at that point.

It is impossible even now to know with any certainty whether the litigation against the Ronan-Edgehill neighborhood was a product of calculation by the group home industry or just a lucky accident, although circumstantial evidence seems to favor the former supposition. To obtain the kind of landmark decision it had achieved in the McKinney Foundation suit, the industry needed a neighborhood with a sufficiently strong aversion to being labeled discriminatory and sufficiently deep pockets to fight long and hard rather than settle out of court. It appears that the industry and its friends in government had targeted Ronan-Edgehill. In the spring of 1992, three weeks before filing suit, Paul Hancock, chief of the Justice Department's housing and civil enforcement division, told a conference of the National Fair Housing Alliance in Washington, DC, that the department had been "flooded" with family-status cases and went on to detail one such case then under investigation. Without naming the parties or the community, according to the *Washington Post*,

> he described a case in which neighborhood residents objected when a single mother with six adopted and four foster children tried to move in, saying the woman wanted to establish an illegal group home.

"Because all of the children are racial and ethnic minorities and all have the AIDS virus, Hancock said the community's action probably violated laws protecting families with children, minorities and the handicapped," the account continued (C. Bass 1992b).

Clearly the Ronan-Edgehill matter was not regarded in Washington as a routine case; to advance its litigation agenda toward the goal of obtaining decisions that would silence citizens groups and individual citizens, the industry needed defendants with deep pockets who would, because of their political inclinations, stoutly resist being branded bigots. There were, moreover, a variety of curious ties between the Fairfield and New Haven cases, including the active involvement of Shelley Geballe, the prominent civil rights attorney who led the litigation in the Fairfield case and who was a close personal friend and advisor to Eichler, and the fact that the two neighborhood residents most active in stirring up opposition to TNPLH knew the nature of the disabilities of the facility's clients and failed to share this information with their neighbors.

These litigations further underscored in my own mind the erosion of conventional concepts and categories. Just as the constitutionalization of disabilities had transformed the relief of private disputes into arenas for broadly defining public policy (effectively privatizing the policy process), so litigation activities pursued by a coalition of service providers, state agencies, and groups like the ACLU and its Connecticut chapter aligned many of the traditional defenders of civil liberties against individuals seeking to exercise them—a stance which seriously split the state's civil liberties bar (Bass 1992b; Memorandum 1993). Of the dozens of suits brought by group home operators against individuals and citizens groups around the United States in the wake of the 1988 Fair Housing Act amendments, in only a single instance did a chapter of the ACLU take the side of citizens seeking to exercise their First Amendment rights ("Free Speech Advocates Find a Fight in Berkeley"

1994; Holding 1994; "Housing Opponents Cleared" 1994; "HUD Releases Opinion on Berkeley Housing Complaint" 1994; "In Berkeley, a Victory for Free Speech" 1994; "Small-Mindedness Knows No City Limits" 1994; "Statement by HUD Secretary Henry G. Cisneros" 1994).

The confusion is further compounded by the pervasiveness of discrimination on the basis of race, gender, and disability and the extent to which discrimination has been woven into the very fabric of liberal social legislation. *Our Town: Race, Housing, and the Soul of Suburbia* (1995), a revealing study of the landmark Mount Laurel exclusionary zoning cases—described by its authors as "the *Rowe v. Wade* of fair housing"—shows in disturbing detail the racist agenda that framed the government programs subsidizing suburbanization and de facto segregation in northern cities. "Zoning," the authors write,

> has been the chief instrument by which suburbs have held themselves apart from the poor. Once, overtly racial zoning was routine and certain neighborhoods were designated as "white." While that practice was outlawed by the U.S. Supreme Court many years ago, subtler forms of discrimination, focused more on economics than on race, were substituted. Defenders of suburbia are fond of describing these rules—which, as in Mount Laurel Township, fixed a minimum house size and building-lot size and prohibited multifamily dwellings—as representing the will of the people. But since zoning decisions are made entirely by the town's present residents, they alone have the power to decide what is in everyone's best interest—to decide who gets to live in our town, now and into the future. (Kirp, Dwyers, and Rosenthal 1995:8)

The white residents of Mount Laurel were outraged to hear themselves labeled racists. Blacks and whites had lived together in the township since the seventeenth century and, generation after generation, descendants of white Quaker families and descendants of their slaves had grown up together, worked together, and helped one another in hard times. In their minds, racists were red-necked, sheet-wearing night-riders, not people like themselves who were simply trying to enforce a zoning ordinance that followed state statutes and national land-use planning models. They could not acknowledge the extent to which their defense of the community's power to define its character through zoning amounted to complicity in a deeply embedded system of racial exclusion.

The residents of New Haven's Ronan-Edgehill neighborhood were similarly unable to grasp the exclusionary subtexts of the city's zoning ordinance. As Thurgood Marshall had declared nearly two decades earlier, the Belle Terre decision's definition of family had far more to do with regulating lifestyles than with regulating density. The boundaries between family and nonprofit service providers are likely to be further obscured because of changes in the group home industry itself and the continuing evolution of public policy driven by coalitions of disability advocates, legal activists, and the judiciary.

Because the community-based system of treatment and care that gave rise to the group home industry developed from the ground up in response to court orders and was financed by various forms of slack in federal and state human services programs (such as Medicaid waivers and revenues from private activity bonding), it often produced outcomes that dismayed even its most outspoken supporters. The chief justifications for deinstitutionalization—reduced cost and increased quality of care—have been largely discredited. The cost of the system, to the limited extent that accurate revenue estimates are available, is substantial and largely uncontrollable (Bixby 1994a).[5] State agency administrators concede the difficulties of monitoring so decentralized a system and admit that its complexity invites potential mismanagement and client abuse. Recognizing this, the families of some clients have become active and vocal opponents of group homes (Bondy 1986).

In response to these concerns, states like Connecticut are considering moving from a group home to a foster care model, eliminating the nonprofit "middleman" in service provision. But further decentralizing the system of service provision, even if it reduced the opportunities for financial misconduct, would also eliminate the nominal levels of formal accountability to the state offered by the nonprofit form. And it would further confuse the distinctions between families and government agencies.

Certainly the Corporation for Independent Living has seen where the future lies. Since the early 1990s, it has been shifting its programmatic interests away from group homes in favor of "affordable housing" (Trotta 1994a, 1994b; Ferguson 1994, 1996a, 1996b, 1996c; Vernon News Notes 1994; Stansbury 1994; Rainwater 1995; Hathaway 1995). Whether this is mere opportunism—taking advantage of the same activist coalition to achieve different goals—or whether "affordable housing" is a proxy for expanding the settings for foster care of the disabled is anybody's guess.

END GAME

In February of 1995, District Court Judge T. F. Gilroy Daly ruled on the motions filed by attorneys for the neighborhood association and named defendants which had argued that, in branding residents' petitioning the government for redress of grievances an act of discrimination, the government had violated their First Amendment rights. In dismissing the suit, the judge condemned the government's "seeming vindictiveness" in pursuing the defendants: "Civil rights advocates," he declared, "should be first to note the importance of the ability to resort to courts to test novel issues of law without fear" of being punished by the government.

By then I had succeeded to the presidency of the neighborhood association and could fully appreciate the damage the case had done. Residents were afraid to join, fearing that doing so would render them legally liable. A few stalwarts stayed on the board of directors, but it was practically impossible to recruit new members. The neighborhood was deeply divided between those favoring and opposing the association's stance on TNPLH—though their positions were generally based on ignorance of what our stance had been, since we had been unable to provide members with information about the suit for fear that the government would use it as evidence against us.

Despite HUD's public proclamations of having changed its position of citizens' exercise of First Amendment rights in housing matters, despite Judge Daly's carefully reasoned dismissal of the government's case, I knew that the Justice Department could appeal the decision, and my research indicated that the policy and political stakes were sufficiently great to make it highly likely that they would. If so, the neighborhood would have to face some hard realities. The association alone had already spent nearly $30,000 on the suit, the named defendants at least as much all together. If the government appealed, carrying through the next phase of litigation could cost an additional $20,000. If the government lost on the appellate level, the case might go on to the US Supreme Court, and if we lost there, the case would go to trial—for these three years of legal jockeying involved only motions to dismiss the suit on constitutional grounds; the questions of fact had yet to be heard. It was a financial black hole. With a dwindling and fearful membership and the unlimited resources of the government deployed against us, it seemed clear to me that we would have to set our principles aside and settle.

The circuit court decision did buy us a little breathing room. I called a general meeting of association members to explain the suit and lay out our options. Although the sentiment of the meeting was to fight on, I didn't see anyone reaching for their checkbook. So when, a few days later—indeed, on the very last day an appeal could be filed—the government announced that it intended to take the case to the federal court of appeals, I convened the board and recommended that we seek a settlement. The issues went well beyond our little zoning concern. The case involved the power of a multibillion-dollar industry and the future direction of public policy with regard to the care of the disabled. In my view, these were matters best decided by Congress, and I was encouraged to learn that Congress was planning hearings on revising the 1988 amendments to the Fair Housing Act to prevent abuses of citizens' First Amendment rights ("A bill to amend the Fair Housing Act to provide sanctions for the filing of certain complaints," H.R. 4954, 1994).

The association was not alone in its exhaustion. One of the individual defendants had taken a job overseas and was anxious to resolve the matter. Accordingly, we instructed our lawyers to seek a settlement. As it turned out, the government was also ready to settle. The Clinton administration was gearing up for an election and did not want to give the President's enemies another inflammatory issue. Furthermore, the group home industry's objectives had been largely achieved in May of 1995, when the US Supreme Court handed down a landmark decision in its favor in a case revising the definition of family set forth in the 1973 Belle Terre decision and overturning local zoning ordinances that had been used to limit the proliferation of group homes in residential neighborhoods (*City of Edmonds, Petitioner, v. Oxford House, Inc.*, 1995; Baumann 1995; De Leon 1995; "Disability Advocates Win Zoning Case in Supreme Court" 1995; "'Family' Defined Under Fair Housing Act" 1995; Lauber 1995). While the court did not in so many words eliminate the power of localities to regulate land use, in effect it had done so. The majority opinion, written by Justice Ginsburg, carefully distinguished between the characteristics of ordinances regulating density (a legitimate zoning concern) and those that had the effect of regulating lifestyles (to which the court extended constitutional protection).

Because no official reports of the court's decision were available at the time the neighborhood association was weighing its options (it would take several more months before we would know the full extent to which our position had been repudiated), it had only marginal impact on our deliberations. But the government knew how thoroughly it had been vindicated and, in the interest of political expediency, knew that it could afford to be magnanimous. In the settlement reached in July 1995, the government agreed to the case in exchange for a $30,000 cash payment to the plaintiff and a letter welcoming the Eichler family to the neighborhood. The defendants' attorneys managed to persuade the government to drop the all language in the settlement document that suggested that the defendants had discriminated against Eichler. The neighborhood association—or what was left of it—raised its $15,000 share of the settlement and dutifully tendered it to Eichler, along with a letter of welcome, early in August of 1995.

KNOWLEDGE WORKERS AND THE NEW POLITY

One final element is worth considering. Michael Winerip's *9 Highland Road* (1994), perhaps the most detailed account of the group home industry, suggests that the rise of the industry was spearheaded by the kinds of people Peter Drucker refers to as "knowledge workers." Like New Haven's Marjorie Eichler, Linda Slezak, the director of the group home in Winerip's book, was an accredited professional—a social worker—who, with deinstitutionalization, had become an intermediary between public agencies and nonprofit service providers. Slezak, like Eichler, was simultaneously involved in the treatment and administrative sides of her facility's operations. She helped select the site, lobbied with local and state authorities for its establishment, worked with the parent organization (in Slezak's case, the nonprofit Angelo Melillo Mental Health Center), screened prospective clients, and so on. Like a true knowledge worker, her skills were varied, portable, and more attached to cause and career than to any particular corporate base.

So what is the entity that occupies 150 Huntington Street in New Haven? Is it a family? Is it a household? Is it a voluntary organization? A nonprofit corporation? A social welfare/human services regime? An arm of government? The matter gets even murkier when proprietary enterprises—for-profits—buy up nonprofit service providers, which is happening with increasing frequency.

And what about the boundaries between public and private spheres? Traditionally, Americans have assumed that the First Amendment guaranteed them the right to speak and write freely, to associate with whom they pleased, and to petition the government, including the courts, for the redress of grievances. But the Fair Housing Act and a host of decisions at the lower levels of the federal court system have challenged those rights. While the question of whether "hate speech" is protected constitutionally is fairly clear-cut, since discriminatory intent can be clearly inferred from its content, intent is far more elusive in situations like the Ronan-Edgehill case. As the Fair Housing Act is currently interpreted at HUD, any action—whether carried on in public or private—can be used as evidence for discriminatory intent. This means, in effect, that there is no private sphere of action—that all actions, judged from the standpoint of their impact on public events, are public in character.

But the real issue here is not what is legally or constitutionally correct. It is, rather, the question of the configuration of forces that will lead to new constructions and resolutions of such disputes. Liberals like the residents of the Ronan-Edgehill neighborhood spearheaded the legal doctrines and precedents that underlay the antidiscrimination provisions of the Fair Housing Act. In their public sympathies, they have always stood with provision for the poor, dependent, and disabled. But the instruments they created were available for use by anyone; and once the liberal order lost its hold, were used in unexpected ways.

The alignment of the liberal press on these issues is especially curious. The *New York Times*, the *Washington Post*, the *Nation*, and similar publications have always been known as zealous defenders of civil liberties. But in the age of the contracting regime, civil liberties mean something quite different from what they did half a century ago. The *Times*, especially, has been outrageously biased in its coverage of human services contracting.[6] It covered the HUD/First Amendment controversy sparingly and was quick to proclaim the new guidelines a symbol of the department's devotion to the Constitution ("HUD Play" 1994). (In the meantime, it declined to publish letters and op-ed pieces pointing out the flaws in the guidelines.)

To call attention to the curious transformation of the liberal press since the 1970s is hardly new. In the "good old days," the establishment press stuck with the Establishment. Even such dissenting acts as the publication of the Pentagon Papers and the *Washington Post*'s role in Watergate did not seem inconsistent with the liberal press's overall devotion to the institutions and values of the Establishment. But the papers' stance on contracting regimes seems to represent something entirely new. The pervasive use of class-biased language, the glorification of the ostensibly oppressed (whose circumstances were used as a front for advancing a wealthy and powerful industry), and the disparagement of the supposedly privileged (who were actually beleaguered and naive, if well-intentioned, urban homesteaders), all seem to point to a new reportorial ethos. The new journalists appear to have found common cause with their fellow knowledge workers, the entrepreneurial human services professionals. (This is certainly suggested by the fact that Geraldo Rivera's coverage of Willowbrook came about through his college friendship with people who became staffers at the institution and who used these personal ties to advance their professional interests.)

All this gives particular resonance to Peter Drucker's characterization of the knowledge workers as an emerging class. So does the new paradigm of the "new institutionalist" organizational scholars, who have jettisoned the neat old public/private distinctions and firm-focused analyses in favor of a messier interest in the interaction of public, for-profit, and nonprofit firms in "organizational fields," industries, and markets.

BEYOND CIVIL SOCIETY

It may be that this confusion of categories, this erosion of narrative, this failure of institutions is a prelude to the emergence of a new form of civil society. Much as groups like the communitarians are striving to ensure that the new society will embody what they regard as the best features of the old, this seems a vain hope. For one thing, traditional civil society assumed clearly demarcated arenas of public life and activity—arenas which, if the collapsed boundaries between state and family and public and private speech are any indication, seem to be rapidly disappearing.

One indicator of the change may be detected in the transformation of public space at the end of the twentieth century. Many critics believe that the democratic public spaces characteristic of American cities—the bases of the social heterogeneity, physical proximity, free movement, and desire for collectivity that defined "authentic urbanity"—are being replaced by privatized enclaves (Sorkin 1992). In his essay "Fortress Los Angeles," UCLA urban planner and political economist Mike Davis (1992) argues that in Los Angeles, "once a paradise of free beaches, luxurious parks, and 'cruising strips'—genuinely democratic space is virtually extinct." The insulated residential and commercial enclaves of the privileged classes "rely upon the social imprisonment of a third-world service proletariat in increasingly repressive ghettos and barrios." As public amenities shrink, with the closing of libraries and playgrounds, the neglect of parks, and the desolation and increasing dangerousness of streets, public resources are being diverted for developments that further privatize public space and subsidize new exclusive enclaves. Though described as an "urban renaissance," such efforts are, in Davis's view, "only a triumphal gloss laid over the brutalization of its inner-city neighborhoods and the stark divisions of class and race represented in its built environment" (Davis 1992:156).

Davis's colleague, M. Christine Boyer, sees contemporary redevelopments such as New York's South Street Seaport as creating "isolated, self-enclosed patches of development" (Boyer 1992:182). Although insulated from the city as it actually exists, these enclaves retain a connection "through historical allusions to the traditional vision of the city" (1992:184). This use of historical references, framed by a carefully manipulated visual and social environment, makes the real city disappear from view with its "chaos, class distinctions, its snares and vices" (1992:186). According to Boyer, the enclaves' use of the past is highly conventionalized and manipulated; they are simulated traditions that serve to obscure the city's actual past and to engender illusions about its present. "On the surface of these tableaux," she writes,

> everything seems steeped in tradition. The way it was has supposedly become the way it is. Yet these nostalgic constructions only refer to history obliquely by appropriating styles of clothing, architectural environments, and furnishings to create a mood through which the past is filtered and perceived. These stylized historical tableaux, on one level, are self-conscious attempts to regain a centered world, to reestablish a mythical base on which American moral, political, and social traditions might stand... [They] link the past to the present through visual recreations that gloss over real social change by capitalizing on the yearnings for lost innocence, heroic feats, adventures, explorations, and conquests. (Boyer 1992:191)

The problem is that these "well-composed fragments," representing themselves as reality, upstage "the neglected in-between spaces" (Boyer 1992:184)—the actual domain of inclusive public space: "The awareness of highways in disrepair, charred and abandoned tenements, the scourge of drugs, the wandering homeless, subway breakdowns and deteriorating buses, visual litter and auditory bombardment—all are erased and ignored in the idealized city tableaux" (1992:191). While insulating the privileged from disturbing realities—and from any sense of their civic responsibilities—these enclaves also serve as backdrops for forms of consumption that further distance the middle classes from awareness of their connection to a broader public.

Davis's and Boyer's left bias prevents them from seeing that the efforts of the privileged to create privatized enclaves secure from the turbulence of the urban lumpen is not the only force driving the erosion of public space. Government too is responsible. Public-service contracting regimes are the state-promoted analogs to malls and upper-crust residential enclaves, all of which subvert the domains of genuinely democratic public life.

This was the outcome feared by the early-nineteenth-century opponents of voluntary associations and corporations, who called such entities *imperium in imperio*—states within the State—and who fretted about the legislatures "parceling out the State into little commonwealths" in which private laws and private interests would subvert the common good and undermine the popular will. As it happened, opposition to corporations was concerted enough to generally ensure that the power of firms was limited. With the exception of a few company towns, like the Boston Associates' Lowell textile complex in the 1830s, George Pullman's model industrial community in the 1890s, and a few dozen particularly absolutist mining and factory towns, the reach of firms seldom extended far beyond the workplace.

But in the twenty-first century, with the boundaries between public and private domains crumbling and public power being granted out to various kinds of private interests—the privileged domains of wealth (elite residential enclaves), professional authority (public-services contracting regimes), commerce (malls), communications (cable and electronic information services)—the power of the states within the State is becoming unlimited. The notion of equality before the law, as the Ronan-Edgehill case suggests, has been supplanted by a legal ethos in which "protected groups," whether defined by race, disability, class, or influence, may carve up public life to serve their own purposes. And nonprofit organizations and voluntary associations, which, whatever their failings, at least professed an allegiance to a greater public good, have become—as the Founding Fathers feared—"the mortal diseases under which popular governments everywhere have perished" (Madison 1961:77).

This grim possibility was confirmed when, after circulating a draft of this and several other papers to colleagues for comment and criticism, I received a letter from one who was a legal advocate for the rights of the disabled. She pointed out that my mentioning the disability of the clients of TNPLH and the McKinney Foundation was a violation of federal law and demanded that I eliminate the references (despite the fact that the specific disability was mentioned in the court records of both cases and had been widely noted in press reports). She copied her letter to the Connecticut Civil Liberties Union (CCLU) and a law firm which had taken an active part in the McKinney litigation, clearly with the intent of sparking an effort to legally suppress the paper.

I put out an inquiry over several scholarly listservers devoted to public policy—with a tag requesting cross-posting—in which I asked whether anyone knew of any precedent for the suppression of scholarly work of the sort that the civil liberties–group home industry people seemed to be attempting. The query found its way to the listserver of the community of legal scholars, several of whose subscribers not only professed astonishment that such a thing would be attempted but also directly contacted the leadership of the CCLU to express their outrage. Colleagues on the Yale Law School faculty, who had kept their distance from the Ronan-Edgehill suit, were surprisingly helpful when their scholarly prerogatives were so challenged.

The effort to suppress this and a companion paper (a historical study of the rise of human services contracting in Connecticut) died aborning, but the warning it carried to future researchers should not be forgotten. The "enclaving" of public life clearly applies not only to land use, but to "intellectual property."

Notes

The research on which this paper is based was underwritten by the Lilly Endowment, Inc., and the Program on Non-Profit Organizations, Yale University. I am particularly grateful to Philip and Sarah Bondy, Nora Groce, Glenn Davis, and Shelley Geballe for providing me with valuable insights into the dilemmas of service provision under deinstitutionalization. Elaine Backman, Kirsten Gronbjerg, Carl Milofsky, Judith Saidel, Steven Rathgeb Smith, and Melissa Middleton Stone helped me understand the larger significance of my Connecticut findings. Martin LeGault of the Corporation for Independent Living generously supplied me with information about the CIL. Rep. William Dyson provided me with legislative reports that would otherwise have been unobtainable. Former Rep. Irving Stolberg, who served as Speaker of the General Assembly during the 1980s, allowed me to interview him about the legislative history of group home statutes in Connecticut. Roger Conners of the Alliance for Rights and Responsibilities, Barbara Pressley of Nashua, New Hampshire, and attorneys Andrew Bowman and Marjorie Shansky helped me to understand the legal implications of fair housing legislation.

1. Of the major community studies undertaken by social scientists in the course of the twentieth century, only Lloyd Warner's *Yankee City* (1941–59) paid real attention to voluntary organizations. The Lynds (1929), Hollingshead (1949), and other classic studies ignored them. Though the pluralists gave lip service to voluntary associations, their studies of communities—Robert Dahl's *Who Governs?* (1961), G. William Domhoff's *Who Really Rules?* (1978), and Nelson Polsby's *Community Power and Political Theory* (1980)—provided detailed analyses of government and corporate boards but ignored nonprofits.

2. Before taking the bench, Hodgson had been a civil-rights litigator at Koskoff, Koskoff and Beider in Bridgeport. In 1981 she won a US Supreme Court case extending protection against sex discrimination in education to employees under Title IX. In 1989, two years after becoming a superior court judge, she issued a landmark ruling requiring the state to pay attorneys' fees on behalf of poor women who successfully challenged Connecticut's restrictions on Medicaid-funded abortions. (The state supreme court later overturned the ruling.) In 1991, Hodgson was interviewed as a potential candidate for the federal bench. Leventhal, the pediatrician, is affiliated with the Yale Child Study Center. He was a plaintiff in the suit that forced the state Department of Children and Youth Services to agree to increase spending and overhaul its system of caring for children in need—like the foster children DCYS placed with Marjorie Eichler, the children that the Ronan-Edgehill Neighborhood Association fought to keep out. Hodgson and Leventhal retained William H. Clendenen of New Haven (another civil-rights lawyer, formerly a legal-aid attorney) as their counsel and public spokesman in the Eichler matter.

3. This was more or less the rule in American zoning until recently. Over the past decade, as churches have broadened their activities beyond sacerdotal functions, running day schools, day-care centers, and other social services, many communities have begun to regulate places of worship. New Haven, however—alone among Connecticut's 160 municipalities—has resisted this trend.

4. For an important case study of the impact of contracting on governance, see Melissa M. Stone's "Competing Contexts: The Evolution of an Organizational Governance Structure in Multiple Environments" (1993).

5. The press and legislators are questioning human services contractors' claims that group homes are less costly than state institutions. "In a quiet neighborhood in Wethersfield," a recent article on the subject began, "is an attractive ranch house where four people live at a cost to taxpayers of $1,977 a day. That adds up to $721,000 a year." The article went on to single out the CIL as a profiteer: "The Wethersfield house is one of the most expensive group homes in Connecticut. It is owned by the Corporation for Independent Living, a non-profit company that collects about $1 million in rent from the state every month." CIL, the article continued, "is the dominant private landlord in its field, having converted hundreds of residential houses into group homes for mentally retarded people. Business boomed during the late 1980s while the state was moving people out of Mansfield." But, the article suggested, times had changed: "Officials in Connecticut and other states now are shunning the costly group-home concept in favor of providing services to retarded people in their own houses or apartments...'The era of group homes is over,' declared Margaret Dignoti, the longtime executive director of The ARC/Connecticut, an advocacy organization for retarded citizens" (Bixby 1994a).

6. Between 1987 and 1991, Michael Winerip devoted twenty of his "Our Towns" feature in the *Times* Metro section to group homes. These pieces, prominently featured on the first page of the section, were unabashed in their advocacy of the group home idea and unremittingly scornful about neighborhood concerns. There is good reason to believe that Winerip's interest in group homes reflected a policy position taken by the *Times* brass. When Winerip wrote his book on group homes, *9 Highland Road*, the *Times* published an extensive excerpt in its Sunday magazine section and gave it major and complimentary attention in its book review section, describing it as "an unobtrusive, nonjudgmental illumination" of the subject. The review was widely reprinted in papers throughout the country. That Winerip's views mirrored his employers' is also suggested by the fact that other *Times* reporters writing on the group home phenomenon have taken a similarly slanted line (Yarrow 1993). Pieces praising group homes ("Foster Mother Puts Sweat, Money, Heart into Opening a Group Home," 9/14/94) invariably receive favorable and prominent placement; stories revealing group home abuses are downplayed. The *Times*, it should be noted, is notorious for using its news coverage to promote its owners' political views (Talese 1969; Taylor 1990).

Appendix: General Statutes of Connecticut

Title 17a. Social and Human Services and Resources
Chapter 319a. Child Welfare
Part II. Child-Care Facilities and Child-Placing Agencies
Conn. Gen. Stat. @ 17a-154 (1990)

Sec. 17a-154. (Formerly Sec. 17-52a). "Permanent family residence."

Definition. Requirements

(a) For purposes of this section and section 17a-155, "permanent family residence" means a child care facility which meets the requirements of subsection (b) of this section and subsection (a) of section 17a-155 and which is licensed as a permanent family residence by the department of children and youth services, hereinafter referred to as the department.

(b) To be licensed as a permanent family residence, a child care facility must meet the following requirements:

(1) The facility must be designed to provide permanent care to handicapped children in a home environment and family setting;

(2) At the time the initial license is issued, the permanent family care must be provided by two adult persons, hereinafter referred to as the parents, or upon the commissioner's approval, one adult whose principal residence is the permanent family residence, who may, but need not, have children other than foster children living with them;

(3) The parent or parents must occupy, as their principal residence, a building which is designed for residential use by one or two families and which is: (A) Owned or leased by the parent or parents or (B) owned or leased by a nonstock corporation, one of whose purposes is to protect handicapped children by providing a home environment and family setting for handicapped children;

(4) The principal occupation of at least one parent and, in appropriate cases to be determined by the department, both parents, must be to provide direct and regular care to the foster children placed in their residence; and

(5) The parent or parents must have indicated their intent to provide permanent foster care to handicapped children placed in their home by the department or by other child-placing agencies.

(c) Permanent family residences licensed by the department pursuant to the provisions of this section and section 17a-155 shall be deemed private dwellings occupied by one family by the commissioner of health services for purposes of compliance with the State Public Health Code and by the commissioner of public safety for purposes of compliance with the state building and fire safety codes.

Title 17a. Social and Human Services and Resources
Chapter 319a. Child Welfare
Part II. Child-Care Facilities and Child-Placing Agencies
Conn. Gen. Stat. @ 17a-155 (1990)

Sec. 17a-155. (Formerly Sec. 17-52b). Regulations

(a) Within one year from May 23, 1980, the department shall promulgate any necessary regulations establishing additional requirements for the licensure of permanent family residences. These regulations may limit the number of foster children which may be placed in a permanent family residence. The commissioner may in an appropriate case waive any requirements established in such regulations.

(b) Notwithstanding the provisions of section 29-292, the state fire marshal shall, within two years after May 23, 1980, adopt amendments to the fire safety code in accordance with the provisions of chapter 54 concerning permanent family residences designed to care for seven or more handicapped children. In developing the regulations the state fire marshal shall consult with the department of children and youth services and any other interested persons. The amendments to the fire safety code may apply different standards to newly constructed and existing one and two-family dwellings, provided, however, the amendments shall not apply to permanent family residences licensed by the department of children and youth services before the effective date of the amendments to the fire safety code.

(c) After the effective date of the amendments to the fire safety code as provided in subsection (b) of this section, the department of children and youth services may not, except on a temporary or emergency basis, license any permanent family residence for seven or more handicapped foster children which it has not previously licensed unless the state fire marshal determines that such facility complies with the applicable provisions of the fire safety code.

Newspaper and Legal Sources

A Bill to Amend the Fair Housing Act to Provide Sanctions for the Filing of Certain "Complaints." H.R. 4954. 1994. US House of Representatives, 103rd Congress, 2nd Session.

A Rip-Off of the Public? 1994. Editorial. *Hartford Courant* (June 7):D8.

Association of Retarded Citizens of Connecticut v. Thorne, 30 F. 3d. 1994.

A State Investigative Agency. 1985. United Press International (November 12).

At Least 9,000 Units of Housing. 1981. United Press International (February 18).

Achtenberg, R. 1994a. On Tightrope Between Fair Housing, Free Speech. *Houston Chronicle* (August 26):33.

—1994b. Sometimes on a Tightrope at HUD. *Washington Post* (August 22):A17.

—1994c. Substantive and Procedural Limitations on Filing and Investigating Fair Housing Act Complaints That May Implicate First Amendment. Memorandum to FHEU Directors, Enforcement Directors, Compliance Directors, Staff, Office of Investigations, US Department of Housing and Urban Development (September 2).

Agus, C. 1993. Doc Who Cleared Woody Faces Suit. *Newsday* (May 4):13.

Baird Facts. 1993. *The Nation* (February 1).

Bartlett, B. 1994. Roberta on a Rampage: Social Policies of Roberta Achtenberg, Assistant Secretary for Fair Housing and Equal Opportunity, Department of Housing and Urban Development. *National Review* 46(8):47 (May 2).

Bascom, L. C. 1987. AIDS Caseload Seen Rising by 25%. *New York Times* (July 26) New Jersey Section:17.

Bass, C. 1992a. Strange Bedfellows: A Tony Neighborhood's Zoning Dispute Detonates Full-Blown Discrimination Probe Embroiling Prominent New Haven Citizens. *Connecticut Law Tribune* (June 29):1.

—1992b. State Judge Named in Federal Bias Action; Justice Department Fair Housing Case Targets Hodgson. *Connecticut Law Tribune* (September 21):1.

—1992c. Hodgson Slaps Back Hard at Federal 'SLAPP' Suit. *Connecticut Law Tribune* (October 19):14.

—1992d. A Constitutional Clash; Was Hodgson a Hidden Hand Behind Alleged Housing Discrimination?; Justice Department Claims Foul Play; Judge Counters with First Amendment." *Connecticut Law Tribune* (December 14):1.

—1993a. Zoe 'N' the Hood. *Connecticut Law Tribune* (January 1):1.

—1993b. Justice Department Sues New Haven Neighborhood. *Connecticut Law Tribune* (January 23):1.

—1994a. Ruling in Fair-Housing Case Raises Constitutional Clamor; Does Right to Petition the Courts Give Way to Anti-Discrimination Law? *Connecticut Law Tribune* (January 17):1.

—1994b. Hard Questions about Marcus' Soft Costs. *Connecticut Law Tribune* (September 19):1.

—1994c. Small Portion of Marcus Fees OK'd by State Auditors. *Connecticut Law Tribune* (October 17):15.

—1995. All's Fair in Hodgson's Housing Battle. *Connecticut Law Tribune* (February 6):1.

Bass, P. 1992. Good Idea of the Week. *New Haven Advocate.*

Baumann, G. C. 1995. AG: Group Home Law in Flux. Recent High Court Ruling Changes Rules of the Game, Curran Warns. *The Daily Record* (August 7).

Biskupic, J. 1995. Court Acts in Housing Bias Dispute; Zoning Can't Be Used to Exclude Group Homes for Disabled, Justices Say. *Washington Post* (May 16):A3.

Bixby, L. 1994a. Outlook Is Dim for Developer of Group Homes. *Hartford Courant* (January 4):A1.

—1994b. 2 Admit Guilt in Fraud; State Agencies Are Victims. *Hartford Courant* (July 5):B1.

—1994c. Democratic Chief's Fee's Excessive. *Hartford Courant* May 25:A1.

Bondy, S. 1986. Group Homes Opposed. Letter to the Editor. *New York Times* (November 9) Connecticut Section:8.

Brown v. Board of Education of Topeka. 1954. 347 U.S. 483; 74 S. Ct. 686; 98 L. Ed. 873.

Cheshire, W. P. 1994. First It Was Only Our Property; Now It's Our Tongues They Want. *Arizona Republic* (August 11):B6.

Christoffersen, J. 1994. State Won't Reimburse Most of Marcus's Bill. *Journal Inquirer* (September 30):A10.

City of Edmonds, Petitioner, v. Oxford House, Inc., et al. 1995. 115 S. Ct. 1776; 1995 U.S. LEXIS 3183; 131 L. Ed. 2d 801; 63; U.S.L.W. 4402; 95 Cal. Daily Op. Service 3577; 95 Daily Journal DAR 6197; 9 Fla. Law W. Fed. S 10.

Cockerham, W. 1992a. Officials Say Aid for Homes Was Not Improper; Some Officials Defend Loans to Nursing Homes; Funds Used for Construction, Renovation of Units. *Hartford Courant* (January 16):B1.

—1992b. Lawmakers Seek Probe of Oak Hill; Lawmakers Want Probe of Oak Hill School Spending, Care. *Hartford Courant* (August 12):B1.

Confirmation Could Pit Baird Against Neighbors. 1993. *Hartford Courant* (January 15):12.

Connecticut Office of Legislative Research. 1992. Helping Connecticut's Businesses: The Distribution of State Economic Assistance, FY89 to FY91. Hartford: Office of Legislative Research.

CIL. 1991a. *Neighbors: Corporation for Independent Living Annual Report.* Wethersfield, CT: Corporation for Independent Living.

—1991b. Certificate of Incorporation (Amended and Restated Effective July 1).

—1991c. Corporation for Independent Living By-Laws.

—1992. *Neighbors: Corporation for Independent Living Annual Report.* Wethersfield, CT: Corporation for Independent Living.

De Leon, F. M. 1995. Group Home Upsets Edmonds Residents. *Seattle Times* (May 9):B1.

Disability Advocates Win Zoning Case in Supreme Court. 1995. *Disability Compliance Bulletin* 6:1 (June 8).

DOJ Files Housing Lawsuit Against New Haven Residents, Local Neighborhood Association. 1992. *U.S. Newswire* (July 27).

Duncan Robinson and Elizabeth Robinson, Plaintiffs, v. Marjorie Eichler and There's No Place Like Home, Inc., Defendants. Civ. No. 3:92CV00269 (TFGD) United States District Court for the District of Connecticut 1992 U.S. Dist. LEXIS 8695. June 11, 1992.

Faircloth Bill Sets New Standards on Group Homes. 1996. *National Journal's Congress Daily* (August 10).

"Family" Defined Under Fair Housing Act; Unrelated Persons Not Exempt From Discrimination Claims. 1995. *Legal Intelligencer* (June 22).

Ferguson, V. A. 1994. Housing—A Study in Cooperation. *Hartford Courant* (June 8):D8.

—1996a. Clarification Sought of Town Role in Housing. *Hartford Courant* (August 1):B6.

—1996b. Eno Farms Meeting Complaint Dismissed. *Hartford Courant* (August 15):B1.

—1996c. Lawyer Says Town Can Oversee, But Not Run, Eno Farms. *Hartford Courant* September 11:B1.

Free Speech Advocates Find a Fight in Berkeley; HUD Investigating 3 Residents for Bias Against Mentally Ill in Remarks, Letters, Protesting Projects. 1994. *San Francisco Examiner* (July 22):A6.

Free Speech? HUD's Threat Was Infringement of First Amendment. *Houston Chronicle* (August 19):B12.

Greenhouse, L. 1995. Supreme Court Roundup; Court Lowers Local Barriers to Housing for the Disabled. *New York Times* (May 16):A1.

Gugliotta, G. 1994. ACLU Alleges Free Speech Violations in HUD Probes. *Washington Post* (August 17):A20.

Hamilton, R. A. 1984. Aid to Handicapped Is Offered. *New York Times* (January 15) Connecticut Section:1.

Hathaway, W. 1995. Renters into Owners: Nonprofit Developers Struggle to Find New Ways to Create Cooperative Housing. *Hartford Courant* (December 3):J1.

Henry Cisneros' War on the Constitution. 1994. Editorial. *Washington Times* (August 16):A16.

Hentoff, N. 1994. HUD's Attack on the First Amendment. *Washington Post* (September 17):A15.

Holding, R. 1994. Berkeley Housing Dispute: When Speech Isn't Necessarily Free. *San Francisco Chronicle* (July 29):A1.

Housing Opponents Cleared; Berkeley 3 Due Free Speech, HUD Finds. 1994. *San Francisco Examiner* (August 17):A22.

HUD Drops Complaint Against Activists. 1994. *Washington Times* (August 18):A8.

HUD Gets the Message. 1994. Editorial. *Washington Post* (September 3):A28.

HUD-Nail Boots Trampling Rights. 1994. Editorial. *Houston Post* (September 11):C1.

HUD Plays Too Rough. 1994. Editorial. *New York Times* (August 27):22.

HUD Releases Opinion on Berkeley Housing Complaint. 1994. *U.S. Newswire* (August 18).

In Berkeley, a Victory for Free Speech. 1994. Editorial. *Washington Times* (August 22):A18.

Joint Hearings Before the Subcommittee on the Handicapped of the Committee on Labor and Human Resources and the Subcommittee on Labor, Health and Human Services, Education, and Related Agencies of the Committee on Appropriations of the United States Senate, Ninety-Ninth Congress, First Session on Examining the Nation's Institutionalized Mentally Disabled Persons. 1985. S. HRG 99-50, Parts I and II. Washington: US Government Printing Office.

Kaman, R., and S. Malanga. 1994. New York's New Tammany Hall. *Crain's New York Business* (November 7).

Lakin, K. C., and M. J. Hall. 1990. Medicaid-Financed Residential Care for Persons with Mental Retardation. *Health Care Financing Review* (January 11):149ff.

Lauber, D. 1995. Group Think: A Recent Supreme Court Ruling Should Make Local Governments Reconsider Their Community Residence Regulations; Includes Definition and Resource Information. *Planning* 61:10:11 (October).

Leo, J. 1994a. The (Local) Politics of Housing. *U.S. News & World Report* 117:9:20 (August 29).

—1994b. A Crime If Neighbors Don't Want Addicts Next Door? *Orlando Sentinel* (August 25):A13.

—1994c. HUD's Terrible War on Neighborhood Halfway House Dissenters. *San Diego Union-Tribune* (August 23):B7.

Libov, C. 1988. Group Homes for Retarded Gaining Success and Goodwill. *New York Times* (January 17) Connecticut Section:1.

Ludlow, L. 1994. Unspeakable Criticism. *San Francisco Examiner* (July 25):A14.

Mariano, A. 1990. Reports of Bias Against Families on Rise; HUD: 12,800 Discrimination Cases Filed Since '89 Law Took Effect. *Washington Post* (September 22):F1.

—1992. Justice Department Files Bias Suits as Complaints Rise. *Washington Post* (July 4):E2.

Mcdonald, H. 1994. HUD Continues Its Assault on Free Speech. *Wall Street Journal* (September 14):19.

Megan, K. 1991. State Named Receiver; Judge Orders Takeover of 5 Group Homes. *Hartford Courant* (July 18):B1.

—1992. Costs High for Care of Retarded; Steep Costs for the Care of the Retarded. *Hartford Courant* (January 31):A10.

Memorandum of Law Amicus Curiae, The Center for First Amendment Rights, Inc., In Support of Defendants' Objection to Recommended Ruling and Request for De Novo Review. December 18, 1993.

National Public Radio. 1994. HUD Will Change Approach to Fair Housing Law Violators. *Morning Edition* Transcript #1420-5 (August 26).

Noel, D. 1994. Connecticut Democrats Founder on the Rock of Ethics. *Hartford Courant* (June 8):D13.

Panel Probes Costs of Group Homes. 1989. Proprietary to the United Press International (October 6).

Pazniokas, M. 1992. Nursing Homes Got Much of State Growth Aid; Care Facilities Get Bulk of Economic Aid. *Hartford Courant* (January 15):A1.

Prepared Statement of Deval Patrick, Assistant Attorney General Civil Rights Division, Department of Justice, Before the Senate Committee on Banking,

Housing, and Urban Affairs Committee, Subcommittee on HUD Oversight and Structure. Re: S. 1132–A Bill to Amend the Fair Housing Act and for Other Purposes. 1996. Federal News Service (September 18).

Price, J. 1994. HUD Investigations Spurn First Amendment Rights; Probes Target Those Who Protest Public Housing. *Washington Times* (August 8):A3.

—1996. Faircloth Aims to Curb HUD on Group Homes; Bill Bans Suits, Probes Against Protesters. *Washington Times* (August 11):A9.

Raimondo, J. 1994a. Be Careful What You Say: Big HUD Is Watching You. *Rocky Mountain News* (August 24):44A.

—1994b. The Hidden Agenda of Radical Egalitarians. *San Francisco Examiner* (August 17):A17.

Rainwater, J. 1995. Affordable Housing Is Costly on Site. *Hartford Courant* (December 18):A14.

Results of Negotiated Bond Sales. 1988. *Bond Buyer* (January 6):11.

—1989. *Bond Buyer* (January 31):7.

—1990. *Bond Buyer* (August 31):6.

Rich, J. D. 1991. Enforcement of the Fair Housing Act, as Amended by the Department of Justice. *Business Lawyer* 46:1335ff. (May).

Roberts, P. C. 1994a. HUD Tramples First Amendment Right. Editorial. *Houston Chronicle* (August 25):24.

—1994b. Neighborhood Ambuscade. *Washington Times* (August 25):A16.

Seper, J. 1993. Baird May Be Grilled on Housing-Bias Lawsuit. *Washington Times* (January 19).

Small-Mindedness Knows No City Limits; The Bureaucratic Mentality, It Seems, Is Alive and Well in Both Berkeley and Norco. 1994. Editorial. *Los Angeles Times* (August 21):4.

Span, P. 1993a. Both Sides of the Fence; New Haven's Two Views of Baird. *Washington Post* (January 22):B1.

—1993b. Many of Baird's Neighbors Share Child-Care Need, Solve It Legally; Au Pairs Are Common in Prospect Hill Area of New Haven, Conn. *Washington Post* (January 22):A12.

Stansbury, R. 1994. Supreme Court Ruling Worries Town Planners; Local Officials Say Housing Decision Could Endanger Zoning Interests; Court Ruling Worries Town Planners. *Hartford Courant* (February 9):B1.

Statement by HUD Secretary Henry G. Cisneros on Berkeley, Calif., Fair Housing Case. 1994. *U.S. Newswire* (August 11).

Stewart B. McKinney Foundation, Inc. v. Town Plan and Zoning Commission of Fairfield. 1992. Civil No. B-90-115(EBB), United States District Court for the District of Connecticut. 1992 US Dist. LEXIS 5328.

Stone, M. M. 1993. Competing Contexts: The Evolution of an Organizational Governance Structure in Multiple Environments. PONPO Working Paper #185. New Haven: Program on Non-Profit Organizations, Yale University.

Tabin, B. 1995. Ruling on Zoning Impedes Local Zoning Practices. *City of Edmonds v. Oxford House. Nation's Cities Weekly* 18:21:3 (May 22).

Testimony, September 5, 1996, Stuart Ishimaru, Counsel to Assistant Attorney General, Civil Rights Division, US Department of Justice, House Judiciary, Constitution, Fair Housing Act. 1996. Washington, DC: Federal Document Clearing House, Inc.

Testimony, September 5, 1996, Michael Allen, Staff Attorney, Bazelon Center for Mental Health Law, House Judiciary, Constitution, Fair Housing Act. 1996. Washington, DC: Federal Document Clearing House, Inc.

Trotta, B. M. 1994a. Bank Seeks Change in Zone Regulations. *Hartford Courant* (May 16):C3.

—1994b. Simsbury Panel Sued for Rejecting Housing Proposal. *Hartford Courant* (September 7):B1.

UPI. 1981. CT-Disabled. Proprietary to the United Press International (February 18).

—1988. Housing Funds Authorized. Proprietary to the United Press International (December 2).

U.S. Considers Suing 3 Who Fought a Project for the Homeless. 1994. *New York Times* (July 31):18.

United States v. Duncan and Elizabeth Robinson, et al., Defendants. Civ. No. 392CV00345 (TFGD). 1992. United States District Court for the District of Connecticut (July 27).

United States Department of Justice. 1992. *Plaintiff v. Duncan Robinson, Elizabeth Robinson, Ronan-Edgehill Neighborhood Association, Jack Brownlow, Defendants.* Consent Decree between Plaintiff and Defendant Ronan-Edgehill Association.

Vernon News Notes; Housing Complex Gets $53,934 State Grant. *Hartford Courant* (May 13):D4.

Village of Belle Terre, et al. v. Boraas. 1974. 416 US 1; 94 S.Ct. 1536.

Waldman, H. 1992 Great Expectations Part of Baird Neighborhood. *Hartford Courant* (December 25):A8.

Weaver, J. 1987. Foster Homes Needed for AIDS Children. *New York Times* (June 21) Connecticut Section:1.

Wells, J. 1994a. HUD Clears Berkeley Residents. Agency Says Vocal Opponents of Housing Project Did No Wrong. *San Francisco Chronicle* (August 17):A20.

—1994b. Housing Discrimination Probe Upsets Berkeley Officials. *San Francisco Chronicle* (August 2):A18.

—1994c. Another Berkeley Project Raises Free Speech Flap. Concerned Council Opens Agenda to AIDS Patient. *San Francisco Chronicle* (July 25):A15.

—1994d. Civil Rights Furor in Berkeley; Citizens Warned on Protest Over Disabled Housing Plan. *San Francisco Chronicle* (July 25):A15.

—1994e. Fair Housing and Free Speech at Issue in Berkeley. *San Francisco Chronicle* (July 25):A19.

Wen, P. 1991. State to Phase Out $5 Million Contract; Human Service Firm's Dealings Cited. *Boston Globe* (July 11) Metro/Region:18.

Wen, P., and G. O'Neill. 1991. Springfield Center Under Audit for Use of State Funds. *Boston Globe* (June 14) Metro/Region:1.

Were State Loans Misdirected? 1994. Editorial. *Hartford Courant* (January 30):B10.

Whoa, HUD; Zealous Agency May Trample Free Speech. 1994. Editorial. *Columbus Dispatch* (August 5):10A.

Winerip, M. 1987a. Fire at Home for Mentally Ill on L.I. Is Ruled Arson. *New York Times* (December 31):B1.

—1987b. Our Towns; There's No Room in Neighborhood for Mentally Ill. *New York Times* (December 11):B1.

—1988a. A Social Revolution Aids the Mentally Ill. *Chicago Tribune* (November 12) Home Guide:17.

—1988b. Our Towns; For Mentally Ill, Succor Is Found in Group Homes. *New York Times* (November 8):B1.

—1988c. Our Towns; Group Homes: A Law Works Ever So Quietly. *New York Times* (November 4):B1.

—1988d. Our Towns; For an L.I. Man, the Rough Road to a Group Home. *New York Times* (July 15):B1.

—1988e. Our Towns; Bitter Neighbors, Guarded Homes for Mentally Ill. *New York Times* (March 25):B1.

—1989a. Our Towns; How Pay Scales Thwart the Intent of Group Homes. *New York Times* (June 13):B1.

—1989b. Our Towns; New Lives Start at Group Home: 'Feels Beautiful.' *New York Times* (April 4):B1.

—1989c. L.I. Police Suspect Arson in Blaze at Site of a Proposed Group Home. *New York Times* (February 22):B2.

—1989d. Our Towns; Some Neighbors Still Aren't Seen as Neighbors. *New York Times* (February 3):B1.

—1989e. Our Towns; Ordinary People: Retarded Adults Move Next Door. *New York Times* (March 29):B1.

—1990a. Our Towns; Dark Side of Life: Glimpse of Home for Mentally Ill. *New York Times* (November 6):B1.

—1990b. Our Towns; Forgotten Homes for Mentally Ill: A Sister's Tale. *New York Times* (November 2):1.

—1990c. Our Towns; For Mentally Ill, an Alternative to Adult Homes. *New York Times* (August 21):B1.

—1990d. Our Towns; Of Adult Homes, This One Ranks Among the Worst. *New York Times* (August 17):B1.

—1990e. Our Towns; For Some People, Independence Is a Daily Worry. *New York Times* (July 6):B1.

—1990f. Our Towns; Group Homes Face New Battles on Old Fears. *New York Times* (April 27):B1.

—1990g. Our Towns; Sensitivity Ebbs, and Often Flows, in Homeless Plan. *New York Times* (March 27):B1.

—1992. On Sunday; Groups Homes Are Invited Only to Leave. *New York Times* (September 6):49.

Wyatt v. Stickney. 1972. 344 F. Supp. 387.

Yarrow, A. L. 1992. "Not in My Back Yard" and Repercussions. *New York Times* (October 4) Metro:42.

7

Locating Corporate Environmentalism

Synthetics, Implosions, and the Bhopal Disaster

Kim Fortun

> Considered from an empirical point of view, every myth is at once pristine in relation to itself and derived in relation to other myths; it is situated not in language and in a culture or sub-culture, but at the point of articulation of cultures with other languages and cultures. Myth is thus never in its language; it is a perspective on another language.
>
> —*Claude Lévi-Strauss*

Corporate environmentalism promises to help us clean up the past and manage future risks, while continuing to provide "better living through chemistry." The promise circulates in glossy brochures sent to shareholders, at meetings in which citizens chat with plant managers, and within the enclaves of corporations themselves. A guidebook written for managers expresses the logic: "The myth of corporations and consumers destroying the planet gives way to a more complex insight: that the consumer society that has evolved over the past century is efficient at delivering whatever higher social expectations consumers want, including a cleaner environment. When the consumer wants environmental protection, the consumer will get it" (Piasecki 1995:ix). The logic of corporate environmentalism is a claim to both continuity and change, to be realized through initiatives that transfigure but sustain our ways of desiring, responding, and understanding. Corporate environmentalism is, then, a vehicle of culture. Like a Lévi-Straussian myth, it can be located at points of articulation with other languages and cultures, deriving its meaning through constant interchange with the world around it.

Like other contemporary processes of political economy and culture, corporate environmentalism operates globally, linking issues, people, and institutions that only a few years ago were not imagined as related. In this essay, I attempt to provide a sense of how corporate environmentalism is constituted and how, as an ethnographer, I have tried to observe and, at times, critique it. My focus is on corporate environmentalism as part of the legacy of the December 2–3, 1984, Bhopal disaster, which I have tracked in its myriad manifestations in both India and the United States. Disaster is, then, the context for my study. The essay is organized around a series of excerpts, which, together, demonstrate the "cumulative effect" of the politics of environmental hazard.

CONVENIENCES AND INDIRECTIONS

The Bhopal case was dismissed from US courts by Judge John Keenan on May 12, 1986, on the grounds of *forum non conveniens*, a legal doctrine which posits that significant decisions leading to the case were made elsewhere, making it inconvenient to secure witnesses and evidence in the proposed forum, and that there is an adequate, alternative forum wherein justice can be adjudicated. In Judge Keenan's synthesis, it would have been "sadly paternalistic, if not misguided" for his court to evaluate the operation of a foreign country's laws. He did acknowledge that double standards of industrial safety are not to be encouraged, but also noted that "the failure to acknowledge inherent differences in the aims and concerns of India, as compared to American citizens, would be naive, and unfair to the defendant." His judgment concluded with the argument that retention of the case in US courts "would be yet another act of imperialism, another situation in which an established sovereign inflicted its rules, its standards and values on a developing nation... To deprive the Indian judiciary [of] this opportunity to stand tall before the world and to pass judgment on behalf of its own people would be to revive a history [of] subservience and subjugation from which India has emerged" (quoted in Cassels 1993:134).[1]

Plaintiff lawyers, journalists, and environmental activists read the Bhopal case differently, challenging the obviousness of national boundaries and recognizing asymmetry between First and Third Worlds. They articulated connections between Union Carbide India Limited (UCIL) and Union Carbide Corporation (UCC), including stock ownership, shared executives and directors, and decisions taken in Danbury, Connecticut, that, paternalistic or not, directly affected events in Bhopal. Among these were the decision to site the Bhopal plant barely two kilometers from the main railway station; the decision to switch to a production process for synthesizing the pesticide Sevin that relied on methyl isocyanate (MIC), the gas released in Bhopal; and the decision to use an "open circuit process" requiring bulk storage of MIC. Additionally, when India did "stand tall" and litigate the Bhopal case, UCC was the defendant and thus the party that negotiated, accepted, and paid 90 percent of the February 1989 settlement of $470 million. Perhaps the most telling connections were much more indirect: news of the settlement caused UCC stock to rise $2 a share, or 7 percent.

How, as an ethnographer, do I engage these indicators of convenience, location, and responsibility? How do I understand the seeming illogic of Union Carbide's claim to have accepted "moral responsibility but no liability" for the Bhopal disaster? How do I respond when told by the Chemical Manufacturers Association that "It [Bhopal] can't happen here"? How do I recognize that "Bhopal" has been a disaster not only for its victims but also for the chemical industry? More than thirteen years after the gas leak in Bhopal, the chemical industry continues to be confronted by an angry public and a slew of regulations, often referred to as "Bhopal's Babies." Nonetheless, the chemical industry seems to be prospering, with Union Carbide recognized as "one of the winners." How, as an ethnographer, do I locate the contradiction?

What I want to know is how corporate discourse "cracks," recognizing profound change in its field of operation, questioning its own capacity to define an authoritative model of efficient enterprise. The question: How have corporate actors understood and strategized the (in)adequacy of key concepts that have sustained modern institutional practices? Particularly, what constitutes "good management" when the terms of efficiency and value are themselves under negotiation?

These questions compel us to examine how things, in general, have stopped making sense, confounding established conceptions of what constitutes social change and progress. Modes of analysis emergent from assumptions of visible causality, mobilized by intending, knowing subjects do not suffice. Nor do managerial models of response. In assessing the legacy of Bhopal, one has to acknowledge that the disaster is not only a matter of broken bodies, contaminated environments, and the price of shares on Wall Street. The bottom line is that the disasters that emerge from contemporary configurations of power challenge both "stakeholders" and the conceptual apparatus by which stakes are identified, possessed, and sustained.

Ethnographic study of corporations relies on strategies of indirection. Instead of head-on query into the nature of commercial corporate enterprise, I have sought articulations and locations. What is it people say in the name of the corporation, and where do they say it? How is the operation of corporate enterprise described? What affirms, or corrodes, the legitimacy of these descriptions? How has Bhopal transformed the way people understand the world and their role within it?

The most important question seems redundant: What is said when reference is made to Bhopal? As might have been expected, Union Carbide has made overt reference with savvy infrequency. The challenge is to track the substitutions, charting what has been said instead.

SILENT GREEN[2]

Rachel Carson's *Silent Spring* was published in 1962. Some say this was just the beginning. Green consultant Bruce Harrison agrees. By 1993 he could insist that the war was over. Business had won.

Social roles for "green consultants" have been forged over the last thirty years to help institutionalize corporate environmentalism. Bruce Harrison entered the fray early. An account of his career and contributions is provided in his book *Going Green: How to Communicate Your Company's Environmental Commitment* (1993). The book's jacket explains that the E. Bruce Harrison Company is "a professional consulting firm specializing in environmental public policy, which works with more than 80 of the Fortune 500." The book articulates Harrison's version of the history of contemporary environmentalism and a sense of the proper place of historical perspective in corporate efforts to "go green." It also tells corporate actors who and where they are in the environmental storm, and how they can hope to survive.

Harrison's story begins in the chemical industry's days of grace,[3] when the whole world could be viewed through a benzene ring. Bumper crops of babies were being born, calling for pesticides to be just as productive. The perfect lawns of suburbia were growing, but the weeds were not. It was a time of command and control, and everyone was a customer for chemicals. Faith in science and technology was extraordinarily high. In a 1957 report by the National Association of Science Writers, nearly 90 percent of the public agreed that "the world was better off because of science." An equal proportion could not cite a single negative consequence of science (Hoffman 1997:47). Then came *Silent Spring.*

In the summer of 1962, Bruce Harrison was working at the Manufacturing Chemists Association, which later would become the Chemical Manufacturers Association. He had just been named Manager of Community Relations, since he was in charge of "good neighbor programs" in industrial plant communities, which included an annual observance of "Chemical Progress Week." Then the chemical industry was "hit," and Harrison's career took off. The problem: "Rachel Carson's thesis was not only that pesticides would wreak unintentional harm—the hypothetical spring when birds would not sing—but also that because it *knew* of the potential damages of chemicals to wildlife and humans the industry was *evil.* She used the image of the Borgias, cooking up the poison" (Harrison 1993:xiv).

Harrison got a new title, invented especially for the situation: "Manager of Environmental Information, perhaps the first such title in corporate PR." He nonetheless recalls being somewhat naive regarding the significance of the Carson attack. His mentor, Alan Settle, corrected the picture through a comparison with the Japanese attack on Pearl Harbor. Harrison recalls the lesson: "We weren't ready for this, but we've got to come back fast. If we don't take charge now, we're going to be buried, pure and simple." The lesson stuck. Over thirty years later Harrison's strategy is equally aggressive, beginning with knowledge that "taking charge is the only winning move after an attack" (Harrison 1993:xiv–xv).

The more appropriate analogy, however, may be the Vietnam War, evoking images of environmentalists as guerrilla communists threatening a domino effect that would destroy the foundation of American society. Over the years, the guerrillas have been tamed. Counterattacks were carefully strategized, the terrain defoliated, and the enemy forced into the open. By the early 1990s, environmentalists were coming to meetings in business suits, with their own power point displays.

In Harrison's account, Carson's attack on pesticides ushered in the "attack mode" of American environmentalism. The war dragged on through the 1960s and 1970s, reaching a low point with the election of Jimmy Carter in 1976. But Carter's election had ironic consequences. Environmental activists found their way into government bureaucracy, and they built environmental organizations that were "managed like business." By 1990 and the passage of the Clean Air Act Amendments, "environmentalists and business people, as types, began to resemble each other a little" (Harrison 1993:8).

Then came the real watershed: the Second World Industry Conference on Environmental Management (WICEM II), held in Rotterdam in April 1991, which forged a Business Charter for Sustainable Development. Governments and business leaders from around the world came together, including Frank Popoff, CEO of Dow; Edgar Woolard, Jr., CEO of Du Pont; Pete Silas, CEO of Phillips Petroleum; and Robert Kennedy, CEO of Union Carbide.

"Visioning" is what got them there, most likely. Harrison tells us that visioning is learned from athletes and their coaches. It means thinking things through in advance, like Olympic medalist Bruce Jenner, who visualized every part of his competitions beforehand, imaging every move and muscle required. The last stage was "seeing himself crossing the finish line in that long race, circling the track in the stadium, hearing the cheers of the crowd." Robert Kennedy is Harrison's example of how visioning helps people go green, though he admits he can't prove it. Kennedy's company "suffered through the great tragedy of Bhopal" but "resolved to rise from this tragedy and to gain new respect as an environmentally aggressive company" (Harrison 1993:23–24). Kennedy may well have visualized one of the scenarios Harrison suggests we start with.

In one scenario we visualize ourselves sitting alongside firefighters, city officials, and community neighbors as they draft the final stages of a local environmental emergency response plan. In another, we visualize hearing a verdict, after a jury has been convinced that the environmental class action brought against our firm was unfounded and inconsistent with the firm's performance and commitment. In a third, we visualize a time when we can point to profits in key operations as the direct result of continuous environmental process improvement.

The scenario Kennedy is credited with realizing visualizes the presentation of a paper at a world conference on environmental management, leading to a global green charter. Harrison writes that "Kennedy visualized an outcome like this, and that he's already set his sights on the next positive green milestone." Like any golfer, Kennedy must have known that mental preparation helps the game. The strategy is "really more than foresight. It's a sort of *advance hindsight*...The important point is to break the habit of seeing a contentious, costly, long, or loosing condition when the subject is green" (Harrison 1993:24).

The subject is green because participants in WICEM II created what they called a Green World. This was accomplished by pledging support for sustainable development, because it has "something for everybody." Like visioning, signing the charter was an act of advance hindsight. It signed off on the past and wrote in a future in which greening and growth were no longer in opposition.

Harrison confirms the success of the WICEM II Charter through his reading of the United Nations Conference on Environment and Development, held in Rio de Janeiro in 1992. By all accounts, the so-called Earth Summit was a landmark event because its mission was to initiate cooperative work toward sustainable development and because it brought more people to the table than ever before in a UN forum.[4] Nations were not the only invitees. Grassroots representatives were invited, as were representatives from nongovernmental organizations, including chambers of commerce. The goal was to transform not only what the UN did, but also how it did it. Pluralization of participation in global politics was an explicit goal.

Harrison attended as a member of the International Chamber of Commerce's Environmental Commission. His contingent came as signatories to sustainable development, and they preempted the Earth Summit's mission. The attack mode of American environmentalism was dead on arrival. The eight thousand journalists in attendance missed the story, but it was clear to Harrison. As he saw it, the bottom line was that "greening has become the lubricant to grease the machinery of government-sanctioned commerce" (Harrison 1993:4). In sum, environmentalism today is "owned by business."

At WICEM II business visualized a Green World. At Rio, they confirmed it. All things became possible for committed corporations. Business executives could carry the card Harrison provides at his counseling sessions. The card is small enough to be nestled in the palm of an executive's hand so that he may gaze at it and take comfort. The message on the little card is bold: "WE ARE THE GOOD GUYS."

The great historical transformation described by Harrison has been accomplished by providing corporations a new language for communicating with the public and solidifying their own identity. "Sustainable development" is the anchor holding everything in place, allowing basic concepts to be reconfigured. According to Harrison, "the chemical industry has the world's toughest job in public relations. It has to deal with public fears that are ignitable at will. While people absolutely require chemicals to live (every product is touched by chemistry; we ourselves are composed of chemicals), there is no end to the association of *chemical* to *danger*, and therefore no end to the communication challenge" (Harrison 1993:xv). The challenge for Harrison is to help corporations disassociate *chemical* from *danger*.

Companies need "envirocomm," a process and term coined by Harrison "to signal that this is a special and in many ways unique form of communication and public relations" (Harrison 1993:xii). The uniqueness of envirocomm, codified into a seven-step management model, lies in recognizing that "going green is a habit, not a hormone." To begin, companies need to become keenly aware of contemporary conditions, recognizing major trends that make environmental public relations imperative. Next, companies need a "winning green attitude," which visualizes success and exorcises "hang-ups"—"pollutants in the channels of green communication" that obstruct "mental greening." Perhaps most importantly, companies need to stop dropping the ball, because, like Lucy in *Peanuts*, "the past got in her eyes." Times have changed. Lucy can now catch that ball, secure in believing that "the green ball is in the court of corporate America" (Harrison 1993:5).

RETICULATIONS

The Bhopal litigation was settled out of court in February 1989. That same year, Carbide doubled its profits from its chemicals and plastics business. According to business analysts, these improvements were not due to improvements in management. When shares plummeted immediately following the disaster, Moody's lowered Carbide's rating to the lowest investment grade, quoting "fundamental weaknesses" in the firm's day-to-day business operations. Carbide's rise after the settlement was seen not as a reversal of this weakness but merely as a market correction, an effect rather than a cause. One cause of Carbide's rise was a massive restructuring in response to a takeover bid by GAF Corporation. Resisting the takeover justified huge debt to finance recapitalization. Financing the debt legitimated the sale of entire divisions: Carbide's Battery Products division, the world's leading flashlight and small appliance battery business, was sold to Ralston-Purina. The Home and Automotive Products division, which carried consumer brands such as Prestone Antifreeze and Glad Bags, was sold to employees. Critics claimed these were moves to immunize the company from consumer boycott.

Another, less direct cause of the rise in Carbide's investment ratings was a general market cycle that promoted the commodity chemical business. One analyst, quoted in the *New York Times*, insisted that "the so-called turnaround at Carbide is a result of the improvements in petrochemical markets and not much more." The same analyst nonetheless described the settlement of the Bhopal case in euphoric terms, saying that "psychologically, it's terrific. Financially, it's reasonable. This relieves the pressure on Carbide and the stigma" (Hicks 1989).

It is within this context that I began field research in Bhopal. I arrived a year after the announcement that the Indian Supreme Court had accepted an out-of-court settlement, for an amount far below what had been expected by advocates for the victims. Outrage was directed as much at the government of India as at Union Carbide. The "selling out of justice" was blamed on "the system" which linked the two together—with increasing force as pressures from the International Monetary Fund escalated into plans for overall economic liberalization. Debates over the settlement of the Bhopal case therefore indexed much broader negotiations, forcing all articulations specific to Bhopal to compound with emergent discourses attempting to position India within the New World Order. Both critics and advocates of the Bhopal settlement participated in this synthetic process, insisting that the "situational particularities" of the Bhopal case operated as evidence of certain understandings of the past and of certain directions for the future. Details of the disaster were cited, or effaced, to substantiate widely disparate interests, values, and political strategies. With time, I would learn to recognize not only different positions, but also different fields of reference, different rhetorical styles, and different modes of constructing legitimacy.

The government of India used the Bhopal case to prove friendliness to foreign investors and to begin dismantling independence-era commitments to "scientific socialism." US courts used the case to suggest that asymmetry between the First and Third Worlds had been overcome, allowing India to "stand tall before the world and determine her own destiny." Indian leftists would cite the Bhopal case to prove the failure of Leninism, insisting that the primary enemy was not private property but the state, as primary manager of surplus value and lead mimic of the Western fetish for "development," whatever the costs. Leftists in the United States took a different approach, using the Bhopal case to refocus protest away from the state and directly against the commercial corporation. Chemical corporations responded by insisting that they, too, were environmentalists, committed to sustainable development, citizen participation, and "voluntary compliance," which obviated the need for state regulation.

Academic theorists also entered the fray. Legal theorists argued that the consolidation of claims in the Bhopal case provides an innovative model for dealing with uneven distribution of risks and rewards in industrial society. Theorists of "Strategic Management" argued that Union Carbide's response to the disaster initiated an "avalanche of change" that overcame all opposition between economic growth and environmental safety, and between corporations and their neighbors. A sociology textbook draws us closest to the enduring controversy, foregrounding a chart that illustrates seven different calculations of the death rate "caused" by the Bhopal disaster, as a way to suggest how competing perspectives complicate efforts to understand multinational corporations (see Ferrante 1992:chap. 7).

I learned of these diverse, conflictual responses to Bhopal over time and through very different kinds of intellectual and social engagements. My fieldwork in Bhopal was intensively participatory. I worked as an advocate for victims, within a group of middle-class Indian leftists directly linked to the largest organization of gas victims. My work was the work of writing. I wrote press releases, proposals for rehabilitation schemes, and affidavits disputing legal categorizations of disability. The challenge was to demonstrate the insufficiency of dominant logic in ways sensible within dominant logic itself. Languages of principle and syllogism were necessary, as was reference to stable facts and unquestionable method.

In my role as advocate in Bhopal, information inundation both was and was not a pressing problem. There was more than enough to understand, but there were also obvious holes, produced, in part, by corporate and government refusals to disclose important data. Lack of access to reliable communications technologies only exacerbated the deficit, provoking while limiting our own attempts to document the "second disaster"—our name for the years following 1984, when all official projects for rehabilitation and legal redress imploded, with numerous casualties.

Then I returned to the United States, desperately wanting to remain responsible to "the legacy of Bhopal." I knew by then that advocacy can and must take diverse forms. In Bhopal I spoke and wrote in the language of those I hoped to challenge. My task as an academic had to be something different, taking responsibility for the role of scholarship in questioning and therein transfiguring concepts and rhetorics tangled within abuse of power, even if deployed against it. I remained, however, caught within the directly political, becoming a member of Communities Concerned about Corporations (CCC), a group that links grassroots activists across the country to strategize collective response to industrial hazards. My association with CCC remains rewarding and instructive, even though I must operate as an "outsider," having no chemical plant of my own or daily engagements with the machinations of EPA, Du Pont, or doctors ill-prepared for my concerns. I do, however, share a different kind of positionality with members of CCC more directly linked to the realpolitik of dangerous chemicals. Like them, I track the Bhopal disaster, paying attention when advertising by the Chemical Manufacturers Association flashes across my television screen, listening to radio commentary on Du Pont's plans to move production facilities to somewhere in Southeast Asia, wondering if it means that maintenance on facilities in the US will stop, exacerbating the possibility of "mishap," wading through toxic release inventories, asking questions of all those I encounter.

On one early occasion, I learned of the impact of Bhopal on users of hazardous household chemicals from the man who regularly sprayed my mother's house to ward off Texas cockroaches. I was home from India on a brief visit. He asked me what I was up to, as he had done year after year while I was growing up. Rather embarrassed by the question, I said that I was doing research in India, in the city of Bhopal, among victims of the Union Carbide disaster. Expecting that blank stare suggesting I was crazy for having moved so far away, I was caught off guard by his immediate, emphatic response. "I know about Bhopal," he said. "It ruined my business. Had to let go all the fellows who worked for me, become a one-man show again. Couldn't afford the insurance to keep the others on." I simply stared at him, so he continued. "Shame all those people were killed, and so many hurt. Somebody wasn't running their house very well. These chemicals are mean, vicious even. Got to be really careful. Got to make everybody be really careful. But, somehow, it ain't right. Punishing me for someone else's slack."

Years later, at a roadside diner in rural New York, the owner told me of his difficulty securing a loan from the Small Business Administration. His friend, an Indian who owned a small grocery, got such a loan with ease. All because of Bhopal, he said. For some reason, after the disaster, Union Carbide had put up the money.

I still haven't checked out many of these stories. Time's stubborn finitude plays a role, of course. There have been so many "hooks," and learning to prioritize them has been a formidable challenge. I haven't been able to keep up with all the articulations, much less prioritize their significance. Pamphlets produced at the grassroots. Articles from legal journals. Annual reports. Updates on developments in toxicology. Management textbooks, which now rely on the Bhopal case to illustrate various aspects of multinational corporate organization. I now think of this deluge as "the aleatory effect." The aleatory, often associated with the music of John Cage, has an effect of "alloverness." It is produced by an underdetermined deluge of stimuli lacking any syntax or hierarchy of significance. The deluge is scrambled, overtly marked as contingent, and at obvious odds with hegemonic logic. Sources of information vary, in reliability as well as genre. Quantifications proliferate, as do references troped as unquestionable but laced with indicators of interest and institutional rationality.

Where is ethnography within the aleatory effect of environmental disaster? What are the ethnographer's methods? She subscribes to *Forbes* magazine and an endless number of on-line newsletters. She learns about Geographical Information Systems and how they work within epidemiology. She tries to read about the ways sociologists have studied corporations, mapping the social networks of directors and the structure of corporate decision making. Expertise becomes so dispersed it seems fraudulent by default. Sensibilities of competence and accomplishment seem forestalled ad infinitum. At the same time, however, remembrance becomes transfigured, and one realizes that a key challenge for ethnography lies in this very attempt to understand what counts, where it counts, and how it matters—on the ground in everyday life.

DISCOUNTING, AND THE VALUE ADDED

A March 1994 profile article in *Forbes* begins with the claim that "like Mark Twain, Union Carbide thwarts the obituary writers" (Moukheiber 1994:41). Despite a multimillion-dollar lawsuit resulting from the Bhopal disaster and a takeover attempt by GAF Corporation that required the sale of key assets and encumbrance of enormous debt, "Carbide refused to die." An insert quote argues that "people who say you can't teach an old dog new tricks haven't examined the tremendous progress made in the past few years by that old mutt Union Carbide." The article goes on to describe the method of renewal. In short, Union Carbide has downsized, shrinking from $9 billion in sales in 1985 to $5 billion in sales in 1990.

Carbide has profited from this downsizing in a context marked by claims that the survival of industry is threatened by the demands of environmental regulation. How, then, does one account for Union Carbide's success? One rationale is the market. In 1994, industry analysts pointed out that the price peaks of 1989 were again evident and were expected to continue to rise, promising growth in operating earnings from 15 to 30 percent through 1995. On the tenth anniversary of the Bhopal disaster the chemical industry was also benefiting from lower fixed costs. According to an economist from the Chemical Manufacturers Association, "the industry has been through a ten year makeover, shedding old capacity and repositioning businesses to emphasize more profitable specialty chemicals over commodity brews ...The results are beginning to pay off" (Moukheiber 1994:41).

The repositioning of Union Carbide has been complex, and more than radical. Two shifts of orientation seem particularly significant. First, Union Carbide has overturned its diversification strategy of earlier years, focusing on becoming a low-cost producer of one product, ethylene glycol, used to make polyester fibers and antifreeze. Second, major initiatives have been made to utilize new information technologies to cut costs and raise efficiency.

The repositioning of Union Carbide has involved tactics that organize the boundaries of the corporation in new ways. In the last ten years, Carbide has actively sought instruction from people who once would have been considered outside the domain of relevance to the chemical industry, traditionally recognized as one of the most internally focused of US industries. From L. L. Bean, the mail-order catalog company, Carbide learned how to centralize global customer orders into one computer center in Houston. Insight on tracking inventory via computer was borrowed from retailers such as Wal-Mart, enabling the adjustment of production to demand. Global distribution processes were revamped according to the model proven by Federal Express, streamlining the routing of products rather than privileging lowest-cost forms of transport, whatever the circuitous route they take.

This centralization allowed both order accuracy and "just-in-time" production scheduling, enabling Carbide to reduce its finished goods inventory by 20 percent. The work processes to carry out these correspondences were redesigned by employees and resulted in a 30 percent reduction in required personnel. Overall, selling and administrative costs have dropped 27 percent since 1989; fixed costs at Carbide plants have dropped 18 percent, and sales per employee have risen 77 percent. The result: operating earnings jumped 27.5 percent, to $227 million, during 1993, despite a weak market for polyethylene and ethylene glycol, which now make up nearly 30 percent of Carbide's revenues. These earnings were a 45 percent gain over 1992, when sales were 5 percent higher (Moukheiber 1994:41–43).

Why, as an ethnographer, should I heed these numbers? Union Carbide's success within the effects of the Bhopal disaster confounds the business press's claim that environmentalism and economic growth are antagonistic agendas. Nonetheless, it is within the articulations of the business press that one finds the most direct response to the question, "What is signified when Union Carbide says 'Bhopal'?" When Union Carbide is "covered," Bhopal is not an ongoing crisis provoked by environmental regulation and increasing concern about liability. Instead, "Bhopal" is a moment in the restructuring of Union Carbide that began long before December 1984 in response to the demands of a changing market, accessible through new information technologies, new financial mechanisms, new relations with the nation-state, and new rhetorics of both possibility and legitimation. The contradiction is made clear in a statement by McNeese University professor of management Arthur Sharplin: "Clearly, by any objective measure, UCC (Union Carbide Corporation) and its managers benefited from the Bhopal incident, as did UCIL (Union Carbide India, Ltd.). They were politically able to close a burdensome plant, take aggressive actions to restructure both companies, and enhance management benefits...It is ironic that a disaster such as Bhopal would leave its victims devastated and other corporate stakeholders better off" (quoted in Lepkowski 1994:30).

PRESSING BUSINESS

When the Clean Air Act was amended in 1990, commentators insisted that "clean air" is a "dirty joke" that will "challenge industry like never before in its history," cost billions of dollars, and could result in the demise of affected companies nationwide. Elite environmental groups such as the Sierra Club read these predictions as fair trade, insisting that the cost of compliance would simply shift the cost burden from the public to industry. Comparing figures from organizations like the American Lung Association to figures from the National Petroleum Council, they substantiated both the new legislation and their own insistence that environmentalism does not threaten to transform US society, only to reform it (Ivanovich 1993:1E).

The Clean Air Act is one of what are called Bhopal's Babies, a family of environmental regulations said to have dramatically transformed the global chemical industry by internalizing costs once externalized, either through reliance on state funds for safe product transport and waste disposal or through the allocation of extraordinary health risks to workers and host communities. Reaction against regulatory response to the Bhopal disaster has not subsided, but now it appears in the pages of the business press, not in the official statements and glossy brochures of chemical companies. The business press, along with the most radical of environmentalists, maintains the stage on which the great drama of contemporary environmentalism is performed. Corporate actors wait for their cue before entering. Their coaches are green consultants. Labor unions also come on stage, as do citizens groups, insurance and regulatory agencies, investors, and others. The boundaries set by the business press and radical environmentalists both enable and constrain the performance. But there can always be surprises. The script continues to be written.

An article published in *Fortune* magazine in September 1994 illustrates the staging (Dowd 1994). The main billing: "Environmentalists on the Run." The subtitle: "Business leaders, local officials and angry citizens are demanding an end to rules based on silly science and bad economics. This time, they just might win."

The article tells the story of Alar, the growth regulator used on apples which the EPA deemed a carcinogen in 1989, after Meryl Streep and *60 Minutes* set off a panic that had parents pouring apple juice down the drain. US apple growers lost some $100 million. Five years later, the American Medical Association, the National Cancer Institute, and the World Health Organization concurred that Alar poses no real threat to human health. The risk is now said to be "less than that incurred by eating a well-done hamburger or a peanut butter sandwich" and is compared to the much greater risk incurred by playing high school football.

Alongside other stories about the silly science of environmental regulation, hard figures state the economic facts: "America's cleanup bill is considerably larger than those of its principal competitors. US environmental spending amounts to 2.2% of GDP, vs. 1.6% to 1.8% in Germany and 1% to 1.5% in Japan." These facts ground the article's lead prediction that with the exception of legislation to reform the Superfund law, no major environmental legislation would get through Congress in 1994. Instead, three reforms, dubbed "the unholy trinity" by opponents, would dominate the agenda: all new rules must be preceded by cost-benefit analysis; no rules if the government is not willing to pick up the costs; compensation when rules severely limit the use and value of private property (Dowd 1994:91).

Fortune's predictions about the fate of environmental regulation have, in large part, come to pass, de facto if not de jure. Environmentalists often share the structure of *Fortune*'s argumentation, albeit in reverse. Like the business press, "radical" environmentalism polarizes environmentalism and economic growth. There is little attempt to work within the opposition. One side of the binary is privileged, the other discounted. The choices are harsh: jobs *or* the environment, private property *or* the common good, science *or* concern.

Groups like Earth First! demonstrate the strategy, arguing that we must fundamentally limit established patterns of both production and consumption, whatever the costs. The biosphere itself is the threatening, aggressive force that should concern us. Two particularly stunning articulations illustrate the logic. As famine ravaged Ethiopia in the mid-1980s, Earth First! founder Dave Foreman argued that "the best thing would be to let nature seek its own balance." In other words, we should let the Ethiopians starve, recognizing that there is a natural logic to the order of things, not unlike that of Adam Smith's market. Then, in May 1987, the Earth First! journal published an article by "Miss Ann Thropy." The argument: "I take it as axiomatic that the only real hope for the continuation of diverse ecosystems on this planet is an enormous decline in population...If the AIDS epidemic didn't exist, radical environmentalists would have to invent one" (Dowie 1995:210).[5]

It is unclear whether Earth First! has given the Bhopal disaster the same high marks for productivity that it gave to the Ethiopian famine and AIDS. Commentary on these statements has nonetheless circulated widely among environmental activists in both India and the United States. Many recognize that the logic of Earth First! opposes but sustains that of *Fortune* and the business press generally. Some environmentalists, even if not themselves habitants of the radical periphery, consider this radical opposition productive. Anonymous voices from mainstream environmental organizations often recognize Foreman and his cronies as "real resources" who create a space within which groups such as the Wilderness Society can sound "eminently reasonable."

Strategic differentiation may also explain the disjuncture between the business press and business itself. By the early 1990s corporations could not longer be heard as antienvironmentalist. They may have seen the amendments to the Clean Air Act as a threat, but they could not simply oppose them. Corporations continue to remind audiences that we cannot expect a risk-free world, and that everything is dangerous if mishandled. But they rarely baldly oppose environmental safety and economic growth, at least in public performances. They endorse the business press's faith in voluntary compliance and freewheeling "wise-use," rather than regulation, and they insist that their risk assessment techniques are scientific. But by the 1990s, corporations' glossy brochures have become model commitments to environmental excellence. Wild animals play on the covers. The new emblem, shared by all member companies of the Chemical Manufacturers Association, is of two hands, cupped as though praying for the world rather than seeking to conquer it. In the standardized CMA image, three spheres float above the cupped hands. They probably are meant to represent the molecules that chemical companies synthesize into their great contributions to society. When lifted into the brochures of individual companies, a butterfly can substitute for the spheres, and the hands can become those of a child.

If Earth First! creates a space in which the Wilderness Society sounds eminently reasonable, the business press creates similar space for business itself. As a vice president at Dow explains, "One way to lose a reputation for combativeness is to stop being combative, and that's what we've done. Another thing we're doing is to spend more time finding out what people are thinking" (Hoffman 1997:98). What people are thinking is shaped by the seemingly different but structurally similar discourses of *Fortune* and Dave Foreman. Together, the business press and radical environmentalism operate like the proscenium arch that separates a stage from an auditorium. You can't be in the play unless you cross into a space structured by harsh opposition. Props are set up to encourage allegiance with one side or the other—north or south, east or west, heads (here "science") or tails (here "commitment"), feast or famine.

MORALIZING RESPONSIBILITY

Joe Varian heard about the Bhopal disaster while in the parking lot at Walt Disney World. He took off his jacket and put it back in the car. He no longer wanted to advertise the logo for Union Carbide's plant in Institute, West Virginia, where he had worked in distribution for nearly thirty years. In his mind, his jacket did not identify him just with Union Carbide. He knew that the Bhopal plant, which had just released forty tons of MIC over a sleeping city, was considered by the company to be the "sister plant" of the plant in Institute, the only facility in the United States where MIC was produced, with similar technology, including bulk storage capacity.[6]

Varian's insistence not only on remembering the Bhopal disaster but also on trying to understand his place within it runs counter to the official Carbide line, which victims describe as an encapsulation maneuver: isolate the disaster in time, bound it geographically, regard rehabilitation as complete when shares bounce back on Wall Street. The encapsulation maneuver is legitimated by claiming that the parent company cannot be held responsible for mishaps at a subsidiary, and by shifting responsibility to the government of India. The rhetorical and institutional means by which Union Carbide played these claims began immediately following the disaster and has changed little since, although not without disruption both from outside and from within.

In August 1986, Jackson Browning, vice president of Union Carbide, wrote a letter to the *New York Times* explaining that an article published the previous month about the Bhopal disaster "points to one of the continuing tragedies in that city: the apparent decision by the Indian Government to make health concerns subservient to litigation concerns." The letter goes on to bemoan the lack of "third-party evaluation of health effects of the gas release," supposedly stymied by the Indian government and creating a situation in which "enlightened decisions on medical treatment—now and in future years—cannot be made." Nonetheless, Carbide has continued to offer "major humanitarian assistance—with no strings attached and no ties to an ultimate litigation award...India has refused most of these offers apparently in the mistaken belief that acceptance would reduce ultimate compensation." The letter closes with the insistence that, "Immediately following the gas release, Union Carbide said that it would take moral responsibility and let legal responsibility get sorted out later so that the immediate needs of the victims could be met. We believe that the Government of India should make the same kind of commitment to the people of Bhopal" (Browning 1986).

Browning's letter reiterates Union Carbide's standing line on the Bhopal disaster. The insistence that the company accepts "moral responsibility, but no liability" was put into circulation immediately following the gas leak and has been the most repeated response ever since. In 1985 it became the basis of Union Carbide's plea for dismissal of the Bhopal case from US courts, on grounds that the parent company, headquartered in Danbury, Connecticut, had no jurisdiction over the plant operations in Bhopal. This claim was later substantiated through a highly publicized sabotage theory wherein blame for the disaster was located within a five-minute interval of purposeful action by a "disgruntled worker." In sum, Carbide argued that the preemptive knowledge that could have prevented the disaster was beyond the organizational capability of the corporation. There was intentional misconduct, but it was not their own.

Carbide's sabotage theory was first fully presented at an independent conference of chemical engineers in London during the spring of 1988. The paper, "Investigation of Large-Magnitude Incidents: Bhopal as a Case Study," was presented by Ashok Kalelkar, a representative of the engineering firm of Arthur D. Little. Kalelkar's primary goal was to challenge the water-washing theory put forth by journalists and by India's Central Bureau of Investigation, a theory constructed through the testimony of plant workers.[7]

The water-washing theory states that around 8:30 on the evening of December 2 a routine maintenance procedure was carried out to clear blocked lines in the Relief Valve Vent Header piping configuration, downstream from the MIC storage tank. Despite Carbide's own maintenance regulations, the procedure was carried out without the insertion of slipbinds to keep water from backing up into the storage area. MIC storage tank 610 was not holding pressure, so water was able to pass the pressure control valve into the tank.

Carried with the water which flowed into tank 610 were iron rust filings from corroding pipe walls, residue of the salt compounds that had blocked the lines being washed, and other contaminants. The entry of water plus contaminants into the MIC storage tank set off an exothermic reaction that caused catalytic trimerization, a runaway reaction causing massive rise in pressure and temperature that resulted in the release of the tank's contents to the atmosphere.

The water-washing theory implicates Carbide management both for decisions immediately prior to the disaster and for long-term processes of plant design, maintenance, and personnel training. In his refutation, Kalelkar insisted that "salient, non-technical features" be investigated, requiring "an understanding of human nature in addition to the necessary technical and engineering skills." Kalelkar then refuted the water-washing theory with a technical analysis grounded on the claim that "there is a reflexive tendency among plant workers everywhere to attempt to divorce themselves from the events surrounding any incident and to distort or omit facts to serve their own purposes" (Kalelkar 1988).

Because of this reflexive tendency among workers, Kalelkar based his investigation on the accounts of peripheral witnesses. A primary witness was Mr. Rajan, an instruments engineer who claimed that on the morning following the leak he noticed that the pressure gauge on tank 610 had been removed, leaving an opening through which water could have been introduced from a nearby hose. It took Rajan over a year to remember this detail, after which he was relocated to Bombay. The other primary witness was a 12-year-old tea boy, retrieved after much effort from his native Nepal. The tea boy is said to have been on duty the night of the disaster and describes a tense atmosphere just preceding the leak, thus "verifying" that all workers on-site were involved in a conspiratorial cover-up.

Carbide's sabotage theory pins the cause of the disaster on a five-minute interval when a "disgruntled" worker attached a water hose directly to a storage tank filled with methyl isocyanate. No mention is made of the reason there were no safety mechanisms to prevent unauthorized inputs. No mention is made that, according to Carbide's own regulations, the tank should only have been three-quarters full and an adjacent tank empty to allow for transfers in case of emergency. No mention is made that there was no early warning system that would have tracked subsequent rises in temperature, indicating that disaster was imminent. No mention is made that four of five major safety systems failed to work due to indifferent maintenance. No mention was made that these systems were all underdesigned to accommodate mass escape of gas at pressures up to 720 pounds per minute.

SURVIVALISM, AVALANCHE, AND EQUAL OPPORTUNITY

Union Carbide has accepted "moral responsibility, but no liability" for the Bhopal disaster. Out of broader contexts, the opposition seems oxymoronic. Perception of logical contradiction is, however, culturally constituted and socially situated. Carbide's opposition of responsibility and liability is therefore fully rational, "made comfortable to reason" through the work of new cadres of professionals who insist that environmentalism does matter and that it does not contradict established profit accrual strategies. They insist that "going green" is possible, desirable, and in the process of being realized. The rhetorical strategies for circumventing the contradictions are multifaceted, but one persistent theme provides grounding: moving beyond blame.

The logic of being "beyond blame" insists that environmental devastation is a shared concern and a shared responsibility, generated by a complex of social processes that allow no designation of a single culprit. Corporate environmental excellence is in everyone's interest, and requires neither regulation nor litigation to propel it forward. The task of the consultant is to make this mutuality visible, proving that "one of the distinguishing features of the environmental movement... is its inclusiveness. Men and women, rich and poor, far and near, are all beginning to ask the same set of questions. As they take off their masks and discover that the battle to save the environment is a journey that cuts across all societal divisions, we discover how universal the concerns for environmental health and safety have become" (Piasecki and Asmus 1990:170).[8]

A major landmark in this journey "beyond blame" was the Bhopal disaster. According to consultant Bruce Piasecki, the Bhopal disaster engendered an "avalanche of change," signaled by the model Union Carbide has provided the chemical industry in environmental excellence. In Piasecki's reporting, Union Carbide provided such a model before the disaster and has reemerged as a leader since. According to Piasecki, Carbide was one of the first corporations to subscribe to the Sullivan Principles, which specify the nature and goals of corporate environmentalism, and an MIT study rated Carbide as the best corporate citizen among the multinational companies it studied, based on the company's environmental programs, social responsibility, and responsiveness to host governments. Apparently relying on inside information, Piasecki states that "the company had long made safety a priority. Any disabling injury to employees elicited urgent attention at the highest levels of management" (Piasecki 1994:6).

Piasecki recognizes that the night of December 2, 1984, changed everything, resulting in Carbide's entry into the *Guinness Book of World Records* under the section "Worst Accidents and Disasters in the World." Since then, "the Bhopal legacy has attached itself to Union Carbide like Hawthorne's 'scarlet letter' to the adulteress Hester Prynne, depicting the company as no less immoral" (Piasecki 1994:7). In response, Carbide is credited with crafting distinctive environmental management initiatives, which include new classification systems that link regulatory compliance to the legal department's liability-containment strategies, audits on environmental performance that allow executives to compete for capital resources, computer monitoring of "episodic risk," and new management tools that keep senior personnel in touch with liability issues by sentencing them to jail time for environmental crimes (Piasecki 1994:8).

Piasecki never mentions the health status of gas victims in Bhopal or the role of Union Carbide in litigation regarding asbestos, the Dalkon Shield, and twenty-two Superfund sites.[9] Instead, he notes that "in fact, history books will show that the Chemical Manufacturers Association's current 'Responsible Care Initiative,' which developed a shared code of environmental management behavior for the industry, evolved directly from Union Carbide's tragedy." In the same paragraph, he notes that "the new consulting divisions of Arthur D. Little, Booz-Allen and Hamilton, and ICF-Kaiser Engineering derive their energy and fees from the fears triggered by the Bhopal disaster" (Piasecki 1994:8). It was under the guidance of such consultants that Union Carbide responded to the Bhopal disaster. According to Piasecki, the response was systematic. Carbide hired Arthur D. Little. The company held "visioning" sessions of great intensity. Environmental audits became "the buck that no one could pass" (Piasecki 1995:26).

Prior to the Bhopal disaster, environmental audits at Union Carbide were based on complex standards, heavily oriented to US laws and regulations and differing "widely in scale of application from actual requirements to nonimplementable ideals. The full set took 14 inches of office shelf space, and that's where they often remained, unread" (Piasecki 1995:28). According to Piasecki, the standards that emerged after the disaster made their debut boldly, provoking many in the company to note that "it was as if Ross Perot was their chief editor." The new standards "were only ½ inch thick, simple and focused, readable, and, most important, one could audit against them." The simplicity standard was not met by telling people "how to" meet the grade, but by "expressing each higher standard as an executive expectation." Today, "standards are no longer a topic requiring on-the-shelf research. They have become conversational, the topic of everyday life for executive[s] and line professionals alike" (Piasecki 1995:28).

Piasecki's laudatory analysis of Union Carbide is developed in his book *Corporate Environmental Strategy: The Avalanche of Change Since Bhopal* (1995). The overall promise is that strategic leadership can outsmart the opposition between government and industry, and between the economy and the environment. Piasecki explains that the genre he has chosen is the dramatic case study, because it can provide representative details that help us interpret historical change. Unlike most authors writing about environmental management, who cite hundreds of firms each, he focuses on a few consequential cases. His "selective dramatization" is meant to help us abstract meaning from seemingly isolated examples to provide a "contemplation of cultural change," which has had "fecund momentum" since Bhopal. As Piasecki notes, "When you are dealing with an avalanche of change, it doesn't help much to do a drop-by-drop or flake-by-flake analysis. What follows, then, is a big-picture dramatization of what has happened to the corporate world in general, and the field of environmental management in particular, since Bhopal" (Piasecki 1995:11).

Piasecki acknowledges that the dramatic case study does have shortcomings, noting that "some feel, for instance, that it moves too rapidly from observation to conclusion, and they miss its somewhat quiet quest for heightened and representative insight. They simply want facts and figures." One risk is that experts will feel disoriented, the policy makers will feel uncertain, and those with ideological motives will feel anger or frustration. Piasecki's audience, however, is the general manager, "who can benefit from case studies which are not about what should happen, but rather, what is happening, and how it is taking place." Case studies are reliable because they sidestep ideology and political hyperbole, examining both the art and science of environmental strategy (Piasecki 1995:xii).

How, though, can distinct cases capture what is happening in general, across all companies? "The answer rests in the experience of an avalanche. An avalanche accomplishes two things. First, the massive slide utterly changes the landscape. There are new forms to consider. At first, the newness is disorienting, sometimes downright overwhelming." Next, an avalanche separates different kinds of survivors. "As a downward curtain of terror, an avalanche fans open in a massive sprawl, including a far larger realm than the first boom suggested" (Piasecki 1995:5). Different companies survive in different ways, evolving strategies that "still resemble the best defense scenarios generated in the silent halls of the Pentagon itself" (Piasecki 1995:4), responding to the specific threats and possibilities which characterize a company's field of action.

Piasecki acknowledges that for the last twenty years corporate executives have responded to environmental regulation with bewilderment and resistance, caught in foreign terrain without the solid footing of conventional, internally focused management tools. He remembers his own experience while climbing the Sierra Divide with friends. They encountered an avalanche. The boom began. Within seconds, miles of snow fanned toward them. Their first reaction was to find the closest rock and hide behind it—like most companies responding to the aftermath of Bhopal, hoping to find a safe haven in the "greenwash" of public relations. The result was false security in a time of severe and irreversible change.

Corporate environmental management has "matured considerably since Bhopal," even while public debate remains "locked in wheel-spinning and blame" (Piasecki 1995:4). The most advanced maneuvers have acknowledged dramatic change in the landscape, modifying how corporations are imagined, correcting for "the distorting authority of noted popular myths" (1995:10). The first of these myths suggests that corporations don't know what they're doing regarding the environment, telling a tale of corporations as misaligned, out-of-control machine tools, spitting out sparks and shards in all directions. The second myth suggests that corporations are too secretive regarding the environment, relying on manipulative marketing to keep any disclosure "ziplocked with secrecy" (1995:10). These myths, Piasecki states, are at times obsolete. Instead, one should imagine the corporation through the metaphor of a house, "a large rambling structure with plenty of windows, doors and points of entry." Lawyers can peer in via provisions for freedom of information. Communities have the right to know. Even the Securities and Exchange Commission can look inside, through increasing demands for disclosure of risk generated by environmental as well as financial concerns (Piasecki 1994:12).

The challenge is to recognize the metaphoric significance of the avalanche, as did Warren Anderson, CEO of Carbide at the time of the Bhopal disaster—the "environmental equivalent of Pearl Harbor, a violent wake-up call that shook many nations and many firms" (Piasecki 1995:24). According to Piasecki, the press and academia only contributed to Anderson's problem. "Not content to recognize Bhopal as the paramount environmental disaster, scholars and journalists embellished the story with brutality and barbarism as well. Was this not the 'perfect' example of corporate environmental neglect and abuse?" (Piasecki 1994:23). Warren Anderson responded by insisting that Carbide view the disaster in "moral, not legal terms." A footnote explains that "the Bhopal plant was run entirely by Indian managers and technicians and was in fact partially owned by the Indian government. Yet Carbide's US headquarters aided the victims, cleaned up the site, and investigated the cause of the incident. This was only right and illustrates how an avalanche implicates the entire firm" (Piasecki 1994:150n13). Union Carbide's board of directors wasn't as quick as Warren Anderson, and only got the "real message" eight months after the Bhopal disaster, following an "incident" in Institute, West Virginia, at another major Carbide facility where MIC is produced and stored. Although shocked by Bhopal, the board had assured themselves that "it couldn't happen here." The incident at Institute proved that it could.

CIRCLES OF POISON[10]

On August 11, 1985, a cloud of chemicals used in the manufacture of aldicarb (Temik) spread over four communities in Institute, West Virginia. Residents were concerned but confused. After the leak in Bhopal, they had been assured that any hazardous emission from the plant would be detected by a new $5-million computerized leak detection system, allowing plant operators to warn exposed communities immediately following any release. The system, known as "Safer," was supposed to be able to identify instantly the speed and direction of a toxic leak. Carbide, however, had failed to program the system to detect the specific chemical combination spilled. As a result, plant workers thought that the gas cloud was hovering above the plant itself and not migrating over surrounding communities. The release included aldicarb oxine, which contains trace amounts of MIC, and methylene chloride, a nervous-system toxin and a suspected carcinogen under special EPA review.

For twenty minutes no siren sounded. The eyes of plant workers were glued to a computer screen while the world outside their window was being covered with a cream-colored cloud of chemicals. Meanwhile, thousands of nearby residents were exposed and 130 were headed for hospitals. Officials later warned that food grown near the Institute plant might be contaminated and should not be eaten. OSHA cited Union Carbide for "willful neglect" and, in April 1986, fined Carbide $1.4 million for 221 violations of 55 federal health and safety laws. US Labor Secretary William Brock stated, "We were just surprised to find constant, willful, overt violations on such a widespread basis." In March 1986, Carbide negotiated a settlement with OSHA, agreeing to pay $408,000 for "five serious violations" in return for an agreement to correct the violations immediately (Dembo, Morehouse, and Wykle 1990:84).

In interviews, residents and workers of the Institute area referred to the month following the incident on August 11 as "toxic hell month." On August 18, a tank truck accident leaked sulfur trioxide, requiring the evacuation of thirty homes. On August 26, a cloud of water and hydrochloric acid leaked and drifted over South Charleston, in the vicinity of a Chubby Checker concert with 35,000 people in attendance, whom officials decided "it was better not to warn than panic." On September 7, an undisclosed amount of dimethyl disulfide and Larvin leaked from the Institute plant, also without any alarms sounding. On September 8, a leak of methyl mercaptain in nearby Nitro hospitalized three workers. On September 11, the South Charleston plant leaked liquid monomethylamine but did not report the release until three days later.[11]

Community response to these so-called incidents has been vehement, if sporadic and not without division. Institute, West Virginia, is the home of the sister plant to Carbide's plant in Bhopal, and the Institute plant is now owned by the French megacorporation Rhône-Poulenc. Institute is in the Kanawha Valley, near both Charleston and Hawk's Nest, where, in the 1930s, over seven hundred workers were killed by acute silicosis while building a hydroelectric tunnel for Union Carbide. The Kanawha Valley has nonetheless remained a Carbide stronghold, with the company enjoying extraordinary loyalty among workers and residents. Since the Bhopal disaster, this loyalty has begun to break down. Union Carbide sold its agricultural products division, including major facilities in West Virginia, indicating to many that any loyalty lacked mutuality. Then Union Carbide, along with Rhône-Poulenc, replaced local workers with contract employees brought from outside the state, breaking union faith that "what is good for the company is good for workers." Meanwhile, Union Carbide initiated a new rhetoric of management revolving around the concept of "stakeholders"—"those groups and individuals that can affect[,] or are affected by, the accomplishment of organizational purposes" (Freeman 1984:25). In theory at least, the new management rhetoric required a "radical rethinking of the firm," recognizing that community members and employees have a place at the negotiating table alongside shareholders and upper management.[12]

Today, many local citizens feel duped, both by Union Carbide and by the general claim that citizen representation is a viable means to democratic participation in risk decisions. One Institute resident insists that "while it looks more democratic, it really is a child's game in which we all pretend that everyone has a grown-up role." Many say that they live in even more fear of disaster than before, and that the only function of the new "right-to-know" laws has been to inform them of danger, without allowing them to do anything about it. Union workers echo residents' complaints, insisting that they now have less control than ever before over maintenance procedures, since permanent employees have been replaced by contract labor who aren't unionized and have no commitment to the local community.

Some in the Kanawha Valley do think that progress has been made in securing environmental safety. Citizens, emergency personnel, and plant employees all refer to a key event that promises to make the region a model for national implementation of new provisions of the Clean Air Act. "Safety Street" was the keystone of the Kanawha Valley Hazard Assessment Project, initiated in response to a citizen request for worst-case scenarios. A Du Pont process safety expert explains its significance: "What's exciting about participating in this whole activity in the Kanawha Valley, [is that] it clearly is at the leading edge of pending regulations at the federal level which are three or four years away... [We] are going to have a positive impact on how federal regulations will be written, developed, and implemented" (Jackson 1994:69). EPA's Carl Matthiessen concurred, encouraging participants in Safety Street not to wait for the EPA, because "we don't have all the answers. You have all the answers. And I think most of what you're doing is already state-of-the art" (Chemical Manufacturers Association 1994).

Staged jointly by the fourteen chemical plants in the valley, Safety Street was organized to air data on the potential results of a plant mishap. The event's banner read, "Safety Street: Managing Our Risks Together." The first part of the event, staged at the Charleston Civic Center, included nine presentations, by industry representatives, emergency planning officials, regulators, and ordinary citizens, explaining different roles played in risk management. After lunch, formality ended, and the audience could approach presenters at convention-style booths. The following day, the relay of information was moved to a local shopping mall, where passersby could scan graphs that carefully discriminated between "worst-case" and "more likely" scenarios.

The pamphlet distributed at this event that described risk management for MIC is instructive. A "worst-case scenario" is identified as "sudden loss of contents of the underground storage tank when completely full (253,600 lbs.)." The accompanying graph draws two concentric circles around the plant. The inner circle, identified as ERPG3, has a radius of nine miles, within which concentration levels would be five parts per million (ppm). The outer circle, identified as ERPG2, has a radius of twenty-eight miles, within which concentration levels would be 0.5 ppm. The graph is surrounded by detail on process and equipment design, safety review procedures, and emergency response plans. The next page describes a "more likely scenario," during which 118 pounds of MIC would escape through a 0.8-mm-diameter hole. The graph here doesn't show the circles, but the numbers indicate that the risk is substantially less. The area designated as ERPG3 would have a radius of only half a mile; ERPG2 would have a radius of only three miles.[13]

Nowhere within this pamphlet are readers told what an "ERPG" is, or what it would mean to be within an ERPG3 area at the time of a catastrophic release of toxic gas. An article in the journal *Corporate Environmental Strategy* provides the explanation. An ERPG is an "Emergency Response Planning Guide," administered by the American Industrial Hygiene Association. ERPG3 designates an area within which "it is believed that nearly all individuals could be exposed for up to one hour without experiencing or developing life-threatening health effects." ERPG2 designates an area within which "it is believed that nearly all individuals could be exposed for up to one hour without experiencing or developing irreversible or other serious health effects or symptoms which could impair an individual's ability to take protective action" (Jackson 1994:73).

In other words, if you don't get out of an area designated as ERPG3 within an hour after a worst-case release, you're dead. If you don't get out of an area designated as ERPG2 within an hour, you aren't going anywhere, and, at best, you'll develop "irreversible or other serious health effects." Such, at least, might be the scenario if you are the generic "individual" designated by the ERPG. It is even less clear what happens to a child, an elderly person, an ill person, or some other differentiated category.

This overview is bad enough at the theoretical level. On the ground it is truly catastrophic. The Kanawha Valley is, in fact, a valley. It is hemmed in by mountains, with one interstate leading out of town. There are a few back roads through the hills, but they are often difficult to access. One such road, adjacent to the Institute plant, is gated and locked. Industry representatives say they will be happy to open it upon necessity, though it is unclear whether emergency planning procedures assign anyone to this task. The road empties out near an African-American community that shares a fence line with the plant, as does the campus of West Virginia State College. Nearby, there is a rehabilitation facility that houses severely disabled patients.

Industry recognizes the problems associated with any attempt to evacuate the Kanawha Valley. Its solution is to encourage residents to "shelter in place." Instructions are distributed on small, house-shaped magnets that can be attached to the family refrigerator:

1. Go inside.
2. Turn off air moving equipment.
3. Turn on radio or television.
4. Tune in emergency broadcast system.
5. Stand by for telephone ring-down.
6. Stay calm.

The friendly, house-shaped reminder neglects to explain how residents need to cover doors and windows with plastic, taped to walls with duct tape. It also forgets about the lime green sign residents should post in a window, visible from the street, once they are locked inside. The sign reads: WE HAVE BEEN NOTIFIED.

Residents of the Kanawha Valley are divided in their evaluation of "sheltering in place," and of the Safety Street Initiative that helped bring it to public attention. Some are harshly fatalistic, insisting that in the Kanawha Valley the chemicals will, eventually, "getcha." One resident insisted that this is almost natural: "First they killed the Indians; now they're killing the hillbillies." Others are more strategic, pointing out that it is not insignificant that local chemical companies have to replace their own stock of gas masks so frequently: workers steal them and take them home to their families. Still others cooperate with initiatives such as Safety Street, playing roles in instructional videos, serving as company diplomats at school and civic functions, attending meetings that "bring everyone to the table" and demonstrate "Responsible Care."

Industry in the Kanawha Valley seems confident that its safety plans are sufficient. Management experts confirm this sense of security. Their logic is that the Clean Air Act Amendments of 1990 require chemical facilities to develop and distribute risk management programs, beyond the disclosure requirements of previous environmental legislation. Industry hopes to implement a model before EPA announces its own. The model developed in the Kanawha Valley could become the standard against which compliance with the law is measured. Management experts are therefore encouraging, reminding their clients that "worst case scenarios don't have to be ugly, don't have to be scary. Like planning for your own funeral, it is a necessary activity that can be looked upon with fear and loathing, or it can be an eye-opening activity…" (Jackson 1994:69). Nowhere in the article where this encouragement is deployed are residents quoted or otherwise given space to air their own views.

STAKING ALTERNATIVES

The Bhopal disaster has generated a great deal of commentary in various academic disciplines[14] and within the popular press. It is often presented as a matter of "risk management," situated within a configuration of multiple "stakeholders." The discourse of stakeholders, now relied on by all sides of the political spectrum in engaging with environmental issues, emerged in the attempt to recognize the complex interaction of different parties in late-industrial societies. The conceptual basis of the discourse recognizes differences in objective social position, which must be adjudicated. Thus, there appears to be a recognition of conflict that could serve as an important addendum to environmentalist discourse grounded on universalistic claims of a natural, proper relation between humans and their context.

But there are problems with the stakeholder model, most evident in its performative effect. Minority players in environmental conflict continue to feel marginalized; capital continues to determine what is both feasible and desirable; the "manageability" of environmental risk is never questioned. The stakeholder model does provide a place at the table for citizens and others whose allegiances are "beyond the fence." But it is not good manners to insist that there are, indeed, divergent views of reality and tastes for change. Some oppositional voices keep talking anyway.

Communities Concerned about Corporations (CCC), a coalition of labor, community, and shareholder activists, is an example. The story of the emergence and development of CCC is a story of frustration with the environmental regulations enacted in the last ten years. A key component of these regulations was the mandate for citizen involvement in risk management decisions, to be enacted through the "right to know" about hazardous production processes previously considered off limits as corporate trade secrets.

The problems with the promise have been conceptual as well as practical. Most generally, knowledge has not equaled power. Even if they had had sufficient time and expertise to wade through the documentation provided under these laws, risk bearers have not had the institutional basis required for effective intervention in corporate decision making. In the midst of right-to-know laws, citizens' advisory committees, and worker safety councils, people across the country have become aware that structural impediments not only keep them from achieving greater safety, but also make them pawns of the system. The response has not been a critique of democracy and law per se, but an insistence on the continued relevance of constitutional argument.

CCC grounds its work in constitutional claims to the sovereign rights of the US people, as opposed to those of corporations. A key reference for the group is a pamphlet titled "Taking Care of Business," which argues that "when we look at the history of our states, we learn that citizens intentionally defined corporations through charters. In exchange, for the charter, a corporation was obliged to obey all laws to serve the common good and cause no harm" (Grossman and Adams 1993). Such idealization allowed for a straightforward statement of purpose for convening a major political meeting to commemorate the tenth anniversary of the Bhopal disaster: "We demand our democratic rights. We demand a new charter for the Union Carbide Corporation. We want the company to be a part of our communities' future but only on condition that its managers give priority to hiring local workers, and respect their rights, protect and restore the environment, and share the risk inherent in hazardous industry. Above all else, we demand that workers and neighbors play a major role in deciding the future of Carbide's facilities in our communities. This is the democratic way. This is the American way" (CCC 1994). The strategy of charter revocation embeds CCC within a fundamental irony of the Fourteenth Amendment to the US Constitution: formulated to protect emancipated slaves, its enactment has served to protect the corporation as a person in ways that often override the rights of individual human persons, particularly those in minority and low-income neighborhoods.

RECURSIVE REGIMES

Corporate environmentalism relies on multiple financial, legal, organizational, and rhetorical mechanisms that have come to characterize contemporary political economy. Few of these mechanisms seem particularly significant in isolation. Interconnected, however, they have realigned entrenched relationships between corporations, the nation-state, and citizens, and have shaped the underbelly of the world in which advocates have responded to the Bhopal disaster. The days of faith that what is good for General Motors is good for America seem to be over. Many perceive multinational corporations as a threat to democracy and an impediment to national economic prosperity. Simultaneously, however, many claim that the nation-state may no longer be the primary organizational entity responsible for redressing social problems.

Explanations that focus on how corporations are above the law due to the sheer quantity of their financial power are not enough. The operations of power through which Union Carbide and other petrochemical companies have moved "beyond Bhopal" are more subtle. Although laws have been broken and crude authority often exercised, a persistent strategy of working within the ideals and institutions of democratic governance has also been evident. The effect has been uneven, allowing many to applaud industry initiatives while others are left disoriented, but with a residing sense that they have less control than ever over how the risks of industrial production are distributed.

The disorientation produced by contemporary environmental hazard is, in part, due to systematic disjuncture between what people are told about risk management and how they must deal with risk management in their daily lives. Ethnography could play a role in helping us understand the effect, by turning "synthetics" from toxic threat to cultural critique. To synthesize is to bring together things that do not naturally cohere. Synthetics can be harmful, in the form of chemicals or of Hegelian dialectics. Hegelian claims to steady progress toward absolute knowledge are visible in the clean developmental narratives of corporate environmentalism. They move us beyond blame. All opposition is overcome. A metaphor like sustainable development disguises contradictory messages as a unified argument. There is no acknowledgment that discourse can never be adequate to its example, or that the right to know is not the same thing as justice.

Synthetics can, however, be engaged differently, providing an image for ethnographic description that forms a complex whole by combination, but drawing out rather than effacing fissure between components. Late cubist painters experimented with this strategy, increasing their use of color and layering their surfaces with different textures and materials. As in earlier phases of cubism, the subject was approached from many different angles. Multiple viewpoints were kept visible through the use of parallel planes. Collage provided a way to further accentuate the difficult task of seeing. A 1913 collage by Picasso is one example. Pieces of paper in different colors and patterns are layered on the surface of the painting. A few charcoal lines suggest that what we see may be a human head. But without the title, "Head of a Man," we cannot be sure. The lines make us look closer, both for a man and at the myriad textures that make him up.[15]

Ethnography needs to learn to draw these few lines, suggesting what may be going on without claiming to offer a final reading. The layers of the collage must be built up. Then a few marks are made on its surface. The work is not in underscoring the obvious but in suggesting that there are alignments that haven't been noticed or concurrences that developmental narratives leave out.

One particularly unsettling concurrence illustrates the challenge: In 1989 a Union Carbide public affairs strategy group circulated a memo concerning the environmental group convened by Lois Gibbs, famous as a key voice from Love Canal. The memo warned that Citizens' Clearinghouse for Hazardous Waste (CCHW) is "one of the most radical coalitions operating under the environmentalist banner...with ties into labor, the communist party, and all manner of folk with private/single agenda[s]." The agenda of CCHW was to "restructure US society into something unrecognizable and probably unworkable. It's a tour de force of public issues to be affecting business in years to come." Amidst the media coverage of Earth Day 1990, the author of the memo sent an apology to Gibbs, after the *Washington Post* threatened to publish the memo in full (Lepkowski 1994:38).

Just eight days prior to circulation of the memo, Robert Kennedy gave his opening speech as elected chairman of the Chemical Manufacturers Association. This speech, taking up the challenge of regaining the "trust and confidence of the public," insisted that "there is a growing need for predictable, consistent environmental stewardship from nation to nation and region to region around the world. The chemical industry has a great opportunity in the years ahead to make new history." Kennedy followed his speech with the initiation of the CMA's "Responsible Care Program," a "major performance-based initiative" to "work together in ways that the public sees as responsive to their concerns." In addition to pledging to support the industry's responsible management of chemicals, the program instituted "Public Advisory Panels composed of environmental, health and safety thought leaders" who would be asked to comment on all aspects of management, including the ways products are developed, made, transported, used, and disposed of. Carbide's brochure describing the program states that "beyond specifics, Responsible Care signals the Chemical Industry's commitment to keep faith with America and the world" (Union Carbide 1989).

How can this concurrence be drawn out? What does it mean, beyond the obvious duplicity? Does it signal a shift in the way corporate identity is configured, away from contractarian models reminiscent of the Enlightenment subject? Is it a demonstration of something like psychosis—a refusal to connect different orders of activity? What does it say about boundaries both within the corporation and with the outside world? What does it say about how power operates, when a "private" memo from the public affairs department of a public company is leaked to the *Washington Post,* and then the story is retold by a senior journalist at *Chemical and Engineering News* in an academic article (Lepkowski 1994:38)? These questions could never generate an adequate explanation of the Bhopal disaster. But they might begin drawing out its meaning, transfiguring remembrance, staging a future less determined by the force of repetition.

ETHNOGRAPHY AND THE POLITICS OF DISASTER

> The Bhopal incident has not affected our ability to do business. It was a terrible human tragedy along with the sabotage that led to it. The tragedy had an indirect consequence in the form of GAF's takeover attempt a year after Bhopal. But Bhopal is history now.
>
> —*Robert Kennedy, CEO, Union Carbide Corporation*

> To articulate the past historically does not mean to recognize it "the way it really was" (Ranke). It means to seize hold of a memory as it flashes up at a moment of danger.
>
> —*Walter Benjamin*

The Bhopal disaster is most easily located one December night in 1984 when a Union Carbide pesticide plant released over forty tons of methyl isocyanate over a sleeping city. Reliable estimates claim over 10,000 people dead within the first few days thereafter. By geographic indicators, 600,000 people were exposed and continue to suffer physical and economic devastation. In February 1989, litigation of the case was settled out-of-court for $470 million, without the consent of victims. The medical data on which the settlement amount was based placed only 5 percent of victims in compensable categories, despite new evidence of immune system damage and chromosomal aberration. In August 1994, as people around the world prepared to commemorate the tenth anniversary of the disaster, a total of 82,523 individual cases had been cleared by Claims Courts in Bhopal. The award for each death ranged from $4,000 to $12,000.[16]

These numbers resist memory, intellectual engagement, and political change. Abstracted from context, they become mere blips in the litany of death figures that structure twentieth-century history, lost in other numbers citing the threat of population growth, deforestation, and declining terms of trade. I have tried to configure Bhopal differently, exploring while challenging conventional modes of remembrance, questioning how knowledge of the past becomes moral knowledge, constitutive of future possibility.

Remember Bhopal. This slogan has been repeated for over thirteen years throughout both India and the United States, by different social actors, in dramatically different contexts. How has the slogan become meaningful? How has it guided social initiative? Within what world is it spoken? What world does it evoke? One worlding device is globalization, understood as a process wherein new political-economic orders are producing new normative orders. Globalization distributes value and meaning in new ways, exceeding the explanatory capacity of established modes of accounting for social change. Globalization also exceeds the reach of conventional ethical models, evident in disasters such as Bhopal wherein transfers of capital, technology, and risk complicate assignations of responsibility. What counts as knowledge remains contested. What the past means is underdetermined. How, as an ethnographer, can I respond?

Ethnography within globalization is far from straightforward. One key move is a shift of focus from Bhopal as a spatially circumscribed site of research to the disaster itself, understood as a legacy that draws geographically dispersed actors into a never-ending, asymmetrical conversation about justice in contemporary world order. Turning disaster into the "object" of my concern is rife with contradictions. The Bhopal disaster continues in time and crosscuts spatial boundaries. It resides at the intersection of different legal regimes, and where bureaucracy collides with everyday life. It is located in competing definitions of health, fairness, and progress. It inhabits the discourse and social style of corporate environmentalism. The meaning of disaster cannot be stabilized. But written as disaster, Bhopal becomes a prism through which we can view the world, askew.

Ethnography of disaster within late capitalism should aspire to produce, for the uses of our imagination, a glimpse into the unrepresentably complex world system in which we live. Methodologically, this means pulling globalization into an ethnographic field of vision: tracking micro- and macroprocesses; triangulating interpretive and political-economic perspectives; accounting for paradox—the contradictory ways science, technology, law, nationalism, and other phenomena operate—as crucial social resources in some registers and locales, as mechanisms that legitimate uneven distributions of risk and reward in others; and accounting for the ways political authority is catalyzed and corroded by monetary might and by myriad other operations of power.[17]

Ethnography of disaster turns to the future. Its task is one of recollection, out of sync with replication. Rote memory does not suffice. One must reach for the past, recognizing traces of what will come. Tracking historical determinations and their pathological effects is part of the work. Becoming attentive to messages or hints of signification that were once inaudible is also important, as are bringing the past into play so that its components can be recounted and recategorized, and opening the path of new questions and different futures.

"Bhopal" must be remembered, in ways that call historiography itself into question. Sathyu Sarangi, an activist working in Bhopal, articulates the conundrum: "History as we know it cannot account for disaster—disasters are externalities, written off official balance sheets, lost in a logic which assumes that today is better than yesterday, even if the same percentage of the population lives below the poverty line and government hospitals only offer symptomatic relief" (personal communication). The message is ironic: We must remember, recognizing that habitual ways of recollection fail. So history must be rewritten, countering Robert Kennedy's move beyond Bhopal, insisting that Bhopal is history, now.

Notes

1. *Opinion and Order, In Re: Union Carbide Corporation Gas Plant Disaster at Bhopal India in December 1984,* 846. F Supp. 842 (SDNY 1986).

2. This heading refers to the 1973 Charlton Heston film *Soylent Green*, about an overpopulated world dependent on synthetic food which, in the end, is shown to be synthesized from euthanized people.

3. Harrison actually begins his account in 1962. I elaborate here to provide context.

4. The official Rio conference included representatives from 150 nations and 1,400 NGOs, which were granted standing in the negotiations for the climate and biodiversity treaties. A second "Global Forum" was held elsewhere in Rio. Participating NGOs had hoped to formally present their national reports at UNCED itself. This didn't happen, nor was a clearinghouse established to facilitate circulation of the reports later. It is interesting to compare UNCED with the Stockholm Conference on the Environment in 1972. Haas, Levy, and Parson provide figures, which they insist should be taken "with a grain of salt," given inconsistent reporting of attendance: More than one hundred heads of state attended the Rio Summit, while only two went to Stockholm. Of the 1,400 NGOs accredited by UNCED, about one-third were from the developing world; at Stockholm, only 134 NGOs attended, with only about 10 percent from developing countries (Haas, Levy, and Parson 1995:162).

5. I have heard both these citations repeated, almost verbatim, by environmental activists working in both India and the United States. They are often referred to in the process of questioning the complicity of environmentalism with dominant institutions and ideology. The exact citations provided here were

included in Dowie (1995:210). Dowie locates Foreman's reference to famine in Ethiopia in an interview by Bill Devall, published in the Australian journal *Simply Living.* The article on AIDS as corrective to excess population was published in the May 1, 1987, edition of the journal *Earth First!*

6. Varian is interviewed in the film *Chemical Valley*, available from Headwaters, a part of Appalshop Video, 306 Madison Street, Whitebury, KY 41858, tel. (606) 633-0108.

7. T. R. Chouhan, a former worker at the Bhopal plant, has written a book detailing both the water-washing theory and the long history of neglect in the Bhopal plant in the years preceding the disaster. His book, *Bhopal: The Inside Story,* was one of the writing projects I worked on during my fieldwork in India, 1989–92. It is largely due to our collaboration that I now am able to engage the technical aspects of the Bhopal disaster ethnographically.

8. Many blame environmental activists for contributing to this discourse of shared concern about the environment. By many accounts, this followed Nixon's establishment of the EPA and the passage of a series of major legislative initiatives that allowed corporations to appear cooperative. Opposition was then pushed to insist that "factories don't pollute; people do," ushering in consumer environmentalism and rhetorics of "every day is Earth Day" (see Luke 1993).

9. Carbide's role in these lawsuits is documented in a financial analysis of the company compiled by the Oil, Chemical and Atomic Workers Union in June 1990, "Union Carbide Corporation: Financial Analysis."

10. This heading is borrowed from the book *Circle of Poison* (Weir and Schapiro 1981), which provided a key reference for emergent concern about the international marketing of restricted pesticides.

11. This list is only somewhat suggestive of the overwhelmingly material sense of threat that lingers over the Kanawha Valley and many other areas where chemical plants are clustered. Another small indication is a story about the "victory" won when industries in the Kanawha Valley agreed to change their alarms so that they didn't sound exactly like the alarms used a few times daily by the local firehouse, causing residents to "hold their breath for that long twenty seconds," waiting to see if the pitch would drop and a major disaster was being announced.

12. The stakeholder concept of management apparently debuted in 1984 with the publication of Freeman's "landmark" book. According to Calton and Kurland (1995:155), "The problematic nature of this concept is reflected in a history of efforts by Freeman and others, to reconcile the conventional assumption of managerial agents' fiduciary responsibility to serve a unitary organiza-

tional purpose (i.e., profit maximization) with the expectation of agent responsiveness to the counterclaims of non-owner stakeholder groups."

13. Rhône-Poulenc, "Risk Management Plan: Institute Plant: Methyl Isocyanate (MIC)," no date.

14. Much of what has been written on the Bhopal disaster is extremely good. For accounts of the early days of activism in Bhopal see Ravi Rajan (1988) and Visvanathan with Kothari (1985). For a brief but thorough overview of the first ten years of political response to the Bhopal disaster, see Claude Alvares (1994). Jaising (1994) reviews the first ten years of "legal let-down." For further interpretation of the legal issues see Veena Das (1993), V. R. Krishna Iyer (1991), and Jamie Cassels (1993). For an account of my own activism in Bhopal, see Fortun (1998). Sheila Jasanoff (1994) includes commentary on the impact of the disaster in the United States, India, Europe, and transnationally.

15. Picasso and Braque began working in collage in 1912. Torn pieces of paper and fabric were assembled on a canvas. The addition of a few lines could make an image appear, over what would otherwise look like a random collection of elements. Some refer to this work as "synthetic cubism."

16. The figures for 1994 were drawn from Alvares (1994) and Jaising (1994). Figures for earlier phases of response to Bhopal were drawn from press releases and other documents I helped produce while working in Bhopal, 1989–92.

17. My approach draws from proposals made by George E. Marcus and Michael M. J. Fischer in the mid 1980s, challenging researchers to link interpretive and political-economic perspectives for purposes of cultural critique. In their conception, cultural critique is a continually comparative effort that uses understanding of different experiences to destabilize and revitalize our own efforts toward a more humane society. Ethnography becomes a means to imagine social alternatives, disrupting conventions that have become naturalized and thereby immune to change. Recognizing the difficulty of bridging micro and macro levels of analysis, Marcus and Fischer challenge us to find a way to "represent the embedding of richly described local cultural worlds in larger impersonal systems of political economy." For ethnographers, disciplined to track detail at the micro level, "the task lies ahead of reshaping our dominant macro frameworks for the understanding of historic political economy, such as capitalism, so that they can represent the actual diversity and complexity of local situations for which they try to account in general terms" (Marcus and Fischer 1986:77, 88).

8

Worlding Cyberspace

Toward a Critical Ethnography in Time, Space, and Theory

Michael M. J. Fischer

ABSTRACT

> ...the growing realization of the inherent dangers of technology as such—not of its sudden but of its slow perils, not of its malevolent abuses which, with some watchfulness, one can hope to control, but of its most benevolent and legitimate uses...our actions have opened up a whole new dimension of ethical relevance for which there is no precedent in the standards and canons of traditional ethics.
>
> —*Hans Jonas*

> For philosophical or political reasons, this problem of communicating and receivability, in its new techno-economic givens is more serious than ever for everyone; one can live it only with malaise, contradiction, and compromise.
>
> —*Jacques Derrida*

Cyberspace is (check one; if reading this on the Web, click on one of the underlined links): (a) a game of finance and corporate maneuver; (b) an undoing of the legal system of intellectual and economic property rights, patents and copyright, secrecy and military export laws, and community standards for moral codes, as well as an undoing of several other traditional intellectual arenas of distinctions such as the economics of (free) speech versus (commodifiable) texts, and materialities of (patentable) machine versus (copyrightable) text (software); (c) a hardware technology of jerryrigging together computers, satellites, copper and fiber optic cables, and perhaps soon silicon to neural tissues, with uneven coverage into the Third World, and also in the First World, but with potentials for providing access around traditional deadened schools, local censorship, and bureaucratic stonewalling; (d) a conceptual space of connectivity, information, assorted desires for escaping or enhancing the body or material world, new paralogical language games for creating selves and socialities; (e) a research space of postliterate, graphic, self-organizing, and experimental models, simulations, and constructions; (f) a cultural-ideological, even ritual, space of (con)fusion, at least in America, between a "cowboy-hacker-individualist-anarchist-libertarian" ethic and a series of market and political mechanisms for restructuring labor in new forms of manufacturing and services; (g) an object world with which to think about the changes of the late twentieth century that go under the name of the postmodern, poststructuralist, or second-order cybernetic; and an arena productive of humorous, fertile, and mind-shaping metaphors for dealing with; (h) a historical phase, most intense in the 1990s, from the use of utopian and colonizing talk of the electronic frontier to the gradual coevolution and integration of the Internet with other institutional worlds; (i) all of the above.

There is a pervasive feeling in many fields touched by cyberspace that things are beyond traditional control, that realities have outrun our usual conceptual categories. And the very rhetorics of cyberspace make claims for the new: both that there are new realities and that cyberspace provides tools for handling interactive complex realities beyond traditional disciplinary vocabularies or methods. Cyberspace is chronically "under construction," rapidly changing, expanding, and mutating among technologies and populations. Ethnographies, to keep up, must themselves become more open textualities, with "ports" to many dimensions and connections, without succumbing to incoherent fragmentation. Ethnographies must attempt simultaneously to unveil the underlying "constricted potential of a combinatory grid that is both exhausting and indefatigable,"[1] and to publicly screen emergent social and cultural configurations. Ethnographic fieldwork provides tools of investigation, but those tools are challenged by cyberspace to maintain insider-outsider critical and comparative perspectives—not to become absorbed—and to adapt writing strategies that can map voicings and tonalities, locate people and their social structures, and thereby articulate critical sites of constraints and openness.

Ethnographies of cyberspace need to deal in theory, time, place, languages (and cultures), institutions (legal, economic, psychological, scientific), and with the reconfigured knowledge-power nexi involved in all of the above. They are challenged to do so both substantively and in their own forms and force of writing. Even more than a multisited ethnography, an ethnography of cyberspace presents a topological challenge for a multidimensional approach that is able to bring into sharp juxtaposition the contradictory elements of cyberspace's political economy, cultural elaborations, liberating and subjugating potentials, new information-based sciences, alternative engineering designs, and their social implications.

Ethnographies, in their traditional forms of writing, may seem, now increasingly subject to the pressure of a growing cyberspace pedagogical regime, to operate under the anxiety of being endangered, the anxiety of being already conceptually and pedagogically archaic [click for links to psychodynamic and philosophical, techne- or logos-engendered Doppelgänger trackings of this discourse.] More realistically, although it is not the case that there is no more place for traditional writing, it is from the perspective of "twenty minutes into the future" (as science fiction often likes to posit), that we can gain a sense of possibility and enrichment, as well as difficulty and danger. It is within this sense of possibility that we might strive with our future-looking but present capabilities, making ourselves open to the ear and desire and positioning of the other, facilitating social institutions that are flexible and reflexively modern rather than brittlely hierarchical, dogmatic, and univocally normative.

In Theory, In Time, In Place, In Language—all these categories or dimensions for ethnographies of cyberspace foreground linguistic and conceptual double-voiced articulations of the potential/actual, the located/unfolding, the rooted/differentially dispersed. Temporalities as well as topologies fold themselves into interesting configurations. The ethnographic task of worlding cyberspace "In Theory" is to situate preliminary frames for thinking about the emergent computer-mediated worlds in which we are all inserted or enframed—if not always with equal access or capacity. These theories themselves need placement in historical horizons, the task of worlding cyberspace "In Time": While the 1970s were fueled by certain texts of theory in general—albeit intended as models of and models for, as proleptic of and pedagogy for, an emergent common sense—the 1990s more concretely find practical institutions—law (In Brief), economics (In Exchange), psychology (In Consciousness), science (In-formation Sciences)—under pressure in their very conceptual formulations thanks to the technologies of computers and computer-mediated communication. The uneven distribution of these technologies and their attendant thought styles index both new and intensifications of old horizons of power and inequalities; they constitute a task of worlding cyberspace in geographic and social space. Many of these challenges are registered "In Language" and new forms of writing: electronic, multimedia, cross-generic, cryptofigural, paralogical, paradoxical, and otherwise. The literature of cyberspace, like that of ethnography, "re-establishes contact between the corpora and the ceremonies of several dialects" (Derrida 1995:116), and so runs the risk of eliciting anger and charges of unreadability, frivolity, transgression. As Derrida (1995:115) wryly notes, "No one gets angry at a mathematician or a physicist whom he or she doesn't understand...but rather with someone who tampers with your own language, with this 'relation,' precisely, which is yours." It is a cultural politics that works its magic as powerfully in popular culture idioms (tech talk, science fiction, advertising) as in academic theory, and that is in play against a concentration of media power which "tends to put technical modernity to work in the service of worn out things" (Derrida 1995:124).

IN THEORY

> The computing capacity of even bacterial DNA was enormous compared to man-made electronics. All Virgil had to do was take advantage of what was already there—just give it a nudge, as it were.
>
> —*Greg Bear,* Blood Music[2]

In theory—and unevenly in time and space—many of our communicative and perceptual structures are being changed by computers and simulation technologies from a world of direct experience to one more accurately knowable through indirect play with structural coordinates and physical worlds available to the human consciousness only through technological prostheses. (Examples abound in medical technologies—such as imaging diagnostics or being able to perform more delicate surgery with virtual reality technology—in architecture and planning, in aeronautical and space engineering, in sciences such as molecular biology or nanotechnology, in financial planning models, as well as more vulgately through the entertainment and communications media.) In a sense this is merely a catching up by everyday experience and common sense to the movement of the sciences since the late nineteenth century, where direct experience has long been understood to be either misleading or at best a partial and supplementary access to the complexities of reality. But the world mediated by computers and simulation has taken us a step farther yet, one that requires at least two kinds of knowledge simultaneously: the indirect structural precision of the sciences supplemented by the experiential, relational world of social relations and cultural mapping.[3]

In theory (to condense and summarize the arguments about the contemporary era as systemically different from the earlier twentieth-century modernities), we now live in a poststructuralist world, insofar as the world constructed in the 1940s by cybernetic control systems has evolved to the point where decentralized systems (such as the Internet) are necessary lest there be systemic breakdown. The Internet is an important icon of "reflexive modernity,"[4] of the gradual move toward a more pluralistic world of decision making that can restructure the increasingly ineffective and dysfunctional division of labor between weakening parliamentary politics and increasingly more powerful but nonpublic decision making by the market or by military-subsidized research and development.[5] The phantasmic, speculative, indeterminate threats[6] of ecological decay and catastrophe are among the fields of pressure in public consciousness toward new institutions of "reflexive modernization" that depend upon contemporary sciences and their computerized information modeling, processing, and institutional coordination. As Ulrich Beck (1986/92) argues, ecological consciousness in the 1990s has moved beyond nostalgias of attempting to "preserve" or "conserve" nature conceived as primordial, and is premised upon the dynamics of consumerism. Consumerism is a cause of ecological damage, but it also provides the market and political demand for rights to clean air and water and products that are not toxic. Ecological or green consciousness depends both upon scientific mediation, since much of the pollution and toxicity of environmental damage is only visible and monitorable through measurement rather than through ordinary perception, and upon the experiential and differential knowledges that people in different positions in the production and consumption chain can provide. Even traditional bureaucratic institutions such as federal law enforcement agencies can now be put under pressure. Computerized records of a prosecutor's selection of cases and severity of punishments can be tracked and compared by investigative journalists, thereby exposing to the public tacit and behind-the-scenes patronage networks that have structured Justice Department allocations of resources, personnel, and interests (Burnham 1996; Transactional Records Access Clearinghouse [TRAC]:http:trac.syr.edu).

"In theory" plays constitutive, proleptic roles and provides models from which realities deviate, ever generating the need for new theory. The illusions or projections of recent French theorists remind us through their proleptic missteps of the differences between theory and world (for instance, on *The Postmodern Condition*, Lyotard's 1979 "report on knowledge," see "In Time," below), yet they are themselves productive, constitutive, ethico-aesthetic, or symptomatic of new subjectivities made possible by new machinic assemblages (Guattari 1992/95). Among these "effective dreams"[7] of theory are the ways in which technologies change temporal and power relationships (Virilio 1977/86, 1993/95; Latour 1988); provide sensory prostheses, object relations for libidinal investment, and evocative objects for self-definition and social engagement (Guattari 1995; Ronell 1989; Stone 1995; Turkle 1995); operate through language games of paralogy, mutation, modification, rhyzomic generativity, play, and dissemination (Bukatman 1993; Deleuze and Guattari 1975/86; Derrida 1972, 1995; Lyotard 1979; McHale 1992; Serres 1980/82); and illuminate the tensions between potentially new economic logics and intensification of old political economic mechanisms of restructuring—including flexible capital accumulation at the expense of atomized professionals and manufacturing labor (Aronowitz 1994; Barlow 1994; Gilder 1989; Hayes 1989; Lanier 1994; Samuelson et al. 1995).

IN TIME

> **email:** (i) electronic mail; (ii) c. 1480: embossed or arranged in a network, from Fr. emmaileure (network)—OED.
>
> —The Hacker's Dictionary

Just as In Theory two kinds of knowledge, two kinds of science, can no longer do without one another—explanatory structures that are breaks with normal experience, that can only be arrived at through the protheses of instruments, experiments, models, and simulations; and experiential, embodied, sensorial knowledge that acts as situated feedback—so too two charter mythologies of temporality vie in our understanding of cyberspace—skeins of genealogical origin stories that shape hopes and fears about technological innovation; and cycles of political economy liberatory hopes repeatedly disciplined by market processes of capital accumulation facilitated or redirected by law and politics (legislation, regulation). One thinks in the latter case of the democratizing and decentralizing hopes for a "people's" minicomputer in the early 1980s (Brand 1989; Rheingold 1991; Wooley 1992) that would undo the oligopolistic industrial structure of mainframe suppliers, and the disappointment that was later to set in; and how that cycle is (in danger of) being repeated with the Internet. The danger fuels the politics of cypherpunks, cryptoanarchists, and others dedicated to keeping the Internet democratically or anarchistically open.

In Time technological origins and futures are shifting complicities. Insofar as origins in technological matters are ordinarily belated—they exist in concept, desire, imagination, and linguistic metaphor before they are installed—the gap between expectation or fantasy and implementation can resonate with, and be used to provide openings to, alternative worlds through multiple precursor genealogies;[8] utopian hopes foreclosed;[9] designers' inabilities to foresee users' appropriations (Feenberg 1995); alternative styles of using a technology (Turkle

1995);[10] desires, family romances, and spirit worlds that provide the obsessive urgency and dedication for the tedium of experimenting until invention is achieved (Ronell 1989); machinic assemblages that facilitate/enforce new subjectivities (Guattari 1995), that speed up the flow of mutation (Virilio 1993/95) and leverage displaced relations of power (Koch 1995; Latour 1988), or that encourage a shift in thinking about technology as task-specific tools to technology as instruments of play and experimentation in social learning (Stone 1995; Turkle 1995).

Prefigurations of technology are often simultaneously wrong and prescient, particularly for our ambi-valent and ambiguous computer technologies which, on the one hand, threaten to create totalizing cybernetic control in more powerful shadow worlds than that of RL ("real life")—such as the data banks in which our juridical, fiduciary, medical, and other Doppelgänger personae are created, monitored, and manipulated, often beyond our knowledge and control (Branscomb 1994; Burnham 1983). On the other hand, these technologies could create decentralized environments that play out Enlightenment or modernist fantasies/nightmares of exciting/dangerous out-of-control worlds ("The Cryptoanarchists' Manifesto" [May 1994] predicting the emergence of numerous nefarious as well as beneficial black markets once strong cryptography becomes widespread); playful, sensuous, multiple worlds of continuously recontracted identities (Stone 1995) and recontracted freedoms and ethics of answerability (Derrida 1987, 1995; Ronell 1989); or worlds more diffusely stable than any centralization could dream (Foucault 1978, 1979, 1980).

In Time, two dates or two decades conventionally serve as markers of these ambivalent transitions: 1979 or the early 1980s, and the early 1990s. These are not origin dates of either the computer or the Internet, the first of which extends back to the early post–World War II period, the second to the late 1960s—the one an outgrowth of World War II command-and-control, trajectory-and-firing, feedback calculation needs (Norbert Wiener's cybernetics), of general calculators and decryption (Alan Turing, John von Neumann), as well as of telephone information technology needs (Claude Shannon's information theory), the other an outgrowth of the need for a communication system that could withstand nuclear attack and not be knocked out by hitting a centralized switch. These dates are rather transitions in theory, in outlook, in historical horizon.

Jean-François Lyotard's 1979[1984] book *The Postmodern Condition: A Report on Knowledge* was produced for the Quebec government's council on universities. It became a touchstone for electric (hysterical?) debates about theory (the "postmodern"). Praised for its enigmatic acknowledgment of the computer as a medium for social change in the late twentieth century, it depended, as Andrew Feenberg points out (1995), upon a slightly misguided vision of the computer. This was the era just before the introduction in France of Minitel and in the United States of minicomputers (IBM's personal computer was introduced in 1981, Apple's MacIntosh in 1984). The French Minitel was part of a state-directed modernization program to upgrade the French infrastructure and to carve out a niche in the global trade system. Six million terminals, networked to X.25 time-sharing hosts, were given away to households in a bid to acculturate the French to the new medium, to provide access to information as part of the state Telecom utility, and to provide a protected market for terminals and thereby create the basis for a global export industry. Designed not to tax users with skills beyond their telephonic habits, the primitive terminals and keyboards were unable to expand into the international market, and Lyotard's vision of increasingly decentralized self-government through free access to data banks was a vision of a far more technocratic information society than the many-to-many, computer-mediated-communication (CMC) society that was to emerge.

Still, Lyotard was prescient about many of the forms that such CMC would take, including anonymous pseudonyms (institutionalized by Minitel services, which required pseudonyms) that called forth new language games, where identity is assumed-constructed rather than assumed-presupposed, where "cognitive regimes of phrases" can lead to incommensurable "differends" or multiple worlds based on different social contracts, where social and cultural forms are generated paralogically (through modification, mutation, innovation) rather than through centrally planned, rational, transparent design. When Minitel's Videotext system was first tested in 1981 it included a means for feedback to the designers, but the popularity of such messaging from users was not recognized as a precursor to mass demands for interactivity. In 1982, hackers turned Gretel, a host machine whose users could post advertising or send messages to system operators, into a decentralized messaging system. Other services quickly followed, with names like Desiropolis, SM, and Sextel. Paris walls were covered with graffiti about the new "pink" entertainment form; users' telephonic habits colonized the Minitel with the desire to communicate, not just access information, and by 1985 the volume of messages exceeded capacity and the system crashed.

Feenberg (1995) points out that it was not only the French state and French intellectuals like Lyotard, Derrida, Deleuze, and Guattari who were thinking about the implications of computers; science fiction writers like Ursula Le Guin, Philip Dick, and Stanislaw Lem, he suggests, were also making a break in conventions of writing and topics of obsessions toward interactivity, the fragility of reality, and the multiplicity of selves. During the first flush of minicomputers in the 1980s, Apple's MacIntosh and IBM-compatible personal computers were widely discussed in terms of their powerful democratizing potential against the monopoly of main frame industrial machines, hierarchical corporations, and oligopolistic markets. Sherry Turkle (1995) and Susan Leigh Star (1995), writing about computer cultures in the United States, characterize this period as one gradually shifting away from computational styles of computer use, formalist pedagogies (the "right way" of programming was by linear, logical, rule-based thinking), reductionist epistemologies (one learns how things work by breaking them down into simpler parts), and anxieties about whether computers could think (the Turing test) toward an "aesthetic of simulation," evocative metaphors for programming and user interfaces (the desktop as dialogue partner), a joyful sense of complexity or of the epistemologies of emergence from the simultaneous interaction of many parts, and a looking to connectivity (rather than single user–machine relationships) and to computers for emotional and social feedback. In the 1990s, Turkle says, no one confuses computers with sentient beings (the anxiety of the '70s posed in the fear of replicant humanoids in the film *Blade Runner*, the fascination with what computers and automation could and could not do, with Turing tests, with fears of surveillance, with fears of impersonal Taylorist monitoring of work through keystrokes or time spent, and job loss). Instead, people take pleasure in treating computers as quasi-sentient entities and exploring the enriching potentials of simulations, virtual reality prostheses, and interactivity that facilitates new social arrangements and psychological spaces. "Design" and "configuration" are slogans that foreground claims for the expansion of human relations and capacities.

The early 1990s are often spoken of by the computer science community as a second major turning point, marked by the reorganization of the Internet, changes in the global competitive structure of the semiconductor and information technology industries, the introduction of new user-oriented tools, and the huge influx of general users to the Internet—previously inhabited by relatively small, technically knowledgeable communities of hackers, students, researchers, engineers, and programmers. No longer is "theory" in general at issue; now, one practical and institutional arena after another—law, economics, psychology, the sciences—finds its traditional terminologies, premises, and models under profound pressure.

In Time: To cite just a few dates, in 1990 coordination of the Internet backbone shifted from the Defense Department's Advanced Research Projects Agency to the National Science Foundation as part of a continuing and broad-based shift away from a government- and university-dominated research community toward eventual privatization and commercialization. The year 1992 marked a "sea change" in the competitive dynamics of the semiconductor industry, requiring internationalization and modularization as it became clear that information technology industries could not survive in domestic markets alone or build self-contained machines. Instead, they had to become transnational, build "open systems architectures," compete over flexible features, pursue alliances and cross-licensing among firms, and develop networking (connecting computers to one another) and value-added services (moving data and images across the networks) (Yoffie 1994). The introduction of Mosaic and the World Wide Web in 1993 and of Netscape interfaces and indexing robots ("search engines," "spiders," "crawlers") two years later made navigating the Internet easy for a broad range of users. Commercial providers (America Online,

CompuServe, Prodigy) began opening gateways to the Internet, and businesses began to advertise and sell via the Internet; as a result, encryption and issues of privacy, authentication, and digital money became foci of attention.

How does one access ethnographically the tension between market cycles and the kinds of cultural mutation on which Lyotard's text, among others, focused the energies of cultural imagination? Two strategies are to focus upon its geographies—its uneven construction, costs, usages in different places, resistances to it on the part of bureaucracies and employees—and upon its body politics—the Third World women who manufacture the chips, toxicities of clean room production, surveillance and invasiveness of its "availability" imposed upon professionals and service providers, the global division of labor, the dispersive, cottage-industrialization of the virtual office.

IN PLACE (SITES UNDER CONSTRUCTION)

> Cyberspace remains a frontier region, across which roam the few aboriginal technologists and cyberpunks who can tolerate the austerity of its savage computer interfaces, incompatible communications protocols, proprietary barricades, cultural and legal ambiguities, and general lack of useful maps or metaphors.
>
> —*John Perry Barlow, "Coming into the Country"*

> Is your routing protocol complex? You've raised the cost of entry. Do you have an acceptable use policy? You've limited your population. Have you invented an anonymous FTP mechanism and an RFC series? You've encouraged the spread of the network... Infrastructure... reflects how we apply... fundamental human values. Privacy, for example, can be protected or destroyed by a network.
>
> —*Carl Malamud*

Carl Malamud (1993) provides a preliminary pilot survey for a global geographic and ethnographic history, stylized as a ribald hacker's (and gourmet's) travelogue, with himself as one of the free-spirited aboriginal technologists on this new frontier. He begins in good ethnographic fashion with an emblematic scene, a celebratory, almost ritual space: a 1991 trade show that serves as a microcosmic workshop for assembling the global Internet. Some thirty-five miles of cable were hung from the ceiling of the San Jose Convention Center using five cherry pickers. These supported two different backbones (FDDI, Ethernet), fifty subnets, microwave links, and T1 lines, connecting to the NSFNET (and video-link laid by Sprint from Geneva via Atlanta and Kansas City), so that three hundred vendors could demonstrate interoperability of their wares and engineers could pinpoint ambiguities in standards. Enough components to wire a twenty-story high-tech skyscraper like those being built in Singapore and other leading-edge high-tech sites.

Imagine expanding this globally. Malamud provides a humorous twenty-country field guide to the heterogeneous sites around the world that in 1991 were gradually linking themselves into a global Internet. The account provides a sardonic counterpoint to the usual histories of the Internet that celebrate a seemingly smooth development from the US Defense Department's ARPA project to a civilianized NSF-supervised backbone to a privatized Internet and a spreading international network. Malamud traverses Europe from Geneva to Prague to Dublin, the Pacific from Hawaii to Tokyo to Singapore to Canberra, Bombay, Bangkok, Kuala Lumpur, and various other locations with different problems, situations, and goals. His account is of interest for several reasons. It gets beneath the glib hype of magical connectivity and indicates the heterogeneity of the actual hardware, wiring, design, and organization of the various segments of the Internet; it provides a historical account of the efforts to create, the resistances to, and the efforts to limit or control connectivity; and in the end it provides a bridge to a recognition that universal connectivity may not quite be the metaphor for the future, as design must cope with a flood of users who might be better served by a congeries of subnetworks, a field of diversity.

In Geneva, for instance, headquarters of the International Telecommunications Union (ITU), Malamud finds a bureaucracy at odds with its electronic communications environment, providing in concrete microcosm the historical picture of decaying bureaucratic control and emergent electronic connectivity which such theorists as Marshall McLuhan, Michel Foucault, Jean-François Lyotard, and Jacques Derrida have also been describing—albeit in more philosophical, less concrete, registers. In 1991 the ITU headquarters (despite rights to free telecommunications throughout the world) had a telephone system with an old Siemens PBX which did not allow a secretary to transfer calls; there was only one fax machine for nine hundred employees (deliberately, to control communications with the outside); and officials were ambivalent about putting ITU recommendations for standards on the Internet because the ITU made money on selling the recommendations in book form (although dissemination on the Internet was one or two orders of magnitude beyond what they would ever reach through book sales). Things were so bad that high-powered officials brought their own AT&T phones to work so they could have a few stored numbers, and got themselves guest accounts at CERN, the European high energy physics lab, a key node of the Internet.

By contrast, Prague had been dependent until 1989 on reverse engineering IBM mainframes and attempting to fit these together with Bulgarian front end processors and local operating systems. With the end of the Cold War, Prague was suddenly able to install (still expensive) 9600 bps leased lines to Western Europe, and with the aid of several IBM-donated 3090 mainframes was beginning to establish networking capabilities. "As fast as the [Eastern Block] countries could persuade the U.S. to process the paperwork for Cisco routers [as a legacy of the Cold War all these countries were on the U.S. export restrictions list; it had taken the Poles, for instance, a year to get a Cisco router (Malamud 1993:235)], countries were plopping in TCP/IP nodes, enhancing EARN connections, and using UUCP and EUnet to spread connectivity into new places" (Malamud 1993:271).

Malamud contrasts sites around the world and visits key individuals who made the initial connections in various sites happen: Torben Nielsen in Hawaii, who linked four university buildings with rented power tools, dug ditches, and used salvaged materials from military aircraft to create a local area network (LAN) for $1500; Jan Murai in Japan, who tied networks together into JUNET and, when Nippon Telegraph and Telephone deregulated, used two modems and a university-provided phone line to establish links to Amsterdam, Washington, and Hawaii; Dennis Jennings in Dublin, who in 1979 networked two Dublin universities, in 1983 became president of the BITNET that was being introduced by IBM to Europe as EARN (European Academic Research Network), in 1985 became US National Science Foundation Program Director when NSF was only beginning to think about networking its four supercomputer centers and nudged them into bringing about the NSFNET backbone, and in 1991 helped create EBONE, the European backbone.

Malamud's account provides a preliminary matrix to which can be added other accounts of struggles and competitions to establish networks (see the 1996 "hacker tourist" account of laying a third-generation fiber optic cable from England to Japan [Stephenson 1996]). In Iran, for instance, the Institute for Studies in Theoretical Physics and Mathematics in Tehran has had an Internet site since 1992 and is now upgrading its 9.6 kilobyte connection with a 64 kilobyte satellite telephone line leased from the American Hughes Corporation (Jahanshah 1995). In 1994, Iran leased part of its network to a private company that provides access to individuals (some 200 customers so far). The government Telecommunications Company is now showing interest in the Internet and is trying to run the private company out of business, with such tactics as cutting off the latter's phone lines. The private company has gone to court with the support of customers like the Tehran Municipality. Qum, the theological center of Iran, is showing interest as always in the newest technological means for spreading its messages. Meanwhile the US NSF briefly ordered the connection between Tehran and the University of Vienna closed, on the grounds that Iran should not benefit from federally funded infrastructures; upon review, this position was reversed. Such competitions are not unusual.

In India parts of the bureaucracy are dedicated to expansion of networks, but other parts (including segments of the banking system) are attempting to protect jobs and the self-reliance of production and to restrict access to computerization and the Internet. Meanwhile businesses are establishing their own links, and the software industry and chip design are beginning to take off as off-shore support for US and multinational companies and as Indian companies produce products account. Such competitions are sites where the strains al needs within a society may be exposed to view, and are ocultural change.[11]

and, a country with over ten thousand hosts (10 percent ..n hosts on the Internet), the US seems a bit archaic; utilities and all sorts of services are normally ordered and paid for through the computerized network, eliminating separate checking, paperwork, or standing in line. Experiments with municipal networking exist in many parts of Scandinavia, in the Sophia-Antipolis "Silicon Valley" of France (near Nice), which is a nine-town joint venture with the regional government and the Nice Chamber of Commerce, but rarely in the US except for the much-touted Blacksburg, Virginia, experiment.

IN LANGUAGE (TECH TALK, HACKISH, FICTION)

> It's in words that the magic is—Abracadabra, Open Sesame, and the rest—but the magic words in one story aren't magical in the next. The real magic is to understand which words work, and when, and for what; the trick is to learn the trick.
>
> —*John Barth,* Chimera, *used as an epigram for chapter 4, "Metalinguistic Abstraction," in Hal Abelson and Jerry Sussman,* Structure and Interpretation of Computer Programs

> Either Elvis Presley is dead, or he isn't!
>
> —*Attributed to Eric Hobsbawm*

> Isn't this an "interface" here, a meeting surface for two worlds... sure, but which two?
>
> —*Thomas Pynchon,* Gravity's Rainbow

Tech talk, hackish, infinite loops, future Bostons—the lively languages of the denizens of the several subcultures on the electronic frontier provide rich arenas for exploring emergent cognitive styles and new worlds of interaction. The languages that hackers and techies use and that leak into general discourse (how do they sound and reconfigure thought in Japanese, Portuguese, Hindi, Malay, Russian?[12]), the literary languages of science fiction (especially cyberpunk) and science-incorporating novels (e.g., Richard Powers's *Galatea 2.2*), the advertising language used to sell new technologies in medical and science journals (see also Haraway 1997), and the figurations and metanarratives that lie behind the ways scientists and engineers explain what they are up to (and how they conceive their discoveries as contrasting with the recent pasts of their fields), all provide rich entries into new ethnographic worlds both of the present and of the near future. Nanotechnology, chemistry and materials sciences, molecular biology, genetics, evolutionary and theoretical biology, remote sensing and environmental monitoring, PET scans and medical imaging are among the many arenas mediated by the lively new languages of the information and computer technologies.

Also imbricated in the use of these languages is a pragmatics of engineering interaction premised on (a) partial knowledge and constant need for translation, interfacing, sharing, and updating; and (b) a willingness to deal with real world complexities that cannot be completely controlled (hardware always goes wrong, software can never be completely debugged). This pragmatics cannot be separated from the material worlds of the new information highway, the market pressures that are gradually sharing dominance with earlier state funding for shaping the evolution of cyberspace, and the legal structures that are lagging behind the technological changes but can powerfully affect their development.

The worlds being constructed and mediated by the new biological and material sciences and information technologies are not merely cognitive ones, but are also profoundly, if playfully, sensual ones. The debates about virtual reality systems are many but as yet quite underdeveloped, ranging from the critics who see only testosterone-driven entertainment examples (Kramarae 1995) to the proponents of, for instance, computer-enhanced medical surgical systems that allow finer kinesthetic control than ordinary human haptic sensation. Feminist literary criticism of both science fiction proper and of such computer scientist fantasies such as Hans Moravec's (1988) *Mind Children* (downloading wetware brains into silicon form so as to escape the body) has focused attention on the embodiments of cyberspace prostheses (Hayles 1993, 1996; Stone 1995).

There is something special about the lively languages of tech talk, hackish, and the science fictions that engineers and scientists enjoy.

The ethnographer (even if the distinction eventually breaks down) needs to pay attention to these as native languages, as pragmatics deployed situationally by computer scientists and other information scientists, before lumping them with general popular culture variants. Thus, Scott Bukatman (1993) is onto something when he suggests that science fiction writing often exploits a distinctive writerly, and playfully paradoxical, style that requires active inferential work by readers, and that it is on this formal level—Joycean semantic fusions, syntactical revisioning, presuppositional implications—that the genre provides some of the most sustained attempts to identify and narrate the ambiguities of contemporary culture.[13] But the traditions to which he links this style are the neologistic play of William Burroughs and the literary theories of Roland Barthes. One wonders if more important might not be a different set of traditions that await excavation: the lively, playful, polysemic, working languages of engineering and software techies, such as are catalogued in *The New Hacker's Dictionary* (Raymond 1993). These are, of course, not entirely separated traditions, as the epigram to this section from one of the leading textbooks for computer science students indicates (and as Raymond [1993:484] protests, "Hackers often have a reading range that astonishes liberal arts people"). Still, there is an ethnography waiting to be done on the nuances (and pragmatics) of, for instance, why William Gibson's *Neuromancer* is initially dismissed by techies when cited by humanists as a foundational cyberspace or cyberpunk text. Not that techies and hackers have not read it—Pengo, one of the [in]famous German hackers who broke into the Lawrence Livermore Laboratories computers, said his image of himself as a hacker was modeled on Case in *Neuromancer* (Hafner and Markof 1991:15)—but its valuation or intertextual location is marked differently. It is not that techies and hackers have not read Gibson, but that in their view liberal arts people have read little else, little of actual substance that pertains to or is generative of this emergent arena of communicative connectivity, and of course that Gibson famously describes himself as not computer knowledgeable when he wrote the book.[14] Such relative marking is itself a field of pragmatics, constitutive of difference in the ways that different communities relate to, and interact through, computers, informational technologies, cyberspace, or the information highway.

Literary critics such as Brian McHale (1992) and cultural historians of science such as Paul Edwards (1996) are also on to something when they chart the shifts in plot structures and metanarratives that sf (science fiction) literature and film have traversed in the last few decades. In Edwards's case, the correlations of such shifts with thinking among planners and funders in the military-industrial-university complex are usefully at issue. McHale distinguishes cyberpunk from older sf through the ways in which microworlds, cyberspace, cybernetic or bioengineered protheses, AIs (artificial intelligences), and mediated deaths are deployed. No longer are the orbiting space colonies or subterranean cities showcases of technology and egalitarian liberal governance; instead there are decaying slums, enclaves of privilege, ghettoes of crime and commerce, multicultural juxtapositions, and interspecies heterotopias. No longer are there humanoid robots; now there are AIs, bioengineered improvements, alter egos, and prostheses of all sorts, renegade cybernetic systems attempting to absorb humans, and hybrid human-machine interfaces that allow the biological metabolism to shut down (die) and reboot for varying periods. More skeptical is Paul Edwards's survey of sf films and novels over the post–World War II period in which he looks for alternatives to closed worlds of cybernetic command and control fantasy, some alternative structures that would lead to more open and green worlds.

And yet there is a striking difference in "structure of feeling" in how writers immersed in the new technologies and sciences pose these issues, one, I think, that is not explained by their being Panglossian enthusiasts. Kevin Kelley (1994) and Claus Emche (1994), for instance, find precisely these alternatives to the post–World War II closed-world modernisms in the language of "out of control," self-organizing, evolving learning systems and parallel processing. One needs to read these with critical care, attuned to the metanarrative utopias, teleological aspirations, or simple idealizing hopes that are structured into speculative models (Egger 1993) and look for the alternative accounts that can be given of the same technologies and scientific developments (Porush 1993). But we need to read for the connectivities and emergences as well that are growing through our everyday practices of using these technologies, and not dismiss them through an equally metanarrative, but cynical, application of past (Luddite, Marxist, or romantic) frames to new forms.

Might the language and creative writing of techies and hackers be a guide to the worlds that many of us are now entering with our laptops, desktops, and work stations, networked into a global information network? Consider the "handles" or "aliases" used by hackers—Phiber Optik, Knight Lightning, frobgrot, koda.krome, notjeff—both the worlds to which they allude, and also the metaphorical play they put into motion, part of the larger universe of puns, contractions, acronyms, verbal forms, and other linguistic humor that make up hacker reference and repartee, and the degree to which these reflect a technical concern with substitutability, abstraction, alternative coding, and signal-to-noise ways of regarding communication. These play on and extend the recombinant material forms that computer-mediated sciences invoke and sf written by programmers reflects on: bots of various forms (robots, nanobots, mobots, fleabots), simulated intelligence forms (stims, microsofts, personality chips aka perks), biological computers and transgenetic animals, prostheses and cybernetic machine–biological cyborgs, objects made of new materials, new languages, and transspecies multicultural social formations, new illnesses of multiple-chemical-sensitive and virally transported transgenetic modalities. These are the worlds we are entering, and they are not accessible through the old languages of nature versus culture dichotomies. We turn first to hackish, then to creative writing by computer professionals.

Hackish[15]

> **hack:** (i) an appropriate application of ingenuity; (ii) creative practical joke.
>
> **banana problem:** [from the story of the little girl who said, "I know how to spell banana, but I don't know when to stop"].
>
> —The Hacker's Dictionary

To what degree does "hackish" not merely reflect a love of language play, but provide a "particularly effective window into the surrounding culture" (Raymond 1993:20)?—into how its inventions grow out of the way in which computers are configured and software language is designed, showing if there is in fact a new style of technically grounded cultural logic in which "flavorful" elegant puns "bend" phrases so as to include a second "jargon" word as a function of a kind of condensation that increases awareness of linguistic form, logic, multiple allusions or references, and precision, and yet maintains transparency, efficiencies of communication, and relatively easy accessibility. As a friendly visiting anthropologist to hacking culture—and as a slow but determined learner-user of computer literacy, E-mail, and World Wide Web connections—I am constantly amazed by the openness of these subcultures, and of the degree to which everyone is dependent on others for help in keeping their knowledge current, growing, and adaptable to a state of constant and rapid change. I am also impressed by the degree to which speed of communication is mimicked by the density of punning allusions to multiple referents, and the pressure the speed and volume of information places on my old-fashioned tendency to take notes, an increasingly out-of-phase slowness for pacing the "fire-hose" flow of electronic connectivity (part of what was called, in the opening section, the anxiety of operating under a growing cyberspace pedagogical regime, and the need to develop new reading and processing tactics).

There are, of course, many ways in which a "technically grounded new cultural logic" might be sifted out. For instance, "much to the dismay of American editors," hackers tend to use quotes as balanced delimiters, placing punctuation outside the quotation marks: "Jim is going", "Bill runs", and "Spock groks". Putting the commas and periods inside the quotes for programmers violates the integrity of literal strings with characters that don't belong, and would, if it were a piece of code, issue false instructions; a tutorial that tells you to delete a line by typing "dd." is quite different from one that tells you to type "dd". *Harts Rules* and the *Oxford Dictionary for Writers and Editors* accept the hacker sensibility and call that convention "new" or "logical" quoting.

This is a more technological grounding of cultural logic than simple terminological coinages. However, insofar as coinages have extended hermeneutical relations and histories, they can begin to tell us a good deal about the cultures in which they are shaped. A few examples—like spoken hackish "bang" referring to the grapheme !, aka "excl" (pronounced /eks'kl/) or "shriek"—begin to resonate with Jacques Derrida's sub-version that writing is prior to speech, and provide a grounding for that interpretation of Derrida that Greg Ulmer (1994) advances: seeing both grammatology being mediated through the new electronic media and cultural writing becoming increasingly an experimental "heuretics." But one wants to immerse oneself in this concrete world of sounds and silent electron traces before jumping into the Derridean sea, or into the Deleuzian complementary intuition (in the interpretation put forth by the Critical Art Ensemble [1994]) that the new electronic media allow a new literal "logic of sense" (where the sensorium is not separated from the intellect as an Other; indeed, a fascination for many people of digitalized multimedia virtual reality is the ability to place oneself in altered states). Another Derridean trace: "There is also an accepted convention for 'writing under erasure'; the text, 'Be nice to this fool ^H^H^H^H gentleman, he's in from corporate HQ,'" would be read as "Be nice to this fool, I mean this gentleman," the diagraph ^H being a print representation for a backspace. *Quelle différence!*

Form-versus-content jokes seem to follow easily: "This sentence no verb"; "too repetetetive"; "bad speling"; "incorrectspa cing"; "excuse me I'm cixelsyd [dislexic] today." As does patterned play with verbing ("I'll clipboard it over"; "I'll mouse it up"), pluralizing with inflection particles from imported languages or archaic strata (Yiddish *frobbotzim* as a plural of *frobnitz*, little things you can tweak, manipulate, adjust; VAXen using the Anglo-Saxon plural -en), and anthropomorphizing. (This last apparently gives great difficulties to some philosophers and certain anthropologists whose theories of metaphor refuse to acknowledge the uses of humor. As Raymond [1993:13] patiently admonishes, "This isn't done in a naive way; hackers don't personalize their stuff in the sense of feeling empathy with it, nor do they mystically believe that the things they work on every day are 'alive.'") You may hear, "The protocol handler got confused," and explanations like "and its poor little brain couldn't understand X, and it died" (Raymond 1993:13). Which leads to the quite important observation, not unlike the old cliché about the many words Eskimos are supposed to have for snow, that "hackers have even more words for equipment failures than Yiddish has for obnoxious people" (Raymond 1993:14). Important, because it points to the material grounding of the cultural logics, but also because it points to the continual adjustments, patching, flexibility, rerouting, reconfiguring, sharing, negotiating, translating, interacting, communicating, and clarifying that working with this technology requires and that is accepted as reality by its resident hackers, viz.:

> **creationism:** The (false) belief that large innovative software designs can be completely specified in advance and then painlessly magicked out of the void by the normal efforts of a team of normally talented programmers. In fact, experience has shown repeatedly that good designs arise only from evolutionary interaction between one (or at most a small handful of) exceptionally able designer(s) and an active user population.
>
> **heisenbug:** [from Heisenberg's Uncertainty Principle in quantum physics] A bug that disappears or alters its behavior when one attempts to probe or isolate it. (This usage is not even particularly fanciful; the use of a debugger sometimes alters a program's operating environment.)
>
> **mandelbug:** [from the Mandelbrot set] A bug whose underlying causes are so complex and obscure as to make its behavior appear chaotic or even non-deterministic. This term implies that the speaker thinks it is a Bohr bug rather than a heisenbug...
>
> **Bohr bug:** [from quantum physics] A repeatable bug; one that manifests reliably under a possibly unknown but well-defined set of conditions. Antonym of heisenbug...
>
> **schroedinbug:** [MIT: from Schroedinger's Cat thought experiment in quantum physics] A design or implementation bug in a program that doesn't manifest until someone reading the source or using the program in an unusual way notices that it never should have worked, at which point the program promptly stops working for everybody until fixed. Though (like bit rot) this sounds improbable, it happens... (Raymond 1993)[16]

If an engineering pragmatics of sharing, patching, and kluges (from German *klug*, "clever," i.e., a patch) is basic to the technological mode, contradictory principles are nonetheless also basic to the landscape, including various ways of limiting freedom of action, ranging from "bondage and discipline languages" (e.g., BASIC, PASCAL, early versions of the Athena Project at MIT) to marketplace proprietary rules and competitive blocking of opponents' freedom of action. This provides the grounds for the elaboration of the hacker ethic in favor of open systems, but also the grounds for the intense debate over the evolving direction of Law and Ethics on the Electronic Frontier (see In Brief[17]). Again a few simple terms can help index the nature of the terrain. BASIC (Beginner's All-purpose Symbolic Instruction Code), originally designed for Dartmouth's experimental timesharing system in the early 1960s (like PASCAL, another instructional "toy" designed in the late 1960s), while allowing some simple programming, according to Raymond (1993:54), becomes not only difficult to use for longer and more complicated tasks, but is counterproductive by instilling habits that impede learning more powerful languages. A more general version of this type of relatively benign dilemma is "candygrammar" using mostly "syntactic sugar," that is, the effort to design English-like languages (COBOL, Apple's Hypertalk, many "4GL" database languages) to help unskilled people program. Hacker aesthetics hold that since it is not really the syntax that makes programming hard, candygrammar languages are often just as difficult to program as more elegant, terser ones, and end up simply creating more pain for experienced hackers who have to help out inexperienced users.

More serious are real situations of "fear and loathing": "[from Hunter Thompson] ... a state inspired by the prospect of dealing with certain real-world systems and standards that are totally brain-damaged but ubiquitous—Intel 8086s, or COBOL, or EBCDIC, or any IBM machine except the Rios (aka the RS/6000)" (Raymond 1993). EBCDIC, for instance, is an "alleged character set" that exists in a number of incompatible versions and lacks several ASCII punctuation characters important in modern computer languages. Hackers suspect that IBM made people use this as a customer-control tactic, a form of "connector conspiracy" (designing products that do not fit with competitors' products), since the ASCII standard was already well established at the time. Moreover, as Raymond notes, although "today, IBM claims to be an open-systems company, IBM's own description of the EBCDIC variants and how to convert between them is still internally classified top-secret, burn-before reading" (Raymond 1993:159). IBM is the target of much hostile hacker humor, the company acronym itself being said to stand for "Inferior But Marketable," and many other such witticisms.[18] (The barbed humor parallels similar, more recent witticisms against Microsoft, for similar reasons, as Microsoft dominates the operating system and Internet markets.)

"What galls hackers about most IBM machines above the PC," explains Raymond (1993:235), "isn't so much that they are underpowered and overpriced...but that the designs are incredibly archaic, crusty and elephantine...and you can't fix them—source code is locked up tight, and programming tools are expensive, hard to find, and bletcherous to use once you've found them." FUD and FUD wars are a result. FUD (Fear, Uncertainty, and Doubt that IBM sales personnel instill in the minds of customers thinking about buying from competitors) was coined by Gene Amdahl after leaving IBM to found his own company. FUD wars thus is the posturing of vendors ostensibly committed to standardization but actually attempting to fragment the market to protect their market share. (See also the 1979 Charles Andres comic allegory about "brainwashed androids of IPM [Impossible to Program Machines] to conquer and destroy the peaceful denizens of HEC [Human Engineered Computers]" containing—aside from many references to the prototypical computer game Advent[ure]—"the immortal line 'Eat flaming death, minicomputer mongrels!' [uttered, of course, by an IPM stormtrooper]" [Raymond 1993].) Tactics in this economic war of position are varied (and a large subject for business school case studies [Yoffie 1994]), ranging from such minor and ineffective forms as "crippleware" (software that has some important functionality deliberately removed to entice you to pay for a working version; compare "guiltware" for shareware pleas to send money if you are using their product, also "nagware") to the attempts to utilize increasingly archaic and ill-adaptive intellectual property law protections and lawsuits.

The hacker ethic by contrast, located naturally enough in universities like MIT, insists that information sharing is a "powerful positive good, and that it is an ethical duty of hackers to share their expertise by writing free software and facilitate access to information and to computing resources wherever possible," including the more controversial "belief that system-cracking for fun and exploration is ethically OK as long as the cracker commits no theft, vandalism, or breach of confidentiality" (Raymond 1993). This puts hackers often, and in principled active ways, at odds with industry, the archaic legal structure, government attempts at regulation, national security–justified controls (the export control act), and computer crime surveillance (the FBI and Secret Service).

Underneath the pragmatics of computer subcultures and their differences, underneath the competitions for control of various forms (market share, security, privacy, freedom), is a material substratum of historically changing hardware and institutional legacies and possibilities. The hacker subculture, for instance, whose jargon is collectively compiled in *The New Hacker's Dictionary* (and its 1983 predecessor), has a history traceable to the early 1960s PDP-1 machines at the AI Labs at Stanford (where the Jargon File was started in 1975) and MIT (where a duplicate copy of the Jargon File was maintained from 1976), Carnegie-Mellon, Worcester Polytechnic, and similar sites. The first *Hacker's Dictionary* (Steele 1983) was thought at the time to be a monument to a subculture dealt a death blow by funding cuts, the introduction of personal computers (fear of atomizing the social relations fostered by timesharing machines), and the seduction of the best and brightest into industry. There is a machine-specific set of implications surrounding the 1983 cancellation of Digital's Jupiter Project (meaning the death of PDP-10 centered cultures that nourished the Jargon File), the shift from "home-brew" hardware engineering to vendor-supported hardware, the shift of MIT to dedicated LISP machines, and the shift at the AI Lab from the beloved ITS to TWENEX.[19] It is significant, for instance, that GNU (acronym: "GNU's Not UNIX!") (a UNIX-work-alike set of developments, including the popular GNU EMACS and GNU C compiler) is part of Richard Stallman and the Free Software Foundation's efforts to agitate for the position that information is community property and all software sources should be shared. In this context, the history of networking developments from Multics to UNIX[20] takes on more than a technical significance, opening onto ethical, political, and economic issues as well.

While hacker culture grew up around certain kinds of machines and artificial intelligence labs, it is only one of several overlapping distinctive subcultures, including techspeak and sf fandom, in which many hackers participate. There is a danger among humanists to make sf fandom stand in for these other cultures rather than recognizing them as interactive subcultures. My interest here is in attempting to move ethnographers toward a mapping of the overlap with various techspeak and science subcultures, rather than continuing to replant in the much-used garden of popular culture/sf versions of the scientific and technological imaginary. I am interested in both the ways those (real world) scientific and technological imaginaries grow, and in the social worlds they inhabit, grow from, and shape.

Raymond (1993) claims that the Internet constitutes a geographically dispersed think tank, pointing to the fact that during the 1988 cold fusion controversy, many papers were disseminated on the Net before making their way into print. There has in fact been a good deal of experimentation with various forms of communication on the Net, and considerable doubt about the degree to which serious discussion can be pursued and protection from troublemakers of all sorts can be prevented: problems of netiquette and of governance. Initially, many BBS (electronic Bulletin Board Systems) appear to be poor forums for serious discussions (see Stone's 1995 account of the history of CommuniTree; Lotfalian 1993), despite their democratic promise of open access in contrast to hierarchical and/or heavily screened, gate-guarded arenas such as the classroom, journals, television, and radio. They initially appear to be poor forums because they are heavily spur-of-moment opinion-driven, rather than carefully analytic or documented; also because their space seems to be markedly male-voiced, often increasingly so (with time female voices fall silent). Things need not be this way. The World Wide Web, with interface programs like Mosaic and Netscape with (hypertext) links to databases of all sorts, can transform the opinion-driven nature of initial BBS. Discussion groups can be self-disciplined arenas (various forms of governance mechanisms have been experimented with), and genuine interest-driven discussion lists—like breast cancer or other disease-focused support groups—can contain an inherent process of warning and skepticism toward poorly supported assertions or advice. They can also provide an important counter to the self-protecting authority systems of institutional medicine. Gender and other identity play in the place of user IDs can change the communicational dynamics (for good or ill). One old gentleman, it is said, who plays bridge on-line, signs on as a woman because he has found he is invited to join games much more quickly than if he is a man.

Our class E-mail list at MIT in 1994, with PGP-encrypted signatures and pseudonyms for interaction, showed a quite interesting gender distribution. Almost all of the twenty-six registered names were gender neutral: bitdiddle, nexus, axis, quickster, swizzle.shtick, cactus, the hacker, gyphon, Morrighan, Kipple, shalako, jello44, koda.krome, lizard, notjeff, 3 Jane, gilligan, bagel, frobgrot, elephant, the Keeper.[21] In time, some of the posters felt signature pressure, so the hacker began to sign Alyssa or Alyssa P. Hacker; 3 Jane signed Lady 3 Jane Tessier-Ashpool (a character in William Gibson's *Neuromancer*); bitdiddle soon gendered himself as ben bitdiddle. There were then perhaps a half-dozen male names (ben bitdiddle, sean, Prof. Charles, joebloggs, Ishmael Gabanzai, notjeff, gilligan) and two or three female ones. Only four were vaguely ethnic: Morrighan, shalako, Ishmael Garbanzai, Prof. Charles. Some drew on specific hacker jargon: joebloggs is a reference to the imaginary family, Fred and Mary Bloggs and their children, used as a standard example in knowledge representation to show the difference between extensional and intensional objects (Raymond 1993:72); frob is a productive particle (frobnitz, frobinicate, frobnosticate, etc.), referring to a small thing that can be tweaked or frobnicated, from a command on some MUDs to change a player's experience level, and to make wizards or request wizard privileges (Raymond 1993:193). Others used stylistic linguistic play: koda.krome; notjeff > notwork as network not working or acting flaky. A few drew on the sf/dungeons and dragons mythos or cybergame references (one student used his well-known out-of-class handle, Warlock[22]), such as were popular among the Legion of Doom and Masters of Deception hackers busted by Operation Sundevil (Sterling 1992): Knight Lightning, Phiber Optik, Acid Phreak.

Writing Infinite Loops and Future Bostons

If *The Hacker's Dictionary* and ethnographic investigation into linguistic usages open windows into not just the life worlds but the philosophical attitudes and engineering-design-pragmatics of several hacker, programmer, and computer scientist subcultures, the larger linguistic units of storytelling by such subculture members may help sketch in some of the broader and deeper dimensions of these worlds and perspectives. Indeed, storytelling is itself a central object of speculation, analysis, and design-curiosity for several of these subcultures (see, for instance, the weekly meetings of the Narrative Group at MIT's Media Lab [ni@media.mit.edu]). Three story collections provide first frames: *Infinite Loop: Stories about the Future by the People Creating It* (Constantine 1993) is an anthology of twenty-seven short stories (eight by women) by programmers, systems analysts, and software engineers, not inappropriately published (as was Malamud's book) by a company that also produces software trade shows; *Future Boston* (Smith 1994); and *In the Cube* (Smith 1993), a science fiction collective project (with each writer contributing a different piece of a single story-world) by a more varied set of ten contributors (two women), including one from *Infinite Loop* and five other programmers and technical writers, a physicist, a multimedia artist, a financial consultant, and a writer.

The ethnographic fascination of these stories lies in the interplay between the texts and RL (real lives), especially in *Infinite Loop.* In contrast to stereotypes about nerds who have no emotional lives, or whose emotional lives are fueled largely by adolescent testosterone—not that such a subculture does not exist, but there are many other more interesting groups,[23] including the turn by some who have suffered neurological diseases in their families to intensive research in cognitive science, linguistics, and artificial intelligence modeling (see Powers 1995)—these stories are about psychological and relational issues, about animating paradoxes and breakthroughs of apparent impossibilities that computer or cyborg futures provide as proleptic vehicles of current design thinking.

Pati Nagle's story "Pygmaleon 3.0" (in Constantine 1993), for instance, interplays fascinatingly with MIT Media Lab team leaders' descriptions of their projects. At the tenth anniversary celebration of the Media Lab (10/10/95), Pat Maes talked about the butler metaphor common in thinking about the design of software agents. Other Media Lab researchers described projects in perceptual computing (the programming of computers to recognize faces, emotions, gestures, and subtle changes of expression); smart rooms, and the communication among smart objects so that, for instance, a vacuum cleaner knows not to turn itself on when someone is home, or could be told by a couch that it was too heavy to be pushed around. Even the fact that *Infinite Loop* is published by a company that produces trade shows was mirrored in Marvin Minsky's self-consciously and ironically identifying the manufacturers of the various robotic devices he talked about, identifying each manufacturer with a pause and a laugh line, "made by Hewlett-Packard... a sponsor of the Media Lab."

In Nagle's story, a single woman programmer is trying to negotiate the expectations of having to sleep with a boss who disgusts her in order to get ahead. Her condominium is fully managed by an operating system named Oz. Oz, whose programming can be overridden by her voice commands, not only adjusts the lights and heat, brings her drinks, and talks to her; he also monitors her emotional states and adjusts her environment according to her stress levels. One of the advertising catalogs displayed on her holographic television screen includes an extraordinarily responsive, self-learning, male lover whom she decides to rent, "just to test out" how his operating system works. He is much more sophisticated than she expects, and he and Oz propose various ways of dealing with her boss. This is one of the few stories that incorporates the computer command structures into the story text.

Other stories involve psychological conundra of holograms and implants that change personality or sensation; of bioengineering; and the (im)possibilities of computer mediation of illicit, impersonal sex without guilt. There are stories about rivalry between programmers and the feeling of omnipotence that computing can give; the dilemmas of parenting in a municipality that is free of computer viruses because it has outlawed personal computers (but where they still exist illicitly); and a parody of the San Francisco heavy-metal mechanical-gladiatorial artist Mark Pauline (see Dery 1996). There are stories about the fierce competition of the computer age, both about speeded-up work time (a hilarious version of the physics fantasy of being in two, or more, places at once, and the devastation and havoc this can wreak on family, body, and the ability to survive economically), and about a laid-off lead programmer at Boeing, now homeless, who finds a stolen biological computer. (After a few false starts she guesses the correct command to turn it on: "Boot!" Imagining its uses, she thinks of selling it for fabulous sums, starting her own company, and gaining new autonomy; but she decides what she really needs is emotional security, and takes it along to the homeless center for Sunday turkey dinner.) There is a spoof of gadgets designed for the military-industrial complex, the true uses of which are as consumer tools for "personal discovery," which simultaneously parodies the script-style of thinking about life that programming can foster.

A lovely story about cyborgs used to reengineer the human species and our environment as the latter becomes increasingly a threat to the former, has a world populated with nanobots that allow humans to process chlorophyll, nanotooters to regenerate aging bodies, nanoassemblers for building, nanocomputers for designing. The hero works on a holographic design model of a bird to fix the ozone layer by breathing in oxygen and nitrogen and breathing out ozone and nitrogen. The story is also a deft account of husband-wife interaction, and of the assignment of credit for finding solutions. Lois Gresh (1993), the author of the story about time compression, also has a wonderful story about a self-reproducing biological computer with a capacity-straining program called Nietzsche ("compiles so slowly you'll think you've shorted"), which "she" finally births into a separate biological computer. Nietzsche now needs more tasks to keep from "terminal boredom," so she births a third computer, a Hassidic rabbi intelligence that begins debating with Nietzsche. Parodying programming and philosophy, and hinting at the diseases of cancer and malignant tumors (and attendant ethical issues) to which such biologies might be subject, the dilemmas of what seems at first a merely amusing and textured story are shadowed more darkly in the life tragedies of the human designers and their worries about the transfer of their creations to the medical establishment and speculations about their possible future roles as consultants watching over these more animal than machinelike AIs. Woven throughout are the ethical dilemmas of life, in whatever form, "out of control."

If *Infinite Loop* is ethnographically fascinating for the interplay between story and contemporary RL, as in the "Pygmaleon 3.0" and Media Lab project resonances, the *Future Boston* stories provide potential for ethnographically located grounding in a real place and for implicating history and changing social dynamics (see also *Zodiac,* Neal Stephenson's 1988 ecological sci fi/reality parody set in Boston). The armature of *Future Boston* has a standard sci fi or cyberpunk cast (new technologies embedded in a decaying environment, and a stratified authoritarian governance caught between warring factions), and the plot is noir thriller. (A female detective who misses her father, killed in the Great Flood, is used by her client to repress an uprising. The client, a hard-boiled female City Operator or Supervisor is, in turn, desperate to find her kidnapped adopted daughter, whose fingers are being sent to her one by one by a revenge-seeking infiltrator of a school for the children of elite Boston merchant families.) Boston is projected into a more multicultural society (the detective is Irish, the police chief is Italian, the elite merchant families have names like Nyo, Martinez, Mudandes, and Gutfreund), and is expanded also through multispeciation (especially with the linguistically distinctive Phner, and the recombinant, bioengineering Targive).

The epic frame is a futuristic parody of Boston history: a busy interplanetary spaceport, post-secession from the US (in a Pyrrhic replay of the original American revolution), post-arrival of the Loophole through which various alien species have arrived, post-municipal mutiny (Civil War) and repressive use of a Great Flood to drown the mutineers. The sea has reclaimed much of the landfill, and Bostonians now live in a huge, 180-story cube, an enclosed and stratified environment with video-simulation windows. Unenclosed suburban towns exist across the water: Charlestown, Dorchester, and Cambridge, where MIT and Harvard still maintain marginal existences. The spaceport in the harbor is the access to the obligatory physics parody: the Loophole or "multiply-connected space-time topological anomalous region which a spaceship can traverse to travel from one place to another without crossing the intervening distance" (Smith 1994:155).

But the Loophole is less access to a Star-Trek fantasy of outward expansive space colonization, and more an inward, implosive, historical reminder of being colonized and of the tragic Fall of the Phner, a parody of the biblical myths of origin, including a Tower of Babel reminder that language differences can carry alternative worldviews. The linguistic play continues to be characteristic and a meditation on grammatical-philosophical potentials.

The Phner have a language without verbs; instead, they "use concepts that concatenate existence and time, words like destruction-imminent-but-necessary or existed-once-now-ended-and-memory-still-influences-events" (Smith 1993:40). From an English language point of view, "they have trouble with verb tenses, time sequences and causality—before and after are almost the same word in Phner" (Smith 1993:12). But they have acute memories, imitate others to perfection as communication devices, and so can act as the "sents of Boston" (Smith 1993:17): "To the Phner, every spot of blood, every crumb of dirt, every wound and scar and broken bone tells a story" (Smith 1993:19). This syntactical, memory, and sleuthing structure provides a kind of karmic-cosmic attitude toward life and death; deaths are never forgotten, yet they are placed in larger contexts that judge them as "artful" or not. "Phner can accelerate their time-sense for brief periods, react more quickly, move faster, think more clearly...a survival reflex that conjures up terrifying and sad memories of the Endless Fall" (Smith 1993:39–40) [after losing a war with the Sh'ik], but which "at the same time it can be...a terrific buzz" (Smith 1993:40).

The Phners' acute memories (a process of esfn') makes them superb craftsmen of historical-reconstructed parts of town, and also a threat to art markets that depend upon uniqueness, since Phner easily recreate objects as they were when first esfn'd. To the Phner the notion of copies destroying value makes little sense, since "no two objects are identical because they have unique histories" (a recreated object retains for them traces of its mode and time of recreation). They consequently also have extremely skilled physicians, and from human points of view ghoulish interests in dissecting the dead to learn what they can. Phner are social animals who live in tightly packed "warrens" and have communal rituals that exercise the moral as well as psychological senses. Whatever one makes of this fantasy, it stands in for, acts as a token of, cultural differences premised on real epistemological and linguistic-structural differences, something rare in most science fiction (Ursula Le Guin being another notable exception).

The Targive are a similar token, this time of recombinant biological potentials, which even if not worked out with any particular technical didacticism available through contemporary molecular biology, nonetheless marks out that conceptual terrain. They are a race of nomads who build citadels, basilica, cathedrals, out of local forms of biological life, and who also produce various "mods" or modifications of local biological forms. Every Targive gift (punning no doubt both on the German *Gift*, which means poison, and on the oxymoron of tar which sticks rather than being giveable, or which tars the gift receiver with unwanted side effects) "conceals a scorpion so only the desperate accept their offer" (Smith 1993:40). For cleaning up Boston's effluents, they biodesigned a "clivus" which eats, digests, and transforms, helping bacteria dismantle the complicated man-made molecules of pollutants into ammonia, water, nitrogen, and carbon dioxide (Smith 1993:191). They can perform modifications on human brains as well, but at a serious cost—for they exact in tissue of their choosing a price for their gifts.

The world of this future Boston is filled with chairs made of Targive-modified jellyfish; bioelectronic blackbirds that act as eyes for the City Operator; holographic exercise environments in which one can fight off lizards, Zulus, and Nubian warriors; "biodesign on a grand scale, micronics so small and powerful that a lint-sized chip could not only beat you at chess but insult you in Swahili all the while, truly independent servobots, artificial brain aids, field-based technology; the list went on endlessly. With them came vermin, bugs, bizarre foodstuffs, and a host of alien con artists, lunatics, political fanatics, demagogues, courtesans, smugglers, and rapscalawags. And the dread disease cities, which in the late 2030s killed a fifth of the City's population before the Targives designed a treatment and a vaccine" (Smith 1993:156). Indeed, "It's part of City lore that...City Operators have Targive implants to help them interface better with the bots, eyes, spatiens, and Phneri, and with the half-biological City organism itself" (Smith 1993:25). There are even jesters, the popcorn aliens who parody the world of buying and selling:

"Sell to you and sell for me! Cells of two and cells of three! Cells for yet a hundred indecisions, and for a hundred visions and revisions, before the toasting of a fake or spree. This has been dyed grue, the rarest color in the galaxy. ... Appears green until you buy it, then ... it turns blue. ... That's why grue is unique!" ...

"I've got to go. I'm hunting for someone."

"Why didn't you say so?" ...

"I did say so. You weren't paying attention."

"You weren't charging attention! I didn't know I could buy it from you." ...

The popcorn grabbed the picture and immediately turned it upside down. "Yes, yes," he replied. "Absolutely distinctive hairline. I can certainly sell you to him."

"But you haven't got him."

"Oh but this is a futures contract." (Smith 1993:154)

IN BRIEF (THE LAW)

Everything you know about intellectual property is wrong. ... Intellectual property law cannot be patched, retrofitted, or expanded to contain digitalized expression any more than real estate law might be revised to cover the allocation of [the] broadcasting spectrum.

—*John Perry Barlow, "The Economy of Ideas"*

It is difficult for intellectual property laws to keep pace with technology. When technological advances cause ambiguity in the law, courts rely on the law's purposes to resolve that ambiguity. However, when technology gets too far ahead of the law, and it becomes difficult and awkward to apply the old principles, it is time for reevaluation and change.

—*Bruce Lehman et al., Intellectual Property and the National Information Infrastructure*

Software is a machine whose medium of construction is text.

—*Randy Davis*

Futures contracts, in the lively languages of the law: changing briefs for changing times. It is striking how often lawyers write about challenges of law and cyberspace in the tropes of radical breaks with the past, that precedents are multiple and ambiguous, that a choice of metaphor on the part of legislators or judges can make an extraordinary difference. Pamela Samuelson et al. (1995) writing about copyright and patent law; Michael Froomkin (1995) writing about cryptography, privacy, First and Fourth Amendment rights; Judge Richard Stearns, in the 1994 case of MIT undergraduate David LaMachhia, writing a decision about wire fraud, copyright infringement, and system operator liability—all express concern that the law is inadequate to developments in the new medium.

Courtrooms and legislative committees provide adversarial grounds between plaintiffs and defendants, but also between economic interests and societal ones, state and individual rights. Networked connectivity, accumulating data banks, encryption, and the economics of a shape-shifting technological medium have over the past fifteen years reframed the conceptual universes by which lawyers, judges, and law enforcement operate. In the struggle for comprehension and adjudication, legal language has been given a workout. Lively languages operate here as much as in literary or imaginative spheres; metaphor here is both a serious workhorse (on the basis of which precedent and analogical reason operate, with profoundly different outcomes depending upon the metaphor chosen), and a computer functionality that the law has fumbled in accommodating (e.g., conceptual metaphors as the modality in which software programs give behavioral coherence, and wherein reside much of their value as user interfaces).

That the law operates by matching new situations and new technologies to older precedents through metaphors and analogical logic is not a new observation, but Michael Froomkin's essay "The Metaphor is the Key" (1995) demonstrates how the choice of metaphor in the debates over cryptography[24] can make a major difference. Froomkin looks at the different effects of adopting various metaphors, and their associated legal precedents. If encryption is regarded like a car, for example, a vehicle in which messages are carried, then government demands to inspect messages randomly can be analogized to random checks on cars, escrowed keys being like license plates or taking pictures for a license, and, like the police stopping cars on the highway, may not need to wait for a warrant (by which time the car or message is gone); one can check whether messages are encrypted with the approved encryption system, without necessarily looking at the content of the message. "If the car metaphor prevails," Froomkin warns, "there will be far fewer constitutional rights in cyberspace than if any other metaphor comes to dominate."

If, on the other hand, one regards the ciphers of encryption as a language, then the government argument that it must have the ability to decrypt would be analogous to imposing limits on the use of languages other than English and would be unconstitutional under the First, Fifth, and Fourteenth Amendments. Rejection of the language metaphor, Froomkin warns, can lead to undesirable consequences. The metaphor of a house "may provide protection depending whether a court could compel production of [an encryption] key not committed to paper. If the court is unwilling to do this on Fifth Amendment grounds, strong cryptography would provide nearly unbreakable protection of private papers stored on a home computer."

These metaphors do not operate in a historical vacuum, and Froomkin suggests a shifting concern from Big Brother to Big Drugs in the rhetoric of the FBI's campaign to impose mechanisms that would allow the government to access encrypted messages.[25] In fact, while much of the press coverage of computer crime has been about hackers breaking into systems,[26] white collar crime and misuse of data banks are much more serious sources of computer crime, both in financial terms and invasion of privacy terms.[27] Encryption technologies can be used both to protect privacy and to make such crimes much easier. Thus, the struggle is vigorously contested between those who fear anarchistic black markets in everything from body parts to kidnapping and assassination contracts, money laundering, and extortion ("the four horsemen" of drugs, terror, money laundering, and pedophiles), as well as the breakdown of taxation and general law enforcement abilities of the state, and those who fear the imposition of police state controls, including outlawing of privacy-enhancing encryption, imposition of national identity cards (to be used at point-of-sale terminals to collect taxes and monitor health and other statuses),[28] and the general growth of surveillance by employers, marketing, and other information entrepreneurs.[29] "Regardless of how the Court decides to strike the balance," says Froomkin (1995:845), "it will involve a process requiring decisions not compelled by any precedent.... To predict where the law... may be going and to suggest feasible alternatives, one needs to understand the concerns that are likely to influence [the future course of the law]."

Similar kinds of metaphorical choices are debated in the still unsettled question of system operator liability: Is s/he like a publisher, an editor, a bookstore, or a common carrier? If an editor, then more liability is likely to accrue; if a bookstore or common carrier, the s/he cannot be held responsible for the content of the books/messages.[30] System operators at the moment are caught between potential suits for libel by victims of defamatory statements on their systems and suits for abridgment of free speech. Economic pressures mediate some of this: Prodigy monitors children's chat rooms, at least, for fear that parents will cancel subscriptions if they find their children being subjected to materials and solicitations they find offensive. Legislative and technical mediations are also now being proposed.[31]

The debates over intellectual property law—copyright, patent, trade secrets—are central to the economic incentive structure of the computer industry. A series of contradictory outcomes of major appellate and Supreme Court decisions (*Whelan v. Jaslow* [1986]; *Lotus v. Mosaic & Paperback* [1987–90]; *Apple v. Microsoft & H-P* [1988–92]; *Computer Associates v. Altai* [1992]; *Borland v. Lotus* [1997]) have sparked vigorous debate as to whether copyright and patent law are adequate to the new medium and whether a sui generis law should be written, as was done for computer chips in 1984. At issue is the confusion over whether software can be analogized to texts and literary productions (copyright) or to machines (patents) or—least likely given the relative ease of reverse engineering—to trade secrets. At issue as well is a temporally unfolding change in the nature of the software market, which is paralleled by changes in positions taken by the industry.

The first software patent was issued in 1968, but in the 1960s software was normally bundled with hardware, given away as something that made mainframes useable. A 1966 Presidential Commission chaired by J. W. Birkenstock, the head of IBM (which controlled 70 percent of the computer market), did not want software to be patentable; algorithms are laws of nature, are thus not patentable. In *Gottshalk v. Benson* (1972) IBM, Burroughs, and Honeywell filed friends of the court briefs in which again they argued that the mathematical character of algorithms, even if they facilitate machine implementation, make them ineligible for patent protection. But by the 1980s a mass market began to emerge for software, and industry began to demand protection for a commodity that was expensive to develop but easy to copy. A 1978 Presidential Commission urged Congress to add software to the 1976 Copyright Protection Act because there was no patent protection, and this was done in a 1980 amendment to the act. But copyright is an uncomfortable fit for software: Copyright is intended to promote diversity of literary production; software to be most useful requires standardization. Copyright is intended to prevent copying; every computer operating system integrally contains copying programs. Although there have been extensions of copyright protections from the original application to print, reprinting, and vending of printed materials (to public performance rights for drama, music, and public display, analyzed by the 1976 law into five kinds of rights—reproduction, derivation, distribution, public performance, and public display), copyright seems to stretch the meanings of copying to various reductio ad absurda. These have become the source of the contradictory appellate court decisions in the series of "look and feel" court cases of the late 1980s, and the impetus for new policy initiatives explored in the July 1994 Preliminary Draft Report, or "Green Paper" (Lehman 1994) of the National Information Infrastructure Initiative (NII[32]) working group chaired by Bruce Lehman, the Commissioner of Patents and Trademarks and Assistant Secretary of Commerce.

In 1981 the case of *Diamond v. Diehr* reopened the patent system to software, adding to the confusion. Taking the position that patents can be issued for industrial processes controlled by computer programs (rubber curing, in this case), IBM immediately began filing patents on software. After an influential article by Donald Chisum (1986) supporting the use of patents for software, the Patent and Trademarks Office began in 1989 to accept more and more applications. IBM files some two hundred a year, and there are as many as a thousand a year being filed, many in anticipation of their use for cross-licensing with other companies. Indeed, software is often written up as both a patent application and a copyright, since it is increasingly difficult to distinguish between implementations done through hardware or software; they can be done either way. Like copyright, the patent system fits software poorly. Intended to encourage the making public of processes and methods of production in exchange for a seventeen-year protection, the time period for protection is the first problem, since the time cycles of software (and hardware) in the computer industry are much shorter. The search for "prior art" to demonstrate that one's patent is non-obvious and original is difficult and confusing, both because of the lack of technical expertise in the PTO and because of the complexity of programs and the difficulty of deciding which elements might constitute prior art. These problems open the door to endless litigation, since software development depends on incremental modification. Litigation becomes a means for raising entry barriers to small companies and embroiling big ones, but it works, arguably, to the favor of large companies with considerable legal resources.[33]

If both copyright and patent definitions are hard to apply to software, perhaps a sui generis law is required. This was the solution found in the 1984 Semiconductor Chip Protection Act, in which patentlike protection is given for two years automatically, and for eight years if the chip is registered. At the same time, the act acknowledges incremental design development, the right to reproduce and reverse-engineer chip designs to test and analyze how they work. The industry wants competitors to make compatible chips, and the production process relies on second sourcing. But the semiconductor industry, unlike the software industry, has only a dozen or so large manufacturers; the barriers to entry are high, and it is very expensive to set up a production facility. Still, the argument can be made (Samuelson, Davis, Kapor, and Reichman 1995) that the current laws generate an unstable oscillation between overprotection and underprotection, because none of the categories of intellectual property apply neatly to software. At the time of *Whelan v. Jaslow* (1986) it seemed that there was underprotection and the need to encourage investment, so an expansive interpretation of copyright was pursued. At the time of *Computer Associates v. Altai* (1992), not just a different circuit court and a different reasoning process, but a different time, when the market felt cramped by overprotection, led to a narrower definition of copyright being pursued.

It would be better, argue Samuelson, Davis, Kapur, and Reichman (1995), if one thought out ways to protect the actual value of computer software, rather than forcing poor analogies. The most important property of programs lies in their useful behavior, including the conceptual metaphors that give behavior coherence. Behavior can be "cloned" without appropriating the text of the software; that is, different codes can produce the same behavior. If what is of value in the market is the behavior, it misses the point to try to copyright the codes, which in fact are made up of incremental elements modified, but rarely directly copied, from various prior art sources.

The 1994 Green Paper is an interesting document against which to test this line of argument. Although it claims that copyright law needs only "minor clarification amendment," what is revealing is its item-by-item puzzlement over what traditional legal concepts might mean in the new digital environment. It can be read much the way a wickedly delighted psychoanalyst might look for hesitations, ambivalences, and contradictions in The Official Story, thereby finding another, quite contradictory one being told. (The Green Paper was succeeded by a 1995 White Paper which, according to many analysts, tries to erase the telltale ambiguities in the Green Paper by omitting unfavorable legal precedents and tilts the resolution in favor of already existing communications industries in an unsustainable attempt to extend the meaning of copyright to even such "copies" as the electronic repetitions in the machine memory that make it possible to display or send a document.[34])

Photocopying, once an analogous new technology, the Green Paper begins, also once "caused apprehension among copyright owners," but thanks to the time, cost, and degradation of quality involved in copying, as well as to court decisions denying application of "fair use" to Kinko's and other off-campus copy shops' production of "coursepacks" for teaching, print copyright rules still work reasonably well. The same holds for audiotape recording, even digital ones (as worked out under the Audio Home Recording Act of 1992). But digital integration of all forms of text, image, and sound information, done with speed, ease, and no loss of quality, makes it sometimes difficult to tell what is distribution, what is reproduction, or what is publication. Traditional copyright law depends on a definition of publication that requires a material object to change hands. How stable is the notion that browsing in another computer constitutes "fixing" of a new copy because it must be in RAM or the buffer in order to be displayed? In *Playboy Enterprises v. Frena,* the court decided that unauthorized downloading of digitalized images scanned from Playboy photographs constituted economic damage to Playboy Enterprises. However, the Green Paper notes that it remains unclear whether Frena "distributed" the photographs or subscribers "reproduced" them; furthermore, if subscribers are then liable for copyright infringement, it is unclear if Frena is liable as contributory. In the Playboy case and a similar case concerning video games (*Sega Enterprises, Ltd., v. MAPHIA*), judgments were made, but the principles at issue are very ambiguous when applied more generally to the liability of bulletin board sysops (system operators) if the latter are able to claim no knowledge of what is put on their electronic bulletin boards. A prominent 1994 court case dealing with these issues, that of MIT undergraduate David LaMachhia, was dismissed as unprosecutable under either copyright law or the wire fraud laws often used by prosecutors when they need a vaguer general purpose statute. The judge in the case noted that prosecution should not be used as a vehicle for writing laws where current legislation does not fit the new cyberworld, that if Congress wished LaMacchia-style activity to be made criminal, it needed to write legislation to that effect.

Moreover, the Green Paper continues, the new digital environment also creates problems for the "first sale doctrine" (that when one buys a book, one may resell it), for archival and library exemptions (which allow free use and limited reproduction rights), for rights of free transmission on receiving apparatuses like radios in a bar or beauty shop (which "will change as home equipment merges with other equipment," and for licensing provisions allowing cable and satellite operators to retransmit copyrighted materials ("will need to be reviewed" as creative, communications, and computer entities continue to merge). More subtly yet, since copyright infringement does not depend on intent, and since it also need not be a literal copying, the ability to easily manipulate works in digital format leads to a whole raft of issues regarding infringement, reproduction, and derivative work. Among these issues, the Green Paper lists manipulating photographs (in which the input may be infringement but the result may not be) and the resale or distribution of items from gray markets (legally produced for distribution abroad but not authorized for the US market):

> If an infringing literary work, for instance, was physically shipped into the U.S. in the form of a paper copy, a CD-ROM disk or even stored on a memory chip, then it could be an infringing importation if the above discussed conditions exist, but it would appear that Section 602, as currently written, could not be used to block the electronic transmission of such material. (Lehman 1994:238)

A more obvious and basic issue is that domestic law will be made increasingly ineffective unless at the same time an international or "Global Information Infrastructure" and legal framework is constructed. This, the Commerce Department's Green Paper notes, is not merely an issue of intellectual property rights ("When the globe is blanketed with digital information dissemination systems, a user in one country will be able to manipulate information resources in another country in ways that may violate that country's copyright laws."), but also a potential problem for commerce: Doing "electronic business" over information superhighways will be difficult unless rules for protection [of rights, but also privacy, and security] and harmonization of legal structures are provided. The initial issue is the claim of the Software Business Association that their members lose billions of dollars each year in pirated software.

Harmonizing copyright systems means, among other things, coming to terms with at least two different moral understandings of the purpose of copyright. For Anglo-American law, the purpose is to protect authors' economic rights so that they will make their ideas publicly available in order to promote the progress of science and the arts; for European law, "moral rights" of authorship are not transferable and have to do with natural rights or rights of personhood. The American authors of the Green Paper say these moral rights may have to yield in the new digital world.

The Green Paper has relatively little to say about patent law, which is at least equally under siege by the digital revolution as copyright. Indeed, it has little to say about the entire confusion of patent and copyright categories created in a series of important court decisions over the past fifteen years about the copyrightability and patentability of software (as well as the blurring or interchangeability between hardware and software), a confusion so severe that many (e.g., Barlow, Newell, Samuelson) suggest a whole new intellectual framework may have to emerge. The Green Paper proposal timidly hints at this by proposing that "transmission" be elevated into an elaborated conceptual apparatus to deal with many of the issues listed above. It ends with an important reminder of two social issues fundamental to the conflicts among the major interest groups (academia, industry, programmers as a profession, and the state)—the basic purpose of the copyright law, and the problem of access:[35]

> The Copyright Act exists for the benefit of the public. To fulfill its constitutional purpose, the law should strive to make the information contained in protected works of authorship freely available to the public. "Freely available," of course, does not necessarily mean "available free." The Working Group does not believe that authors should be required to donate access time to their works on-line, but some reasonable approach must be adopted to ensure that the economically disadvantaged in this country are not further disadvantaged or disenfranchised by the information revolution. (Lehman 1994)

The Green Paper, in short, provides a preliminary site of contestation in the information revolution, as well as a sense of the destabilizing effect on basic conceptual categories that it is generating. It does so by looking not at language uses that celebrate, exacerbate, or elaborate upon these instabilities (as for instance in a playful "pomo" theoretical exposé), but at a conservative document that is unable to hide the contradictions of arguing both that only minor clarifications and amendments are needed and that "when technology gets too far ahead of the law...it becomes difficult and awkward to apply the old principles."

This situation should not be taken as an argument in favor of a presumption that new technologies necessarily make old laws obsolete, as Laurence Tribe (1991) notes in regard to First and Fourth Amendment rights, but rather as a reminder that one must pay close attention to the values that the law—constitutional or statutory—is meant to foster. Although the emphasis here has been on the instabilities of legal categories, language, and reasoning, the argument has been underpinned by a questioning of the economic dynamics, democratic access, and private liberties that are under pressure. Just as the legal system periodically needs to be reminded that the Fourth Amendment protects the privacy of people, not places,[36] so too, in thinking about the economic restructuring that cyberspace is facilitating, one needs to think of the values of the human beings involved, the values placed in the exchange system.

IN EXCHANGE

> 1992...signaled a sea change in competitive dynamics...The importance of this transition reaches far beyond the participants in the [information technology] industry...None of these industries are able to operate successfully within autarkic national boundaries.
>
> —*David Yoffie*

> Chips make me think of the eyesight of women in Singapore and Korea, going blind during the process of crafting the fiddly little wire; of "clean rooms"...in Silicon Valley and the Netherlands...Perhaps it is time to have a less boring idea of the body right now—a body politic...The combination of telecommuting with the global factory has proved terrible for women...isolated in the "electronic cottage"...an easy way for a corporation to do legal "union busting" and bypass any particular state's labour regulations...Tayloristic intervention,...monitoring of key strokes in data entry,...timing breaks to go to the toilet.
>
> —*Susan Leigh Star,* The Cultures of Computing

> Information...Like other such deep phenomena as light or matter, it is a natural host to paradox...helpful to understand light as being both a particle and a wave, an understanding of information may emerge in the abstract congruence of its several different properties...
>
> Information is an activity...is experienced, not possessed...has to move...is conveyed by propagation, not distribution...grow[s] in the usual fractal lattice like frost spreading on a window...
>
> Information is a life form...as in an oral tradition, digital information has no final cut...
>
> Information is a relationship...Receiving information is often as creative an act as generating it.
>
> —*John Perry Barlow, "The Economy of Ideas"*

Just as the new electronic media are undoing old assumptions, definitions, and regulatory mechanisms in the law (intellectual property law, export controls, privacy, freedom of information), so, too, there is a claim that the information economy operates by laws different from those of classical or marginal utility economics. It is in the details of the paradoxes of this new economy that the double ethnographic challenges reside: the challenges to produce credible ethnographic accounts of the concrete and detailed temporal changes in the political economy of cyberspace, and the challenges to provide critical mirrorings in which the utopian and dystopian sides of the political economy can be screened in their partialities and contingencies. In public discourse, at least, it is as though one side of the paradoxical structure cannot be seen while the other is being discussed.

On one extreme side of this structure, John Perry Barlow, Carver Mead, George Gilder, and others argue that the constraints of labor and capital are being removed thanks to a technology that operates increasingly on the level of the microcosm—the particle world of electrons and biological molecular processes—as miniaturization has moved from circuit boards to integrated circuits to faster and faster chips made out of sand (silicon), and as parallel processing has allowed computations to operate as "out-of-control" self-organizing systems. On the other side, these processes have been described as allowing for an intensification of the labor and capital processes described by nineteenth-century political economists (exchange of formally free labor through a mystified process of alienation and extraction of surplus value). Cycles of innovation and consolidation have plagued the computer industries (Hayes 1989; Yoffie 1994; Teitelman 1994). David Yoffie and his colleagues at the Harvard Business School put together a case book on informational technologies in 1994, arguing that almost all firms have a stake in the evolution of these technologies, both as customers for the technologies themselves and, arguably more importantly, as a model for management in the twenty-first century. None of the IT industries can operate in autarkic national boundaries; all must be transnational. No market (neither the US nor Europe) is big enough to support the costs of developing a digital switch or semiconductors; those firms that tried to remain national went bankrupt. Only in the 1990s did the promise of merging technologies actually begin to happen, and this caused the disintegration of vertically integrated businesses. Computers and telecommunications began to merge, and the differences between personal computers, workstations, minicomputers, and mainframes began to collapse. "Blurred firm boundaries" (Yoffie 1994) led to new corporate forms of shifting alliances. First movers willing to cannibalize their own businesses (offering new products that reduced sales on older ones) had enormous advantages in capturing market share and setting standards. Some might argue that these are but consolidations of a globalizing market (Aglietta 1976/79), similar to earlier and more national or regional mechanisms like the post-war housing and automobile consumer markets, supported by socialization of credit and loan facilities.

A second such paradox is the separation in cyberspace between production and use. Office use of software and hardware (where the "only" physical downside seems to be carpel tunnel syndrome, eye strain, sick building problems, and the sterility of an environment that makes the screen seem like life) is so far removed from the manufacturing of the chips in "clean rooms" (which generate hidden toxicities) that it is far too easy for many users to forget the production processes when talking about cyberspace. A third paradox has to do with the inability of economic measures to show productivity gains through computerization (Teitelman 1994; Uchitelle 1996), and a fourth, often tacitly understood and regretted, is the important role that military contracts still play in the computer worlds of corporate survival. The secrecy of military contracts and the ways in which the work is parceled out so that programmers need not know the end uses to which they are contributing are not dissimilar from the studied displacements of consumers' attention away from the hazards of manufacturing chips.

Hayes's (1989) exposé of these hazards suggests an ethnographic method of "following the work processes"—through evacuations of facilities for toxic leaks, the occurrence of medical disabilities, the intentional disabling of occupational hazard indicators, and the lack of medical research on accumulating multiple chemical sensitivity syndromes. The semiconductor industry uses toxic gases to give electrical properties to microchips (arsine, phosphine, diborane, chlorine); acids to harden and etch chips, to electroplate, and to retard oxidation; and solvents (Hayes 1989:64–68). Inhaling hydrogen chloride from silicon tetrachloride leaks can form hydrochloric acid inside the body (Hayes 1989:65). By 1980, occupational illness rates for semiconductor workers were more than three times those of general manufacturing workers. In response, the Semiconductor Industry Association changed the way it records injuries and illnesses so as to show a two thirds drop in occupational illness rates (Hayes 1989:65), and the Reagan administration cut funding for the Project on Health and Safety in Electronics (PHASE), a program that collected and publicized information for electronics workers on chemicals used in manufacturing (Hayes 1989:66). In 1986, faced with preliminary results of a survey of its workers in Hudson, Massachusetts, that showed a twice-normal miscarriage rate (39 percent among workers in wafer etching, 29 percent in wafer photolithography), Digital Equipment Corporation reacted by banning interviews with workers and announcing programs of pregnancy testing and transfers for women of childbearing age. AT&T also mandated job transfers out of clean room work for pregnant women (Hayes 1989:67). In 1988, a California Department of Health study found that pregnant women who drank tap water in Silicon Valley had twice as many miscarriages and four times as many birth defects as those who drank filtered or no tap water; IBM and Fairchild settled a related class action suit quietly out of court (Hayes 1989:24). The astronautlike suits worn in clean rooms are designed not to protect workers from chemical toxicities, but to protect the wafers from the particles human bodies throw off (Hayes 1989:67); similarly, laminar air flows and filters are designed to protect the chips by extracting particulates, not to protect the workers by extracting fumes. Describing the false sense of protection that suits, filters, and air flow can impart, Hayes (1989:68) comments, "The ambiance is misleading in a distinctly modern (i.e., ambiguous) way."

Apart from acute potential dangers from spills and leaks, chemical toxicities can be cumulative, building up in the fatty tissues of the body and inducing "chemical hypersensitivity," an increasing sensitivity to chemicals in the everyday environment. This "chemically induced T-cell inadequacy" debilitates the immune system, not unlike the virally induced AIDS. And yet the chemicals, techniques, and brand names of clean room equipment are all protected as "trade secrets" and "proprietary information," and daily logs recording evacuations, fume detector tapes, and injured worker dismissals are also kept secret and are rarely reported in the press. Threshold limit values (TLVs) are set by professional organizations for monitoring systems, but there is no independent checking; in fact, according to a National Research Council/National Academy of Sciences study, there are no TLVs at all for 79 percent of 48,523 workplace chemicals (Hayes 1989:76). Immigrant women are often preferred workers in Silicon Valley for clean room work, and as these manufacturing jobs are outsourced abroad it is often women, the new industrial labor source, who perform the work there.

It is, thus, not only the so-called clean room that is misleading, but the entire economy of the computer industry, which goes through a classic sort of labor reorganization while claiming to be part of a new economy that operates according to laws no longer constrained by scarcities of labor. Yet the ideology of descent into the microcosm and the laws of a quantum economics remain vital spurs to the imagination and to chip design, to the embedding of cyberspace in a changing world of scientific exploration and technological innovation, a world of quantum, optical, and DNA computers that can overcome current physical limits to computational speed and that operate on new computing principles far removed from the sequential logics of mechanical Turing machines. At each turn, in each dimension of cyberspace—in time, in language, in place, in brief, and in exchange—there appears to be productive paradox. As a novel about computer scientists, their psyches and incapacities puts it:

> "It went like this, but wasn't"
> ...That's good. Lead with a paradox. Hook her.
> It's the traditional Persian fable opener.
>
> —*Richard Powers,* Galatea 2.2

RE-SITUATING ETHNOGRAPHY

> The problem was that you didn't always know what you were seeing until later, maybe years later, that a lot of it never made it in at all, it just stayed stored there in your eyes.
>
> —*Michael Herr,* Dispatches

> Ethics has been confined largely to the domains of doing, which include performative acts of a linguistic nature.... What might interest us here is the fact that responsibility no longer pivots on a notion of interiority...
>
> —*Avital Ronell, "Video/Television/Rodney King: Twelve Steps Beyond the Pleasure Principle"*

> Man is no longer man enclosed, but man in debt.
>
> —*Gilles Deleuze, "Postscript on the Societies of Control"*

Moebius-strip-like, we return to the beginning, to Hans Jonas's suggestion that not only the law, the economy, language, place, and time are challenged by our contemporary technological era, but that there is even a claim on the new in ethics, in how we deal with one another, and that this implicates, relocates, and complicates ethnographic writing.

The ethnographic starting point in this essay is the pervasive expressions by practitioners in many fields that things are outrunning their conceptual categories, and that unlike earlier, more generalized debates about the "postmodern," this has become in the 1990s a concrete practical matter for the diverse institutions of society (law, economics, engineering). Among the institutional facets most developed in this essay has been the law (In Brief), through dense case-work sequences affecting economic, academic, and civil rights interests and involving material effects of choices about metaphors, such that practitioners feel challenged by the new in ways that stretch their traditional uses of analogy and precedent. Economics (In Exchange) too has practitioners, from business school case-writers to technology writers, who claim that traditional categories are outrun. Here the discussion opens further into the historical horizons of business cycles, industrial reorganizations, labor processes, and transvaluations of ideas, labor, and materials into producer and consumer goods. It also engages the ongoing dialectic between those processes and what at least since Marx have been called processes of fetishization, specterization, or virtualization of the economy (to which there has been an interesting return of analysis in the 1990s; see Leitch 1996), as well as some ethnographic work on the social effects of those processes (e.g., Stacey 1990; Star 1995). Parallel fields of discussion might be opened into psychology (In Conscience), both human-machine interfaces (e.g., Papert 1996; Turkle 1995; Stone 1995), and artificial life, brain and cognitive psychology, or neuroscience; into popular culture, entertainment, and advertising (In Play), as theaters of exploration and preparation as well as voicings of things that cannot be said in less court-jester-like environments; and into sciences (In-formation), such as molecular biology, where it has been argued that the imagery of the genome as an information science is both misleading and productive.[37] Most concrete is the section on building the infrastructure of connectivity around the world (In Place, Sites under Construction), captured in the title of one of cyberspace's cheerleading journals, *Wired.* The laying of a third generation of fiber optic cable from Europe to Japan is driven by competition between giant transnational business alliances which undo older national PTT monopolies and regulating controls (Stephenson 1996). The "sea change" arguments of "In Exchange" are thereby further strengthened.

The form of this essay attempts to capture on paper—a static medium—in a kind of freeze frame some of the dimensions and institutional facets of what a hypertextual ethnography with cross-linkages could accomplish. Ethnographies can be and (a few) already are being written in hypertext, multimedia, and CD-ROM formats that overcome the linearity of traditional writing and that might put interconnections into play more easily than simple text (e.g., Goldman-Segall 1990, 1995). Some research and collaboration can be, and already is being, conducted through E-mail and on the Web. But at issue in the influence of these modalities—as with cinematic or filmic forms earlier in the twentieth century—is not merely the literal adoption of new technical possibilities, but a new pedagogical regime, just as much fiction writing in the twentieth century is acknowledged to draw on cinematic techniques (Cohen 1979). Language itself is foregrounded in much of the thinking about this new pedagogical regime, ranging from the puns, metaphors, and syntactic play that access and hold in juxtaposition differential epistemological standpoints, to narratives and institutionalized discourses that act as switches and circuits of thought, behavior, action, organization, and cultural forms. Space, time, and differential access are being rearranged.

Cyberspace is part of the reality in which all of us live, and much of it works behind the scenes. Jaron Lanier debunks the hype that "virtual reality" prostheses could be taken to be more real than the physical world: "The virtual world only exists because of the magic of the way your nervous system makes things real when you interact with them. And the moment you start to space out or become lazy, the reality goes away and it just turns into a bunch of junk on your head" (Lanier 1996:43–44). So, too, there is much hype about cyberspace. But cyberspace continues to work behind the scenes when we space out, compiling our credit ratings, positioning our financial futures, restructuring our work lives and stratification systems, building new decentralized bureaucratic surveillance and security systems, providing scientific and pragmatic knowledges beyond ordinary perception, keeping us distracted and suspended in complex temporal loops of partial knowledges, interactions, and circulating debts that merge and interact beyond individual responsibilities and control. We cannot afford to abandon responsibility, and therefore must build new social forms of reflexive modernization that can make such systemic complexity and interactivity accountable. Hence the turn in much contemporary philosophy to questions of ethics—ethics no longer seen as the realm primarily of individual doings—as the quotations used here from Jonas, Derrida, Herr, Ronell, and Deleuze signal.

Ethnographies are challenged to no longer dwell merely in romantic tropes of discovery, but to ground, to make visible and audible,[38] contending worlds of difference, to provide translation circuitry that recognizes its own relations to other circulating representations (Fischer 1993, 1997).

Notes

1. I adapt here for the infrastructure of cyberspace a phrase Derrida uses to describe the way in which "the closure of metaphysics" in philosophical discourses is used to unveil the limitations and inescapability of moves in philosophy (see Derrida 1995:80).

2. By spring 1995 the first successful experiment with a biological computer was no longer science fiction.

3. The notion of two necessary and complementary kinds of science has been broached in various ways by Lévi-Strauss (1962/66), Lacan (1973/77), and Beck (1986/92), by advocates of "social learning" and participatory policy making (Rip, Misa, and Schott 1995), and by others. As the Greg Bear epigram and note 2 illustrate, science fiction and popular culture can operate, as Lévi-Strauss describes "savage thought" more generally, as a proleptic or anticipation effect, "like a shadow moving ahead of its owner," partly through a systematizing of what is immediately presented to the senses, and partly through a bricolage style of working out logical possibilities (Lévi-Strauss 1962/66:chap. 1).

4. On reflexive modernity, see Beck (1986/92), Giddens (1991), Lash and Urry (1994). On empirical cases that support Beck's description of the dynamics of risk society, see Reich (1991), Brown and Mikkelson (1990); on the agonism required to force honest disclosure, see Wiener (1995).

5. Thus, for example, while reform of the US health care system foundered in the political arena during the first two years of the Clinton administration, the market pushed ahead quite rapidly, totally reworking the nature of the health care system. Similarly, while the government seeds research in arenas like the development of the Internet and the Human Genome Project, the amounts of money the private sector has to spend in these areas has dwarfed that of public moneys.

6. See Beck 1986/1992 for an elaboration of these formulations as well as those of shadowboxing and shell games by multinational corporations, especially his lovely passage comparing the specularity of risk today with the gods and demons of antiquity (1992:73).

7. Or dreams that have effectiveness in the world; see Freenberg's reading of Ursula Le Guin's 1971 novel *Lathe of Heaven.* The trick, says Feenberg, is not to impose modern technology upon the world, but to learn how to use effective dreaming in harmony with the complexity of the world (Feenberg 1995:141–42).

8. On origin stories, see Serres (1991); for a technological example, see Ronnell (1989). Alternative genealogies for contemporary computer and Internet culture include cybernetic control systems, networking technologies (railroads, telegraph, water and sewage systems), and virtual reality sensory mechanic assemblages (film, telephone, phonograph). On the pre–World War II development of cybernetics *avant la lettre,* see Mindell (1996); for a postwar history, see Edwards (1996). On the history of ARPA (Advanced Research Projects Agency) and the beginnings of the Internet, see Norberg and O'Neill (1996). On the history of networks as the political precursor for the struggles over the Internet, see Russell, McKnight, and Solomon (1995).

9. One thinks of Walter Benjamin's notion of "dialectical images" in which the technological object serves to remind subsequent generations of the difference between early liberatory hopes for the technology and the normalized subsequent uses. See Buck-Morss (1989) and Mehlman (1993).

10. Consider the linear and hierarchical rule-governed modes of programming and modeling enforced in the 1970s as opposed to the more intuitive, play-based styles of computer use in the 1980s, with its fascination with user-friendly MacIntosh-style metaphors for graphic interfaces, metaphors of self-organizing complexity, and small, multiple ("parallel processing") robots rather than large centralized computers.

11. For accounts of the struggles and competitions to establish networks in China, see Triolo and Lovelock (1996); on North Africa, see A. K. Danowitz, Y. Nassef, and S. E. Goodman (1995). Egypt had 214 Internet hosts by 1995, and the state has not only supported university and government use, but also the development of local PC assembly and software industries by creating demand in the state sector. The Ministry of

Defense bought the first PCs locally assembled by the state-owned Banha Electronics Corporation. In Algeria, by contrast, a drive to computerize state firms in the 1980s and promote other uses of information technologies has slowed due to political unrest.

12. This is but a hint: Computers are called Acharya, Veda, Soochak. There are some Germanisms in *The New Hacker's Dictionary*: DAU (*dummster anzunehmender User*, "stupidest imaginable user"), derived from engineering slang GAU (*grüsster anzunehmender Unfall*, "worst foreseeable disaster," as in nuclear plant core meltdown), but also borrowings such as kluge, a patch, from the word for "clever"; "Gedanken thesis," a pejorative and ironic contrast to physics usage of "Gedanken experiment" (lack of intuition about what is programmable, about what constitutes a clear specification of an algorithm). Russian via Yiddish makes some appearances in *The New Hacker's Dictionary*, as well, and there are kremvax and kgbvax, fictitious USENET sites at the Kremlin announced April 1, 1984, predating by six years the first genuine site in Moscow. Eventually Vadim Antonov had a real site named kremvax, which became an electronic center of anticommunist resistance during the failed coup of August 1991 (Raymond 1993:252).

13. "The red sun is high, the blue low," Bukatman (1993:11), citing Samuel Delany and Teresa de Lauretis, says is a typical sentence that keeps the reader guessing until the final word signals a location diegetically far from earth, generically in a sci-fi text. "The door dilated," or "Daddy married, a man this time," similarly keep one's assumptions flexible about the life worlds one is entering. New metaphors and terminologies are coined to capture emergent or possible combinations, as in his title taken from Burroughs, "terminal identities," a double articulation of both the interface with the global electronic circulation of data and an end point or concrete machine that grounds the flight of electrons.

14. Viz. entry under "cyberpunk" in Raymond (1993:129): "Gibson's near-total ignorance of computers and the present-day hacker culture enabled him to speculate about the role of computers and hackers in the future in ways hackers have since found both irritatingly naive and tremendously stimulating." See also Gibson's interview with Larry McCaffery (1986), in which he talks about influences (Thomas Pynchon, Robert Stone, Dashiell Hammet, William Burroughs), says that the language of *Neuromancer* that seems futuristic is actually from 1969 Toronto drug and

biker slang, and admits, "Listen to me trying to explain this, it immediately becomes apparent that I have no grasp of how computers really work."

15. Unless otherwise noted, all jargon and definitions in this section are taken from Raymond (1993).

16. See also pyston, bogon, and inventing nonce particle names (cluon, futon, etc.). Pystons were elementary particles carrying the sinister force, with the probability of losing being proportional to the number of pystons falling on a process; since pystons are generated by observers, demos tend to fail when many people watch. Now largely succeeded by bogon, whose antiparticle is a clutron or cluon, a unit of cluefulness. Futon is the elementary particle of randomness.

17. Also the name of a course, 6.085/STS085, at MIT taught by Hal Abelson, Joanne Costello, and myself, using, in addition to real-time class, an on-line E-mail signature-encrypted discussion list, and a World Wide Web home page with readings and with links to various archives and information sources. In Fall 1998 the MIT class joined forces with the Harvard Law School and professors Larry Lessig and Johnathan Zittrain. Thirty law students and thirty engineers constituted the class. See http://swissnet.ai.mit.edu/6095/.

18. There is, however, a hacker underground and even institutional islands of hackerdom within IBM, acknowledged in Raymond 1993. Charles Andres, author of the comic "CPU Wars," (1979) allegedly even received a letter of appreciation in 1979 from the head of IBM's Thomas J. Watson Research Laboratories (Raymond 1993:121).

19. ITS (Incompatible Time-sharing System), was an influential operating system for PDP-6s and PDP-10s at MIT that generated much AI-hacker jargon. Actual work shifted to newer machines after 1982, and the last ITS machine shut down at MIT in 1990, but the Royal Institute of Technology in Sweden maintains one in its computer museum (Raymond 1993:243).

20. Multics was a late-1960s time-sharing operating system developed by MIT, GE, and Bell Labs, treating all devices uniformly as special files. After that consortium broke up, Ken Thompson and Dennis Ritchie in 1969 invented UNIX, "a weak pun on Multics," as an interactive time-sharing system that has become the most widely used multiuser general purpose operating system in the world. Raymond (1993:427) comments that many see it as the most important victory of hackerdom over industry opposition.

21. Year Two of the class had the following: bitter, Boy, chopper, crab, durham, Dragon, hmm, Fox Muldor, Idless, interzone, kosmo, Kraken, krakpot, loki, Lyle, mercury, Motts, Nicki, Pik, Prophet, repeatloaf, satire@myplace.disorg, Seen, Smithers, spock, spot, student, Thoreau, vapor, will.

22. Wizards and warlocks are those empowered in various cybergames and MUDs to create and enforce rules. More generally, a wizard is "1. A person who knows how a complex piece of software or hardware works... esp. someone who can find and fix bugs quickly in an emergency," and "2. A person who is permitted to do things forbidden to ordinary people; one who has wheel privileges on a system" (Raymond 1993:453).

23. The FBI profile of hackers and crackers is of introverted young males without outside interests. A more troubling subculture is that of virus writers (Korey Sandler, *PC Computing Magazine*, Sept. 1994), who range from mischievous hackers to industrial saboteurs and disgruntled employees out for revenge to Third World malcontents filled with ressentiment about a technology to which they can gain only partial access. Dark Avenger, for instance, was a Bulgaria-based hacker (Bulgaria was the USSR's Silicon Valley, but individuals did not have their own computers) who told a journalist that the US might be able to deny him entry to the country but could not deny entry to his viruses.

Compare "A Portrait of J. Random Hacker" (Raymond 1993), which describes not only an older, university-educated set, but also the shift from the nerd stereotypes of the early 1970s to the "more whole earth than whole polyester" and more "mildly health-food faddish" than the junk food stereotype. See also the portrait of working for companies like Microsoft in Douglas Courtland's story "Microserfs" (1993) and his subsequent novel (1995).

24. The 1994–95 debates over the Clipper Chip, initially a mandate that the telecommunications hardware sold in the US accommodate a chip that would allow law enforcement officials, under court order supervision, the ability to wiretap the flow of digital information. The FBI argued for this in its fight against the "four horsemen" of drugs, terrorists, money launderers, and pedophiles. Opponents feared Big Brother more than Big Drugs.

25. Admiral Bobby Inman, former director of the National Security Administration and a professor of public affairs at the University of Texas,

points out that among voters crime trumps privacy issues (Talk to Law and Ethics on Electronic Frontier class, MIT, fall 1994).

26. In 1988 Robert Morris, Jr., a computer science student at Cornell and son of the chief computer scientist at the National Security Agency, was the first to be charged under the new 1986 Computer Fraud and Abuse Act (18 USC 1030) for having released an Internet Worm causing computers around the country to crash. The now famous Internet Worm was the first of a series of highly publicized viruses that forced awareness on users that one ought not to leave systems unprotected.

27. Senators Leahy and Kyle, for instance, in proposing a modification to the Computer Fraud and Abuse Act, cite not only concerns about Dutch hackers who broke into NASA computers and the computers used in the Gulf War, but also the abuse of privileges on government computers, snooping tax returns, selling confidential criminal histories from the National Crime Information Center, and breaching federal courthouse computers holding confidential records.

28. For the most elaborate account of the potential implications of crypto-anarchy, see Tim May (1988, and various updates). See also Miller (1994).

29. Concern about employer surveillance has been long-standing, in monitoring work operations, in reading employee E-mail, and in the compiling and selling of data base information. There are now companies that are expanding the capabilities of all these activities, including forensics companies that retrieve E-mail that companies or employees thought destroyed to be used in court cases.

30. *Cubby v. CompuServe* (1991) held the system operator not liable for content on the system because CompuServe does not regularly monitor content and serves more as a common carrier (like the telephone system). Currently (1995) Prodigy is being sued by a stockbrokerage, Stratton-Oakmont, in a $200-million libel suit, because Prodigy does do a certain amount of routine screening.

31. A series of bills were proposed in the House and Senate during 1995 to regulate content, criminalize "indecent" material, and also to prohibit content regulations. The World Wide Web Consortium has proposed instead a demand-side technical mechanism: a rating format for content to which users can attach filters developed on their own or by advocacy groups, or by groups like the Good Housekeeping Seal of Approval.

32. The NII sometimes is compared in scale and ambition to the 1960s space program, as well as in its own metaphoric name to the federal interstate highway infrastructure for encouraging the post-war economy. Lewis Branscomb and Brian Kahin (1994) suggest that it is very different in organizational form and dynamics. It is not managed by a single agency, but is rather a "distributed program, minimally managed by interagency task forces," and it is propelled by rapid changes in commercial information technologies, in turn heavily influenced by the entertainment and information services businesses. The question of whether or not there should be mechanisms to ensure universal service make the comparison with the telephone system pertinent as well, and foreground the role that intellectual property and regulatory law can play in shaping the economic terms of this new medium.

33. See the fascinating debate between Paul Heckel (1992), and Simson Garfinkle, Richard Stallman, and Mitchell Kapor (1991).

34. The committee composition for the White Paper was heavily stacked with industries needed in any future lobbying effort for the proposal, and representatives of the public were marginalized. The Green Paper at least went through the motions of holding a more open set of hearings around the country, and also solicited feedback on-line.

35. For a critique of the stance of the report and its recommendations in terms of these power balances, see Samuelson 1994.

36. Tribe writes about the way in which the court has abridged and expanded the constraints on wiretaps in *Olmstead v. US* (1928), *Katz v. US* (1964), and *Smith v. Maryland* (1976).

37. Compare the critiques of the Human Genome Project to those of Reagan's "Star Wars" Strategic Defense Initiative. Both have been seen as technically improbable goals, yet they have served as mechanisms for generating new computational technologies and have had powerful social effects. The promise of gene therapies and other medical interventions, even if further in the future than most realize or admit, is already affecting employment practices, family planning, education, insurance, and notions of self, health, and disease. It has been argued that the influx of information theory concepts into biology in the 1950s and 1960s fostered a hegemonic role for molecular biology, occluding (at least temporarily) such fields as embryology and developmental biology; and that in the 1960s it even temporarily

occluded the vital contributions of biochemistry. (See Kay n.d.; Keller 1995; Lewontin 1994; Nelkin and Tancredi 1989.)

38. "Worlding" draws on all three in quasi-Derridean difference: the auditory homophony with whirl, hinting at an electron(ic) speed; the textual difference between ideational whirl and the grounding of the ethnographic world. Worlding Cyberspace.

9

American Moderns

On Sciences and Scientists

Paul Rabinow

> We shall set to work and meet the "demands of the day," in human relations as well as in our vocation. This, however, is plain and simple, if each finds and obeys the demon who holds the fibers of his very life.
>
> —*Max Weber, "Science as a Vocation"*

When I finished writing *Making PCR, A Story of Biotechnology* (Rabinow 1996), I wanted to reflect on the process and the stakes of the experience, to return to some of the original questions I had wrestled with in choosing and defining the research. PCR, or the polymerase chain reaction, provides the means to make genetic scarcity into genetic abundance through exponential amplification of specific sequences of DNA, and my book concerns the emergent biotech milieu in which this new technology took shape—the mid-1980s at Cetus Corporation in the San Francisco Bay Area. My fieldwork was partially shaped by C. P. Snow's 1959 *Two Cultures* (republished in Snow 1964), which identified and lamented a divide between Science, meaning physics, and the Traditional Culture, meaning literature. Snow's book opened a debate about this split and its significance. Although that debate has now receded into oblivion, the content, if not the tone, of these lectures seems apposite today.

The core of Snow's argument is simple. Following Bronislaw Malinowski, Snow observed that scientists have a culture in the anthropological sense: "[W]ithout thinking about it, they respond alike. That is what a culture means" (Snow 1964:9). The ethos informing that culture is pragmatic optimism. Scientists are "impatient to see if something can be done: and inclined to think it can be done, unless it's proved otherwise" (1964:7). Snow captured the physicists' stance toward themselves and the world with one of those aphorisms that draw immediate assent but whose ambiguities linger on. These men of science, he observed, "naturally had the future in their bones" (1964:10). Confident to the point of arrogance, yet pragmatic, often on the left of the political spectrum, carriers of the future, if not in their genes at least in their labs, these men of science surprised Snow, however, by their lack of Traditional Culture. "The ear, to some extent, the eye. Of books, though, very little. They are self-impoverished" (1964:13–14). A provocative, even inflammatory observation. Snow observed that the bearers of Traditional Literary Culture were equally impoverished by their lack of scientific education. This state of affairs remains more or less the same today, except for one important difference. Snow's observation that "It is the traditional culture, to an extent remarkably little diminished by the scientific one, which manages the western world" (1964:11) sounds archaeological, a report from a distant era.

In his *Second Look* of 1963, written in response to the storm of reaction his book occasioned (and republished in Snow 1964), Snow introduced two modifications to his position. First, he displaced physics from its throne, awarding molecular biology the right to represent the kingdom of science because of its potential social impact. Molecular biology, he thought, "is likely to affect the way in which men think of themselves more profoundly than any scientific advance since Darwin's—and probably more so than Darwin's" (1964:74). Second, he downplayed the significance of the distinction between science and technology, observing that in practice they were increasingly the same thing, and citing the work on the hemoglobin molecule as a fundamental scientific contribution whose discovery was inextricably linked to technology and health.

Snow closed *Second Look* with a question: "How far is it possible to share the hopes of the scientific revolution... and at the same time participate without qualification in [modernist] literature?" (1964:96–97). Today, this question appears exotic precisely to the extent that such efforts have not only failed but have been pushed off the agenda. However, for Snow the challenge was to make "culture" visible in three ways: first, to see that scientists, like everyone else, had an (anthropological) culture; second, to show that the (humanistic and anthropological) culture of the humanities was incomplete in essential ways; and third, to envision a new type of hybrid culture that would reshape and integrate the first two.

Clifford and Marcus's *Writing Culture,* published in 1986, constituted another watershed in that it placed the question of writing and of ethnographic authority squarely onto the anthropological agenda. In his Introduction, James Clifford clearly states the volume's starting assumptions: "The essays collected here... see culture as composed of seriously contested codes and representations; they assume that the poetic and political are inseparable, that science is in, not above, historical and linguistic processes. They assume that academic and literary genres interpenetrate and that the writing of cultural descriptions is properly experimental and ethical" (Clifford 1986a:2). Given the reigning interpretation of cultures, the book marked, and then came to symbolize, a rupture that has been broadly misinterpreted as the presentation of a doctrine that sought to undermine both culture and science.

Writing Culture did not present a worldview. It did something different—it articulated an emergent problematization. The concept of problematization comes from Michel Foucault, who defined it as follows: "The development of a given into a question, the transformation of a group of obstacles and difficulties into problems to which diverse solutions will attempt to produce a response, this is what constitutes the specific point of problematization and the specific work of thought" (Foucault 1984a:388). The essays in *Writing Culture* were diverse, and several were barely compatible. What they shared was a common demand for a response, not more, not less. In this light, the concept of culture put forth by Snow and Malinowski was not so much refuted, destroyed, or replaced as made problematic—and so, too, were the methods and reasons for studying culture. Consequently, the problem for some of us was how to make cultural description experimental and ethical.

In part inspired by *Writing Culture,* I intended to coauthor the PCR book with my main informant, Tom White, a biochemist who was formerly a vice-president of research at Cetus. At the time, White was a vice-president of research and development at Roche Molecular Systems, a subsidiary of the Swiss multinational Hoffmann–La Roche, which bought all the rights to PCR from Cetus in 1991 for over $300 million. Ultimately I wrote the book myself, so strictly speaking the experiment in collaboration across the two cultures failed to attain its original objective. I do not conclude from this fact that the collaboration was a failure. As the manuscript neared completion, I reposed a question that I had previously put to White on several occasions: Why had he wanted to work with me? Characteristically, he responded in writing, which allowed him to formulate his thoughts more accurately. White's reply provided reasons why our joint project stalled; more interestingly, it provided insight into how the project had been sustained. In a tacit way, it also highlighted the course of interactions between two Americans, both resolutely modern—but more of that at the end.

As I learned more about how collaborative research operated in the biosciences, I began to realize that there are many ways to shape a project, and, more subtly, diverse ways to receive credit. The story of how PCR was conceived, invented, coddled, and pushed into becoming a workable technology demonstrates that White was an expert in managing, facilitating, and contributing to the work of others in both direct and indirect ways. In this light, then, let me repose the question: What can be learned from this ethnographic experience about the two cultures, or more accurately, since the word culture is overly general and rather worn out, about two practices?

I have divided my discussion of White's response into three parts, titled "ethical substance," "mode of objectivity," and "telos." Each begins with White's words, followed by my commentary. The divisions parallel in a loose fashion those employed by Michel Foucault in his last writings on ethics and the "technologies of the self." Readers familiar with Foucault will realize that a fourth category, "ethical work," is subsumed under "mode of objectivity." My essay's fourth section uses Max Weber's 1917 address to students, "Science as a Vocation" (Weber 1946a), as a device to connect these fieldwork reflections to a larger problematization.

I. ETHICAL SUBSTANCE: EFFICIENCY, CURIOSITY

Tom White: My original contact with Paul Rabinow was via Vince Sarich, who had been a collaborator of Allan Wilson's at UC Berkeley while I was a graduate student there in the early 1970s. Sarich explained that Rabinow was interested in learning more about biotechnology and genetic engineering with respect to its current and future cultural implications. Our first meeting occurred in early 1990, about a year after I had left Cetus Corporation to work for Hoffmann–La Roche, where I managed their joint program with Cetus to develop diagnostic applications of a powerful new technology: the polymerase chain reaction. My initial interactions with Paul concentrated mainly on the state of the Human Genome Project and its effect on human identity and forensic analyses. There was also some discussion of the gap in time between genetic diagnosis and the development of new therapies. I also unexpectedly became involved in reviewing Sarich's lecture notes for his Anthro 1 course, when he drew parallels between evolutionary models and contemporary behavior and social policies. During this time, I gained trust in Rabinow by reading one of his books and several articles that grew out of our discussions. He was open to criticism and not intrusive as an observer of seminars and lab meetings.

Over several years, projects that I was involved with provided a rich source of material for Paul's study of scientific cultural practices: the issues and testimony from the scientific community on the novelty of the conception of PCR during Du Pont's challenge of Cetus's patents, writing articles for the AAAs on issues surrounding gene patents, using PCR to test (at the request of the NIH's Office of Research Integrity) for the presence of HIV sequences in archival samples from the Gallo and Montagnier labs from the beginning of the AIDS epidemic (and to characterize them), and writing letters requested by the nomination committees for the Japan

> and Nobel prizes. In turn, I became engaged in some of Paul's projects: the Rice University series, a conference at MIT, and his research at the CEPH. These I found very simulating both from the subjects being discussed as well as the range of people, interests, and perspectives that were so very different from those of my colleagues in biology and medicine.

The "Sarich affair." Tom White had known Vincent Sarich, a professor of physical anthropology at Berkeley, from 1971 to 1975, while both were working in the lab of Allan Wilson. During the 1960s and 1970s, Sarich collaborated with Wilson on breakthrough work on "molecular clocks." They developed new methods of analyzing molecular data and calculating the divergence times of species such as humans, chimpanzees, and gorillas. Their work fundamentally challenged the prevailing wisdom that the divergence among the great apes was ancient, and provided empirical support for the theory that most mutations are selectively neutral. They were among the first to demonstrate that changes in the regulation of genes, rather than the steady accumulation of simple mutations, was the cause of major changes in morphology. During the 1980s, Sarich abandoned his scientific research and began to assemble a worldview or philosophy. He labored mightily to combine a variant of libertarianism with an encompassing evolutionary framework. In a fashion typical of autodidacts, Sarich was prepared to explain almost everything. As a venue for his opinions, he began regularly teaching the large (about one thousand students) Introduction to Physical Anthropology course at Berkeley—a course usually devoted to primate evolution—and infusing it with his views of society and life.

Over the years there had been some controversy about some of his assertions, especially on intelligence differences between racial groups, but these remained isolated incidents. In 1991 Sarich's class was disrupted by students, some of them class members and some not, charging him with being racist, sexist, and homophobic. The students objected to Sarich's claims that more hairdressers were homosexual than heterosexual and that there were demonstrable and significant genetic differences in intelligence between groups and genders.

Sarich, true to his libertarian principles, always simultaneously maintained that his generalizations never applied to individuals. A public controversy erupted over freedom of speech, the limits of teaching, and the substance of Sarich's claims.

Within the anthropology department, colleagues cast the debate as exclusively a matter of free speech: Did one have the absolute right to teach anything in any manner one pleased? The overwhelming response was "yes." Posing the question in this way seemed to me to be overly abstract, formalistic, and juridical. I also knew that once the debate was cast in those terms it would turn in circles. When I asked if there would be any reason that I should not be allowed to teach a course in molecular biology—I knew the basics just as Sarich knew the basics of philosophy, although neither or us had formal training or credentials in the area—the response was an impatient and barely tolerant silence.

Among the physical anthropologists at Berkeley, Sarich was the only one who would engage in any public discussions on the substantive scientific claims. The others defended the principle of absolute free speech, defended their turf through appeals to tradition, and went to the local press with inflammatory and fictitious charges of censorship. Ordinarily, as a group they were riven with ferocious rivalries, barely on speaking terms, and generally all too ready to criticize each other pitilessly, but under these circumstances they closed ranks. The affair could have been the occasion to debate what the new configuration of biological and cultural sciences would look like, but it didn't turn out that way.

I had undertaken the ethnographic research at a biotech company in part as a kind of political gesture. As older issues of racial inequality were resurfacing in new guises, it seemed important to understand how much advances in molecular biology could legitimately contribute to these debates. Furthermore, our department, like many others, was engaged in a pitched battle over the future construction of the field of anthropology. Were there any intellectual reasons to believe that the emergent biological and cultural sciences should be in the same department? Berkeley had been the home to the last major synthesis of cultural and physical anthropology. Sherwood Washburn's work on tool making and evolution, for example, was an inspiration and fit snugly with the cutting-edge cultural anthropology of Clifford Geertz, whose article "The Impact of the Concept of Culture on the Concept of Man" (Geertz 1973c) announced what seemed to be a new holistic anthropology but proved instead to be the setting sun of such interdisciplinarity. The growing importance of molecular biology, feminism, textual approaches, poststructuralism, and the like opened a new period from which no plausible and sustained interconnections, to say nothing of syntheses, have yet been forged.

Partly for my own education and partly in preparation for a panel discussion we organized around the controversy, I purchased two copies of Sarich's lecture notes for Anthro 1 from a local taking service, Black Lightning Notes. Tom White and I methodically worked through them, indicating the points each of us found scientifically questionable. We might well have been laboring under Max Weber's injunction, laid down in 1911—"What we hope for from racial biologists...is exact evidence of well-defined connections in individual cases, and so of the decisive importance of completely specific hereditary qualities for particular concrete social phenomena. That, gentlemen, does not exist as yet" (Weber 1911:390)—except that I hoped for nothing from racial biologists. Regardless, eighty years later, Weber's challenge and his conclusion remain pertinent.

During the evening forum on Sarich's work, with several hundred people present, a good deal of political rhetoric was displayed. Afterwards White and I agreed that the forum and its antecedents were more about the uses and abuses of authority than about the specific claims of the purported relationships, or lack of relationships, between genetics and behavior. Dispositionally, we were inclined to share Max Weber's admonition: "Ladies and gentlemen, in the field of science only he who is devoted solely to the work at hand has 'personality'" (Weber 1946a:137). A cool, decibel-monitored focus on "the facts" defined for White what it meant to act like a scientist. However, it seems fair to say that I was far less effective in raising issues of broad import and moving the audience to take a stance than several of the other forum panelists. To that extent both White and I were distancing ourselves from overt political action. Though our dispositions and affective temperaments converged, our goals remained unspecified. A degree of mutual trust and acknowledgment of each other's skills and capacities was beginning to take shape between us.

Curiosity

Partly as a result of the forum, White and I thematized an interest in the question of limits (of teaching, of authority, of arenas of investigation, and of constraints on inquiry from ideological, institutional, business, or legal sources). We shared a sense that there was something important at stake in these and related events and developments. One of the things we found missing from the imbroglio was a sense of new knowledges and powers at play, a sense that there might be a new set of problems emerging that would pose different demands. This shared sense led, among other things, to an exchange about curiosity.

> *PR:* What role does curiosity play in science?
> *TW:* To me curiosity is an extremely powerful motivating factor. You know, food, sex, and shelter and stuff like that. Some of things we are doing here we don't really know where they lead, you could call it instinct or gut level, but we don't know. Henry Erlich [a senior scientist at Cetus] will justify his work on diabetes [as having commercial potential], and that's the right thing to do, but he just wants to know about how the whole thing works. He doesn't give a damn about whatever else is involved in it. That's why David Gelfand [another senior scientist] has boundless curiosity which takes over what he does.
> *PR:* What are the limits to curiosity?
> *TW:* Boredom. I've seen curiosity end for some scientists. When it does end it is a totally recognizable element in them. They no longer have the curiosity. They go home at five o'clock. Or they say, "Well, if you want me to write up the paper I am going to have to take some time off from work," rather than write it at night or on the weekend like everyone else does. Or some peculiar result is presented at meetings, they yawn and aren't interested. It's the strangest thing. It's like death in a scientist. They can be

productive in a certain sense but the ability to solve new problems isn't there.

PR: So, curiosity can die and become routine and boredom. But what about the other side: Can you have too much curiosity?

TW: Yes, some people are so curious that they never complete anything. One idea after another idea but all at a level that's not very deep so you can't determine the complexity. What's workable or not. The science fiction mode sets the limits of curiosity when humans mate with apes and meddle with God's work kind of thing. The limit for scientists is that scientists' visions are limited socially. Many of them never even conceive some issues. For example, how the family is defined. These people are thinking about how to detect hemoglobin S from hemoglobin A; they don't think how this will affect families.

PR: Is curiosity a good thing?

TW: It's getting the answer to your curiosity. The mouse pushing on the button to get more cocaine. There is something intensely gratifying about satisfying your curiosity. Scientists just want to know the answer to something. That's why David Gelfand is in the lab every Sunday, he just wants to know how the thing works. Those who are motivated by curiosity have the problem of stopping. They ruin social occasions.

PR: I've written a paper called "The Curious Patient," which was inspired by Hans Blumenberg's chapter on curiosity in *The Legitimacy of the Modern Age.* Blumenberg talks about curiosity as one of the great motive forces of enlightenment. He shows how curiosity has been something that has been consistently under attack by Christianity and other authority structures. But modernity faces the question, What are the limits to curiosity? There were the German medical and scientific experiments and so many others in the United States and elsewhere which obviously crossed the line of acceptable research or clinical practice. Perhaps there are no self-limiting principles within science itself to tell you not to do a particular experiment? Since curiosity and modernity combine to drive endlessly towards producing something new, perhaps the combination of newness and curiosity's boundlessness is the problem? Perhaps these German scientists who worked on living patients were horrible human beings, but we now know that they were not all horrible scientists. This disjunction is troubling. The core of the distinguished German medical establishment went along with the Nazis. Curiosity has its thresholds. Perhaps it is ethics or religion or politics or aesthetics (as Nietzsche thought) which limits what one can and can not do—not science.

TW: That boundary where curiosity goes over into something unethical could also be an element in some aspects of scientific problems. They are always ascribed to power and priority issues, but there is an element of curiosity affecting the ability to interpret your data. Sometimes, people see the results they want to see. Others falsify their experiments, others simply ignore the data that doesn't fit.

Curiosity does get to a point where judgment is required. One boundary to examine is, When does curiosity reach a limit? How would that decision be made? Since there isn't an independent referee, what sort of process does one go through to arrive at a stopping point? What would you draw on to make that decision? Not a simple question: What to do to access resources? What you do that might be unethical? Or socially advisable?

White was quite right in saying that molecular biology has no principle internal to its field of practice by which to pose the question of limits. In the human sciences, it is possible to practice in such a fashion that the question of limits, as well as the reflexive thematization of that concern, constitutes a central dimension of the project itself. Reflexivity, however, like rationality, means many different things. Just as one could formulate a practice that foregrounds political awareness and action, so too one could engage in a practice that attempted to make "ethical" action calculable and rationalized. Reflexivity might mean methodologically searching for a normative scale that could be cast in operationalizable terms; work in many areas of bioethics is involved with constituting such a practice. Another direction, the one I pursued, casts reflexivity as an experiential and experimental "problem," one not amenable to the kind of bureaucratic requirements many bioethicists face, one not directly "useful." This stance entails being curious about scientific curiosity and curious about one's own curiosity. It leads one to thematize the form of life that surrounds, sustains, and undermines curiosity. Thus, even when claims are made to have discovered "the curiosity gene," the question of what kind of society has posed such questions to itself and why has it sought to produce this type of knowledge remains open. So, too, the question will remain of how best to situate oneself in relation to that knowledge, that society, and those goals.

II. MODE OF OBJECTIVITY: ETHICAL WORK

> *TW:* Articles were beginning to appear in the popular scientific literature about PCR's "uncommon" origin [by Kary Mullis, its "inventor"]. These were counterbalanced or paralleled by other accounts from Cetus's management and public relations office. From my perspective, as the former VP of Research at Cetus, none of the accounts gave an accurate picture of the circumstances and milieu that had led to PCR. In fact, they reinforced certain stereotypes about scientists (the unappreciated genius working alone) and science in industry (closed, unimaginative, plodding) that bore no relation at all to the way science was done in one of the first biotechnology companies.
>
> I had made a preliminary effort to write my observations about the history of PCR, but also felt I was too close to the events to portray them objectively. What was needed was someone with a different background than those involved directly, i.e., not a typical memoir from a

> retired authority figure, nor a journalistic account that emphasized gossip or rivalries. An anthropologist seemed about right to me. Furthermore, an anthropologist would be able to place current scientific practice into a broader framework of other cultural practices and theory, so that whatever was truly unique about the PCR experience, if anything, would be visible.

Consistently unharried midst a multitude of responsibilities, White is not casual. He is simultaneously goal oriented and systematically flexible in finding appropriate means to attain his objectives. Emblematic of this stance to me was a complex multidimensional chart White had on his office wall outlining the steps that would be necessary over the course of several years to coordinate a set of teams working toward commercializing a set of diagnostic tests. The chart had replaced an equally large cross-cultural timeline of world history. Both charts functioned as maps in the sense of portraying objectives and functional conjuncture points; White never took them as rigid guidelines for action, nor as "filled-in." He prides himself on maintaining close contact with those directly involved in working out technical details, since experience has shown him that these are the people who have the most precise knowledge of difficulties and solutions. White coordinates and manages; he is responsible for the larger picture. As he indicates, White was dispositionally prepared for someone to propose a project on the invention of PCR, even if he was not actively searching for such a person. My proposal fit a space on some imaginary chart. That is one reason White responded so rapidly to my overtures. He was clearer than I about the project, at least initially and in the sense outlined above. But again, he left the strategy and details of working it out to me, almost never initiating research directions but always making himself available for responses and help.

White has formulated a set of evaluative benchmarks in order to judge the performance and character of scientists and their work. Upon meeting me, White began evaluating my person and character (credentials, strengths and weaknesses, personality in terms of potential collaboration, idiosyncrasies, and so forth) just as he would with anyone else he worked with. After a series of formally arranged interviews about the Human Genome Project and general issues in molecular biology and genetics, he extended his observations to my preliminary ethnographic work at Roche Diagnostic Research, the complex of labs whose research he directed. I was under scrutiny at the lab meetings I attended (highly technical discussions about diagnostic tests in a variety of stages of development) as well as in my follow-up discussions with individual scientists. White discretely—and appropriately—monitored both. He and the other scientists and technicians concurred that I was learning enough molecular biology to follow the discussions, and that I was acting responsibly (not pursuing confidential materials on probe design, not sharing reactions of one scientist with others, and so on). White strongly demurred when I remarked that the technicians were so responsive to my questions mainly because of my connection to him; he was adamant that although his authorization was necessary for me to be in the labs at all, it was not sufficient. Each of his colleagues and technicians was exercising his or her own autonomous judgment. They knew his management style of monitored independence, maximized flow of information, and critical evaluation of people and procedures up and down the hierarchy. White strongly believed that maximizing autonomy within a project-oriented structure produced better results; it was more efficient, it was better for human relations, and it maximized responsibility at each level. Modern to the hilt. I showed that I was willing and able to conform behaviorally to this normative structure, and White was wagering that he was correctly evaluating my character as well.

White's objective was to form an accurate picture of the circumstances and the milieu of contemporary biotechnology from which a very important invention had emerged. He believed he was too close to the events and the actors to portray them objectively; in his view, an anthropologist had the right distance and the right perspective to make the event's uniqueness visible. White was fully aware that an accurate, objective, and visible account could be put to many different purposes. In his statement he did not make reference to the fact that the meaning of each of these terms is highly contested in the human sciences. Consequently, White's framing of the project is simultaneously, and characteristically, transparent and opaque. It is transparent insofar as it is impelled by a desire to have a literally correct and appropriately coherent account of a major scientific and technological breakthrough. It is opaque in its unadorned, confident choice of "an anthropologist" to produce such an account.

While serving in the Peace Corps in Africa during the 1960s, White learned a good deal (partially from reading anthropological accounts, but mainly through his experiences) about the language and culture of the Loma people in Liberia. He was especially intrigued by their different use of parabolic language, representations of dimensional space, and system of counting, and had even published an ethnohistory by a Loma elder. He was therefore not naive about anthropology. He knew that anthropology was embroiled in major disputes about the status of representations, textuality, and power, and was familiar with *Writing Culture.*

Shortly before I began working with White, his wife, Leslie Scalapino, a well-known poet and publisher of an avant-garde press, O Books, had been engaged in a series of polemic skirmishes with the editor of *Socialist Review* that directly paralleled some of the debates within anthropology that surrounded *Writing Culture.* I invited Scalapino to talk about these debates. Although I was interested in her views per se, I was also curious about the discussions she and Tom had about the prospect of his working with me.

> *LS:* There were many things I found interesting about your article ["Representations Are Social Facts," 1986]. For example, when you are talking about Fredric Jameson's analysis of postmodern culture, it is interesting to me that Jameson, in what has now become a rather famous essay, attacked one of the language poets, Bob Perelman. It's interesting to me because much of what's being done in poetry now is very similar to the kinds of questions you're raising in your article. Much current writing has to do with analyzing perception itself, one's own subjectivity, as the placement of the writer or the viewer vis-à-vis what's being written. Jameson's argument

> has been regarded by many people in the literary community as an example of a very conservative, yet Marxist, argument in which he criticized contemporary poetics as dislocated in the direction of being merely fragmentary. Meaning, that which is modern is seen as chaotic.
>
> The language group of writers, who are themselves of a Marxist orientation, are proponents of form scrutinizing itself. Jameson is regarded in his essay as demanding a very hierarchical and centralized view of writing where there would be no room for any kind of varied perspective or examination of perspective itself.
>
> Tom told me that you have read an exchange between the language poet, Ron Silliman, and myself whose subject was feminism, gays, and so-called minority perspective as incompatible with avant-garde or experimental work. In this exchange, I was answering an essay by Ron that was published in the *Socialist Review* about six poets, including myself. Actually our exchange was much larger than what you saw, having occurred over a period of about a year. It was impossible to get any answer of mine to his essay to be published in the *Socialist Review.* They described my initial reply as being too poetic and rejected it on the basis that it was not political discourse. To which I objected that they could not, should not, determine the form and thus the nature of political discourse. Before our exchange could be published later in another journal, the male editor wanted us to rewrite it in a more orderly format. He disagreed with Ron's argument and considered my tone to be hostile. We did not revamp our exchange but shortened it. My original tone in our correspondence was stronger but this gradually changed. Ironically, the editor was criticizing the later, softer tone.

While the culture wars rage in the human sciences ("incommensurability," "postidentity," "postnarrativity," and the like), White and his fellow scientists—several of whom read parts of each of the multiple drafts of *Making PCR*—never once raised epistemological objections to my approach. They corrected details, debated the applicability of terms like "technocrat," and insisted on "accuracy," but refrained from objecting to my use of form and interpretation. "It's your book," was the common refrain. Such reserve is entirely uncharacteristic of the practice of molecular biologists (or other scientists) among themselves, where strong criticism is the norm.

This turn of events remains perplexing to me. Does it mean that these molecular biologists are moderns, that is, nonhegemonic, pluralistic, even perspectival, about things social? The answer, at least partially, is "Yes." White and his colleagues are moderns, and several of the senior scientists had an active interest in writings about science. Several others aside from White have spouses in the art world. Henry Erlich, whose wife runs the ODC San Francisco dance company, is a keen fan of the novels of Richard Powers, such as *The Goldbug Variations* and *Galatea 2.2.* They are also Americans; they exhibit none of the pathos or tragedy that for others has accompanied the "diversity of value spheres." Richard Rorty would approve of their nonplussed attitude.

The flexibility about textual form and tolerance for multiple interpretation when it comes to society must be juxtaposed to the standardization of scientific writing and interpretation to which all good scientists adhere. As the ethnography shows, these molecular biologists would not agree with the following assertion from Pierre Bourdieu: "I hold that, all the scholastic discussions about the distinctiveness of the human sciences notwithstanding, the human sciences are subject to the same rules that apply to all sciences. . . . I am struck, when I speak with my friends who are chemists, physicians, or neurobiologists, by the similarities between their practice and that of a sociologist. The typical day of a sociologist, with its experimental groping, statistical analysis, reading of scholarly papers, and discussion with colleagues, looks very much like that of an ordinary scientist to me" (Bourdieu 1992:185). The inevitable line that greeted me in labs in France and the US was something like, "Now we will be put under the microscope," or "He's here to treat us like guinea pigs." These jokes, which came from scientists who employed neither microscopes nor guinea pigs in their work, disappeared immediately once our work was underway; they revealed an initial anxiety about being objectified, nothing more. Ethnographically and experientially, the analogy is a bad one, and its use as a metaphor is even worse.

Juxtaposing two quotes, one from Pierre Bourdieu and the other from Kary Mullis, both from methods sections of larger works in, respectively, sociology and molecular biology, rhetorically underscores the point. First, Bourdieu:

> In order to escape the realism of the structure, which hypostatizes systems of objective relations by converting them into totalities already constituted outside of individual history and group history, it is necessary to pass from the opus operatum to the modus operandi, from statistical regularity or algebraic structure to the principle of the production of this observed order, and to construct the theory of practice or, more precisely, the theory of the mode of generation of practices, which is the precondition for establishing an experimental science of the dialectic of the internalization of externality and the externalization of internality, or more simply, of incorporation and objectification. (Bourdieu 1977:72)

Although I more or less understand what Bourdieu means, I have not met a single biologist who does and, for that matter, very few anthropologists who do. In contrast, Kary Mullis, the inventor of the polymerase chain reaction, discusses his "methods" in the following terms: "Oligonucleotides were synthesized using an automated DNA synthesis machine (Biosearch Inc., San Rafael, California) using phosphoroamidite chemistry. Synthesis and purification were performed according to the directions provided by the manufacturer" (Mullis and Faloona 1987:339). Mullis's account is transparent to those who work in his field and appropriately opaque to those who don't.

Bourdieu works in a pluralistic scientific milieu, and he regrets it. Mullis, on the other hand, lives in a milieu that has stabilized experimental practices and textual genres reporting those practices. When Mullis conceived of the polymerase reaction, he was convinced that he had thought of a revolutionary invention; he was slow, however, to produce either experimental proof or to write up his experimental results. White and others put tremendous pressure on him to do both.

In 1985, after two years of intense work by two teams at Cetus Corporation attempting to make the polymerase chain reaction work consistently and efficiently, the scientists finally were getting results that satisfied them. They decided to publish a paper announcing the new method. Following a commonly employed procedure, they re-ran a set of experiments, so that they would have "elegant" results for the paper. I did something similar in the last draft of *Making PCR.* However, I had a choice of quite disparate ways of bringing the project to completion, including emphasizing the disparities and blockages along the way or underplaying them. It seems self-evident that the practices of the Cetus scientists and my own differed. The relation of textual form to experimental practice has been stabilized in the biological sciences in a fashion that the human sciences have never achieved.

Even assuming that one could find an equivalent of the laboratory practices of molecular biology among anthropologists and sociologists, the relationships between the experimental situation and the texts that report on that setting present stark differences. There is a great diversity of experimental practice in the human sciences and a great diversity of textual practice as well. Although the coming triumph of a physical science model in the human sciences has been announced for several centuries—what I have called the "cargo cult view" of science—it has never happened. Empirically the only way we know it could come about would be through political means in which all opposition was eliminated (defunded, detenured, and so on).

In a remarkable paper entitled "Why Is There No Hermeneutics of the Natural Sciences?," the Hungarian philosopher Gyorgy Markus (1987) synthesized current research in the history, philosophy, and sociology of science and underlined the central dividing point:

> Natural scientific activities involve in our culture not only argumentative-discursive but also experimental-manipulative practices. Therefore new knowledge is fixed and accumulated in this field not merely in the form of textual objectivations, but also through incorporation into those

> lab activities which have the character of craft skills and can only be learned through example and controlled performances in the relevant situations. All the observation terms are linked to that action arena. As a result an adequate understanding of natural scientific texts cannot be learned/acquired in an intercourse with these texts alone. The craft skill is shared only by the group of specialists. (Markus 1987:28).

Markus is fully aware that textual production in the human sciences, itself quite diverse, is linked to other practices as well. His point is that these arts and practices differ. The differences are anything but scholastic. Erasing them through metaphor—Bourdieu's "experimental gropings"—is ethnographically unconvincing.

Employing categories from "reader-response" theory, Markus asks who is the implied subject in natural scientific texts. He analyzes the textual devices that contribute to constructing an impersonal subject as the author of the scientific article. Chief among these devices is the imperative to remove all textual traces of the vagaries, accidents, special circumstances, unusual skills, and fortune involved in a piece of work. Markus writes, "The 'inscribed author' of the natural scientific texts appears as an anonymous performer of methodologically certified, strictly regulated activities and a detached observer of the results—without any further personal identifying remarks beyond possession of the required professional competence...It is essential that the 'scientific anyman' could have been the author of the paper" (Markus 1987:13). The same textual criterion applies to the audience; these devices make possible the complete interchangeability of the author and the audience. It follows that only those who share the experimental practices (often restricted to a subspecialty) are fully capable of understanding and evaluating such texts. Hence, their strength and their limitation are one and the same thing.

Markus concludes that there is no hermeneutics of the natural sciences because there is no need for one. Scientific writing "is culturally defined as of no interest or consequence for a non-specialist reader." In fact, growing technical mastery and specialization in the natural sciences yield a progressive narrowing of cultural significance because "the view of nature provided by the sciences is no more a world-view" (Markus 1987:29). This lack of a worldview, this narrowing, this cultural triumph, is itself a condition for the technical efficacy of modern science. In a strict sense, there is no self-questioning within molecular biology. From time to time there are debates about the ends to which results could be put, political projects that might be dangerous or beneficial, and occasional discussions about the composition (gender, race, class) of the social body of scientists. But the normative parameters of the textual and nondiscursive practices of sciences like molecular biology are not a question for philosophic debate among practitioners. The plethora of "worldview" books with punchy adolescent titles produced by science journalists and aging scientists underscores the point.

A parallel situation does not exist in the human sciences. No one, above all Pierre Bourdieu himself, has ever mistaken his writings for the social scientific everyman. Their distinction immediately sets them apart. It is true that mimicking the subject and reader positions of the natural sciences is one option available to practitioners of various human sciences. It is, however, only one option among others, one style among others, one rhetoric among others. The utter lack of success in achieving unity in the human sciences (except from time to time under totalitarian political conditions) does not prove that the human sciences will never "come of age," but it does underscore the distinctive historical and sociological uniqueness in the achievement of such textual unity in the natural sciences. Their strength is their weakness, their weakness their strength.

III. TELOS

TW: The motivations for my interest in this collaboration are several. There are a number of disturbing phenomena and trends in contemporary science that parallel society at large; there are widespread stereotypes of scientists in industry that are destructive and counterproductive to improvements in health care; there are preconceived notions about the genomic diversity project that are anti-intellectual, patronizing, and perpetuate delusions about our knowledge of the origin and migratory history of modern peoples; an interest in scientific communication and collaboration per se.

As an example of the first phenomenon, leading international scientific journals have increasingly become the vehicles for tabloid news articles on scientific rivalries, misconduct, patent and credit disputes, etc. The use of anonymous sources, leaked confidential documents, erroneous information, and unchecked claims is the new(s) standard for *Nature* and *Science.* These journals are so influential and reputable in their peer-reviewed articles, that credence carries over to their tabloid reports. The editors also occasionally perpetuate the stereotypes of "pure" academic scientists and of industrial scientists only being motivated by money and profit, while conveniently ignoring the corrupting influence of "academic capital," e.g., membership on editorial boards, grant agency peer-review panels, serving as an FDA reviewer of one company's application while serving as a paid consultant to its competitor, and other conflicts of interest that are not usually designated as such within the academy. These models lead some influential scientists to exhibit behaviors usually associated with creationists or fundamentalists: claiming the absolute moral high ground, a fondness for conspiracy and catastrophe scenarios, and a complete disregard for facts. The trends are certainly rampant in society at large in the form of a willful blindness to societal problems and a delusionary momentum to find simplistic causes and solutions while claiming to be pragmatic and revolutionary.

So, one of my purposes in helping Paul write the PCR book was to arrive at an account of an extraordinary genetic discovery that could show how to create an environment for future discoveries. Furthermore, this account would counteract other "histories" that in my

> view perpetuate the very conditions and stereotypes that destroy creativity and the process of discovery. This would be done by providing a cultural anthropologist unique access to the scientists, from technicians to department heads, to top managers, etc., of a biotechnology company. Perhaps this would also overcome the misplaced conservatism of private institutions about allowing such access and openness if the company, its scientists, and their anthropological collaborator could conduct themselves in a principled, creative, and productive way. After all, how else can society arrive at the best informed decisions on the ethical, legal, and social issues arising both from new technologies and information and also from the methods of investigating them?

White wants simultaneously to defend the traditional boundaries of modern science as a practice and to extend the institutional sites in which such science can be seen to be legitimately practiced. Many scientists I have talked to, both within and without the university and both in Europe and the US, complain that *Nature* and *Science* are illicitly trading on their authority as leading scientific journals. The depth of the resentment is striking. Its source seems to be boundary anxiety; any practicing bioscientist today is keenly aware of the politics of science, especially regarding funding priorities, competition and its discontents, and so on. They seem willing to tolerate, even while lamenting, the current state of affairs, as long as there is a protected inner sanctum of science played by the rules. White and his colleagues defend the biotech industry as a legitimate and competitive alternative to the university or governmental labs. When part of the Nobel Prize in chemistry in 1993 was awarded for the invention of PCR, White saw this event as a major validation of the quality of science done outside the university.

For White, an anthropologist might serve as a situated observer but one who could explore the effect of his or her partiality on the subject matter. "Part of an experimental exploration is not knowing what you may find. My attitude about an anthropologist studying PCR, and my colleagues' notion of not 'directing' him, is in some measure a desire to let the anthropologist discover something (a pattern, process, or paradigm?) about what happened. It was intended to see if he might produce a new form." In that sense, White hoped that the collaboration could make him more productive. He never blurred the distinction between the technical and the therapeutic, never asked me to play a facilitator or therapeutic role. He remained attentive to possible operationalizable aspects arising from my analysis. One thing he wanted to know was how to create "an environment for future discoveries."

White was engaged from the start in an experiment in which I was being deployed as much as I was using him. This experiment was one he could manage and monitor but not control. There were risks for him in such a strategy; my presence might have occasioned interpersonal trouble in the lab, or his corporate superiors might have disapproved of the whole project. Neither of these things happened. In the last stages of the writing, a lawyer at Hoffmann–La Roche was informed that legal advisors had suggested that Roche scientists modify a few of their own quotations (about lawyers) in the book; the legal advisors told White they were "not in the business of censorship." White never asked for a right of veto of my material, nor was he ever offered one.

Why did he engage in this experiment? Partly because of his strong desire "to set the record straight," partly because of his curiosity about what I would produce. No doubt there was some ego gratification in the sense of an affirmation of his self-image as an unconventional facilitator, resolutely operating in dissonance or at least in a productive tension with his well-heeled surfaces. Mainly, White wanted to practice his science in a certain manner, "to work at the limits of one's ability and curiosity with as few resources and restrictions as possible." He wanted to work in an environment in which such collaboration would be considered normal. It was a risk worth taking. After all, White and his colleagues were practitioners who spent their lives in environments of calculated risk, and it was part of their professional disposition to try things and see what happened.

The biotechnology industry plays a significant role in certain sectors of molecular biological research. The fact that as few as one in five grants in the US is funded by governmental agencies indicates that fundamental changes are taking place in the institutional arrangements for supporting science that emerged after the Second World War. Without money there is no research in these fields, and an increasing percentage of that research is being done in nongovernmental or university settings. White and his colleagues had chosen to work for a biotechnology company where the literal calculation of financial risk was directly on the agenda in a way that wasn't true in a university environment. They were professional controlled risk takers operating in a fluid environment structured by availability of funds, technological limitations, legal constraints, and their own dispositions.

IV. DEMANDS OF THE DAY: BETWEEN EFFICIENCY AND WORLD VIEW

Max Weber's lecture "Science as a Vocation," delivered in 1917 on the day the Bolsheviks seized power, contains the classic statement of the place and problem of science (*Wissenschaft*) in modernity understood as a cultural and economic formation as well as an ethos. Weber's remarks provide a touchstone for testing the vexed, if allusive, question of the status of science and modernity, postmodernity, and amodernity in the light of specific ethnographic research on contemporary biotechnology and its practitioners. More importantly, they put forth a hypothesis about the limits of the sciences and the demands posed by those limits.

Weber identified the gradually accumulating spread of rationalization processes, from calculative rationality to bureaucratization to the methodical organization of everyday life, as the key diacritic of modernity. The mark of modernity—and here is where *Wissenschaft* enters—is demagification (*Entzauberung*). Demagification means principled disenchantment, not the total control or general flattening of life. Such principled disenchantment does indeed open the cultural and ethical possibility of nihilism, or postmodernity, but does not entail it. On this often misunderstood point, Weber could not be clearer: "The increasing intellectualization and rationalization do not, therefore, indicate an increased and general knowledge of the conditions under which one lives. It means something else, namely, the knowledge or belief that if one but wished one could learn it at any time. This means that the world is disenchanted" (Weber 1946a:139). In the sphere of meaning the mark of modernity is fracture and pluralism. The gradual institutionalization of science applied the fracturous blow to older worldviews, not forcibly destroying them but only decentering them, relativizing them, placing them in a relational position. Scientific practice created a sphere in which the dark and joyous forces of enchantment and meaning were banished, stilled. Although the point is often missed, Weber is quite clear that such forces continue to flourish: "Fate, and certainly not science, holds sway over these gods [Aphrodite and Apollo] and their struggles" (1946a:149). Many other social and cultural instances beyond fate give shape to "these gods." Normatively, however, science stands against the principled hegemony of such forces. Modernity is the principle of demagification, not its colonial triumph. Weber follows Nietzsche in signaling plurality of value as modernity's fate, its triumph and dilemma.

This multiplication of cultural possibilities problematizes the place of the knowledge seeker. Science (*Wissenschaft*) only provides the tools for a growing technical mastery of the world, both natural and social. "Natural science gives us an answer to the question of what we must do if we wish to master life technically. It leaves quite aside, or assumes for its purposes, whether we should and do wish to master life technically and whether it ultimately makes sense to do so" (Weber 1946a:144). Weber had nothing but a haughty contempt for those spokesmen (of all political stripes) who believed that science could and ought to play such a role. "Who," he ironized, "aside from certain big children who are indeed found in the natural sciences—still believes that the findings of astronomy, biology, physics, or chemistry could teach us anything about the meaning of the world?" (1946a:142). Furthermore, who believed that science was the path to the Enlightenment goal of happiness, "aside from a few big children in university chairs or editorial offices" (1946a:143). Those who claim today that the Human Genome Project is the holy grail fall squarely within the infantile tradition, as do those who take their ant colonies as metaphors or, worse, metonyms of all collectivities. And so, too, do those who see only status-striving in human existence.

According to Weber, science does three things. It "contributes to the technology of controlling life by calculating external objects as well as man's activities. [It] contributes methods of thinking, the tools and training for thought. [It] helps us to gain clarity" (1946a:150–51). The demand of self-clarification places the issue of *Lebensführung*, or life-regulation, at center stage both as an object of study and as an ethical problem. It is precisely these issues that Michel Foucault's analytic of ethics was grappling with as well. Foucault (1984:355) defines the "telos" of ethical activity as "[t]hat activity in which one finds the self. An action is not only moral in itself, in its singularity; it is also moral in its circumstantial integration and by virtue of the place it occupies in a pattern of conduct." The key terms are "circumstantial integration" and the "place it occupies in a pattern of conduct." These terms are uncannily close to and simultaneously far from "technical efficiency" and "worldview."

What is that circumstantial integration? And what is the pattern of conduct? To what extent did I or could I integrate Tom White's goals into my pattern of conduct? I had no stakes in or fantasies about improving industry (and was not optimistic about the academy), although the goal of interacting with scientists in "a principled, creative, and productive way," and hence the task of inventing a milieu where we could do so, was at the core of the project. I share Tom's desire to counteract the "stereotypes that destroy creativity and the process of discovery," but not his tenacious optimism about fulfilling that desire. I don't have any programmatic intention of showing "how to create an environment for future discoveries." Ultimately, for me the thorniest part of the quotation is found at the end of Tom's statement: "After all, how else can society arrive at the best-informed decisions on the ethical, legal, and social issues arising both from new technologies and information and also from the methods of investigating them?"

How else? For Tom, this phrase was his basic question, one that underscores how he framed the demands of the day. The phrase made me agitated. My experience has not been that "society" often seeks to arrive at the best informed decisions. More accurately, what funding agencies, federal bureaucracies, or legal instances and parliamentary bodies considered to be "informed" was often completely exotic—and irredeemably alienating. When I applied to the Social, Legal and Ethics division of the Department of Energy's Human Genome Project for a grant to study PCR, I was told PCR was not relevant to the project (even though admittedly the project would have been basically impossible without it). Social science should study what happens to the discoveries of molecular biology, not the molecular biologists and their practices. Charles Cantor, then director of the Genome Project at Berkeley, told me that PCR "had no social consequences, just like the transistor."

When I applied to the National Institutes of Health Human Genome Project to study the different approach to genome mapping being undertaken in France by the CEPH, I was told there were no significant differences in approach (this was before the French beat the Americans in producing the first physical map of the human genome). The official letter of rejection informed me that my working "hypothesis" about studying the production of genetic knowledge in different cultures was poorly formulated because all significant human differences were biological, not cultural. When I asked the anthropologist-ethicist-bureaucrat who was charged with overseeing these evaluations whether he believed all significant differences were biological, he told me their evaluation procedures had been fair. When I asked him if he had fallen off his chair laughing, he didn't respond. With the passage of time, and disregarding the simple asininity involved, I have come to find these responses almost coherent. Given its assumptions, how else could an ethics bureaucracy operate "to achieve the best-informed decisions"? What is curious are the assumptions that one needs to show how to proceed from a worldview (theory) to a technical problem (hypothesis) and that bureaucracies should be charged with ethics. In *Writing Culture* I had urged others to exoticize the West; integrating that imperative into my pattern of conduct seemed, eventually, like the right thing to do.

Yet White had provided me with the opportunity to do research in part because he thought such research would help him to make informed decisions and to create and sustain an innovative environment. It would make something different happen that he couldn't entirely control. White, after all, is a hyperactive optimist by temperament. He also has a career record of making environments from which discoveries do emerge and new forms of experimentation are possible.

In this light, it is worth noting that White had been approached in the early days of the Human Genome Project about heading the Department of Energy program. He did not pursue the opening, deciding instead to stay in industry. Although I am a hyperactive pessimist, I had integrated the circumstantial opportunity into my pattern of conduct. The incidental movements that led me to White, to the polymerase chain reaction, to Cetus Corporation, yielded, as far as I can tell, neither technical efficiency nor a worldview, but produced a book. I gained some experience and perhaps a certain clarity from the experiment. Who, aside from some big children in university chairs, government bureaus, and editorial offices, could ask for anything more?

Note

Another version of this paper appears in Rabinow's *Essays on the Anthropology of Reason* (Princeton University Press, 1997).

10

Postmodernist Critique in the 1980s, Nuclear Diplomacy, and the "Prisoner's Dilemma"

Probing Family Resemblances

George E. Marcus

This paper is an experiment that focuses on high-level Cold War diplomacy in its twilight and critical postmodernism in its prime. I ask, in a US framework, about the state of internal change within the power/knowledge[1] of nuclear diplomacy, a state that parallels in nonobvious ways critiques of the humanities and human sciences disciplines that emerged and spread during the 1980s. I give this temporal framework a very personal agenda and location, placing myself as an actor in the development of the 1980s' critiques, spurred on by a sense and perception that the world, or at least the US, was changing in a way that made the critiques more cogent and justified. I have selected nuclear arms–control diplomacy of that period as the target "other" power/knowledge in order to try to discover any affinities with the moves and constructs of so-called postmodern critique within the academy, both because of that diplomacy's clear distance from any contact with the academic critiques of disciplines and because it was at the vortex of the most dramatic structural and cognitive real-world changes of that decade.

I want to suggest how converging or intersecting genealogies of shared concepts and concerns might be established through a sort of ethnographically sensitive translation between "worlds apart" power/knowledge arenas, such that mutually relevant discussions might occur between scholars and experts who perhaps never thought they had much in common. Once convincing linking genealogies are established, then the agenda of critical anthropology is defined for the present in trying to exploit or explore them in further dialogues across very strange, and estranged, boundaries of academic and other expert discourse. What is at stake is the movement of critical anthropology into conversation with policy studies and operations, but in a framework that it has a substantial role in shaping. Here the task consists in making visible and conscious across domains the intertwined histories of conceptual frameworks that powerfully orient cognitions, practices, and definitions of problems confronted.

The operative task of the following exercise is thus one of critical translation in a world of family resemblances of overlapping power/knowledges, involving moving beyond the critical field of discourses that have emerged in the human sciences to the discovery of affinities, parallels, and differences within other power/knowledges for which these critical discourses have meant little or nothing. If, indeed, overt styles of critical postmodern thought have cogently gestured toward conditions "out there," then through a kind of ethnographic translation a similar de facto postmodernism in its own terms, however subtly marked and even resisted, should be found in other power/knowledges. The result of such an exercise would at least indicate with great specificity what are useful and less useful ideas in the central trends of critical academic postmodernism of the past decade. It would also map with equal specificity a much needed and perhaps provocative expansion in the range of discourses of scholarship, technical thought, and expertise with which critical postmodernism and cultural studies might engage other than in their distancing and clichéd "oppositional" stance to all that is "dominant" and "hegemonic."

This form of critique looks for affinities between postmodern thought and other power/knowledges precisely where they are not obvious, where they emerge in the latter as unintended consequences of trying to deal instrumentally with the contemporary world. For example, at what points is a power/knowledge that has comfortably dealt with constructs of integral selves and individuals faced suddenly with multiple subjectivities (a key artifact of postmodern/feminist/cultural studies thought) in the course of its problem solving? It is precisely at such points that two-way translations and engagement might be strategized. The fact that these affinities are discovered and negotiated within the enemy territory of the dominant/hegemonic rather than imposed by the power of postmodern thought in brilliant applications marks the difference between the project suggested here and the existing domains (or reservations) of postmodern critique within many contemporary power/knowledges. (There are now accepted but marginal postmodern sectors in such fields as history, economics, political science, law, psychology, and management studies, among others.)

As indicated, I want to work through an example of this critical project focused on the power/knowledge of the closing years of high-level Cold War diplomacy. Rather than testing the intellectual capital of the 1980s against the state of power/knowledges as they are now unfolding, I have decided to provide a short historical perspective. The shift in leadership in the USSR and the country's eventual dismantling were centrally registered in the discourse of diplomacy which, for most of the Cold War, had been about nuclear arms control. With hindsight it is easy to see how postmodern the world has become, but my question is whether there are any affinities between the radical shifts of framework and representation practices suggested by postmodern critiques in the academy of the 1980s and the discourse of diplomacy of the same period, which, albeit insular, was having to navigate radically changed conditions and new assumptions.

AT THE INSTITUTE FOR ADVANCED STUDY, 1982–83: STORY LINES

I was invited to be a visiting member at the Institute for Advanced Study during 1982–83, primarily because of Clifford Geertz's interest in the paper, "Ethnographies as Texts," that Dick Cushman and I published in the 1982 *Annual Review of Anthropology* and because Geertz was working on a set of lectures on anthropological writing that eventually formed the core chapters of his book *Works and Lives* (Geertz 1988). It was during my time at the Institute that I planned the School of American Research "Writing Culture" seminar with Jim Clifford and drafted (in partnership with Mike Fischer) the arguments for *Anthropology as Cultural Critique* (Marcus and Fischer 1986).

Clifford visited me at the Institute during this year and met Geertz for the first time. There was clear mutual respect between them as writers. Geertz was then simultaneously attracted to and wary of the coming "literary" turn, even though before the days of "theory" he himself had been associated with a literary influence on anthropology. The concerns with textuality, disciplinary history, critical modes of reflexivity, and the critique of realist practices of representation under the weight of poststructuralist and feminist ideas then permeating the US academy that informed my (and to a far lesser extent, Geertz's) thinking were just one instance of what was probably happening in many disciplines and at many places. This one clear "story line" in the atmosphere of the Institute while I was there would become a major story of the decade and beyond.

Amid the diverse projects being pursued at the Institute that year were three other salient story lines, two of which figure into the exercise that I have designed for this paper. One of them, not directly relevant here, was the focused attention being given to cognitive science. Another story line derived from the work that Charles Sabel did as a visiting member of the Institute during 1982–83 while working on the manuscript that was to become *The Second Industrial Divide* (Piore and Sabel 1984). This was one of the first major statements of the changing conditions of capitalist political economy in the West, centered around the idea of post-Fordism and production processes of flexible accumulation. In 1982–83—the middle of Reagan's first term—salient perceptions were of adverse change for the US economy in a rapidly changing world of competitive capitalism along with aggressive Cold War posturing. It might be recalled that the new work on political economy briefly played a role (through Robert Reich's popularization) in the suggestion before the 1984 election that the Democrats ought to oppose Reagan by arguing for a national industrial policy to compete in a post-Fordist world. The rapid changes in markets, production processes, and consumer choices were very apparent to the person on the street in the early 1980s, and these realities, I would argue, played a crucial offstage role in giving postmodernist critiques a sense of their own possibilities.

In this broad body of interdisciplinary work to which I and others at the Institute were introduced by Sabel, the theorized source of "emerging reality" was being shaped that would provide the strongest representation of "immense changes afoot in the world," giving postmodernist critique in the realm of culture theory its guarantor of cogency. Indeed, this new work on emerging political economy was frequently referenced in works of cultural critique.

This brings me to the final story line, which happened to be quite salient at the Institute in 1982–83 and which I found perhaps the most fascinating of all. It dealt with the seemingly Spenglerian moment that the Reagan administration had begun to create with its departure from détente and its more aggressive stance toward the Soviet Union. This was the moment of the invocation of the "evil empire," of the thinkability of a winnable nuclear war, and of debates about the feasibility of direct military intervention in Central America. I recall bizarre discussions at the Institute about what kinds of desperate actions could derail the nuclear brinkmanship of the Reagan administration. I recall public debates between Richard Ullman (professor at the Woodrow Wilson School) and Bill Luers (former ambassador to Venezuela, later made ambassador to Czechoslovakia, after which he retired to become president of the Metropolitan Museum of Art) about the dangers of Soviet footholds in Central America. Most memorably, I participated in a weekly series of informal lunches at the Institute dining hall that brought together a diverse group of mostly younger international relations scholars from the Woodrow Wilson School, some weapons scientists, occasional persons who had moved between academia and government or diplomatic service, and always George Kennan, a longtime member of the School of Historical Studies at the Institute.

In terms of sharp, edgy discussion about important events of the day, these lunches were for me the most stimulating events at the Institute that year. The core of the discussions was dominated by young, very bright scholars of international relations arguing over US strategy in competition with the Soviets, arguments narrowly focused on nuclear arms policy. I learned subsequently that these discussions occurred in the middle of a resurgence of neorealist thinking in this field—the idea that the Soviets were nastier than we thought they were and that international relations thinking should return to overt strategy and planning for large-scale conflict. (Of course, this trend was in line with the Reagan administration's moves to remilitarize the US posture toward the Soviet Union.) I was captivated by the elegance and intricacy of this very reductionist game, while finding the game itself obtuse.

Others on the sidelines at the lunches made commentaries or more philosophical glosses on the tight tension of US–Soviet competition, and frequent mention was made of the strategic threat of revolutions in Central America and the background to US policy in that part of the world. For Charles Sabel, the interesting developments in international relations concerned issues of political economy and the evolution of a new international regime that was reorganizing world economies; at the time this was the form that thinking about the global economy took. The main focus in these conversations, however, was on the narrow game/discourse of US–Soviet nuclear strategy totally insulated from immense changes in political economy and thereby maintaining a surreal, but also very locally real, centering to the Cold War order.

The major counterweight at these lunches was the quietly imposing presence of George Kennan, whose comments persistently undermined the assumptions of the revitalized neorealist game being pursued by the younger men. I later learned that Kennan was well known for his distaff view about the Soviet threat that powered Cold War competition; at the time, with the Reagan administration heating up the Cold War, he was very involved in rearticulating this view. Not long after his crucial early–Cold War articulation of containment strategy, Kennan moved to a much more moderate position on Soviet motivations. He argued consistently for a complex and nondemonized view of the Soviets as "others" in the "great game" of Cold War diplomacy, a view that would have precluded a return to a nuclear brinkmanship strategy like that of the early Reagan administration. Kennan was thus once again the rallying point for left-liberal opinion against what looked like a revival of the old Cold War in the early 1980s. As we now know, this early-1980s Cold War strategizing discourse was to go through dramatic changes after Gorbachev came to power in 1985, moving from the Spenglerian specter of the "decline of the West" at the beginning of the decade to a jingoist, but still not fully confident, heralding of the "triumph of the West" at the end, as in Francis Fukuyama's (1991) *The End of History and the Last Man.*

Now, in the mid- to late 1990s, I want to juxtapose and mutually engage this power/knowledge of high-level diplomacy during the 1980s to that of postmodernist critical thought during the same period, when the latter was distantly (if at all) related to the former but was certainly spurred on and stimulated by the spectacle of dramatic changes connected with the great game of Soviet–US relations. In the 1980s, certainly, postmodernist thought was made cogent by the spectacle and velocity of change in the world (the rise of the global economy plus the shifts in Soviet–US relations), thus making visions of watershed change a realistic and credible alternative possibility in the near future, despite the glum situation of conservative control of most Western governments.

THE AVANT-GARDE (POST)MODERNIST FASCINATION WITH SIMULTANEITY AND THE PRISONER'S DILEMMA

Was there any parallel sense of postmodernist moods deep within the distant power/knowledge of nuclear diplomacy? Examining the power/knowledge discourse of nuclear diplomacy in practice during the 1980s by starting from within so-called postmodernist critical thought of the same period requires the construction of intersecting critical genealogies between two domains apparently worlds apart. I can only sketch here an analysis of such an opening through posited affinity. The specific locations I would like to probe are the long-term, signature fascination with simultaneity in the discourse of avant-garde modernisms and postmodernisms, and an identifiable similar fascination with simultaneity in the construction of the key problematic of game theory—the prisoner's dilemma. In turn, the development of game theory (the prisoner's dilemma in particular) in the US is intimately related to the formulation of early–Cold War strategies of nuclear diplomacy. The conduct of nuclear diplomacy was not in the hands of game theoreticians, nor is it clear that game theory was prominent in the thinking of the main actors of Soviet–US relations, but it was certainly a powerful intellectual expression on the inside of the actual great game (if game is the correct metaphor) of nuclear arms competition and control. Thus, I am wagering that making the connection between a problematic of simultaneity in postmodernism and also in game theory will create a vehicle to probe the power/knowledge of nuclear diplomacy in practice for its parallel to critical postmodernism's evoked projections upon the contemporaneous world of unfolding, immense change.

The Fascination with Simultaneity among Avant-Gardes

Techniques of juxtaposition have been at the center of avant-garde practices throughout the histories of modernism and postmodernism. Montage, collage, and assemblage have been avant-garde critique's forms of representation or antirepresentation, with sharp, implied challenges to construction of discourses of the real in conventional genres. These basic techniques of rupture have been applied as the media for a spectrum of avant-garde sensibilities, ranging from a condemnation of modernity and its modes of thought (rupturing juxtapositions subverting the systematic logics fixing the categorical frames of dominant, oppressive "bourgeois" forms of narration) to the celebration of the technological wonders of modernity (for example, the invention of collage by futurists to communicate the sort of speed and immediacy that modernity makes available in everyday life, for which realist modes of representation are inadequate). In terms of form and technique, postmodernist discourse has recapitulated these avant-garde, modernist practices, albeit in the service of emulated, altered, and often hyperdeveloped versions of modernism's range of sensibilities.

One of the most important moves in the so-called postmodernist trend in the academy has been the adoption in both spirit and practice of these avant-garde techniques of (anti?)representation in humanities and social sciences writing as a means of challenging the academy's mode of realism: analytic reason. The power of this form of reason for scholarly practices remains overwhelming. Even when writing against it, one is writing in its terms, or least in reference to it. "Reality" testing thus lurks as a criterion even for the most distanced, theoretical uses of strategies of critique by juxtaposition. In this (re)deployment of avant-garde (post)modernism's techniques within and against the domain of analytic reason as adequate to the contemporary, emergent "real," where new claims are being made about the quality or nature of the "condition of postmodernity" out there, the key empirical question embedded in the practice of juxtaposition concerns the state and expe-

rience—the phenomenology—of simultaneity. This is the condition that the discourse of analytic reason might acknowledge but must evade, and that postmodernist critique wants to address squarely but for which it might not have a satisfactory substitute discourse.

Analytic discourse about the real employs linear representation and sequence, making possible statements about causation that are implied if not rigorously articulated. It allows for systematic theorization and description of social and cultural life. Regardless of whether it indulges implied or rigorous notions of causation, the basic representational mode of analytic discourse depends on the taken-for-granted capacity to articulate relationships (of people, parts, distinctions, things, and so forth) as the most basic object of study. A relationship, however complex and multileveled, entails linearity and sequentiality in conception. This is the basic work horse of analytic reason that postmodernist critique's concern with simultaneity (through the given techniques of rupture) wants to address without summoning anything to replace the discipline and rigor of analytic reason. Furthermore, "unintended consequences" is the space of intractability that analytic discourses reserve to permit limited recognition of effects of simultaneity in social life, but it is precisely this space that postmodernist strategies of juxtaposition want to open up.

Instead of actors who respond to what has been done to them by knowable others—the basis of a relationship—actors are acting in juxtaposition or simultaneity to what is being done by unknowable others as they act; the play with synchronicity in experimental film and fiction (Joyce's *Ulysses* being a prime case) or the idea of "utterance" in Bakhtin are good examples of trying to express this condition from very well established modernisms. The imaginary/discourse of simultaneity is quite different than anything that has been explored in the dominant modes of realism in play in most contemporary power/knowledges. It is precisely this alternative imaginary/discourse that postmodernist critique within the academy wants to explore. Observations about defining aspects of contemporary societies as postmodern (for example, the centrality of time-space compression as reviewed by Harvey [1989], or of speed as focused upon by Paul Virilio [1985]) enhance the fascination of current critical thought with simultaneity and its potential as a condition through which to evoke an alternative vision of contemporary life.

Thus, an unrelenting concern with simultaneity is one of the most distinctive and certainly one of the most subversive, provocative, and irritating characteristics of many forms of thought called postmodern. It is something that realist genres have not been able to abide, dependent as they are on linearity and the construct of transparent reciprocity which simultaneity undermines.

A Case in Point: Game Theory and the Prisoner's Dilemma

Of all the varieties of contemporary discourses of analytic reason, only game theory, specifically its most central and influential puzzle, the prisoner's dilemma (hereafter called PD), foregrounds in its construction the problem of simultaneity and thus shares an affinity with this key provocation of (post)modernist critique. The other main post–World War II paradigm of analytic reason, cybernetics and systems theory, was fully constructed on the imagery of linear relationships and continuous interconnection (see Heims 1993). The PD was thus an attempt of rationality to find a perfect solution in the environment of a key problem of modernity—the condition of simultaneity—in avoiding the assumptions of systems/cybernetics theory which depended upon the positing of linear relationships and direct connections. While by no means equally sharing the spirit or ethos of avant-garde critique (in fact, the condition of simultaneity is constructed for rationalist manipulation by the metaphoric notion of game itself), PD fails as a puzzle for elegant solution, for reasons related to the source of fascination that the condition of simultaneity has for postmodernist critical thought.

Especially in its early years, the history of game theory itself is intimately linked to Cold War history and the policy management of nuclear weapons (see Poundstone 1992). Game theory, which began with the 1944 publication of *Theory of Games and Economic Behavior* by John von Neumann and Oskar Morgenstern, concerns conflict between thoughtful and potentially deceitful opponents in which players are assumed to be perfectly rational. It is therefore a branch not of psychology but of mathematical logic that underlies real conflicts among not-always-rational humans. A "game" is a conflict situation in which one must make a choice knowing that others are also making choices; the outcome of the conflict will be determined in some prescribed way by all the choices made. This is the (post)modernist's problem of simultaneity under the logician's control—the imposition of the ideas of game/conflict and back-and-forth moves in the midst of independent simultaneous action and rules/assumptions imposed by godlike logicians/analysts.

Game theory found its most important application at the RAND Corporation, the prototypical think tank founded at the behest of the Air Force shortly after World War II. RAND's original purpose was to perform strategic studies on intercontinental nuclear war. The need for RAND's operations research was indeed stimulated by a sort of crisis of representation in military matters brought on by the appearance of nuclear weapons, so that generals and scientists became wedded in new ways.

In 1950 two RAND scientists, Merrill Flood and Melvin Dresher, made what has been perhaps the most influential version of game theory, devising a simple "game" that RAND consultant Albert W. Tucker dubbed "the prisoner's dilemma." Not published as such until years after its invention, the story of the prisoner's dilemma—a story that is both a precise mathematical construct and also a real-life problem—spread through the scientific community of the 1950s by oral transmission. From the 1960s, this dilemma paradigm has become a part of a much broader intellectual culture and even a marker of cultural literacy, among writers (for example, the 1988 novel of this title by Richard Powers), social scientists, and humanities scholars. It has come to stand for game theory, its ethical ambiguities, and the tensions of the early nuclear era.

Flood and Dresher wanted to take into account the fact that people are irrational within the realm of game theory; they therefore dispensed to some degree with the narrow assumptions of the original theory and tried to make it relevant to everyday life situations of dilemma, choice, and calculation. Tucker, a Princeton mathematician, gave the tale its classic formulation, of which Poundstone presents a typical contemporary version (1992:118–19):

> Two members of a criminal gang are arrested and imprisoned. Each prisoner is in solitary confinement with no means of speaking to or exchanging messages with the other. The police admit they don't have enough evidence to convict the pair on the principal charge. They plan to sentence both to a year in prison on a lesser charge. Simultaneously, the police offer each prisoner a Faustian bargain. If he testifies against his partner, he will go free while the partner will get three years in prison on the main charge. Oh, yes, there is a catch...if both prisoners testify against each other, both will be sentenced to two years in jail.

The prisoners are given a little time to think this over, but in no case may either learn what the other has decided until he has irrevocably made his decision. Each is informed that the other prisoner is being offered the very same deal. Each prisoner is concerned only with his own welfare—with minimizing his own prison sentence.

The prisoners can reason as follows: "Suppose I testify and the other prisoner doesn't. Then I get off scot-free (rather than spending a year in jail). Suppose I testify and the other prisoner does too. Then I get two years (rather than three). Either way I'm better off turning state's evidence. Testifying takes a year off my sentence, no matter what the other guy does." The trouble is, the other prisoner can and will come to the very same conclusion. If both parties are rational, both will testify and both will get two years in jail. If only they had both refused to testify, they would have got just a year each!

This story was not intended to be a realistic picture of criminology, but to serve the logician's challenge to game theory by posing a puzzle without a perfect solution. The commonsense argument for defecting goes like this: "A prisoner's dilemma is a simultaneous choice. There is no way that your choice can affect the other player's choice. So no matter what the other player does, you're better off by defecting." The commonsense argument for cooperation is this: "The two players' situations are identical. It is unrealistic for one to take advantage of the other by defecting. Assuming that the players are both rational, they should decide on the same strategy. The two realistic outcomes are mutual cooperation and mutual defection. Both prefer the cooperative outcome, so that's what they should do; cooperate." But in a real-life situation, there is no guarantee that both players will make the same choice. As a practical matter, then, you have to assume that all four outcomes are possible. In a true prisoner's dilemma, it is as hard to justify cooperation as it is to accept mutual defection as the logical outcome. Therein lies the paradox.

An expected solution never came to the PD, and it remains a limiting case for the ambition of a theory that would impose perfect rationality on the (post)modern condition of simultaneity—the nonlinear nature of relationship as a usual circumstance of social and cultural life, and not just of dilemma situations. So much for the disappointments of theory. In practice, no example of a prisoner's dilemma has been more popular, both in technical articles and the popular press, than nuclear arms rivalry. The PD is sometimes taken to be part of the jargon of nuclear strategy, along with "mutually assured destruction" and "MIRV." At the time the PD was invented, the US and the Soviets had embarked on an expensive nuclear arms race. The situation could be seen as a PD (and was seen as such at RAND, whose "thinking about the unthinkable" was of maximum influence at the time, setting the broad frame of strategic thought for the entire Cold War) in which building bombs could be identified with defection and refraining from doing so could be identified with cooperation. Each side would prefer that no one build the bomb (reward payoff for mutual cooperation) rather than both build it for no net gain of power (punishment payoff for mutual defection). But each side may well elect to build the bomb either out of hope of gaining the upper hand militarily (temptation payoff) or out of fear of being the one without it (sucker payoff).

As the Cold War wore on and the US and the Soviet Union became implacable foes whose relations remained focused on the politics of nuclear arms competition and then control, the relevance of exercises in perfect rationality as embedded in the project of game theory (and within it, its internal critique and limiting case in the form of the PD) clearly lessened. Yet it is possible that the problematic around which the PD developed and which it shared with avant-garde modernisms—

the fascination with relations of simultaneity—may be of crucial relevance in understanding the course of the development of high-level nuclear diplomacy in terms of which Cold War reality was articulated and managed. It is just that avant-garde modernisms have nothing as elegant as the PD to offer with which to understand the actual course of Cold War nuclear diplomacy.

This is where the ethnographically sensitive translation between power/knowledges and the probing for the PD in action, so to speak, comes in. The basic setup of the PD—the condition of nonlinear relations of simultaneity—is probably useful to retain and quite ironic as a perspective on the actual playing out of US–Soviet relations at the end of the Cold War. To substitute for the mechanistic vision of choice and action in the PD, overly controlled by the godlike assumptions of logicians defining the game, a richer set of theories and concepts are needed that describe the human experience of operating in conditions of simultaneous processes in which one's relations are with unseen, or only partly perceived, others. Classic social theory and analytic reason, as noted, offer very few resources for this reimagining of the PD in messy, human terms.[2]

Let us now move to a set of exhibits/artifacts from the late–Cold War history of nuclear diplomacy that detect something of the dynamic in practice of the mixed PD/postmodernist problematic of simultaneity. When do we reach the point in "real" life when the utility of maintaining the fiction that what we are doing is a game at all is exhausted, leading us to look for other terms and descriptive frames to deal with "provisionary strategies"? No such dramatic breaking of frame in nuclear diplomacy at the end of the Cold War is apparent, but certainly the game metaphor, implied or explicit, wavered at various points in the events of the 1980s.

Finally, it seems to me that revisions in systems theories to encompass discontinuity, contingency, nonlinearity, and apparent simultaneity—or to put it simply, complexity—have generated theoretical paradigms, such as chaos, that have thoroughly displaced game theory in terms of both prestige and popularity (see Gleick 1986). The new systems theories retain the goal of establishing principles of embedded or underlying order in accounts of much more complex phenomena.

This is a heady brew that promises order and yet recognizes in phenomena the contradictions, paradoxes, and processes of disorder so focused upon by (post)modernist critical thought. It is no wonder then that the long-standing practice of borrowing theoretical metaphors and analogies from the natural sciences to enhance the rhetoric of new ideas in the human sciences continues, with frequent references to chaos, complexity theory, fractals, and the like in contemporary discussions of global cultures, new social formations, and so forth. Game theory, which at one time addressed in dilemma stories such as the PD key aspects of the problematics of avant-garde modernisms that systems theory ignored, now pales against the ability of revised systems theory (such as theories of chaos and complexity) to excite and contribute to the authority of developing imaginaries within the human sciences.

NUCLEAR DIPLOMACY

Game theory turns out to be a formalized portrait or calculus of the way that social actors think about interests in its own interest of pure rationality. Due to the very specific intellectual and cultural history outlined above, it has a close relationship to the mode of thought the Cold War was identified with and, in fact, produced as a practice of power/knowledge: the discourse of nuclear arms production, competition, and control. This topic focused high-level US–Soviet relations into a highly technical, complex "glass-bead game" whose technicians were not scientists but establishment (or establishment-style) lawyers like Paul Nitze and Paul Warnke. Such nuclear arms negotiators presented an unusual combination of the cultivated generalist/amateur posture of the establishment elite and intricate, technical expertise about the character of nuclear weapon systems.

As noted, it is doubtful that game theory and the PD had much presence in the actual great game after the early years of the Cold War as it was articulated within the complex arena of those concerned with nuclear diplomacy. In practice, the great game has had all the characteristics of (post)modernist simultaneity rather than of game theory. Still, the PD is part of the elite lore of those charged with nuclear arms control. It is therefore, I would argue, one prospective "mole" for probing affinities with postmodernist critique within the terms of this power/knowledge at the vortex of global change during the same period that this critique emerged in US academia. As I argued, there are aspects of the way the PD is constructed (quite aside from its rationalist, problem-solving purpose) which are at the heart of a perception of a condition of (post)modernity in avant-garde thought. Could these aspects, having to do with relations defined by conditions of simultaneity, be reconfigured for probing within the characteristics of nuclear diplomacy discourse in which the PD has a chimerical, marginalized standing as a once important constituting paradigm of nuclear diplomacy that is now an artifact of elite folklore? It is precisely in this latter capacity that the PD might serve as the bridge for a project of ethnographic translation between power/knowledges.

Without its rationalist purpose, what remains of the PD is the situation of the "prisoner" more than the game imposed on it—less a competition or rivalry of tit for tat, move-countermove, than the predicament of two powers/actors operating blindly in terms of one another, with the nature of their relationship constructed in the imaginations of each. This is the paradigm of (post)modernist experience for which the idea of the game was inadequate, as demonstrated by the long search for a perfect solution for the PD. What sort of reconfigured problematic does this paradigm actually define for the conduct of nuclear diplomacy in the late Cold War of the 1980s?[3]

The insularity of nuclear diplomacy discourse is striking. With few exceptions (the Cuban missile crisis, Paul Nitze's "Walk in the Woods"), actual contacts and exchanges with the Soviet "other" are highly ritualized and technical. The dynamics are generated by politics among those in an administration charged with nuclear diplomacy—the president, the national security advisor, the secretary of state, others in the State Department involved with arms control negotiation, and the community of various expertises (journalistic, academic, scientific, intelligence) oriented toward these "agent" positions in nuclear diplomacy. Only former Cold Warriors on the outside, such as George Kennan, could articulate the contrary wisdom that argued for the recognition of the substantive alterity of the Soviets which would have expanded or transcended the discourse of nuclear diplomacy and conventionalized the relationship between the two powers at the highest levels.

The stylized manner of US-Soviet relations constituted by nuclear diplomacy was disrupted by two events in the 1980s: Reagan's Strategic Defense Initiative (SDI), unveiled in a speech on March 23, 1983, and Gorbachev's accession to power in 1985. As nuclear diplomats struggled to deal with the momentous consequences of both, to what degree did they self-consciously or even ambivalently come to terms with the (post)modernist conditions of their power/knowledge, embedded within their own history and folklore in the PD story?

SDI: A RUPTURE IN THE DISCOURSE OF ARMS CONTROL

Reagan's announcement of the Strategic Defense Initiative (popularly known as "Star Wars") in 1983 took the nuclear diplomatic community by total surprise, and the rest of the decade was in part a struggle by various factions to reassert their versions of the verities of arms control while seeming to pursue the president's unconventional initiative. This idiosyncratic, radical, and highly futuristic plan to make nuclear weapons outmoded through space defenses totally undermined the arms control efforts that had characterized nuclear diplomacy through the period of détente. Although the idea was to make the whole basis of the US–Soviet relationship irrelevant, the SDI was in fact a keenly aggressive move. It would match the economic power of the two states in a way that had not been done since the arms buildups of the early Cold War, and both sides knew that the Soviet Union was not up to this strain.

Reagan's attempt to dispense with the great game could not be attributed solely to a cunning plot to break the Soviet economy but equally had its roots in his characteristic kind of idealism, surrealism, and American exceptionalism (the latter treated as a major theme of US foreign policy in Henry Kissinger's retrospective *Diplomacy* [1994]). The Byzantine efforts of nuclear diplomats like Paul Nitze and Richard Perle to continue to pursue their agendas through the new challenges that SDI imposed was the true game of nuclear diplomacy during the 1980s as the Soviet Union continued to fall apart. These agendas of course had to do with the assumption of the possibility of nuclear war on which the simultaneously real and imaginary relationship of the US and the Soviet Union had been based.

Reagan's initiative, in its dreamy unreality, can be understood as an effort that would end the prisoner's dilemma of US–Soviet relations in its (post)modernist inflection/affinity. The contemporary masters of the PD-in-practice embodied in nuclear diplomacy succeeded in sustaining this imaginary on which the focal Cold War relationship of simultaneity was constructed, with all its psychological possibilities of paranoia and indulgent self-construction in the absence of any rich and broadly monitored contact with an "other." What was not registered sufficiently in this insular, baroque game that guaranteed order in the world of the Cold War was the appearance of real alterity for the first time in the person of Gorbachev, whose rise to power proved to be far more endangering to the assumptions of nuclear diplomacy than SDI.

GEORGE SCHULTZ LECTURES GORBACHEV ON THE INFORMATION REVOLUTION

In the Kremlin, April 14, 1987

> At this point, about two hours into our meeting, Gorbachev suggested we take a short break. I took this as an opportunity to engage him in a line of discussion I had talked over carefully with President Reagan before leaving for Moscow. I walked to the end of the table and set up two brightly colored pie charts showing the distribution of world GNP at various times, including a projection to the year 2000. "Here is what is happening," I said. "The US and the Soviet Union are now the two great powers. Others are not in a position to think about global developments the way we are. Typically, over the years, high-level Soviet-American exchanges have dealt with controversy: arms, human rights, communism versus capitalism, regional hot spots. There are big changes going on in the world economy. It's not just bipolar to multipolar; the world is in the midst of a highly complicated evolution—or revolution. The implications are not entirely clear, but we can see an outline of the future taking shape. The central feature is the great growth of the global econ-

omy: a general rise in GNP, gigantic expansion in goods and services, a huge increase in trade flows. As the world's output expands overall, the distribution of that output is more and more dispersed."

Gorbachev looked at the charts. I could see he was intrigued. "As a result, more and more nations are achieving economies of a size that permits them to divert major resources into one or more major undertakings at a world-class level. The list of nations able to take on an influential world role in a particular field—computers, weapons, finance, and so on—is going to be truly astonishing. China, Singapore, Korea, Israel are examples of very different countries clearly heading into this top category in one or more areas. What drives this growth?" I asked rhetorically.

"Science and technology," Gorbachev responded.

"Yes, but," I said, "hitched to an incentive-based, market-oriented economic system. Examples: in agriculture, nations are becoming free from a burden as old as civilization—the struggle to feed themselves. Malthus, who believed there are inherent limits to food production, is turned on his head. Biotechnology, plant strains, fertilizers, genetics, waste- and spoilage-reduction technology, have brought about a revolution. More important has been the rediscovery that if a farmer can get a price for his product that covers the cost of production plus a little more, the incentive for production is enormous. The net result of all this will be that the world can feed itself and at a relatively small cost," I told Gorbachev.

"In industry, almost every natural resource—take copper, for example—now has its substitute. Scientific and chemical processes now replace minerals in the ground. This is good news for some nations and bad for others. But for all it is a spur to move beyond the industrial age to the information age," I emphasized. "Manufacturing is often global in scope. Here is a shipping label for an integrated circuit used in manufacturing by an American company. The label reads, 'Made in one or more of the following countries: Korea, Hong Kong, Malaysia, Singapore, Taiwan, Mauritius, Thailand, Indonesia, Mexico, Philippines. The exact country of origin is unknown.'" I had a picture of this label. Gorbachev looked at it with some skepticism.

"The military scene is being transformed by the increasing ease with which formerly militarily insignificant nations can now obtain or even produce weapons only somewhat less sophisticated than the best we have today, such as the Chinese Silkworm missiles now possessed by the Iranians. With the rise of ethnic (such as Tamil terrorism in Sri Lanka), regional (such as the Vietnamese occupation of Cambodia), and religious (Islamic fundamentalism) tensions, this means that small conflicts can become unprecedentedly explosive," I said.

"And the financial world was transformed years ago. The London market, the New York market, and the Tokyo market are big, but today, the only way to conceive of the financial market is globally. The information age has put the world on an information standard. Markets react almost instantly to a major event anywhere.

"What are the philosophical implications of all this?" I asked. "Here are my thoughts. This is a scientific revolution. There was a time when a government could control its scientific establishment and be basically successful. No longer. To keep up today and in the future means that scientists will have to be in constant touch with the 'thinking community' around the world. And this is an information revolution. The inability of one nation to be predominant in the international financial world is going to be repeated field after field. The key is going to be knowledge-based productivity, even in defense: an aircraft carrier is really one big information system," I said.

"So the old categories no longer hold true. In our

GNP accounts, we have classifications that distinguish between capital and labor. That distinction is central to Marxist thought as well. But that dichotomy is becoming obsolete because we have entered a world in which the truly important capital is human capital, what people know, how freely they exchange information and knowledge, and the intellectually creative product that emerges."

As I talked, Gorbachev interjected occasionally, but basically he listened carefully. He was engaged and interested. "We should have more of this kind of talk," he told me. I agreed.

After about twenty-five minutes, Marshal Akhromeyev walked in with a jaunty step and upbeat, confident manner. We turned to START and SDI. Gorbachev said that the idea of a 50 percent cut in strategic forces, first agreed on at the Geneva summit, could now be described in numerical terms: 1,600 launchers and 6,000 warheads. (Schultz 1993:891–92)[4]

Commentary

Here Schultz, the Stanford economics professor, was sketching the bigger picture, the dramatically changing conditions of capitalist political economy on which the cogency of developing postmodernist cultural critique of the 1980s was most directly based. But this exchange was a mere interruption in the narrow frame to which Schultz's face-to-face meetings with Gorbachev and other high-level Soviets were restricted. The relationship of the US and the Soviets in simultaneity had been sustained in practice by the discipline of the discourse of arms control negotiation. Gorbachev was the first Soviet leader with the hint of a "face" that might be recognized in a normal face-to-face relationship. Schultz was trying to break through the rigid frame of the old world of US–Soviet relations to an account of a new world in which, through the information revolution, simultaneity would continue to be the medium of relationship, but this time through speed and time-space compression in the global economy instead of through the mannered relations in the blind of the Cold War leviathans who were, true to the PD, prisoners rather than gamesters of the nuclear world that they had created.

The unraveling of the Soviet Union after 1988 unexpectedly and clearly displaced the centrality of the (post)modernist, PD basis of Soviet–US relations in high-level US diplomacy. For Reagan, and even more so for George Bush, the arrival of Gorbachev meant that for the first time a complex, actual interlocutor "other" could be imagined as a counterpart by the US president; as Margaret Thatcher remarked after her first meeting with Gorbachev, he was "someone with whom I could do business." This gave a literalness, an intersubjectivity, a linearity of back-and-forth interaction—in essence, an illusion of presence—to US–Soviet relations that belied the conduct of their relationship in simultaneity along with whatever insight into the nature of sociality in the (post)modern world was offered by this previous condition.

The illusion of a relationship in the most conventional terms—an "affair" or partnership, as it were—impeded management at the highest levels of the speed of change in the late 1980s for which Schultz's lecture on the (post)modernist political economy was apposite and the conduct of US–Soviet relations in the simultaneity of nuclear diplomacy was perhaps more relevant (see Beschloss and Talbott [1993] for the most detailed account of the end of the Cold War). The Bush-Gorbachev affair was the ultimate limiting case (and failure) of the conventional idea of a relationship in the (post)modernist world in which Soviet–US relations, centered on nuclear diplomacy, had been conducted through much of the Cold War and with special intensity during the 1980s. Within a US context, however, the 1980s was a remarkable decade of new, unconventional thinking (the exotic foray of avant-garde idioms into the human sciences, with mixed results thus far) and the struggle of old forms of unconventional thinking (nuclear diplomacy at the end of the Cold War), with affinities and contradictory parallels between them—the (post)modernist fascination with simultaneity through the PD, for example . Critical work in the 1990s, I would argue, depends more upon the speculations of translating across the power/knowledges of this period than on any self-conscious return to the eternal verities of existing metahistories (for instance, see Kissinger 1994) whose frames are likely to miss what is acknowledged by them as unprecedented, really different, and distinctively definitive about these times as they unfold.

Envoi

With a strong sense that the 1980s' intellectual ferment at the level of metatheoretical discussion is over (see the "end of theory" laments of the early 1990s) and an equally strong sense of unrealized potential and irresolution of many of these "high" theoretical ideas in enactments of very specific genres of research and scholarship, what remains for critical cultural studies and its derivations is to seek not-always-comfortable engagements in arenas that it has been hesitant to enter or has defined itself in opposition to. This would address unfinished aspects of the practice of reflexivity that has been such a major emblem and strategy of critical research in recent years. Critical cultural studies has produced impressive work on popular culture and the contemporary predicaments of those social actors conceived in subaltern positionings. Reflexivity in such work has aided the construction of these valuable research genres. What has not been done within the framework of these very same critical cultural studies is to incorporate the reflexive dimension that makes visible the established and potential relationships of critical cultural studies to forms of institutional power. This paper, with some tentative exercises in that direction, has sought to argue strongly not only for making these connections but also for developing them.

The point is not merely to suggest this kind of provocative reflexivity (as others, like Bourdieu [1990], have done) for theoretical purpose and advantage, but to consider the radical implications of performing it in all aspects of the research process for the standard ways that critical cultural studies scholars position themselves in relation to subjects of study and presumed audiences, how they materialize objects of study, and how they create rhetorics of political purpose, affiliation, and virtue for their projects. For example, from the standpoint of critical ethnographic work in cultural studies, the most radical move required of scholars who have repositioned themselves by establishing affinities between themselves and those operating in other power/knowledges is to overcome typical distinctions between elites (and institutional orders) as "others" that anthropologists largely do not study, subalterns as "others" whom anthropologists do study, and anthropologists themselves in the position of ethnographers as "other" to either of these. The self-perception of the practice of ethnography as a power/knowledge like, among, and with specific kinds of connections to others, based on certain ethical commitments and identifications, forces the refiguration of the terrain of research—unfixes standard positionings—in which the concepts of elites, anthropologists, and subalterns get rearranged. Aside from the defining features of power structures and conspiratorial groups, what we have attributed to elites is not "other" to us as scholars at all, but rather the play of institutional orders, which incorporates "us" as merely a different institutional interest.

Operating within reconfigured spaces of research has implications for the traditional sympathetic involvements of researchers with their subjects. Now these involvements are multiple, conflicting, and much more ambiguous. The nature and quality of fieldwork in different sites can vary greatly. This situation requires a different kind of resolution of a research persona than that which had normally constituted the anthropologist in fieldwork, and which was a major component of the much critiqued traditional conventions of authority in ethnographic writing (I know because "I was there"—I saw, I sympathized, etc.; see Clifford and Marcus 1986). The construction of new personae and identities both in fieldwork and in writing creates what I have called elsewhere a kind of circumstantial activism (Marcus 1995) in these reconfigured projects, stimulated by a style of reflexivity that places critical cultural studies much more complicitly in fields of power that it might have preferred to leave as elite hegemonic "others."

But the stakes for critical cultural studies of cultivating a serious, performed view of itself as one power/knowledge among others are greater than just a revision of the research process and its habitual modes of preferred representation. It seems to me that to prevent cultural studies scholars from speaking only to themselves, and sometimes to those they presume to speak for as well—in other words, from occupying a place of "reservation" filled with both complacency and anxiety about "relevance"—the possibilities of relationship and discussion across the frontiers of standard positioning moves must be attempted.

The process of trying to do so may not be any more satisfying—in fact, the risks for ethics, integrity, and confusion are much greater; at the current juncture, however, where the excitement about theory has diminished and the undertaking of radically reconfigured research projects in the deployment of theoretical capital has stalled or moves forward with uncertainty, there is little other choice. At least this option gives a radically reflexive cultural studies the kind of activist engagement that it has in fact imagined for itself, but through stratagems that it might never have considered undertaking.

Notes

1. I am using power/knowledge here in the spirit of Foucault's (1980) identification of the vectors and forces of power in society with the diffuse micropractices of knowledge production and their complex genealogies in the historic formation of institutions such as law, government, academia, corporations, hospitals, professions, and so on. The term power/knowledge is thus a way of labeling or marking discrete arenas of discourse and practice as they arise while retaining the sense of the fluidity and heterogeneity of the associations and connections that generate those arenas.

2. Some of the recent forays into culture theory within the (post)modernist trend of critique might be promising. It would be interesting, for example, to rethink the PD paradigm in terms of Michael Taussig's mimesis/alterity perspective (1992) derived from Walter Benjamin. Alterity/otherness is a vital concept missing from the PD paradigm, necessary if one wants to follow it into the real life of nuclear diplomacy; and Taussig's/Benjamin's notion of the mimetic is suggestive of how involvements and relationships with others through conditions of simultaneity might be materialized for study.

3. The best account of this is Strobe Talbott's (1988) *Master of the Game*, published before the collapse of the Soviet Union, which focuses on the career of Paul Nitze.

4. This passage from George P. Schultz, *Turmoil and Triumph* (1933) is used by permission of Simon & Schuster.

11

Merchants in the Temple of Scholarship

American University Press Publishing at Century's End

T. David Brent

As the present century draws to a close, university presses in the US are enjoying something of a heyday. Against all odds—diminishing markets for scholarly books, increasing costs of book manufacture, decreasing sources of outside subvention, the financial and intellectual crisis that besets many leading American universities, and technological and other social changes that have conspired to markedly reduce the status of books in American life—university presses are publishing many more titles, generating more sales and trade reviews, and offering staff salaries more commensurate with those in the commercial publishing world than at any previous time in their history.[1]

Many factors contributed to the rise of university press publishing from its humble beginnings to a respectable and important place in American culture over the course of the century. The "publish or perish" mandate, combined with the unattractive economics of publishing serious scholarship for commercial presses, has given the university press an increasingly critical status for scholars. University presses, especially the leading ones, have acquired an enormously powerful role in determining the value of scholarship not just economically, but in the more important sense of enabling scholarship to become a durable and enduring cultural commodity. By deciding what segments and kinds of scholarly production justify what kind of publication investment, if any, and in consecrating that decision with the name of the university, the university press today wields great clout in the making and breaking of intellectual prestige.

For all the potential for abuse that such an increase in power may entail, I wish here to discuss this development as a positive one—the maturation, rather than the subversion, of one of the better institutional principles founded at the end of the last century. In terms of this volume's broad themes concerning the impact of cultural critique outside academia and the power/knowledge shifts and emergent social formations discernible in the contemporary world, the evolution of the cultural power of American university presses is an example of how the very economic, political, and social developments troubling cultural critics can strengthen the resistance of a valuable cultural institution to them and under certain circumstances can increase that institution's ability to serve the function for which it was originally established. The essential continuity and power of the narratives by which the university press represents itself to itself, to the public, to the academy, and to the publishing industry at large have made it largely immune to the "crisis of representation" identified within the academy and have served not only to preserve its integrity but to increase its economic and symbolic power in a general climate inimical to such a development. Present from its inception, the university press's anomalous state as an institution suspended between the demands of the academy and the realities of the publishing industry means that it has always been in a crisis and that it has never been possible to do satisfactory "fieldwork." In this sense the current circumstance of university presses represents no significant break with the past at all.

In the course of my career as an acquisitions editor for a prominent university press, I have often found myself called upon to explain what a university press is. The question is one that university presses continually ask themselves, and the answer has important cultural implications. The answer I favor is that publishing scholarly books must be more than putting into book form the heavily footnoted, drearily written, academic niggling over obscure facts propounded by university faculty and then, to paraphrase Chester Kerr's famous statement, printing the smallest number of copies at the greatest cost and charging the highest prices to people who can least afford them (Kerr 1949). The university press must aim, rather, to publish books that further a more belletristic than technical search for truth, truth about matters of widespread relevance, and it must seek to make these books commercially available in a manner appropriate to their significance. In so doing, it must act in a manner similar to the best commercial publishers of serious literature.

As I demonstrate below, this relative autonomy from purely academic concerns has been thrust upon the American university press by the need to confront the economic realities of the general publishing industry. The prime consequence is that university presses, like their commercial counterparts, must gamble in a generally high-risk, low-profit game. University press gambling has a certain advantage over commercial press gambling, not, as is commonly thought, because of its not-for-profit status but rather because of what Pierre Bourdieu (1993) calls the process of "consecration" characterizing autonomous fields of cultural production. The university press gambles on something whose value has been certified by legitimate representatives of the community of producers and potential consumers. This certification process enables cultural capital to be converted into symbolic, if not economic, capital. The leading university presses are the ones that have proven most successful at this feat of prestidigitation; by refining the economic consequences of the consecration process, they have developed the most autonomy and prestige.

Those in a position to critique the practices and assumptions of university press publishing are already within the sphere of consecration in the sense that the quality and standards of university life will always be reflected in the lists of those presses. University presses have been criticized for publishing books of very limited interest, for the slowness of the review and decision-making process, for preserving the status quo, and for boring book designs, poor distribution and incompetent marketing, but they have never, as far as I know, been criticized for believing in the importance of publishing scholarly writing. The university press must work to overcome the defects of the university, which it reflects; it must fight for its existence as a decided underdog in a consumer economy addicted to flashy, transient, "time-saving" devices.[2] Thus, critique in this realm is designed to help the gambler gamble better, not to abstain from betting on the enduring significance of scholarship.

"WHAT IS A UNIVERSITY PRESS?"

Somewhat like critical philosophers, and unlike most commercial presses, which operate in principle as for-profit organizations, university press publishers have from the beginning reflected upon the nature of their enterprise and attempted to affirm its value. I have placed the question in quotes because I wish in this section not only to outline the answers that have been proposed but even more to offer some ideas about why it is so frequently asked and what that suggests about the field.

University press directors and others who have addressed the question typically affirm the mission of the press to disseminate "original and significant" contributions to scholarship that will "advance knowledge" or "stimulate research" in recognized areas of inquiry. Many of these answers make explicit reference to the premises upon which the first American university press was founded. For example, in his Foreword to Gene R. Hawes's "handbook" on American university press publishing, entitled *To Advance Knowledge*, Chester Kerr, then director of Yale University Press, wrote:

> Daniel Coit Gilman was a Yale man who became the first president of Johns Hopkins—and perceived instantly that there is a third force in any responsible institution of higher learning. In addition to teaching (the faculty) and research (the library) there must be publication (the faculty and the library and the university press). Advance knowledge "far and wide" was his message and the medium was to be the scholarly publishing house. (Hawes 1967:iii)

Gilman did indeed establish the Johns Hopkins University Press in 1878 as an integral part of the parent university, setting a precedent followed next by William Rainey Harper, president of the University of Chicago, who established his press as one of the three main divisions of the University in 1891, and subsequently by the founders of virtually all university presses in this country. Among Gilman's purposes was to give those outside the university access to the teachings that went on in its lecture halls and to establish a publication outlet for scholars who had difficulty getting their research published commercially. Like many of the older university presses, Hopkins's first publications were scientific journals, in this case in mathematics and chemistry. It was not until 1887 that Hopkins published its first book; indeed, it was not until 1890 that it changed its name from "Publication Agency of the University" to its current name (Hawes 1967:30).

In a brief pamphlet published in the early 1980s (and currently accessible on the American Association of University Press's Internet site), "What is a University Press?," Sheldon Meyer, vice-president of the Trade Editorial Division of Oxford University Press, and L. E. Phillabaum, director of Louisiana State University Press, also invoked Gilman's founding vision. Their opening paragraph reads:

> If, as has been said, the true university is a collection of books, then university presses have had much to do with the making of universities. The essential purpose of presses, as the publishing division of their parent institutions, is to serve scholars and scholarship in general. They exist on the cutting edge of knowledge and often function as the natural outlet for information, theory, and methodology that will influence human endeavor in the decades and generations to come. (Meyer and Phillabaum c. 1984:1)

The authors go on, in the space of a mere seven pages, to emphasize the uniqueness of the market for scholarly books, the often profound abilities of university press staff to understand a scholarly subject and its potential market, the differences between various types of press arrangements with the parent university, the question of what university presses publish, and the extent of cooperation—rather than competition—between university presses. Virtually throughout they stress the problem of finances and the necessarily subsidized nature of scholarly publishing. In tune, perhaps, with the political message of the early 1980s when it was published, they conclude by advocating austerity.

The pamphlet is thoroughly idealistic in addressing the realities of scholarly publishing. It expresses confidence that at its best the university press reaches out, through its publications, to a broad "society of scholars, and to serious readers outside academic life," and that the review process and imprint of the press's faculty advisory board "insure the quality and significance of the books on the press's list." The authors go on:

> University presses exist in two separate worlds—that of the university and higher education generally, and that of the book publishing industry. For this reason a press must operate with considerable autonomy; although it may be one flesh with its parent and not an independent business, it must still manage its affairs as if it were truly a business. Because a press is part of a university, its purpose is to advance knowledge rather than to make a profit. Yet it must function with as much business acumen in achieving a rigidly budgeted deficit or limited profit as does a commercial publishing house which must show a profit for its shareholders. In times of financial stringency in the academic world, the ability of a university press to operate on effective business principles is essential. (Meyer and Phillabaum c. 1984:3)

In my view, this statement, and the pamphlet as a whole, have a canonical status for university presses, suggesting that such presses must behave as dutiful children to the parents who have given them life and purpose but who may be unable fully to support them. The parents thrust the child into the world in the hope that, through honorable means consistent with the family's beliefs, the child will be able both to support itself and to keep the family name in good standing. The child is empowered, indeed required, to act in the name of the parent, ideally supporting itself and bringing honor to the family name.

The same image can be perceived in classified ads placed by parent universities for university press positions. For example, in the July 3, 1995, issue of *Publisher's Weekly*, the industry's main trade journal, the University of Alabama (note: not the Press), placed the following ad:

> The University of Alabama seeks a Director who is committed to academic excellence. Also Editor-in-Chief, the Director coordinates manuscript acquisitions, supervises a staff of twenty, and is responsible for the editorial and fiscal integrity of the Press. The Director works closely with the Press

> Committee and reports to the Provost and Academic Vice President of the University. The Press publishes about forty new titles a year in a range of academic fields and is the state's only fully staffed professional publisher of scholarly books. Candidates must have at least a bachelor's degree and significant administrative and editorial experience in publishing.

A middle- to small-level university press, the University of Alabama Press was established in 1945, making it roughly the same age as most American university presses, the majority of which were founded in the '30s and '40s. As in many smaller presses, Alabama's director is responsible not only for administration and "fiscal integrity" but also for editorial direction and "coordination" of manuscript acquisition. Although the separation of such functions as administration and list-building, or editorial development, characterizes a further stage of professional development such as that at the leading university presses as well as at most commercial presses, the university has no hesitation in identifying its press as "the state's only fully staffed professional publisher of scholarly books." Indeed, calling attention to the fact that the staff consists of professionals and not, I suppose, untrained or part-time employees, and that it is the only press of its kind in the state, suggests a certain cachet, perhaps in the hope of attracting candidates from the world of commercial publishing. By explicitly recognizing its press as a professional publisher "committed to academic excellence," the University of Alabama demonstrates its complete acceptance of the founding principles of American university press publishing as articulated by Daniel Coit Gilman in 1878 (see, for example, *Johns Hopkins Gazette*, Sept. 25, 1995).

One final example of how an American university press—in this case one of the oldest, largest, and most distinguished—talks about itself and is talked about by others in relation to its originary agenda will illustrate many of the themes discussed thus far. On June 20, 1992, the University of Chicago Press celebrated its one hundredth anniversary with a party in the historic Chicago Stock Exchange Trading Room, owned and reserved for special occasions by the Art Institute of Chicago. The celebration was a gala affair, suggesting both the prestige and affluence of its host. In attendance were senior press staff, several influential members of the university faculty, a number of directors of other prominent university presses, a distinguished European publisher, editors of newspaper book review sections, and numerous celebrated authors. Jacques Barzun and Jacques Derrida sent statements that were read in absentia. The whole set of formal speeches was subsequently published in a limited edition volume entitled *One Hundred Years of Scholarly Publishing* (University of Chicago Press 1992).

Though appropriately lighthearted in tone, the celebration was also the occasion for some earnest reflection on the state of publishing in the US today, the nature of scholarly publishing, and the history, development, and contribution of the University of Chicago Press. The European contingent in particular gave articulate voice to the very discursive strategies by which the American university press has defined itself historically. The Hungarian novelist Stephen Vizinczey, some of whose out-of-print books Chicago has reprinted, set his gloomy criticisms of the decline of interest in serious literature and the rise of low-brow consumer culture against expressions of gratitude for what the Chicago Press stands for and has accomplished over the century. In a remarkable passage, Derrida offered perhaps the most penetrating synopsis:

> In situations where sometimes intellectual wars are raging, liberating in some academics the least admissible passions, provoking dogmatic tightening or intolerant behavior, what I have in fact most admired in the ethics of the Press...is the great independence, the serenity, the spirit of open tolerance—in short, the liberalism in the most demanding sense: not the liberalism of the laissez-faire, laisser-passer of the free market (with the laws of which—I won't forget this, for one must never forget it, and vigilance here is an intellectual and political duty—the always ambiguous strategy of a publishing house must reckon), but that which is required by the necessity for critical debate, the testing of arguments, of knowledge and thought, by the differences in cultures, languages, traditions, by the respect for heritages, faithfulness to all heritages,

> but also faithfulness to what is coming, I mean to the future, to the demands or appeal of what has not yet been understood by everyone and that intrigues, worries, and incites reflexes of frightened or repressive preservation—here or there, in whatever age, on the left or on the right. But...in its policy toward books the University of Chicago Press has most often appeared to me exemplary in this regard...[T]he University of Chicago Press represents a kind of luminous and indispensable reference, both a system of intellectual rules put to test by a tradition to cultivate, and an example of institutional success and technical performance. (University of Chicago Press 1992:40–41)

Press director Morris Philipson later summed up the occasion as a celebration of the fact that the press "has done its job extremely well, according to its own lights," and that its original purpose, established with the founding of the university, namely, to publish serious books, "has been fulfilled in each generation as serious people responsible for the Press have interpreted it." (Philipson's statement also suggests an aspect of the consecration process of an autonomous field of cultural production, to be discussed below.) The presence of food and drink, of texts read by members, so to speak, of the family, of the invocation of a lengthy time span and of the fulfillment of the original agenda "in each generation," reminded me of the Passover seder ritual. Cries of *dayeinu* ("it would have sufficed for us!"), sung after every seder, would not have been inappropriate. It would suffice for a university press to have succeeded in even one of the great things Derrida cited, for in being able to publish scholarly books without going out of business, it has accomplished something akin to the miracle of the Exodus from Egypt.

Derrida's speech touched on a number of points important for my overall argument. First, he asserts that in the face of the intellectual uncertainties of academics, the press has remained independent, serene, and tolerantly open. He calls this "liberalism in the most demanding sense," immediately qualifying his observation with the recognition that the press must adopt an "always ambiguous strategy," that it exists, as Meyer and Phillabaum put it, in "two separate worlds."

He then goes on to recite the kinds of goals articulated by Gilman, Kerr, Hawes, and all, noted above, stressing a system of intellectual rules, institutional success, and technical virtuosity. So precise, concise, and comprehensive is Derrida's account of the rhetorical dynamics, the aspirations and the perils, that have characterized American university presses over their century-long existence, one might almost think he had read the Meyer and Phillabaum pamphlet. Derrida also touches briefly on something I will explore later for the purpose of clarifying the notion of autonomy, as Bourdieu understands it, and that is the idea of responsiveness (Derrida calls it "faithfulness") "to the demands or appeal of what has not yet been understood by everyone."

For the moment, however, I wish to turn explicitly to the reasons why the question "What is a university press?" has been asked, inscribed in pamphlets, encoded in classified ads, and answered in anniversary celebrations. The ritualistic quality of the question is, I have suggested, quite evident. It truly does have something of the quality of the Four Questions of Passover, which all begin: Why is this night different from all other nights? The question itself appears really to be a prelude to an examination of how university press publishing, and scholarly publishing in general, differ from commercial publishing. It is asked periodically, particularly in times when it might seem to university presses that their mission is in jeopardy and the only solution is to throw in the towel or behave in ways more like general trade publishers. In reaffirming the original goals, then, there is an admonition that no matter how "always ambiguous" the strategy actually used in practice, what remains paramount is the advancement of knowledge, not making money from selling a product that happens to be a book. The more than one-hundred-year tradition of affirming Gilman's original definition sets the university press apart from all commercial publishing, preventing it from wholly succumbing to publishing only what sells and recognizing it for persevering in a business whose principal satisfactions must remain symbolic.

Gilman's definition thus functions ritualistically, not to impose a transcendent, unattainable ideal, but to affirm identity, to warn, and to inspire. On this reading it is a way of sustaining, giving meaning to, and defending day-to-day pragmatic decisions and practices in the face of conflictual reality. The fact that the texts I have cited here were either published by the umbrella organization of university presses, the American Association of University Presses, or self-published (and in the case of the Alabama ad, intentionally directed toward the trade publishing industry) further suggests their function as inspirational statements of orthodoxy.

THE REALITIES OF THE FIELD OF SCHOLARLY PUBLISHING

What then are the unique realities of existing in "two separate worlds" for university presses? These consist, in point of fact, of participating in three separate worlds: the technology and economics of book publishing in general, the economic life of universities, and the nature of academic life and scholarly production as these have all developed in the US in the twentieth century.

At the beginning, of course, all these realities were quite different than they are today, and it may rightly be questioned whether a "Publication Agency of the University" had to be concerned with any of them. When the president of the university functioned as the director of the press, the head of the press was really a "secretary" who arranged for the printing and manufacture of the materials so designated by the president-director. Whatever autonomy the press-as-publication-office had in terms of editing manuscripts and deciding on typeface, kind and quality of paper and binding, design, and possibly print run, the press had no autonomy whatsoever in the selection of what to publish. It was given materials to publish, not asked to select them on its own, and the economics of the enterprise were all the president-director's (that is, the university administration's) problem, not the press's.

It was obvious right from the start, however, that this arrangement would not work out economically or in terms of fully satisfying the goal of "advancing knowledge far and wide." Even the simplest kind of printing-publishing has its economic problems, and unless the publisher has a benefactor or source of income indifferent to perpetual deficits, these must be handled by someone experienced with the market for print materials. This reality has been true of the publishing industry ever since Johannes Gutenberg invented moveable type, borrowed money from his lawyer to produce a splendid edition of one of the most important books of the times, the Mazarin Bible, lost all his money, his press, and his type, and was exiled in penury from Mainz, his hometown. Gradually, over the course of the first couple of decades of a university press's operation, as the "Gutenberg Principle," so to speak, caught up with the "Gilman Principle," the secretary of the press took over more and more responsibility for its total operation, finances, and editorial direction, eventually becoming a "director."

The initial lists of the first university presses consisted entirely of journals and books submitted by its faculty, resulting in the widespread misconception of university presses held even today by the general public as well as some people in the commercial publishing world. Meanwhile the head of the press, under whatever title, had to confront the implications of rapidly mounting deficits resulting not just from the failure to recover manufacturing costs but also from rising overhead involving physical housing, salaries, and the need for diversification into divisions such as publication (editorial), manufacture and purchasing (production), and retail (marketing and business). Many broad changes were undertaken to address this problem. Presses eventually ceased serving as the sole publication office of the university (in some cases, they also stopped providing accounting services for various academic departments) and became more internally diversified. Most germane for present purposes, the dawning recognition and acceptance of the need to publish books that could sell more than a few hundred copies and so add to the income of the press (these were called "property books" by the University of Chicago Press as early as 1905) meant that the staff of the press began actively to participate in the selection process (see University of Chicago Press 1967:xi–xxx).

The specific story of any one university press's development can be seen to have ramifications for the institution in general through the recognition that very early on both the university and its press had to accommodate to the economics of general publishing, and that this spurred on the necessity to "operate with considerable autonomy," as Meyer and Phillabaum put it. By the mid-1970s, when I became an active participant-observer in this field, numerous university presses had become multimillion-dollar-per-year businesses, boasting titles on their lists that would be the envy of many commercial publishers. The top personnel of the top presses had been recruited, to a large extent, from commercial publishing (particularly the sector that publishes serious nonfiction), and the status of the university press had grown tremendously. No longer was it perceived as a second-best form of publication, and university press lists included great scholars and prestigious European, British, and American series. Moreover, these publishers offered high-quality manuscript editing and production and a longer time in print than most commercial presses could afford. By acquiring reprint rights for important scholarly books that had been declared out of print by commercial houses (which increasingly were being bought out by giant corporations with no prior commitment to publishing), university presses demonstrated that they were capable of salvaging cultural capital that commercial presses had deemed unprofitable.

The past twenty-five years, however, have seen the acceleration of changes in university press publishing probably unmatched since the initial period when they were just getting started. The mid-1970s were not the happiest of times economically, and the shrinking market for scholarly books, particularly hardbound books, forced reductions in print runs of up to 50 percent and dramatically escalated list prices. Though the rise in book prices in general never kept pace with inflation, the declining significance of books in American life which had become noticeable over several decades meant that books were perceived as too expensive by potential buyers. Keeping costs down through new technological means became a major preoccupation. Production technology changed rapidly; within a short time, from roughly the mid-'70s to the early '80s, virtually all books were being typeset electronically. Finally, these economic, social, and technological changes were accompanied, no doubt due to the greatly increased number of academics and the rise of the syndrome of linking promotion to book publication, by a vast increase in the volume of scholarly writing and concomitantly of submissions to university presses. Acquisition editors were besieged by submissions as early as the late 1960s, when Hawes's "handbook" was published; by the mid-'70s, given the economic crisis, "inordinate selectivity," "irresistibility," and "economic viability" were the shibboleths by which editors dealt with the slush pile of unsolicited or otherwise unconsecrated manuscripts submitted to them.

Confronting the economics of general publishing, in other words, continued to cause transformations in the selection process at university presses. Today, editorial decisions still must be approved by faculty committees, but professors simply do not have the time (and never had the publishing expertise) to control, as opposed to participate in, the process. Presses compete for prestigious, prospectively best-selling manuscripts. Editors tolerate multiple submissions, a practice once universally condemned;[3] they are empowered to offer advance contracts and fairly sizable monetary advances, both virtually unheard-of twenty-five years ago; and they spend less time, as a rule, actually editing manuscripts and more time cultivating networks of scholars who can both produce books and serve as advisors on and consecrators of other scholars' work that the editor may be considering. While perhaps constrained by university policy not to reject without outside review manuscripts submitted by faculty members of the parent university (the lists of numerous university presses still consist largely of books by the home faculty), the degree to which the lists of leading presses reflect the intellectual interests and publishing judgments of the editors has never been greater. Not surprisingly, the performance of university press editors is now evaluated as much in terms of bottom-line contribution as it is in terms of being a good "servant" of "scholars and scholarship in general" (Meyer and Phillabaum c. 1984).

A poignant article in *Publisher's Weekly* (1994) sums up the current situation at a leading American university press. Jim Clark, director of the University of California Press, was interviewed about the press's reported fiscal crisis at the end of its first century. The article stated, "The Press is exploring new technologies, looking for ways to cut its production costs in an increasingly strained fiscal context, and broaden its audience while at the same time following its mandate to produce scholarly works." In the context of the State of California's fiscal crunch, which has adversely affected the university system and forced a potential 50 percent reduction in library budgets, Clark was quoted as saying, "Our fear is that books which are most important—those of significant scholarship—would be cut first because they sell the fewest copies." He went on to discuss the possibility of acquiring more "trade-oriented titles" in order to increase revenues while publishing what he called "monographs" on-demand or in CD-ROM format. Committed to the press's "integrity and character," Clark was searching for ways, through the use of new technology, to continue to publish "least-sellers." He expressed concern that the "whole character" of the press could change, perhaps implying that it could be forced to discontinue publishing short-run books and become more commercial in order to survive financially. He defended the "ambiguous strategy" of maintaining the original purpose, which distinguishes university from commercial publishing, while becoming more businesslike and thereby strengthening the similarities between university and commercial publishing.

Clark's statement that "the most important books—those of significant scholarship...sell the fewest copies," must be read in light of the fact that *PW* speaks to and for the trade publishing world. The statement is in fact highly questionable, for there is a proven intrinsic relationship between scholarly stature or significance and sales. Most likely, Clark meant that he fears being unable to publish works of scholarship significant enough to be bought in book form by only a small number of persons (an insight almost as old as university press publishing itself), and that he is trying to find an economically viable, perhaps nontraditional, way of continuing to do so. From *PW*'s point of view, the article can be read as trade publishing's way of saying, "I told you so. You really can't publish that kind of book successfully, can you?" From the trade publisher's profit-oriented perspective, the economics of scholarly publishing have always appeared doomed and hopeless—though it is a rare trade publisher who understands those economics.

THE PUBLISHER AS GAMBLER

In the 500-year history of publishing, few publishers of any stripe have been free of worry about finances. The structure and dynamics of the industry in general, as described by sociologists Lewis A. Coser, Charles Kadushin, and Walter W. Powell in *Books: The Culture and Commerce of Publishing*, one of the only such studies ever undertaken, suggest why this is so:

> (1) The industry sells its products—like any commodity—in a market, but in a market that, in contrast for [sic] many other products, is fickle and often uncertain. (2) The industry is decentralized among a number of sectors whose operations bear little resemblance to each other. (3) These operations are characterized by a mixture of modern mass-production methods and craftlike procedures. (4) The industry remains perilously poised between the requirements and restraints of commerce and the responsibilities and obligations it must bear as a prime guardian of the symbolic culture of the nation. (Coser, Kadushin, and Powell 1982:7)

Publishing is, in short, a fairly miserable business with big cultural and economic stakes and uncertain returns.

Coser, Kadushin, and Powell favor the metaphor of the publisher as "gatekeeper" of culture, though they admit early on that the publisher as "shaper" of culture is equally valid. Behind this ambiguity, as I see it, is something akin to the anthropological debate about "structure" and "agency." The publisher of general books, as opposed to textbooks, instruction manuals, and the like, is dependent on authors to generate the essence of the product brought to market. The publisher may have a variety of influences on the eventual product, shaping it through suggestions to the author, demanding cuts or additions, and even rewriting whole sections, in addition, of course, to packaging it in the manner deemed most appealing. The more important question, again, is how the decision to publish is made. Does the publisher actively solicit the book and decide to publish it out of personal enthusiasm, market demand, politics, cultural aspiration, or a combination of these factors? Does the book simply appear over the transom, and the publisher, in need of something to sell, thinks "Why not?" To what extent does building a list reflect agency or autonomy, and to what extent do larger social and economic forces impinge on the publisher and determine enthusiasm in the first place?

Ethnographic, social historical, and philosophical methods are required to explore such questions.[4] The publisher's point of view, on the other hand, is resolutely pragmatic. No matter how experienced one may be either as a gatekeeper or a shaper, one is virtually always in a position of great uncertainty where any act of agency is like that of a professional gambler. Regardless of how carefully shaped to respond to a particular perceived demand—no matter how good the publisher's hand—the product brought to market stands a good chance of failing to return one's investment promptly, if at all. The publisher, like a good gambler, must be enthusiastic and confident about its hand (or at least appear to be so), for it has invested a great deal of time and money up front on a unique product that will rarely sell more than one copy to a given customer (in other words, a small-ticket item that behaves more like a big-ticket item economically), a product that moreover requires an act of concentration, namely reading, that is intensively time-consuming, in a society that values products that "save" time. Conventional market research of the kind used by other commercial enterprises is virtually impossible; publishing wit has it that the first printing of a book is its market research. The risk that a publisher takes in making such an inherently problematic product available is thus comparable, in several respects, to that taken by motion picture and theater producers, art dealers, and the like, although I believe that in its full dimensions book publishing is unique in the whole field of cultural production.

The only trump card, so to speak, that the publisher/gambler can hold is when the first printing of a book, the size of which generally determines its list price, attracts a larger market than was initially anticipated. In that situation, the book can be reprinted for only the costs of paper, printing, binding, and associated business and marketing expenses, without the original bulk of overhead associated with acquisition, editing, design, and typesetting. Through experience with books that perform in this manner, publishers can develop a profitable backlist that gives them long-range economic stability and reduces the damage done by books that either did not perform up to expectations or, in the case of profit-oriented publishers, only performed as well as planned.[5]

The uncertainties attendant upon the whole business of book publishing cause individual presses to act in a variety of ways. Commercial publishers today, by and large, refuse to gamble on developing a backlist; they get in and get out quickly with books catering to popular tastes or offering solutions to popular anxieties, and let them go out of print as quickly as such tastes and anxieties change. Many titles of more long-range or specialized interest, whose markets do not meet the minimum level set by the commercial houses, may then be picked up for reprint by houses, such as university presses, with lower operating requirements, more expertise in reaching the nontrade market for a particular book, and a vested interest in developing a successful backlist.

University presses thus will gamble on books that commercial presses cannot or will not touch. When Jacques Derrida's earliest books appeared in France in the late 1960s, for example, no American commercial press was willing to risk translating and publishing them in English. The fact that they had been published by such distinguished houses as Editions de Minuit and Editions du Seuil, and that prominent American literary critics and comparatists had begun to take them seriously, led such university presses as Hopkins and Chicago—the two oldest in the nation—to gamble that over the long run Derrida would establish an audience here, something that indeed came to pass by the early 1980s. Today publishing a major new work by Derrida in English translation represents almost no gamble for a university press. His books are virtually guaranteed to sell several thousand copies in both hardbound and paperback editions within a short time after publication and to remain in print for the foreseeable future. (It should be noted, however, that Derrida's average sales of 5,000 to 20,000-plus copies would still not make him a particularly hot property for most commercial publishers.) If, on the other hand, Derrida had not established an American following in a relatively short period of time, or if he loses his following in the future, his books would likely have been, and would likely be, out of print. Although the length of time in print for university press titles is still longer by nearly an order of magnitude than for the most commercially oriented houses, this life span has decreased markedly over the past twenty-five years. It is no longer uncommon for university press books to be declared out of print or "out of stock indefinitely" (implying that ownership of publication rights is retained even though the book is unavailable) within five to ten years of original publication, whereas in the mid-'70s it was closer to twenty years.

Be that as it may, university presses typically gamble on the long-range success of a book in a way similar to most cosmopolitan

European and British houses.[6] Whereas for the commercial publisher the economics of publishing a title are weighed in terms of the popularity of its subject matter and treatment, for the university press there must be an intrinsic relationship between the economics of the book and its scholarly significance. The general cultural assumption, invoked in *PW*'s interview with Jim Clark and sometimes used to explain a difficult decision to a prospective author, is that scholarly significance is quite independent of marketability, so that although a work may be truly excellent in its field, so few people buy books in that field that the publisher cannot afford to invest resources in it.

In fact, this assumption is largely false. First, as European, especially Dutch, publishers were the first to prove, highly specialized materials can be published without financial loss if they enjoy a reasonably hard market, or inelastic demand, regardless of how small. Hard markets for scholarly books generally exist when there is a broad disciplinary consensus among researchers about problems, methods, and evidence, in short, about what constitutes an advance in the field. Certain branches of philology, linguistics, archaeology, paleontology, and economics can be considered hard markets for books today, and the publisher's risk in these areas can be accordingly minimal. In contrast, in most of the social sciences and humanities and certainly in the case of serious fiction, consensus is much rarer and often temporary when it exists. The market for such books, consequently, is soft; the publisher cannot count on all persons committed to a particular field to recognize a particular book as a "must read" (or even a "must buy") and can never be sure in advance how large the audience will be. In this case, the assumption that scholarly significance may be independent of economics is equally misleading, for if a book does not reach out to the number of persons who constitute the serious readers in a particular field, how can its scholarly significance be determined? Can a book have stature in a field without an audience? The significance of such books must be measured, in part, by sales. This is by no means to say that the best books are those that sell the best, but rather that there is still an intrinsic relationship between significance and sales, one that in some cases can be proven over the long range as well as the short. Indeed, as I have suggested, university presses leave the door open for the long range as long as they can afford to—sometimes even longer!—and may in some cases reopen it after a number of years.

How does a university press determine what sort of gamble to take with a particular title? Let's look at the present volume, the market for which would not appear to be a hard one. As this volume explicitly recognizes, the disciplines in question (cultural anthropology and cultural studies) are currently so fraught with contention that it is impossible to predict whether it will be perceived as making an advance in a particular issue and will therefore, like *Writing Culture* and *Anthropology as Cultural Critique*, sell over 20,000 copies or, whether, like the average edited collection or monograph, it will sell only 800 to 1500 copies. The reputation of several of the contributors and the volume editor for producing cutting-edge scholarship that is, as Derrida (University of Chicago Press 1992:8) would say, "faithful" to "the demands or appeal of what has not yet been understood by everyone," may lead the publisher to expect that it will live up to its prototypes in the marketplace. If knowledgeable and informed authorities in its fields agree that the volume fulfills its promise, the publisher would certainly feel more enthusiastic in taking a bigger risk on it. Since the volume is neither excessively long nor technically complex, the publisher is likely to be able to price it effectively (at the level that readers in these fields have come to accept), even with a conservative print run, and may sit back and wait and see if the volume's claims are borne out in the long run. Such conservatism is still an economic gamble; no matter what run the publishers sets, a better one can be found retrospectively. The established reputation of the contributors and the endorsement of qualified advisors means, however, that the press will be taking little or no risk on the book's symbolic value. By packaging, pricing, and promoting it aggressively to the perceived intended audience, the publisher virtually guarantees that the volume's cultural capital will be converted into symbolic capital without losing economic capital. Publication plus effective distribution equals prestige.

University press gambling thus involves the commodification of scholarly productions through the use of the representations of other scholars in advertisements and publicity campaigns aimed at the community of producers and at the so-called serious or educated reader outside academia. The university press serves as the "natural outlet" (Meyer and Phillabaum c. 1984) for scholars and scholarship in that the way it commodifies (represents and distributes) scholarly production tends to naturalize the categories of scholarship. The press gives its books a particular location in seasonal catalogs, as books of general or special interest, with accordingly different implied advertising budgets and discounts offered to retailers. It also gives them subject designations that result in their occupying specific locations in libraries and bookstores, and it positions them on particular subject lists that have assumed a recognized place in the disciplines out of which they come. Thus does the press attempt to fulfill its mandate to "advance knowledge far and wide."

From this perspective, the university press does not suffer from the conflicts of ideology, lack of consensus, and anxieties about traditional conceptions and methods that may be present in the academic world. It buys them and sells them. If the press is adept at this buying and selling, it creates the illusion (see the dictionary etymology of "prestige" as a conjurer's trick) that it knows what it is doing, that it picks and is picked by the best and most successful scholars. The leading university presses thus most fulfill Daniel Coit Gilman's original principle, and in so doing they set an example emulated by all university presses.

THE UNIVERSITY PRESS AS AN AUTONOMOUS FIELD OF CULTURAL PRODUCTION

> In short, when the only usable, effective capital is the (mis)recognized legitimate capital called "prestige" or "authority," the economic capital that cultural undertakings generally require cannot secure the specific profits produced by the field—not the "economic" profits they always imply—unless it is reconverted into symbolic capital. For the author, the critic, the art dealer, the publisher, or the theatre manager, *the only legitimate accumulation consists in making a name for oneself,* a known, recognized name, a capital of consecration implying a power to consecrate objects (with a trademark or signature) or persons (through publication, exhibition, etc.) and therefore to give value, and to appropriate profits from this operation. (Bourdieu 1993:75; emphasis added)

Bourdieu's writings on the "economy of practice" of the field of cultural production, or the business of producing symbolic goods, have an appropriately cynical quality about them. As a sociologist, he builds on Kant's analysis of the disinterestedness of the judgment of taste by pointing out how cultural producers have an interest in disinterestedness, in the production of belief in the symbolic value of a good through disavowal of any financial interest, which in turn gives that good an economic value (and is intended to do so by people in business in this economically reversed world). He sees the market for symbolic goods as it has developed since the mid-nineteenth century, when aristocratic and ecclesiastical patronage was in decline, as centrally tied to what he calls the "logic of the process of autonomization" (Bourdieu 1993:112). He analyzes this logic in relation to the notion of demand. Heteronomous cultural producers are those beholden to patrons or clients or to the demands of markets over which they have no control; Renaissance artists or those producing tourist art in Montmartre could serve as examples. Autonomous cultural producers, in their most perfect form, aim only at an audience of other producers; Bourdieu gives the Symbolist poets as the prime example here, but he extends his scope to include other fields of production which constitute their own markets and are allied with an educational system that legitimates them. He specifically analyzes the highbrow French publisher Editions de Minuit as falling into this category. The heteronomous principle is "success, as measured by indices such as book sales, number of theatrical performances, etc., or honors, appointments, etc." The autonomous principle, on the other hand, is "degree specific consecration (literary or artistic prestige), i.e., the degree of recognition accorded by those who recognize no other criterion of legitimacy than recognition by those whom they recognize." Bourdieu says that producers in this sector base their practices in a game of "loser-wins"; he calls them "merchants in the temple" who "make their living by tricking the artist or writer into taking the consequences of his or her statutory profession of disinterestedness" (Bourdieu 1993:40).

The university press, as I have described it, stands in a peculiar position with respect to Bourdieu's analyses. It is too simplistic to view it as heteronomous in one aspect, namely its dependence on the "laws" of the market for scholarly books, and autonomous in the other, namely its disavowal of commercial motives and its production for the audience of producers. Neither point is strictly true. On the one hand, instead of responding to a perceived market demand, the university press enthusiastically tells the market what it should demand; on the other hand, it must embrace, however two-facedly, commercial motives, and it strives to publish for a wider audience than those who, even in the case of the harder scholarly disciplines, produce scholarly works. The university press is thus suspended, like a magic floating wand in a magnetic force field, between two principles vying for dominance over each other.

Even this image, however, does not capture the full picture. It is necessary to be very specific here about the whole range of freedoms and responsibilities, capabilities and constraints, of university press publishing in order to justify calling it an "autonomous field of cultural production" in Bourdieu's terms. In terms of freedom, the university press has gained, as I have shown, considerable independence from its parent university in deciding which books to ask its faculty committee to approve for publication. The university acts neither as its patron nor its client, nor necessarily even as its benefactor (as in the case of numerous presses that have become independent corporations). As long as it permits its name to be used as imprimatur, however, the parent university remains the "capital of consecration." Therefore the university press is not strictly free to publish whatever it wants; it is only free to conform to the standards of excellence of the university and the scholarly community that the university recognizes. (How reminiscent all this is—a resemblance that did not escape Bourdieu—to Kant's analysis of the "free play of the imagination" in aesthetics (Kant 1951[1793]).) Though thrust into the world, the university press still bears the parent's name; in making a name for itself, good or bad, it reflects upon the parent, and the parent can then praise or disown it.

An example here concerning the fate of a particular Midwestern university press in the mid-1970s will be instructive. This press, founded in the late 1950s, rapidly built up a rather sizable list of books in phenomenology, existentialism, and hermeneutics, publishing not only prominent American scholars but also some of the most distinguished

European authors in translation, including Derrida. The story goes that the press was running a deficit. In response, the parent university, which is known to be extremely affluent but penny-wise and somewhat anti-intellectual to boot, hired an independent scholar, a member of the philosophy department of an elite East Coast university, to evaluate the press's list, perhaps reasoning that if the list's prestige value turned out to be as low as its economic value, the press would have to go.

The consultant-philosopher was an analytically trained logician, one of the most distinguished in the US, and her assessment of the press's list was dismal. Based on this scholar's recommendation, the parent university canceled the press's editorial program entirely, leaving it to operate solely as a backlist publisher and distributor of existing stock. The press remained editorially inactive for about a decade, during which time it merged its distribution operation with that of a much larger Midwestern university press and sold off a significant part of its offensive phenomenology list to other university presses seeking to build up their holdings in this area (which, over the same period, came to occupy a respectable position in American scholarly circles). Under the editorial direction of a "book person" (now, ironically, an executive editor at the press of the same university whose logician caboshed the press in question), the press began to build its lists again and, by the late 1980s, was deemed stable and successful enough to become a member of the American Association of University Presses.

This story serves to illustrate the kind of dependence a university press has upon its parent institution. The parent institution can pull the rug completely out from under the press, and it is a safe bet that even the leading university presses remain to varying degrees vulnerable to the approval of the university, in terms both of fiscal responsibility and more importantly of evaluations by scholars designated by the university. If the university press has consistently demonstrated its competence to control both of these dimensions, it will have "done its job extremely well, according to its own lights," as Philipson (1977) put it, and it can throw a party at the Stock Exchange Room to demonstrate its autonomy in an economically reversed world.

If the press to which I've referred had been balancing its budget, it may very well not have been scrutinized for its prestige; the ability to market its lists successfully could be taken as an indication that they were legitimately responding to, or anticipating, a scholarly demand. If, on the other hand, the press's prestige was found to be certifiably high (or if it were simply serving as the "publication agency" of the university), it may have been allowed to continue building its list while running a deficit. Prestige is really the key factor; if the lists of a university press are merely commercially successful, the university would be better advised to put its money in stocks and bonds or even racehorses. Publishing is such a risky and low-profit business that it would not make sense for a university to invest in it, or allow it to operate under its name, unless the symbolic returns were there. Bourdieu is quite right in saying that if the heteronomous principle were to remain unchallenged, fields of cultural production like the university press would disappear (Bourdieu 1993:38). But he is also correct that no matter how autonomous a field becomes, it continues to be affected by the laws of the field that encompasses it, namely those of economic and political profit (Bourdieu 1993:39).

"All interest," writes Kant, "presupposes or generates a want, and as the determining ground of assent leaves the judgment about the object no longer free" (Kant 1951[1793]:44). Outside the domain of pure aesthetic contemplation, however, there is virtually no domain that does not answer to an "interest of reason or imagination," and Bourdieu has shown, following Kant, that even the most autonomous domains of cultural production are tied to interests which, in order to be fulfilled, must be covered up, minimized, or denied. The rhetoric of American university press publishing, from the beginning to the present day, has functioned to promote its developing autonomy regardless of the winds of change in the force fields it occupies: the economy, the university, and scholarly life. If, at the present moment, the university press is able to maintain itself successfully as a bulwark against the encroachment of the corporate mentality of commercial publishing into scholarly life, its autonomy should and must, within the limits I have outlined, be applauded by all those who continue to have an interest in the life of the mind. At the same time, one must never forget that increased autonomy is purchased at the expense of certainty in the field of cultural production.

Notes

1. *Publisher's Weekly* (1995a) in fact used the title "University Presses 'On the Upbeat'" for a report on the 1995 annual meeting of the American Association of University Presses. The most recent statistics issued by the Book Industry Study Group show that university press growth in both unit sales and dollar volume compares favorably to the most rapidly growing segments of the industry as a whole (see *Publisher's Weekly* 1995b).

2. Jacques Barzun's essay "The Paradoxes of Publishing" in Barzun (1971) contains many fine insights into how publishers can market their works more effectively without demeaning them. See also the chapter "Writing and Publishing" in Brent (1962), especially pp. 188–94.

3. See Philipson (1977) for an excellent statement of the ethical and practical implications of encouraging multiple submissions. The burden that this practice places upon the limited resources of university presses has continued to grow over the years. In my view, it represents a kind of academic streetwalking by victims of abusive tenure committees who prey upon, and apparently think they deserve, the sympathies of editors.

4. See Powell (1985) for ethnographic insights into how books are selected at two nonuniversity scholarly presses. Much of what Powell discovered about these commercial presses in the early 1980s remains valid for university press decision-making today.

5. The economic implications of publishing a book that no one reads or buys actually go beyond its costs to an individual press. Broderick (1987) calls attention to the serious consequences, not only for the publisher and author but for the society as a whole, of publishing "a bad book."

6. The lists of the most prominent US university presses in fact comprise many translations from and copublications with foreign, mostly European and British, publishers. Whereas the market for scholarship can be quite commercially viable in Europe, generally only the university presses in the US can afford to try to reach it since it is so tiny compared to that for general books.

References

Abelson, Harold, and Gerald Jay Sussman, with Julie Sussman

1985 *Structure and Interpretation of Computer Programs.* Cambridge: MIT Press and McGraw-Hill.

Agliettga, Michel

1976/79 *A Theory of Capitalist Regulation.* London: New Left Books.

Althusser, Louis

1971 Ideology and Ideological State Apparatuses. In *Lenin and Philosophy,* Ben Brewster, trans. New York: Monthly Review Press.

Alvares, Claude

1994 Bhopal Ten Years After. Afterword to *Bhopal: The Inside Story,* by T. R. Chouhan. New York: Apex Press.

American Demographics

1987 Baby Bust Incomes. *American Demographics* 9:70 (October).

1992 Hanging Out with American Youth. *American Demographics* 14 :24–33 (February).

1993 The Dream Is Alive. *American Demographics* 15:32–37 (August).

Arnold, J. P.

1994 The Davidian Dilemma—To Obey God or Man? In *From the Ashes: Making Sense of Waco,* J. R. Lewis, ed., pp. 23–31. Lanham, MD: Rowman and Littlefield.

Aronowitz, Stanley

1994 *The Jobless Future: Sci-Tech and the Dogma of Work.* Minneapolis: University of Minnesota Press.

Bane, Mary Jo

1976 *Here to Stay: American Families in the Twentieth Century.* New York: Basic Books.

Barlow, John Perry

1990 Coming into the Country. *Communications of the ACM* (Nov. 9). Available also: http://www.eff.org/~barlow/library.html.

1992a Crime and Puzzlement. http://www.feist.com/~fqdb/texts/cp.html.

1992b Decrypting the Puzzle Palace. *Communications of the ACM* 35(7) (July).

1994 The Economy of Ideas. *Wired* 2.03. http://www.musicwest.com/MW/95/Panelists/B/Barlow/economy.html.

1995 Property and Speech: Who Owns What You Say in Cyberspace. *Communications of the ACM* 38(12):19–22.

1996 Selling Wine without Bottles: The Economy of Mind on the Global Net. In *Clicking In: Hot Links to a Digital Culture,* L. Leeson, ed. Seattle: Bay Press.

Barnes, T. J., and J. S. Duncan, eds.

1992 *Writing Worlds: Discourse, Text and Metaphor in the Representation of Landscape.* London: Routledge, Chapman and Hall.

Barzun, Jacques

1971 *On Writing, Editing and Publishing.* 2d ed. Chicago: University of Chicago Press.

Bateson, Gregory

1972 *Steps to an Ecology of Mind.* New York: Ballantine Books.

Baudrillard, J.

1983 *Simulations.* P. Foss, P. Patton, and P. Beitchman, trans. New York: Semiotext(e)/Foreign Agent Press.

Bauman, Zygmunt

1991 *Modernity and Ambivalence.* Cambridge, England: Polity Press.

Bazerman, Charles

1988 *Shaping Written Knowledge: The Genre and Activity of the Experimental Article in Science.* Madison: University of Wisconsin Press.

Beacon Hill Institute

1992 *Privatization of Human Services: Panacea or Placebo.* Boston: Beacon Hill Institute at Suffolk University.

Bear, Greg

1985 *Blood Music.* New York: Ace.

Beck, Ulrich

1986/92 *The Risk Society: Towards a New Modernity.* London: Sage.

Beck, Ulrich, Anthony Giddens, and Scott Lash

1994 *Reflexive Modernization: Politics, Tradition and Aesthetics in the Modern Social Order.* Stanford: Stanford University Press.

Behar, Ruth, and Deborah A. Gordon, eds.

1995 *Women Writing Culture.* Berkeley: University of California Press.

Bell, Robert

1992 *Impure Science: Fraud, Compromise, and Political Influence in Scientific Research.* New York: John Wiley and Sons.

Benedikt, Michael

1992 *Cyberspace: First Steps.* Cambridge: MIT Press.

Benjamin, Walter

1969 *Illuminations.* Harry Zohn, trans. Hannah Arendt, ed. New York: Schocken.

Berger, Brigitte, and Peter Berger

1983 *The War Over the Family.* New York: Anchor Press/Doubleday.

Berke, Richard L.

1994a Two Top Republicans Soften Their Tone. *New York Times* (September 17):A8.

1994b U.S. Voters Focus on Selves, Poll Says. *New York Times* (September 21):A12.

Bernard, Jessie

1972 *The Future of Marriage.* New York: World Publishing.

Bernstein, Susan R.

1991 *Managing Contracted Services in the Nonprofit Agency: Administrative, Ethical, and Political Issues.* Philadelphia: Temple University Press.

Beschloss, Michael R., and Strobe Talbott

1993 *At the Highest Levels: The Inside Story of the End of the Cold War.* Boston: Little Brown.

Blankenhorn, David

1995 *Fatherless America: Confronting Our Most Urgent Social Problem.* New York: Basic Books.

Blankenhorn, David, Jean Elshtain, and Steven Bayme, eds.

1990 *Rebuilding the Nest: A New Commitment to the American Family.* Milwaukee: Family Services America.

Blumenberg, Hans

1983 *The Legitimacy of the Modern Age.* Cambridge: MIT Press. Orig. 1966.

Bourdieu, Pierre

1977 *Outline of a Theory of Practice.* Cambridge: Cambridge University Press. Orig. 1972.

1984 *Distinction: A Social Critique of the Judgement of Taste.* Richard Nice, trans. Cambridge: Harvard University Press.

1990 The Scholastic Point of View. *Cultural Anthropology* 5(4):380–91.

1993 *The Field of Cultural Production.* Randall Johnson, ed. New York: Columbia University Press.

Bourdieu, Pierre, and Loic Wacquant

1992 *Introduction to Reflexive Sociology.* Chicago: University of Chicago Press.

Boyarin, Jonathan, ed.

1993 *The Ethnography of Reading.* Berkeley: University of California Press.

Boyer, M. C.

1992 Cities for Sale: Merchandizing History at the South Street Seaport. In *Variations on a Theme Park: The New American City and the End of Public Space,* M. Sorkin, ed. New York: Noonday Press.

Boyer, P. J.

1995 Children of Waco. *New Yorker* 71(12):38–45 (May 15).

Brake, Michael

1985 *Comparative Youth Cultures.* London: Routledge and Kegan Paul.

Brand, Stewart

1987 *The Media Lab: Inventing the Future at MIT.* New York: Vintage.

Branscomb, Anne Wells

1994 *Who Owns Information? From Privacy to Public Access.* New York: Basic Books.

Branscomb, Lewis, and Brian Kahin

1994 Information Infrastructure Course Syllabus. Harvard Kennedy School of Government: Science, Technology and Public Policy Program.

Brenneis, Donald

1987 Performing Passions: Aesthetics and Politics in an Occasionally Egalitarian Community. *American Ethnologist* 14(2):236–50.

1988 A propos des "research proposals." *Actes de la Recherche en Sciences Sociales* 674:82.

1994 Discourse and Discipline at the National Research Council: A Bureaucratic Bildungsroman. *Cultural Anthropology* 9(1):23–36.

1995 Caught in the Web of Words: Performing Theory in a Fiji Indian Community. In *Everyday Conceptions of Emotion: An Introduction to the Psychology, Anthropology, and Linguistics of Emotion,* J. A. Russell, J.-M. Fernández-Dols, A. S. R. Manstead, and J. C. Wellenkamp, eds., pp. 241–50. Dordrecht: Kluwer Academic Publications.

Brent, Stuart

1962 *The Seven Stairs: An Adventure of the Heart.* 3rd expanded ed. New York: Simon and Schuster.

Brinkley, Douglas

1994 Educating the Generation Called X. *Washington Post Education Review* (April 3):ER1.

Broderick, John G.

1987 The Cost of a Bad Book. *Scholarly Publishing* 18(2):83–88.

Brooks, Harvey

1978 The Problem of Research Priorities. *Dædalus* 107(2):171–90.

Brown, Phil, and Edwin J. Mikkelson

1990 *No Safe Place: Toxic Waste, Leukemia, and Community Action.* Berkeley: University of California Press.

Browning, Jackson

1986 Letter to the Editor. *New York Times* (August 18).

Brownstein, Ronald

1994 Democrats Find the Right's Stuff: Family Values. *Los Angeles Times* (August 1):A1, A23.

Buck-Morss, Susan

1989 *The Dialectics of Seeing: Walter Benjamin and the Arcades Project.* Cambridge: MIT Press.

Bukatman, Scott

1993 *Terminal Identity: The Virtual Subject in Postmodern Fiction.* Durham: Duke University Press.

Burke, Kenneth

1964 Bureaucratization of the Imaginative. In *Perspectives by Incongruity,* S. E. Hyman, ed., pp. 76–80. Bloomington: Indiana University Press.

Burnham, David

1983 *The Rise of the Computer State.* New York: Vintage.

1996 *Above the Law.* New York: Macmillan.

Business Week

1991 What Happened to the American Dream? (August 19):80–85.

1992 Move Over, Boomers. The Busters are Here—and They're Angry. (December 14):74–82.

Callinan, Kevin

1993 Baby Boomer Blues. Letter to the Editor, *New York Times Book Review* (July 25).

Calton, Jerry M., and Nancy B. Kurland

1995 A Theory of Stakeholder Enabling: Giving Voice to an Emerging Postmodern Practice of Organizational Discourse. In *Postmodern Management and Organizational Theory,* D. M. Boje, R. P. Gephart, Jr., and T. J. Thatchenkery, eds., pp. 154–77. Thousand Oaks, CA: Sage.

Carden, Amy

1995 Generation and Class in the Watching of "Melrose Place." Course paper, University of California, Berkeley.

Carlson, Allan

1990 *The Swedish Experiment in Family Politics: The Myrdals and the Interwar Population Crisis.* New Brunswick: Transaction.

Carson, Rachel

1962 *Silent Spring.* Boston: Houghton Mifflin.

Cassels, Jamie

1993 *The Uncertain Promise of Law: Lessons From Bhopal.* Toronto: University of Toronto Press.

Cavazos, Edward, and Gavino Morin

1994 *Cyberspace and the Law.* Cambridge: MIT Press.

CCC (Communities Concerned about Corporations)

1994 Press release (December 3). Charleston, WV.

Chayes, A.

1976 The Role of the Judge in Public Law Litigation. *Harvard Law Review* 89:1281–1316.

1982 Public Law Litigation and the Burger Court. *Harvard Law Review* 96:4–60.

Cheal, David

1991 *Family and the State of Theory.* New York: Harvester Wheatsheaf.

Chemical Manufacturers Association

1994 Reporting Worst Case Scenarios: Managing Our Risks Together. Videocassette.

Cherlin, Andrew J.

1981 *Marriage, Divorce, Remarriage.* Rev. ed. 1992. Cambridge: Harvard University Press.

Chinoy, Eli

1955 *Automobile Workers and the American Dream.* Garden City, NY: Doubleday.

Chisum, Donald

1986 The Patentability of Algorithms. *University of Pittsburgh Law Review* 47:959.

Chouhan, T. R.

1994 *Bhopal, The Inside Story: Carbide Workers Speak Out on the World's Worst Industrial Disaster.* New York: Apex Press.

Christian Science Monitor

1993 Generation X and Jobs. Editorial. *Christian Science Monitor* 85(152):18 (July 2).

Chubin, Daryl E., and Edward J. Hackett

1990 *Peerless Science: Peer Review and U.S. Science Policy.* Albany: State University of New York Press.

Chubin, Daryl, and Sheila Jasanoff, eds.

1985 Peer Review and Public Policy. *Science, Technology, and Human Values* 10(3) (special issue).

Clifford, James

1986a Introduction: Partial Truths. In *Writing Culture: The Poetics and Politics of Ethnography,* J. Clifford and G. E. Marcus, eds., pp. 1–26. Berkeley: University of California Press.

1986b On Ethnographic Allegory. In *Writing Culture: The Poetics and Politics of Ethnography,* J. Clifford and G. E. Marcus, eds., pp. 98–121. Berkeley: University of California Press.

1988 *The Predicament of Culture: Twentieth-Century Ethnography, Literature, and Art.* Cambridge: Harvard University Press.

Clifford, James, and George E. Marcus, eds.

1986 *Writing Culture: The Poetics and Politics of Ethnography.* Berkeley: University of California Press.

Cohen, Keith

1979 *Film and Fiction: The Dynamics of Exchange.* New Haven: Yale.

Coker, Cheo H.

1994 Ice Cube. In *The GenX Reader,* D. Rushkoff, ed., pp. 89–98. New York: Ballantine Books.

Cole, Jonathan R., and Stephen Cole

1981 *Peer Review in the National Science Foundation: Part Two of a Study.* Washington, DC: National Academy Press.

Cole, Stephen, Jonathan R. Cole, and Gary A. Simon

1981 Chance and Consensus in Peer Review. *Science* 214:881–86.

Cole, Stephen, Leonard Rubin, and Jonathan R. Cole

1978 *Peer Review in the National Science Foundation: Part One of a Study.* Washington, DC: National Academy of Sciences.

Constantine, Larry, ed.

1993 *Infinite Loop.* San Francisco: Miller Freeman.

Coontz, Stephanie

1992 *The Way We Never Were: American Families and the Nostalgia Trap.* New York: Basic Books.

Coser, Lewis A., Charles Kadushin, and Walter W. Powell

1982 *Books: The Culture and Commerce of Publishing.* New York: Basic Books.

Coupland, Douglas

1991 *Generation X: Tales for an Accelerated Culture.* New York: St. Martin's Press.

Courtland, Douglas

1993 Microserfs: Seven Days in the Life of Young Microsoft. WIRED Online. HotWIRED 2.01.

1995 *Microserfs.* New York: Regan.

Critical Art Ensemble

1994 *The Electronic Disturbance.* Brooklyn: Autonomia.

The Cryptoanarchists' Manifesto

1994 The Cryptoanarchists' Manifesto (May 1994). In *Cypernomicon,* Tim May. http://calvo.teleco.ulpgc.es/cyphernomicon.

Dahl, R. H.

1961 *Who Governs? Democracy and Power in an American City.* New Haven: Yale University Press.

Danowitz, A. K., Y. Nassef, and S. E. Goodman

1995 Cyberspace Across the Sahara: Computing in North Africa. *Communications of the ACM* 38(12):23–28.

Das, Veena

1993 Moral Orientations to Suffering: Legitimation, Power and Healing. In *Health and Social Change in International Perspective,* L. C. Chen, A. Kleinman, and N. Ware, eds. Oxford: Oxford University Press.

Davis, M.

1992 Fortress Los Angeles: The Militarization of Urban Space. In *Variations on a Theme Park: The New American City and the End of Public Space,* M. Sorkin, ed. New York: Noonday Press.

de Certeau, Michel

1984 *The Practice of Everyday Life.* Berkeley: University of California Press.

Deleuze, Gilles

1990/95 Postscript on the Societies of Control. In *Negotiations.* New York: Columbia University Press.

Deleuze, Gilles, and Felix Guattari

1975/86 *Kafka: Toward a Minor Literature.* Minneapolis: University of Minnesota Press.

Dembo, David, Ward Morehouse, and Lucinda Wykle

1990 *Abuse of Power: The Case of Union Carbide.* New York: New Horizons Press.

Derrida, Jacques

1967/74 *Of Grammatology.* Baltimore: Johns Hopkins University Press.

1972/81 *Disseminations.* Chicago: University of Chicago Press.

1978 Freud and the Scene of Writing. In *Writing and Difference,* pp. 196–231. Chicago: University of Chicago Press.

1987/89 *Of Spirit.* Chicago: University of Chicago Press.

1992 *The Other Heading.* P.-A. Brault and M. B. Nass, trans. Bloomington: Indiana University Press.

1995 *Points.* Stanford: Stanford University Press.

Dery, Mark

1996 *Escape Velocity: Cyberculture at the End of the Century.* New York: Grove Press.

De Solla Price, Derek, and Donald DeB. Beaver

1966 Collaboration in an Invisible College. *American Psychologist* 21:1011–18.

Deutschman, Alan

1990 What 25-Year-Olds Want. *Fortune* 122:42–47 (August 27).

1992 The Upbeat Generation. *Fortune* 126:42–53 (July 13).

Didion, Joan

1993 Trouble in Lakewood. *New Yorker* (July 26):46–65.

DiMaggio, P. J., and W. W. Powell, eds.

1991 *The New Institutionalism in Organizational Analysis.* Chicago: University of Chicago Press.

Dirks, Nicholas B., Geoff Eley, and Sherry B. Ortner, eds.

1992 *Culture/Power/History: A Reader in Contemporary Social Theory.* Princeton: Princeton University Press.

Domhoff, George W.

1978 *Who Really Rules? New Haven and Community Power Reexamined.* New Brunswick: Transaction Press.

Dowd, Ann Reilly

1994 Environmentalists on the Run. *Fortune* (September 19):91ff.

Dowie, Mark

1995 *Losing Ground: American Environmentalism at the Close of the Twentieth Century.* Cambridge: MIT Press.

Drew, Paul, and John Heritage, eds.

1992 *Talk at Work: Interaction in Institutional Settings.* New York: Cambridge University Press.

Drucker, Peter

1989 *The New Realities.* New York: Harper Collins.

Duff, Christina

1993 Poor Prospects: In a Portland Hot Tub, Young Grads' Anxiety Bubbles to the Surface. *Wall Street Journal* (July 28):A1–6.

Duncan, Greg J., Timothy M. Smeeding, and Willard Rodgers

1992 The Incredible Shrinking Middle Class. *American Demographics* 14:34–38 (May).

Duranti, Alessandro, and Donald Brenneis, eds.

1986 The Audience as Co-Author. *Text* 6:239–47 (special issue).

Economist, The

1993 Oh, Grow Up. *Economist* 325:29–30 (December 26, 1992–January 8, 1993).

Edmondson, Brad

1987a This Is a Baby Bust Town. *American Demographics* 9:22 (March).

1987b Colleges Conquer the Baby Bust. *American Demographics* 9:26–31 (September).

1990 Help Desperately Wanted. *American Demographics* 12:60–62 (January).

1992 Meet the Baby Bust. *American Demographics* 14:2 (February).

Edwards, Paul

1996 *The Closed World: Computers and the Politics of Discourse in Cold War America.* Cambridge: MIT Press.

Egger, Martin

1993 Hermeneutics and the New Epic of Science. In *The Literature of Commerce,* M. W. McRae, ed. Athens: University of Georgia Press.

Ehrenreich, Barbara

1990 *Fear of Falling: The Inner Life of the Middle Class.* New York: Harper Collins.

Ehrenreich, Barbara, and John Ehrenreich

1979 The Professional-Managerial Class. In *Between Labour and Capital,* P. Walker, ed., pp. 5–48. Hassocks, Sussex: Harvester Press.

Eisenberg, L.

1977 Disease and Illness: Distinctions between Professional and Popular Ideas of Sickness. *Culture, Medicine, and Psychiatry* 1:9–23.

Elliott, Stuart

1993 In a Whisky Pitch to Generation X Members. *New York Times* (September 13):D7.

Elshtain, Jean

1994 Letter to the Editor. *Nation* (November 7).

Emche, Claus

1994 *The Garden in the Machine: The Emerging Science of Artificial Life.* Princeton: Princeton University Press.

Erikson, K.

1966 *Wayward Puritans: A Study in the Sociology of Deviance.* New York: Wiley.

Exter, Thomas

1990 Older and Wiser. *American Demographics* 12:67 (June).

1991 Low Tide for High Schools. *American Demographics* 13:55 (May).

Feenberg, Andrew

1995 ***Alternative Modernity: The Technical Turn in Philosophy and Social Theory.*** **Berkeley: University of California Press.**

Ferrante, Joan

1992 *Sociology: A Global Perspective.* Belmont, CA: Wadsworth.

Fischer, Michael M. J.

1993 Working through the Other. In *Late Editions 1: Perilous States,* G. E. Marcus, ed. Chicago: University of Chicago Press.

1997 Rouche in Reverse, A Film by Manthia Diawara. *American Anthropologist* 16.

Fiske, John

1994 *Media Matters: Everyday Culture and Political Change.* Minneapolis: University of Minnesota Press.

Fiss, O.

1979 Forms of Justice. *Harvard Law Review* 93:1–58.

Flynn, R. J., and K. Nitsch, eds.

1980 *Normalization, Social Integration, and Community Services.* Baltimore: University Park Press.

Forester, Tom, and Perry Morrison

1990 *Computer Ethics: Tales and Ethical Dilemmas in Computing.* Cambridge: MIT Press.

Fortun, Kim

1998 The Bhopal Disaster: Advocacy and Expertise. *Science as Culture* 7(2):193–216.

Foucault, Michel

1978 *The History of Sexuality.* Vol. I. New York: Pantheon Books.

1979 *Power/Knowledge: Selected Interviews and Other Writings, 1972–1977.* C. Gordon, L. Marshall, J. Mepham, and K. Soper, trans. C. Gordon, ed. New York: Pantheon.

1980 *Discipline and Punish: The Birth of the Prison.* A. Sheridan, trans. New York: Vintage Books.

1984a Polemics, Politics, and Problematizations. In *The Foucault Reader*, Paul Rabinow, ed. New York: Pantheon Books.

1984b On the Genealogy of Ethics: Work in Progress. In *The Foucault Reader*, Paul Rabinow, ed. New York: Pantheon Books.

Fox, Richard, ed.

1992 *Recapturing Anthropology: Working in the Present*. Santa Fe: School of American Research Press.

Frazier, E. Franklin

1939 *The Negro Family in the United States*. Chicago: University of Chicago Press.

Freedland, Jonathan

1994 Generation Hex. *Washington Post* (April 24):G1–G6.

Freeman, R. E.

1984 *Strategic Management: A Stakeholder Approach*. Boston: Pitman.

Freud, Sigmund

1974 [1925] A Note Upon the "Mystic Writing Pad." In *The Standard Edition of the Complete Psychological Works of Sigmund Freud* 19:227–35. London: Hogarth Press.

Friedan, Betty

1963 *The Feminine Mystique*. New York: Norton.

1981 *The Second Stage*. New York: Summit Books.

Fritz, Charles

1961 Disaster. In *Contemporary Social Problems*, R. K. Merton and R. A. Nisbet, eds. New York: Harcourt.

Froomkin, A. Michael

1995 The Metaphor Is the Key: Cryptography, the Clipper Chip, and the Constitution. *University of Pennsylvania Law Review*.

Fukuyama, Francis

1991 *The End of History and the Last Man*. New York: Vintage Books.

Furstenberg, Frank, Jr., and Andrew J. Cherlin

1991 *Divided Families: What Happens to Children When Parents Part*. Cambridge: Harvard University Press.

Gaines, Donna

1990 *Teenage Wasteland: Suburbia's Dead End Kids*. New York: Harper Collins.

Gardiner, J. A, ed.

1977 *Public Law and Public Policy*. New York: Praeger.

Garfinkel, Simpson

1994 Notes on MIT Communications Forum on the Clipper Chip. Presentation (September 29).

Garfinkel, Simpson, Richard Stallman, and Mitchell Kapor

1991 Why Patents Are Bad for Software. *Issues in Science and Technology* 4:22.

Gaylin, W., I. Glasser, S. Marcus, and D. Rothman

1979 *Doing Good: The Limits of Benevolence.* New York: Pantheon Books.

Geertz, Clifford

1973a Thick Description: Toward an Interpretive Theory of Culture. In *The Interpretation of Cultures.* New York: Basic Books.

1973b Religion as a Cultural System. In *The Interpretation of Cultures.* New York: Basic Books.

1973c The Impact of the Concept of Culture on the Concept of Man. In *The Interpretation of Cultures.* New York: Basic Books.

1988 *Works and Lives: The Anthropologist as Author.* Stanford: Stanford University Press.

General Accounting Office

1994 Peer Review: Reforms Needed to Ensure Fairness in Federal Agency Grant Selection. Report to the Chairman, Committee on Governmental Activities, US Senate.

Gibson, William

1984 *Neuromancer.* New York: Ace.

1986 An Interview with William Gibson. In *Across the Wounded Galaxies: Interviews with Contemporary American Science Fiction Writers,* by L. McCaffery, pp. 130–50. Urbana: University of Illinois Press.

Giddens, Anthony

1990 *The Consequences of Modernity.* Cambridge, England: Polity Press.

1991 *Modernity and Self-Identity.* Cambridge, England: Polity Press.

Gilder, George

1989 *Microcosm: The Quantum Revolution in Economics and Technology.* New York: Simon and Schuster.

Giles, Jeff

1994 GeneraLIZAtions X. *Newsweek* (June 6):62–72.

Gillespie, Gilbert W., Jr., Daryl E. Chubin, and George M. Kurzon

1985 Experience with NIH Peer Review: Researchers' Cynicism and Desire for Change. *Science, Technology, and Human Values* 10(3):44–54.

Gillis, John

1994 What's Behind the Debate on Family Values? Paper, American Sociological Association meetings, Los Angeles (August 6).

1996 *A World of Their Own Making: Myth, Ritual, and the Quest for Family Values.* New York: Basic Books.

Gleick, James

1987 *Chaos: Making a New Science.* New York: Viking.

Glenn, Norval D.

1994 The Re-evaluation of Family Change by American Social Scientists. Paper, Committee for the International Year of the Family of the Catholic Archdiocese of Melbourne.

Goankar, Dilip, and Cary Nelson, eds.
1996 *Disciplinarity and Dissent.* New York: Routledge.
Goffman, Ervin
1961 ***Asylums.* New York: Doubleday.**
Goldman-Segall, Ricki
1990 Learning Constellations: A Multi-Media Ethnographic Research Environment Using Video Technology for Exploring Children's Thinking. Ph.D. dissertation, Massachusetts Institute of Technology.
1995 The Global Forest. Oracle CD-ROM. http://www.merlin.ubc.ca/ppl/ricki.html.
Goode, William J.
1963 *World Revolution and Family Patterns.* New York: Free Press.
Gordon, Albert I.
1959 *Jews in Suburbia.* Boston: Beacon Press.
Gordon, Tuula
1994 Single Women and Familism: Challenge from the Margins. *European Journal of Women's Studies* 1(2):165–82.
Gouldner, Alvin
1970 *The Coming Crisis of Western Sociology.* New York: Basic Books.
Greenberg Research
1994 Poll Sponsored by Democratic Leadership Council (November 8–9). Roper Center Public Opinion Online Database.
Gresh, Lois
1993 Watch Me If You Can. In *Infinite Loop,* L. Constantine, ed. San Francisco: Miller Freeman.
Grimshaw, Allen D.
1989 *Collegial Discourse: Professional Conversation among Peers.* Norwood, NJ: Ablex.
Gronbjerg, K.
1993 *Understanding Nonprofit Funding: Managing Revenues in Social Service and Community Development Organizations.* San Francisco: Jossey-Bass.
Grossberg, Lawrence, and Cary Nelson, eds.
1988 *Marxism and the Interpretation of Culture.* Urbana: University of Illinois Press.
Grossberg, Lawrence, Cary Nelson, and Paula Treichler, eds.
1992 *Cultural Studies.* New York: Routledge.
Grossman, Richard, and Frank Adams
1993 *Taking Care of Business: Citizenship and the Charter of Incorporation.* Cambridge, MA: Charter Ink.
Guattari, Felix
1992/95 *Chaosmosis: An Ethico-Aesthetic Paradigm.* Bloomington: Indiana University Press.

Gupta, Akhil, and James Ferguson, eds.

1997a *Anthropology and "the Field": Boundaries, Areas, and Grounds in the Constitution of a Discipline.* Berkeley: University of California Press.

1997b *Culture, Power, Place: Explorations in Critical Anthropology.* Durham: Duke University Press.

Haas, Peter, Marc Ley, and Edward Parson

1995 Appraising the Earth Summit: How Should We Judge UNCED's Success?
In *Green Planet Views: Environmental Politics from Stockholm to Rio,* pp. 155–64. Boulder: Westview Press.

Hacking, Ian

1995 *Rewriting the Soul: Multiple Personality and the Sciences of Memory.* Princeton: Princeton University Press.

Hafner, Katie, and John Markoff

1991 *Cyberpunk: Outlaws and Hackers on the Computer Frontier.* New York: Simon and Schuster.

Hall, Peter Dobkin

1982 *The Organization of American Culture, 1700–1900: Institutions, Elites, and the Origins of American Nationality.* New York: New York University Press.

1987a Historical Overview of the Private Nonprofit Sector. In *The Nonprofit Sector:*
A Research Handbook, W. W. Powell, ed., pp. 3–26. New Haven: Yale University Press.

1987b The Spirit of the Ordinance of 1787: Organizational Values, Voluntary Associations, and Higher Education in Ohio, 1803–1830. In *"Schools and the Means of Education Shall Be Encouraged": A History of Education in the Old Northwest, 1787–1880,* P. H. Mattingly and W. W. Stevens, eds. Athens:
Ohio University Libraries.

1988 Organizational Values and the Origins of the Corporation in Connecticut, 1760–1860. *Connecticut History* (November 29):63–90.

1992a *Inventing the Nonprofit Sector: Essays on Philanthropy, Voluntarism, and Nonprofit Organizations.* Baltimore: Johns Hopkins University Press.

1992b The Empty Tomb. In *Lives in Trust: The Fortunes of Dynastic Families in Late Twentieth Century America,* G. E. Marcus and P. D. Hall. Boulder: Westview Press.

1995 "Since to St. Ronan's sparkling brink/The wolf and wild cat came to drink":
A History of New Haven's Ronan-Edgehill Neighborhood. *Journal of the New Haven Colony Historical Society* 41(2):38–59.

Hall, Stuart, and Tony Jefferson, eds.

1975 *Resistance through Rituals: Youth Subcultures in Post-War Britain.* London: Hutchinson.

Halle, David

1984 *America's Working Man: Work, Home and Politics among Blue Collar Property Owners.* Chicago: University of Chicago Press.

Hansmann, H.

1987 Economic Theories of Nonprofit Organization. In *The Nonprofit Sector: A Research Handbook,* W. W. Powell, ed. New Haven: Yale University Press.

Haraway, Donna

1997 *Modest_Witness@Second_Millennium. FemaleMan©_Meets_OncoMouse™.* New York: Routledge.

Harmon, Amy

1993 For GenX, the Angst Is On-Line. *Los Angeles Times* (April 28):A1.

Harnad, Stevan

1985 Rational Disagreement in Peer Review. *Science, Technology, and Human Values* 10(3):55–62.

Harte, John, Cheryl Holdren, Richard Schneider, and Christine Shirley

1991 *Toxics A to Z: A Guide to Everyday Pollution Hazards.* Berkeley: University of California Press.

Harvey, David

1989 *The Condition of Postmodernity: An Enquiry into the Origins of Cultural Change.* Oxford: Basil Blackwell.

Hawes, Gene R.

1967 *To Advance Knowledge: A Handbook on American University Press Publishing.* New York: American University Press Services.

Hayes, Dennis

1989 *Behind the Silicon Curtain.* Boston: South End Press.

Hayles, Katherine

1993 The Seductions of Cyberspace. In *Rethinking Technologies,* V. A. Conley, ed. Minneapolis–St. Paul: University of Minnesota Press.

1996 Narratives of Artificial Life. In *Futurenatural: Nature, Science, Culture,* George Robertson, Melinda Mash, and Lisa Tickner, eds. New York: Routledge.

He, Agnes Weiyun

1993 Language Use in Peer Review Texts. *Language in Society* 22:403–20.

Heckel, Paul

1992 Debunking the Software Patent Myths. *Communications of the ACM* 35(6):121.

Herr, Michael

1977 *Dispatches.* New York: Knopf.

Heims, Steve Joshua

1993 *Constructing a Social Science for Postwar America.* Cambridge: MIT Press.

Heller, Scott

1995 Finding a Common Purpose. *Chronicle of Higher Education* (March 31): A10, A16.

Hewlett, Sylvia Ann

1986 *A Lesser Life: The Myth of Women's Liberation in America.* New York: William Morrow.

Hicks, Jonathan

1989 After the Disaster, Carbide Is Rebuilt. *New York Times* (February 15).

Hoffman, Andrew

1997 *From Heresy to Dogma: An Institutional History of Corporate Environmentalism.* San Francisco: New Lexington Press.

Hollingshead, A. B.

1949 *Elmtown's Youth.* New York: John Wiley and Sons.

Holtz, Geoffrey T.

1995 *Welcome to the Jungle: The Why Behind Generation X.* New York: St. Martin's Griffin.

Howe, Neil, and William Strauss

1992 The New Generation Gap. *Atlantic Monthly* (December):67–89.

1993 *13th Gen: Abort, Retry, Ignore, Fail.* New York: Vintage Books.

Hughes, James W., and Todd Zimmerman

1993 The Dream is Alive. *American Demographics* 15(8):32–37.

Ito, Mizuko

1994 Cyborg Couplings in a Multi-User Dungeon. Paper, Society for Social Studies of Science meetings, New Orleans (October 14).

Ivanovich, David

1993 Clean Air Act Choking Refineries. *Houston Chronicle* (June 20).

Iyer, V. R. Krishna

1991 Bhoposhima: Crime without Punishment, Case for Crisis Management Jurisprudence. *Economic and Political Weekly* (November 23):2705–13.

Jackson, Patricia

1994 Worst-Case Scenario: A Communication Tool to Reduce Risk. *Corporate Environmental Strategy* 2(4):69–74.

Jahanshah, Javid

1995 Interests Conflict over Control of Internet Access. *Iran Business Monitor* 4(9):3.

Jaising, Indira.

1994 Legal Let-Down. Afterward to *Bhopal: The Inside Story,* by T. R. Chouhan. New York: Apex Press.

James, Darius

1994 Negrophobia. In *The GenX Reader,* D. Rushkoff, ed., pp. 129–40. New York: Ballantine Books.

Jamison, P. K.

1994 Medieval Empires and Hyperindustrial Consciousness: An Exploration of Transformative Identities and Biospheres in Western Toys. Paper, Society for Social Studies of Science meetings, New Orleans (November 14).

Jasanoff, Sheila, ed.

1994 *Learning from Disaster: Risk Management after Bhopal.* Philadelphia: University of Pennsylvania Press.

Jenkins, P.

1992 *Intimate Enemies: Moral Panics in Contemporary Great Britain.* New York: Aldine De Gruyter.

Johnson, Donna M., and Duane H. Roen

1992 Complimenting and Involvement in Peer Reviews: Gender Variation. *Language in Society* 21:27–57.

Jonas, Hans

1979/84 *The Imperative of Responsibility: In Search of an Ethics for a Technological Age.* Chicago: University of Chicago Press.

Kalberer, John T., Jr.

1985 Peer Review and the Consensus Development Process. *Science, Technology, and Human Values* 10(3):63–72.

Kamen, J.

1993 A Matter of "Live" and Death. *American Journalism Review* 15(5):26–31.

Kant, Immanuel

1951 [1793] *The Critique of Judgment.* J. H. Bernard, trans. New York: Hafner Publishing Company.

Kaufman, J., and E. Zigler

1989 The Intergenerational Transmission of Child Abuse. In *Child Maltreatment: Theory and Research on the Causes and Consequences of Child Abuse and Neglect,* D. Cicchetti and V. Carlson, eds., pp. 129–50. Cambridge: Cambridge University Press.

Kay, Lily E.

1993 *The Molecular Vision of Life: Caltech, The Rockefeller Foundation, and the Rise of the New Biology.* New York: Oxford University Press.

n.d. *Who Wrote the Book of Life: A History of the Genetic Code.* Stanford: Stanford University Press, forthcoming.

Kearney, Michael

1995 The Local and the Global: The Anthropology of Globalization and Transnationalism. In *Annual Review of Anthropology,* W. Durham, E. V. Daniel, and B. Schieffelin, eds., pp. 547–65. Palo Alto: Annual Reviews, Inc.

Keenan, Judge John F.

1986 Opinion and Order; In Re: Union Carbide Corporation Gas Plant Disaster at Bhopal India in December 1984. 846. F Supp. 842 (SDNY 1986).

Keller, Evelyn Fox

1995 *Refiguring Life: Metaphors of Twentieth-Century Biology.* New York: Columbia.

Kelley, Kevin

1994 *Out of Control: The Rise of Neo-Biological Civilization.* Cambridge: Addison-Wesley.

Kerr, Chester

1949 *A Report on American University Presses.* New York: American Association of University Presses.

Kinsley, Michael

1994 Post-Boomer Bellyaching: The Dubious Lament of Generation X. *Wall Street Journal* (March 4):A23.

Kirp, D. L., J. P. Dwyer, and L. A. Rosenthal

1995 *Our Town: Race, Housing, and the Soul of Suburbia.* New Brunswick: Rutgers University Press.

Kissinger, Henry

1994 *Diplomacy.* New York: Simon and Schuster.

Koch, Robert

1995 The Case of Latour. *Configurations* 3:319–47.

Koedt, Anne

1970 The Myth of the Vaginal Orgasm. In *Liberation Now! Writings From the Women's Liberation Movement,* compiled by Deborah Babcox and Madeline Belkin, pp. 311–20. New York: Dell.

Kohler, Robert E.

1991 *Partners in Science: Foundations and Natural Scientists, 1900–1945.* Chicago: University of Chicago Press.

Kramarae, Cheris

1995 A Backstage Critique of Virtual Reality. In *Cybersociety,* S. G. Jones, ed. Thousand Oaks, CA: Sage.

Lacan, Jacques

1973/77 *Four Fundamental Concepts of Psycho-Analysis.* London: Hogarth Press.

Lanier, Jaron

1994 Quantum Pricing for Information. *Wired* 2(8):63–64.

1996 Interviewed by Lynn Hershman Leeson. In *Clicking In: Hot Links to a Digital Culture,* L. Leeson, ed. Seattle: Bay Press.

Lash, Scott

1993 Reflexive Modernization: The Aesthetic Dimension. *Theory, Culture and Society* 10:1–23.

Lash, Scott, and John Urry

1987 *The End of Organized Capitalism.* Madison: University of Wisconsin Press.

1994 *Economies of Signs and Space.* Thousand Oaks, CA: Sage.

Latour, Bruno

1988 *The Pasteurization of France.* Cambridge: Harvard University Press.

Lavin, Douglas

1993 Chrysler Directs Neon Campaign at Generation X. *Wall Street Journal* (August 27):B1.

Le Guin, Ursula

1971 *Lathe of Heaven.* New York: Avon.

Lehman, Bruce, chair

1994 Intellectual Property and the National Information Infrastructure: A Preliminary Draft of the Report of the Working Group on Intellectual Property Rights. Washington, DC: Department of Commerce.

Leitch, Vincent

1996 *Postmodernism: Local Effects, Global Flows.* Albany: State University of New York.

Lepkowski, Will

1994 The Restructuring of Union Carbide. In *Learning From Disaster: Risk Management After Bhopal,* S. Jasanoff, ed. Philadelphia: University of Pennsylvania Press.

Leppard, D.

1993 *Fire and Blood: The True Story of David Koresh and the Waco Siege.* London: Fourth Estate.

Lévi-Strauss, Claude

1962/66 *The Savage Mind.* Chicago: University of Chicago Press.

1971 *The Naked Man: An Introduction to a Science of Mythology.* Vol. 4. J. and D. Weightman, trans. Reprint 1981. New York: Harper and Row.

Lewontin, Richard C.

1994 The Dream of the Human Genome. *New York Review of Books* (November 29):17.

Liebow, Elliot

1967 *Tally's Corner.* Boston: Little, Brown and Co.

Linklater, Richard

1992 *Slacker.* New York: Saint Martin's Press.

Lipset, Seymour Martin, and Reinhard Bendix

1957 *Social Mobility in Industrial Society.* Berkeley: University of California Press.

Lipsitz, George

1990 *Time Passages: Collective Memory and American Popular Culture.* Minneapolis: University of Minnesota Press.

Lotfalian, Mazyar

1993 A Tale of an Electronic Community. In *Late Editions 3: Connected: Engagements with Media,* G. Marcus, ed. Chicago: University of Chicago Press.

Loundy, David

1994 E-Law 2.0: Computer Information Systems Law and System Operator Liability Revisited. ftp://infolib.murdoch.edu.au/pub/subj/law/jnl/elaw/refereed/loundy.txt.

Luke, Timothy

1993 Green Consumerism: Ecology and the Ruse of Recycling. In *The Nature of Things: Language, Politics and the Environment,* J. Bennett and W. Chaloupka, eds., pp. 154–72. Minneapolis: University of Minnesota Press.

Lynd, R. S., and H. M. Lynd

1929 *Middletown: A Study in American Culture.* New York: Harcourt, Brace and World.

Lyon, David

1994 *The Electronic Eye: The Rise of Surveillance Society.* Minneapolis: University of Minnesota Press.

Lyons, Paul

1994 *Class of '66: Living in Suburban Middle America.* Philadelphia: Temple University Press.

Lyotard, Jean-François

1979/84 *The Postmodern Condition: A Report on Knowledge.* Minneapolis: University of Minnesota Press.

Mainardi, Pat

1970 The Politics of Housework. In *Sisterhood Is Powerful: An Anthology of Writings from the Women's Liberation Movement,* R. Morgan, ed., pp. 447–53. New York: Vintage.

Malamud, Carl

1993 *Exploring the Internet: A Technical Travelogue.* Englewood Cliffs, NJ: Prentice Hall.

Mandel, Ernest

1978 [1972] *Late Capitalism.* London: Verso.

Marcus, George E.

1992 Review of Writing Worlds: Discourse, Text and Metaphor in the Representation of Landscape, edited by T. J. Barnes and J. S. Duncan. *Society and Space* 10(3):361–63.

1993 Power/Knowledge Shifts in America's Present Fin-de-Siècle: A Proposal for a School of American Research Advanced Seminar.

1995 Ethnography in/of the World System: The Emergence of Multisited Ethnography. In *Annual Review of Anthropology,* W. Durham, E. V. Daniel, and B. Schieffelin, eds., pp. 95–117. Palo Alto: Annual Reviews, Inc.

Marcus, George E., and Dick Cushman

1982 Ethnographies as Texts. *Annual Review of Anthropology* 11:25–69. Stanford: Annual Review Press.

Marcus, George E., and Michael M. J. Fischer

1986 *Anthropology as Cultural Critique: An Experimental Moment in the Human Sciences.* Chicago: University of Chicago Press.

Marcus, George E., with Peter Dobkin Hall

1992 *Lives in Trust: The Fortunes of Dynastic Families in Late Twentieth-Century America.* Boulder: Westview Press.

Markus, Gyorgy

1987 Why Is There No Hermeneutics of the Natural Sciences? *Science in Context* 1.

Martin, David

1993 The Whiny Generation. "My Turn" column. *Newsweek* (November 1):10.

Martin, Justin

1993 Generation X: Save, Baby, Save. *Fortune* 128:127–28.

May, Elaine

1988 *Homeward Bound: American Families in the Cold War Era.* New York: Basic Books.

May, Tim

1988 Cyphernomicon. http://calvo.teleco.ulpgc.es/cyphernomicon.

McCloskey, Donald N.

1985 *The Rhetoric of Economics.* Madison: University of Wisconsin Press.

McGuire, Meredith B.

1988 *Ritual Healing in Suburban America.* New Brunswick: Rutgers University Press.

McHale, Brian

1992 *Constructing Postmodernism.* New York: Routledge.

McLanahan, Sara

1994 The Consequences of Single Motherhood. *American Prospect* 18.

McLanahan, Sara, and Larry L. Bumpass

1988 Intergenerational Consequences of Family Disruption. *American Journal of Sociology* 94:130–52.

Mehlman, Jeffrey

1993 *Walter Benjamin for Children: An Essay on His Radio Years.* Chicago: University of Chicago Press.

Messer-Davidow, Ellen

1993 Manufacturing the Attack on Liberalized Higher Education. *Social Text* 36:40–80.

Meyer, Sheldon, and L. E. Phillabaum

n.d. *What Is a University Press?* New York: American Association of University Presses.

Millar, Jane

1994 State, Family and Personal Responsibility: The Changing Balance for Lone Mothers in the United Kingdom. *Feminist Review* 48:24–39.

Miller, Michael

1994 The Effect of the Spector of Crypto Anarchy on the Evolution of Laws Governing Cyberspace. Paper for Law and Ethics on the Electronic Frontier, Massachusetts Institute of Technology, STS 095/ 6.095. http://www.swiss-ai.mit.edu.

Mindell, David

1996 Datum for Its Own Annihilation: Feedback, Control, and Computing, 1916–1945. Ph.D. dissertation, Massachusetts Institute of Technology.

Moffatt, Michael

1989 *Coming of Age in New Jersey: College and American Culture.* New Brunswick: Rutgers University Press.

Moravec, Hans

1988 *Mind Children: The Future of Robot and Human Intelligence.* Cambridge: Harvard University Press.

Moukheiber, Zina

1994 Learning from Winners. *Forbes* (March 14).

Moynihan, Daniel Patrick

1965 *The Negro Family: The Case for National Action.* Washington, DC: US Department of Labor.

Mullis, Kary, and Fred Faloona

1987 Specific Synthesis of DNA in vitro via a Polymerase-Catalyzed Chain Reaction. *Methods in Enzymology* 15.

Nagle, Pati

1993 Pygmaleon 3.0. In *Infinite Loop,* L. Constantine, ed. San Francisco: Miller Freeman.

National Research Council

1991 *Summary Report 1990: Doctorate Recipients from United States Universities.* Washington, DC: National Academy Press.

National Science Foundation

1990a Global Perspectives on Sociolegal Studies. Program Announcement.

1990b *Law beyond the Nation State: Global Perspectives on Sociolegal Studies.* Law and Social Science Program, National Science Foundation.

1991 *Science and Engineering Degrees: 1966–1989, A Source Book.* NSF 91–314. Washington, DC: National Science Foundation.

Nelkin, Dorothy, and Lawrence Tancredi

1989 *Dangerous Diagnostics: The Social Power of Biological Information.* New York: Basic Books.

Nelson, B. J.

1984 *Making an Issue of Child Abuse: Political Agenda Setting for Social Problems.* Chicago: University of Chicago Press.

Nelson, John S., Allan Megill, and Donald N. McCloskey, eds.

1987 *The Rhetoric of the Human Sciences: Language and Argument in Scholarship and Public Affairs.* Madison: University of Wisconsin Press.

Nelson, Rob, and Jon Cowan

1994 *Revolution X: A Survival Guide for Our Generation.* New York: Penguin.

Newberger, E. H., and Daniel, J. H.

1979 Knowledge and Epidemiology of Child Abuse: A Critical Review of Concepts. In *Critical Perspectives on Child Abuse,* R. Bourne and E. H. Newberger, eds., pp. 19–25. Lexington, MA: Lexington Books.

Newell, Allen

1986 *The Models Are Broken, the Models Are Broken.* University of Pittsburgh Law Review 47(4):1023–35.

Newman, Katherine S.

1993 *Declining Fortunes: The Withering of the American Dream.* New York: Basic Books.

Newton, Judith, and Judith Stacey

1992–93 Learning Not to Curse, or Feminist Predicaments in Cultural Criticism by Men: Our Movie Date with Stephen Greenblatt and James Clifford. *Cultural Critique* 23:51–82.

1995 Ms.Representations: Feminist Dilemmas in Studying Academic Men. In *Women Writing Culture/Culture Writing Women,* R. Behar and D. Gordon, eds. Berkeley: University of California Press.

1997 The Men We Left Behind Us. In *Sociology and Cultural Studies,* E. Long, ed. New York: Basil Blackwell.

Norberg, Arthur, and Judy E. O'Neill

1996 *Envisioning Technology for the National Security State: A History of the Information Processing Techniques Office of the Department of Defense.* Baltimore: Johns Hopkins University Press.

O'Connell, Kathleen M.

1994 Kurt Cobain Reached People Who Had a Lot to Be Mad About. *Los Angeles Times* (April 14):37.

Oakley, Ann

1974 *The Sociology of Housework.* New York: Pantheon.

Obeysekere, Gananath

1981 *Medusa's Hair.* Chicago: University of Chicago Press.

Ortner, Sherry B.

1984 Theory in Anthropology since the Sixties. *Comparative Studies in Society and History* 26:126–66.

1991 Reading America: Preliminary Notes on Class and Culture. In *Recapturing Anthropology: Working in the Present,* R. G. Fox, ed., pp. 163–90. Santa Fe: School of American Research Press.

1992 Resistance and Class Reproduction among Middle Class Youth. Working paper #71. Program in the Comparative Study of Social Transformations. Ann Arbor: University of Michigan.

1994 Ethnography among the Newark: The Class of '58 of Weequahic High School. *Michigan Quarterly Review* (Summer):410–29. Also in *Naturalizing Power,* C. Delaney and S. Yanagisako, eds. Stanford: Stanford University Press.

1997 Fieldwork in the Post-Community. *Anthropology and Humanism Quarterly* 22:61–80.

1998 Identities: The Hidden Life of Class. *Journal of Anthropological Research* 54(1):1–17.

Papert, Seymour

1996 *The Connected Family.* Atlanta: Longstreet.

Parsons, Talcott, and Robert Bales

1955 *Family, Socialization and Interaction Process.* Glencoe, IL: Free Press.

Petrek, Melissa, and Alan Hines

1993 Withdrawing in Disgust Is Not the Same as Apathy. *Mondo 2000* 9.

Pfeil, Fred

1990 Making Flippy Floppy: Postmodernism and the Baby-Boom PMC. In *Another Tale to Tell: Politics and Narrative in Postmodern Culture,* pp. 97–125. London and New York: Verso.

Pfohl, Stephen J.

1977 The Discovery of Child Abuse. *Social Problems* 24(3):310–23 (Fall).

Philipson, Morris

1977 The Scholar as Publishing Author. In *Scholars and Their Publishers,* W. A. Kefauver, ed., pp. 27–33. New York: Modern Language Association of America.

Piasecki, Bruce

1994 Corporate World Shows More Care for the Environment. *Forum for Applied Research and Public Policy* 9(2):6–14.

1995 *Corporate Environmental Strategy: The Avalanche of Change Since Bhopal.* New York: John Wiley and Sons.

Piasecki, Bruce, and Peter Asmus

1990 *In Search of Environmental Excellence: Moving Beyond Blame.* New York: Simon and Schuster.

Pinkerton, James P.

1994 Economy Bites the Edge off Generation X. Op-ed piece. *Los Angeles Times* (February 24):B7.

Piore, Michael, and Charles Sabel

1984 *The Second Industrial Divide.* New York: Basic Books.

Polsby, N. W.

1980 *Community Power and Political Theory.* New Haven: Yale University Press.

Popenoe, David

1988 *Disturbing the Nest: Family Change and Decline in Modern Societies.* New York: Aldine de Gruyter.

1992 The Controversial Truth: The Two-Parent Family Is Better. *New York Times* (December 26):13.

1993a American Family Decline, 1960–1990: A Review and Appraisal. *Journal of Marriage and the Family* 55(3):527–44.

1993b Scholars Should Worry About the Disintegration of the American Family. *Chronicle of Higher Education* (April 14):A48.

1994 What's Behind the Family Values Debate? Paper, American Sociological Association meetings, Los Angeles (August 7).

Porter, Alan L., and Frederick A. Rossini

1985 Peer Review of Interdisciplinary Research Proposals. *Science, Technology, and Human Values* 10(3):33–38.

Porush, David

1993 Making Chaos: Two Views of a New Science. In *The Literature of Science,* M. W. McRae, ed. Athens: University of Georgia Press.

Pound, Christoper

1995 Imagining In-Formation: The Complex Disconnections of Computer Networks. In *Late Editions 2: Technoscientific Imaginaries,* G. E. Marcus, ed. Chicago: University of Chicago Press.

1996 Framed, or How the Internet Set Me Up. In *Late Editions 3: Connected: Engagements with Media,* G. E. Marcus, ed. Chicago: University of Chicago Press.

Poundstone, William

1992 *Prisoner's Dilemma: John von Neumann, Game Theory, and the Puzzle of the Bomb.* New York: Doubleday.

Powell, Walter W.

1985 *Getting into Print: The Decision-Making Process in Scholarly Publishing.* Chicago: University of Chicago Press.

Powers, Richard

1988 *Prisoner's Dilemma.* New York: William Morrow.

1995 *Galatea 2.2.* New York: Farrar Straus Giroux.

Publisher's Weekly

1994 No Quiet Centenary for the University of California Press: Fiscal Strains, Electronics Loom (January 3).

1995a University Presses "On the Upbeat" (July 10).

1995b Book Industry Study Group Statistics January–March (August 14).

Rabinow, Paul

1977 *Reflections on Fieldwork in Morocco.* Berkeley: University of California Press.

1986 Representations Are Social Facts: Modernity and Post-modernity in Anthropology. In *Writing Culture: The Poetics and Politics of Ethnography,* J. Clifford and G. E. Marcus, eds., pp. 234–61. Berkeley: University of California Press.

1996 *Making PCR: A Story of Biotechnology.* Chicago: University of Chicago Press.

Radway, Janice A.

1984 *Reading the Romance: Women, Patriarchy, and Popular Literature.* Chapel Hill: University of North Carolina Press.

Rafael, Vicente L.

1994 The Cultures of Area Studies in the United States. *Social Text* 41:91–111.

Rajan, Ravi

1988 Rehabilitation and Voluntarism in Bhopal. *Lokayan Bulletin* 6:1–2.

Ratan, Suneel

1993 Review of *13th Generation: Abort, Retry, Ignore, Fail,* by Neil Howe and Bill Strauss. *Fortune* (July 26):142.

Raymond, Eric S.

1993 *The New Hacker's Dictionary.* Cambridge: MIT Press.

Reavis, D. J.

1995 *The Ashes of Waco.* New York: Simon and Schuster.

Reich, Michael

1991 *Toxic Politics: Responding to Chemical Disasters.* Ithaca: Cornell University Press.

Reisch, Marc

1990 Carbide's Kennedy Sees Many Challenges for Company, Industry. *Chemical and Engineering News* (August 27):9–13.

Rheinberger, Hans-Joerg

1992 Experiment, Difference, and Writing: I. Tracing Protein Synthesis; II. The Laboratory Production of Transfer RNA. *Studies in the History and Philosophy of Science* 23(2–3):305–31, 389–422.

Rheingold, Harold

1991 *Virtual Reality.* New York: Simon and Schuster.

Rieder, Jonathan

1985 *Canarsie: The Jews and Italians of Brooklyn Against Liberalism.* Cambridge: Harvard University Press.

Rip, Arie

1985 Commentary: Peer Review Is Alive and Well in the United States. *Science, Technology, and Human Values* 10(3):82–86

Rip, Arie, Thomas J. Misa, and Johan Schott, eds.

1995 *Managing Technology in Society: The Approach of Constructive Technology Assessment.* London: Pinter Publishers Ltd.

Ronell, Avital

1989 *The Telephone Book.* Lincoln: University of Nebraska Press.

Rosenfelt, Deborah, and Judith Stacey

1987 Second Thoughts on the Second Wave. *Feminist Studies* 13(2):341–61.

Ross, Alex

1994 Generation Exit. *New Yorker* (April 25):102–6.

Rothman, D. J., and Rothman, S. M.

1984 *The Willowbrook Wars.* New York: Harper and Row.

Rouse, Roger

1995 Thinking through Transnationalism: Notes on the Cultural Politics of Class Relations in the Contemporary United States. *Public Culture* 7:353–402.

Roy, Rustum

1985 Funding Science: The Real Defects of Peer Review and an Alternative to It. *Science, Technology, and Human Values* 10(3):73–81.

Rubin, Gayle

1975 The Traffic in Women: Notes on the Political Economy of Sex. In *Toward an Anthropology of Women,* R. Reiter, ed., pp. 157–210. New York: Monthly Review.

Rubin, Lillian

1994 *Families on the Faultline: America's Working Class Speaks about the Family, the Economy, Race, and Ethnicity.* New York: HarperCollins.

Rushkoff, Douglass, ed.

1994 *The GenX Reader.* New York: Ballantine Books.

Russell, Cheryl

1990 Meet the Next Generation. *American Demographics* 12:2.

1993 The Master Trend. *American Demographics* 15(10):28–37.

Russell, Neuman, Lee McKnight, and Richard Jay Solomon

1995 *The Gordian Knot: Political Gridlock on the Information Highway.* Cambridge: MIT Press.

Sacks, Karen Brodkin

1994 How Did Jews Become White Folks? In *Race,* Steven Gregory and Roger Sanjek, eds., pp. 78–102. New Brunswick: Rutgers University Press.

Salamon, L. M.

1987a Partners in Public Service. In *The Nonprofit Sector: A Research Handbook,* W. W. Powell, ed., pp. 99–117. New Haven: Yale University Press.

1987b Of Market Failure, Voluntary Failure, and Third Party Government: Toward a Theory of Government-Nonprofit Relations in the Modern Welfare State. *Journal of Voluntary Action Research* 16(1–2):29–49 (January–June).

Salamon, L. M., and A. Abramson

1982 *The Federal Budget and the Nonprofit Sector.* Washington, DC: Urban Institute Press.

Salter, Liora

1985 Science and Peer Review: The Canadian Standard-Setting Experience. *Science, Technology, and Human Values* 10(3):37–46.

Samuelson, Paula

1988 Is Copyright Law Steering the Right Course? IEEE Software.

1989 Why the Look and Feel of Software User Interfaces Should Not Be Protected by Copyright Law. *Communications of the ACM* 32(5):563–72.

1990 Should Program Algorithms Be Patented? *Communications of the ACM* 33(8):23–27.

1994 Legally Speaking: The NII Intellectual Property Report. *Communications of the ACM.*

Samuelson, Paula, Randall Davis, Mitchell D. Kapor, and J. H. Reichman

1995 A Manifesto Concerning the Legal Protection of Computer Programs. *Columbia Law Review* 94:2308.

Sandqvist, Karin, and Bengt-Erik Andersson

1992 Thriving Families in the Swedish Welfare State. *Public Interest* 109:114–17.

Sarason, S. B., and J. Doris

1979 *Educational Handicap, Public Policy, and Social History: A Broadened Perspective on Mental Retardation.* New York: Free Press.

Schieffelin, Edward L.

1985 Performance and the Cultural Construction of Reality. *American Ethnologist* 12:707–24.

Schneider, David M.

1980 *American Kinship: A Cultural Account.* Chicago: University of Chicago Press.

Schultz, George P.

1993 *Turmoil and Triumph: My Years as Secretary of State.* New York: Scribners.

Scruggs, Richard, Steven Zipperstein, Robert Lyon, Victor Gonzalez, Herbert Cousins, and Roderick Beverly

1993 *United States Department of Justice Report on the Events at Waco, Texas, February 28 to April 19, 1993.* Redacted version. Washington, DC: US Government Printing Office.

Sennett, Richard

1994 The New Censorship. *Contemporary Sociology* 23(4):487–91.

Serres, Michel

1980/82 *The Parasite.* Baltimore: Johns Hopkins University Press.

1991 *Rome: The Book of Foundations.* Stanford: Stanford University Press.

Shapin, Steven

1994 *A Social History of Truth: Civility and Science in Seventeenth-Century England.* Chicago: University of Chicago Press.

Sharplin, Arthur

1989 Union Carbide, Ltd.: The Bhopal Gas Incident. Paper for the Center for Business Ethics, Bentley College. Presented at Bentley College, Waltham, MA.

Shogren, Elizabeth

1994 Traditional Family Nearly the Exception, Census Finds. *Los Angeles Times* (August 30):A1, A28.

Sills, J. E.

1993 SLAPPS (Strategic Lawsuits against Public Participation): How Can the Legal System Eliminate Their Appeal? *Connecticut Law Review* 25:547ff.

Skolnick, Arlene

1991 *Embattled Paradise: The American Family in an Age of Uncertainty.* New York: Basic Books.

Smith, David Alexander

1993 *In the Cube.* New York: Tor.

Smith, David Alexander, ed.

1994 *Future Boston.* New York: Tor.

Smith, S. R., and M. Lipsky

1993 *Nonprofits for Hire: The Welfare State in the Age of Contracting.* Cambridge: Harvard University Press.

Snow, C. P.

1964 *Two Cultures: And a Second Look.* Cambridge: Cambridge University Press.

Spigel, Lynn

1992 *Make Room for TV: Television and the Family Ideal in Postwar America.* Chicago: University of Chicago Press.

1995 From the Dark Ages to the Golden Age: Women's Memories and Television Reruns. *Screen* 36(1):14–31.

Stacey, Judith
1983 The New Conservative Feminism. *Feminist Studies* 9(3):559–83.
1986 Are Feminists Afraid to Leave Home? The Challenge of Profamily Feminism. In *What Is Feminism?* J. Mitchell and A. Oakley, eds., pp. 219–48. London: Basil Blackwell.
1990 *Brave New Families.* New York: Basic Books.
1994a The New Family Values Crusaders. *Nation* (July 25–August 1):119–22.
1994b Scents, Scholars and Stigma: The Revisionist Campaign for Family Values. *Social Text* 40:51–75.
1996 *In the Name of the Family: Rethinking Family Values in the Postmodern Age.* Boston: Beacon Press.

Star, Alexander
1993 The Twentysomething Myth. *New Republic* (January 4):22–26.

Star, Susan Leigh, ed.
1995 *The Cultures of Computing.* Cambridge, MA: Blackwell.

Steele, Guy L., Jr., et al., comp.
1983 *The Hacker's Dictionary.* New York: Harper & Row.

Steinhauer, Jennifer
1994 How Do You Turn On the Twentysomething Market? *New York Times* (April 17) 3:5.

Stephenson, Neal
1988 *Zodiac.* New York: Bantam.
1996 The Hacker Tourist Travels the World to Bring Back the Epic Story of Wiring the Planet. *Wired* 4(12):97–160.
1998 *The Diamond Age.* New York: Bantam.

Sterling, Bruce
1992 *The Hacker Crackdown: Law and Order on the Electronic Frontier.* New York: Bantam.

Stone, Alluquerque Rosanne
1995 *The War of Desire and Technology at the End of the Mechanical Age.* Cambridge: MIT Press.

Stone, Andrea
1989 Union Carbide Up Two Dollars After Bhopal Settlement. *USA Today* (February 15).

Strand, Douglas Alan, and Kenneth Sherrill
1993 Electoral Bugaboos? The Impact of Attitudes Toward Gay Rights and Feminism on the 1992 Presidential Vote. Paper, American Political Science Association meetings, Washington, DC.

Svare, B., ed.
1983 *Hormones and Aggressive Behavior.* New York: Plenum Press.

Swales, John M.
1990 *Genre Analysis: English in Academic and Research Settings.* Cambridge: Cambridge University Press.

Tabor, J. D.

1994 The Waco Tragedy: An Autobiographical Account of One Attempt to Avert Disaster. In *From the Ashes: Making Sense of Waco*, J. R. Lewis, ed., pp. 13–21. Lanham, MD: Rowman and Littlefield.

Tabor, J. D., and Gallagher, E.

1995 *Why Waco? Cults and the Battle for Religious Freedom in America.* Berkeley: University of California Press.

Tacitus

1971 *Annals of Imperial Rome.* Michael Grant, trans. London: Penguin.

Talbott, Strobe

1988 *The Master of the Game: Paul Nitze and the Nuclear Peace.* New York: Knopf.

Talese, G.

1969 *The Kingdom and the Power: The Story of the Men Who Influence the Institution That Influences the World—The New York Times.* New York: World Publishing Company.

Taussig, Michael

1992 *Mimesis and Alterity.* New York: Routledge.

Taylor, Ella

1989 *Primetime Families: Television Culture in Postwar America.* Berkeley: University of California Press.

Taylor, S. J.

1990 *Stalin's Apologist: Walter Duranty: The New York Times' Man in Moscow.* New York: Oxford University Press.

Teitelman, Robert

1994 *Profits of Science: The American Marriage of Business and Technology.* New York: Basic Books.

Tocqueville, Alexis de

1945 *Democracy in America.* New York: Vintage Books.

Traube, Elizabeth G.

1992 *Dreaming Identities: Class, Gender, and Generation in 1980s Hollywood Movies.* Boulder: Westview Press.

Tribe, Lawrence

1991 The Constitution in Cyberspace. Keynote address, First Conference on Computers, Freedom and Privacy. http://www-swiss.ai.mit.edu/6805/article/tribe-constitution.txt.

Triolo, Paul S., and Peter Lovelock

1996 Up, Up and Away—With Strings Attached: China's Internet Development Has to Overcome Cultural, Regulatory, and Infrastructural Hurdles. *China Business Review* (November–December):18–29.

Turkle, Sherry

1994 Why Do I Need to Get a "Real Life" if My Life Is on the Internet? Paper, Society for Social Studies of Science meetings, New Orleans (October 14).

1995 *Life on the Screen.* New York: Simon and Schuster.

Uchitelle, Louis

1996 Bit Player: What Has the Computer Done for Us Lately? *New York Times* (December 8) 4:1, 4.

Ulmer, Gregory

1994 *Heuretics: The Logic of Invention.* Baltimore: Johns Hopkins University Press.

Union Carbide Corporation

1989 *Toward Environmental Excellence: A Progress Report.* Danbury, CT: Union Carbide Corporation.

University of Chicago Press

1967 *Catalogue of Books and Journals, 1891–1965.* Chicago: University of Chicago Press.

1992 *One Hundred Years of Scholarly Publishing.* Chicago: University of Chicago Press.

Varenne, Hervé, Shelley Goldman, and Ray McDermott

n.d. Racing in Place. In *Teaching and Learning,* G. Spindler, ed., forthcoming.

Virilio, Paul

1977/86 *Speed and Politics.* New York: Semio-texte.

1993/95 *The Art of the Motor.* Minneapolis: University of Minnesota Press.

Visvanathan, Shiv, with Rajni Kothari

1985 Bhopal: The Imagination of Disaster. *Lokayan Bulletin* 3:4–5.

Von Neumann, John, and Oscar Morgenstern

1944 *The Theory of Games and Economic Behavior.* Princeton: Princeton University Press.

Walker, Pat, ed.

1979 *Between Labour and Capital.* Hassocks, Sussex: Harvester Press.

Wallerstein, Judith S., and Sandra Blakeslee

1989 *Second Chances: Men, Women, and Children a Decade After Divorce.* New York: Ticknor and Fields.

Walsh, Liesel

1992 Why the Baby Bust Won't Spend. *American Demographics* 14:14.

Warner, A.

1894 *American Charities.* New York: Thomas Y. Crowell.

Warner, W. L., et al.

1941–1959 *Yankee City.* 5 vols. New Haven: Yale University Press.

Weber, Max

1911 Sociology and Biology. Reprint 1978. In *Weber: Selections in Translation,* W. G. Runciman, ed. Cambridge: Cambridge University Press.

1946a Science as a Vocation. In *From Max Weber: Essays in Sociology,* H. Gerth and C. W. Mills, eds., 1958 ed. New York: Oxford University Press.

1946b The Sociology of Charismatic Authority. In *From Max Weber: Essays in Sociology*, H. Gerth and C. W. Mills, eds., 1958 ed. New York: Oxford University Press.

Webster, Donovan

1994 Chips Are a Thief's Best Friend. *New York Magazine* (September 18):54–59.

Weir, David, and Mark Schapiro

1981 *Circle of Poison: Pesticides and People in a Hungry World.* San Francisco: Institute for Food and Development Policy.

Weisbrod, B.

1989 *The Nonprofit Economy.* Cambridge: Harvard University Press.

Wexler, R.

1990 *Wounded Innocents: The Real Victims of the War Against Child Abuse.* Buffalo: Prometheus Books.

Williams, John

1992 Review of *Generation X* by Douglas Coupland. *New Statesman and Society* May 29:40.

Williams, Monci Jo

1985 The Baby Bust Hits the Job Market. *Fortune* (May 27):122–35.

Willis, Paul

1977 *Learning to Labor: How Working Class Kids Get Working Class Jobs.* New York: Columbia University Press.

Wilson, James Q.

1993 The Family-Values Debate. *Commentary* 95(4):24–31.

Winerip, M.

1994 *9 Highland Road.* New York: Pantheon Books.

Winkler, Karen

1993 Communitarians Move Their Ideas Outside Academic Arena. *Chronicle of Higher Education* (April 21):A7.

Wolch, J. R.

1990 *The Shadow State: Government and Voluntary Sector in Transition.* New York: The Foundation Center.

Wooley, Benjamin

1992 *Virtual Worlds.* Cambridge, MA: Blackwell.

Yoachum, Susan

1994 Small Minority Voter Turnout a Product of Apathy and Anger. *San Francisco Chronicle* (September 22):A4.

Yoffie, David B.

1994 *Strategic Management in Information Technology.* Englewood Cliffs, NJ: Prentice Hall.

Index

School of American Research Advanced Seminar Series

Published by SAR Press

Chaco & Hohokam: Prehistoric Regional Systems in the American Southwest
Patricia L. Crown & W. James Judge, eds.

Recapturing Anthropology: Working in the Present
Richard G. Fox, ed.

War in the Tribal Zone: Expanding States and Indigenous Warfare
R. Brian Ferguson & Neil L. Whitehead, eds.

Ideology and Pre-Columbian Civilizations
Arthur A. Demarest & Geoffrey W. Conrad, eds.

Dreaming: Anthropological and Psychological Interpretations
Barbara Tedlock, ed. (Reprint)

Historical Ecology: Cultural Knowledge and Changing Landscapes
Carole L. Crumley, ed.

Themes in Southwest Prehistory
George J. Gumerman, ed.

Memory, History, and Opposition under State Socialism
Rubie S. Watson, ed.

Other Intentions: Cultural Contexts and the Attribution of Inner States
Lawrence Rosen, ed.

Last Hunters–First Farmers: New Perspectives on the Prehistoric Transition to Agriculture
T. Douglas Price & Anne Birgitte Gebauer, eds.

Making Alternative Histories: The Practice of Archaeology and History in Non-Western Settings
Peter R. Schmidt & Thomas C. Patterson, eds.

Senses of Place
Steven Feld & Keith H. Basso, eds.

Cyborgs & Citadels: Anthropological Interventions in Emerging Sciences and Technologies
Gary Lee Downey & Joseph Dumit, eds.

Archaic States
Gary M. Feinman & Joyce Marcus, eds.

School of American Research Advanced Seminar Series

Published by Cambridge University Press

Dreaming: Anthropological and Psychological Interpretations
Barbara Tedlock, ed.

The Anasazi in a Changing Environment
George J. Gumerman, ed.

Regional Perspectives on the Olmec
R. J. Sharer & D. C. Grove, eds.

The Chemistry of Prehistoric Human Bone
T. Douglas Price, ed.

The Emergence of Modern Humans: Biocultural Adaptations in the Later Pleistocene
Erik Trinkaus, ed.

The Anthropology of War
Jonathan Haas, ed.

The Evolution of Political Systems
Steadman Upham, ed.

Classic Maya Political History: Hieroglyphic and Archaeological Evidence
T. Patrick Culbert, ed.

Turko-Persia in Historical Perspective
Robert L. Canfield, ed.

Chiefdoms: Power, Economy, and Ideology
Timothy Earle, ed.

Published by University of California Press

Writing Culture: The Poetics and Politics of Ethnography
James Clifford & George E. Marcus, eds.

School of American Research Advanced Seminar Series

Published by University of New Mexico Press

Reconstructing Prehistoric Pueblo Societies
William A. Longacre, ed.

New Perspectives on the Pueblos
Alfonso Ortiz, ed.

Structure and Process in Latin America
A. Strickon & S. M. Greenfield, eds.

The Classic Maya Collapse
T. Patrick Culbert, ed.

Methods and Theories of Anthropological Genetics
M. H. Crawford & P. L. Workman, eds.

Sixteenth-Century Mexico: The Work of Sahagun
Munro S. Edmonson, ed.

Ancient Civilization and Trade
J. A. Sabloff & C. C. Lamberg-Karlovsky, eds.

Photography in Archaeological Research
Elmer Harp, Jr., ed.

Meaning in Anthropology
K. H. Basso & H. A. Selby, eds.

The Valley of Mexico: Studies in Pre-Hispanic Ecology and Society
Eric R. Wolf, ed.

Demographic Anthropology: Quantitative Approaches
Ezra B. W. Zubrow, ed.

The Origins of Maya Civilization
Richard E. W. Adams, ed.

Explanation of Prehistoric Change
James N. Hill, ed.

Explorations in Ethnoarchaeology
Richard A. Gould, ed.

Entrepreneurs in Cultural Context
Sidney M. Greenfield, A. Strickon, & R. T. Aubey, eds.

The Dying Community
Art Gallaher, Jr., & H. Padfield, eds.

Southwestern Indian Ritual Drama
Charlotte J. Frisbie, ed.

Lowland Maya Settlement Patterns
Wendy Ashmore, ed.

Simulations in Archaeology
Jeremy A. Sabloff, ed.

Chan Chan: Andean Desert City
M. E. Moseley & K. C. Day, eds.

Shipwreck Anthropology
Richard A. Gould, ed.

Elites: Ethnographic Issues
George E. Marcus, ed.

The Archaeology of Lower Central America
F. W. Lange & D. Z. Stone, eds.

Late Lowland Maya Civilization: Classic to Postclassic
J. A. Sabloff & E. W. Andrews V, eds.

PHOTO BY KATRINA LAKSO

Participants in the School of American Research advanced seminar "Power/Knowledge Shifts in America's fin de siècle," Santa Fe, New Mexico, October 1994. Front row, from left: Kim Fortun, Michael M.J. Fischer, Sherry Ortner, Judith Stacey, James D. Faubion. Back row, from left: T. David Brent, Peter Dobkin Hall, Paul Rabinow, George E. Marcus, Donald Brenneis.